The COMMUNIST REVOLUTION in ASIA

Prentice-Hall International, Inc., *London*
Prentice-Hall of Australia, Pty., Ltd., *Sydney*
Prentice-Hall of Canada, Ltd., *Toronto*
Prentice-Hall of India (Private) Ltd., *New Delhi*
Prentice-Hall of Japan, Inc., *Tokyo*

The
COMMUNIST
REVOLUTION
in ASIA

Tactics, Goals,
and
Achievements

Edited by Robert A. Scalapino

University of California
Berkeley, California

Prentice-Hall, Inc.   *Englewood Cliffs, New Jersey*

Current printing (last digit):
11   10   9   8   7   6   5   4   3   2

Library of Congress Catalog Card No.: 65-26708

Printed in the United States of America
C-15303

Contributors

Robert A. Scalapino

Dr. Robert A. Scalapino is Professor of Political Science and Chairman of the Department at the University of California, Berkeley. He is also Editor of the *Asian Survey*. He has written a number of books and articles on Asian politics and American Far Eastern policy. Among his works are: *Democracy and the Party Movement in Pre-War Japan*, 1953; "Neutralism in Asia," *The American Political Science Review*, March, 1954; "The United States and Japan," in *The United States and the Far East*, The American Assembly, 2nd edition, 1962; Section 4 of the *United States Foreign Policy—Asia*, a Study for the Senate Foreign Relations Committee, November, 1959; *Parties and Politics in Contemporary Japan* (with Junnosuke Masumi), 1962; *The Communist Revolution in Asia*, 1965. He has undertaken a number of field studies in Asia and has served as guest lecturer at Asian universities. He has also served as Consultant to the Ford Foundation and to the Rockefeller Foundation. He has been the recipient of grants from the Carnegie Foundation, the Social Science Research Council, the Rockefeller Foundation, and the Guggenheim Foundation.

John H. Badgley

John H. Badgley is currently Visiting Professor of Political Science at Kyoto University's Southeast Asian Center and is Assistant Professor, Department of Government, Miami University, Oxford, Ohio. He is the author of the forthcoming volume, *Burma's Revolutionary Process* and a number of articles in *Asian Survey, Pacific Affairs,* and *Problems of Communism.*

Hans H. Baerwald

Hans H. Baerwald is Associate Professor of Political Science at the University of California, Los Angeles. He is the author of *The Purge of Japanese Leaders under the Occupation; Chinese Communism: Selected Documents* with Dan Jacobs; and *The American Republic: Its Government and Politics* with Peter H. Odegard; and articles on Japanese politics in *Asian Survey.*

John C. Donnell

John C. Donnell is a staff member of the RAND Corporation. Previously, he served the State Department and U. S. Information Agency in several Asian countries and taught at Dartmouth College. He has written papers on Vietnamese politics for publication and presentation at scholarly conferences.

Bernard B. Fall

Bernard B. Fall, Professor of Government at Howard University, Washington, D.C., is the author of *Street Without Joy: Indochina at War; The Two Viet-Nams;* and other books and publications dealing with Southeast Asia and revolutionary warfare operations.

M. T. Haggard

M. T. Haggard is an American student of political develompents in Asian Communist countries. He has written several articles on the Mongolian Communist movement.

Chalmers Johnson

Chalmers Johnson is Associate Professor of Political Science at the University of California, Berkeley, and a member of the Executive Committee of the University's Center for Chinese Studies. He is the author of *Peasant Nationalism and Communist Power* (1962); *An Instance of Treason: Ozaki Hotsumi and the Sorge Spy Ring* (1964); and *Revolution and the Social System* (1964).

Robert N. Kearney

Robert N. Kearney is Assistant Professor of Political Science at Duke University. He conducted research in Ceylon during 1961-62 and 1965 and is the author of a number of articles on the politics of Ceylon.

Chong-Sik Lee

Chong-Sik Lee is Associate Professor of Political Science at the University of Pennsylvania and the author of *The Politics of Korean Nationalism*. He has contributed numerous articles to scholarly journals on Korean Communism and various aspects of Korean politics.

Guy J. Pauker

Guy J. Pauker is Senior Staff Member and Head of the Asia Section in the Social Science Department of the RAND Corporation, Santa Monica, California. Previously he was Associate Professor of Political Science and Chairman of the Center for Southeast Asia Studies at the University of California, Berkeley. His research has taken him to Southeast Asia annually over the last decade. He is the author of numerous articles and studies on Southeast Asian affairs.

Ralph H. Retzlaff

Ralph H. Retzlaff is Assistant Professor of Political Science at the Department of Political Science, University of California, Berkeley. He is the author of *Village Government in India: A Case Study* and various other articles on Indian politics.

Leo E. Rose

Leo E. Rose is a member of the research staff of the Institute of International Studies at the University of California, Berkeley, and is Director of the Himalayan Border Countries Project and Associate Editor of the *Asian Survey*. He is the author of *Politics in Nepal: A Case Study of a Traditional Society in Transition* with Bhuwan Lal Joshi, and several other studies of political developments in the Himalayan area.

Frances L. Starner

Frances L. Starner, most recently Lecturer in Political Science at the University of Malaya, Singapore, is the author of *Magsaysay and the Philippine Peasantry; The African Impact on Philippine Politics;* and a large number of articles on Southeast Asian politics and international relations.

Contents

Communism in Asia

Toward a Comparative Analysis

Robert A. Scalapino

Communism in Asia is not a new phenomenon.
Its earliest beginnings extend back into the late nineteenth
century, when a handful of young Asian intellectuals
first came into contact with Marxism. The initial communist
parties were established much later,
but even this development took place nearly
a half century ago. Many of the veteran
Asian communists still alive are now in their mid-seventies and,
as we shall note, are presently giving way to a new
generation of leaders. Despite this rather
extensive history, however, the great communist gains in Asia
are products of the last two decades, and centrally
connected with the events surrounding World War II.

Undoubtedly this is one reason why most Asian communists, of whatever generation, tend to be of a different type than the contemporary Russian leaders, and espouse different policies.

Marxism and the Asian Intellectual

Asian communism began as an intellectual movement and, while it has become vastly more complex, the intellectual element is still an important one. As we shall presently observe, ideologues continue to play a significant leadership role in most Asian communist parties. Moreover, the good communist, of whatever station, is expected to study and learn. He is supposed to master the Marxist classics, search his mind in order to root out error, supplant it with truth, and then apply this truth "creatively" to the circumstances of his own society.

It might not be amiss, therefore, to commence this analysis with some attempt to understand the appeal of Marxism-Leninism to the Asian intellectual. At the outset, however, it should be emphasized that at no point has communism represented the dominant political trend among the modern Asian intelligentsia, except when Marxian doctrines have been imposed by state fiat. Even then, the degree and nature of intellectual adherence to communism is debatable. One must appreciate both sides of the coin: The great majority of Asian intellectuals have never espoused communism; and a small but significant minority have either supported communism or been strongly influenced by Marxist-Leninist doctrines. This latter group, moreover, has included some individuals who have occupied commanding heights in the intellectual firmament of their societies.

The Marxist-Leninist appeal has been intimately connected with the massive problems of confrontation with and independence from the "advanced" West. It has been a part of the quest for political, economic, and social modernization. Thus the Asian Marxist, in certain critical respects, has not seen or interpreted his creed in the manner of Marx. Revisionism, of course, is implicit in the journey of any doctrine from theory to practice, but few doctrines in human history have undergone more extensive revisions than Marxism in Asia. Let us then explore the wellsprings of Marxist appeal to the Asian intellectual, noting both the themes that Marx would have appreciated and those he would have regarded as strange or unacceptable.

Marxism as a Progressive, Avant-Garde Theory

The modern Asian intellectual has accepted drastic change as essential for his society, and he has tended to accept also the Western model of change. Indeed, his goals have been governed to a major extent by the teleological insights derived from Western experience. The Asian intellectual has seen—or thinks he has seen—the future of his own society mirrored in the "advanced" Western world. (In this, he may well be partly mistaken, but that is beside the point.)

To understand the burdens imposed by being thus able "to see the future" is to appreciate the enormous intellectual and psychological gap separating the intelligentsia of those societies which pioneered in modernization from the intelligentsia of Asia and Africa. The latter were placed in a position of being perpetual followers, a position tending to frustrate creativity and abet resentments against Westernism even as it bound at least two generations to the Western model. The great nationalist upsurge in the Afro-Asian intellectual world today, including the attack by Asian Marxists upon Western Marxists, is in some measure connected with this problem.

In an earlier period, however, intellectual independence was even more difficult for the modern Asian to attain than national freedom. For him, to be progressive was imperative, and to be progressive was, in essence, to be "Western." Hence, the goal became to grasp the latest developments, the furthermost reaches of Western thought. At the end of the nineteenth century, the latest developments were reflected in liberalism and the parliamentary system; by the early twentieth century, to be *avant-garde,* one had to espouse socialism. The most radical Asian intellectuals had discovered anarcho-syndicalism, an extreme expression of Western dissidence currently in vogue. It was natural that, as anarchism declined and Marxism-Leninism rose in Western radical circles, the Asian intellectual vanguard would be swept toward a new "wave of the future." The successful Bolshevik Revolution redefined for the Asian radical the essence of futurism.

Marxism-Leninism as the "New Democracy"

The West implanted in the modern Asian intellectual a profound commitment to the concept of democracy—the ideas of freedom, equality, representation, and above all, the central importance of "the people." Most Asian intellectuals have retained those commitments, but their philosophic and practical expression of the concepts has taken drastically different forms. At first the dominant, almost sole, model was that of Western parliamentarism. In one Asian society after another, however, disillusionment with parliamentary democracy arose. It was already strong in Japanese and Chinese intellectual circles shortly after World War I. To many, parliamentarism had become synonymous with corruption, special privilege, factionalism, and continuous political crisis.

Wherever and whenever such disillusionment occurs, the "new democracy" of Marxism-Leninism is likely to have a certain appeal. It enables the Asian intellectual to retain his commitment to the broad, theoretical values of democracy—to invoke the sacred words—while freeing him from the traditional democratic forms and practices. The "new democracy" is based upon a tutelage of the masses by a highly organized elite most logically drawn from the intellectual class itself. Theoretically, the people continue to be the objects of worship, the source of supreme authority, the fountainhead of truth. In practice, however, they become the subjects of intensive indoctrination, mass mobilization, and total commitment to the purposes of state as defined by their "vanguard."

Thus, the "new democracy" is not hobbled by concepts of freedom, equality, and popular sovereignty. Without abandoning claim to these principles, the communists build an elitist-controlled, fully mobilized state geared to execute rapid and drastic changes. The central paraphernalia of democracy are retained: supreme people's congresses, parties, and elections. Indeed, the people are caused to participate in politics on a more intensive scale than at any time in the past. But this is organized participation, under the supervision of the vanguard party. Hence, representation is scientific; participation is positive; elections are ceremonies of support. The confusion, uncertainty and chaos surrounding the "old democracy" are avoided.

With this organizational structure goes a program of revolutionary socioeconomic changes intended to make democracy total and complete. Can man be politically free if he is permanently bound by caste or class lines, or if he is the victim of continuous economic exploitation? Utilizing these powerful themes, the Marxist-Leninists promise to unite social, economic, and political democracy, producing true equality and total liberation.

This is the blueprint of the "new democracy." It is not surprising that it has attracted a number of Asian intellectuals, particularly during the period when it is still a blueprint, not yet a reality.

Marxism-Leninism as a Technique of Nation-Building

The Asian communists have harnessed Marxism-Leninism to the climactic stages of the Asian nationalist revolution, making of it an instrument for the swift, thorough, and purposeful creation of a nation-state where none previously existed. Disparate peoples, divided by ethnic, class, and regional ties, are given a common party, a common set of political values, and common tasks so stupendous as to blur most past sources of separateness and identity. The old loyalties to family, tribe, and region are put under sustained and heavy assault. Every effort is made to forge new loyalties to the party and to the People's Democratic Republic. A decade or more after independence, most noncommunist Asian states are weak and fragmented, torn by many social and political fissures. How many of them can be compared, in terms of national unification, state power, or military strength, with Communist China, North Korea, or North Vietnam? [1]

Marxism-Leninism as the Science of Rapid Modernization

For the Asian Marxist, communism represents not the culmination of the modernization process but its potential means. Now it is Hegel who has been righted, and Marx turned on his head. The latter-day Asian communist has as his goal a one-generation industrial revolution, a concentrated thrust toward modernity. He sees in communism a method of mobilizing manpower, allocating resources, providing the power and organization for this purpose. Many intellectuals at least inwardly acknowledge that great sacrifices will be involved in such a rapid pace, but they have rationalized these sacrifices as temporarily necessary to provide prosperity and equality with the advanced world.

Marxism-Leninism as an Ideology in Harmony with Selected Aspects of Asian Traditionalism

The pattern of personal and group behavior in any society is intimately connected with cultural traditions not easily nor quickly overturned. In Asia, political behavior has often clashed sharply with the institutional and ideological requirements of Western-style democracy. In the view of most Asians, including many within the intellectual class, Western parliamentarism is based upon types of behavior contrary to custom and extremely difficult to acquire.

The ideological-organizational structure of communism, however, provides a certain comfort and sense of familiarity. The communist premium is upon elitist tutelage and the educative state, two concepts deeply implanted in Asian tradition. There is a certain sense in which Marxism-Leninism represents a continuation of the classical traditions of Asian scholarship. Moreover, communism emphasizes collectivism and group responsibility, striking out against the "selfishness" of individualism. It provides for decision making on the basis of consensus rather than majoritarianism. Its final goal is a unified, harmonious, classless society instead of a state tolerating differences, espousing minority rights, and placing its greatest stress upon the dignity of the individual. Consciously or unconsciously, many modern Asian intellectuals have found in communism certain revitalized elements of a tradition with which they retain very strong ties.

Marxism-Leninism as a Universalist Creed and a Philosophy of Optimism

In his contact with the West, the Asian intellectual has often suffered from an acute sense of separateness; a despair of overcoming his intellectual isolation. In this context, Marxism appears as a philosophy of hope. It asserts that all societies are united by the same basic truths, the same fundamental social laws. It guarantees that all societies will go through the same broad stages of development and reach the same ultimate position with respect to values and institutions. In an era when the Asian intellectual has desperately wanted to "belong," Marxism poses as a universal creed and a doctrine of certainty in the midst of a very troubled, uncertain world.

Marxism-Leninism as an Advanced, Scientific Methodology

In Asia, political Marxism cannot really be separated from academic Marxism. The forerunners of most Asian communist parties were Marxist study societies, and when the communist movement has been truly powerful, it has often been underwritten by a favorable academic atmosphere—"progressive scientific" journals, Marxist professors, left-oriented student movements, and similar assistance.

Most classical scholarship in Asia took the form of the baldly factual chronicle, the textual exegesis, or the legalistic tone. Suddenly—and in the context of an overpowering faith in "science"—a new "scientific" approach to human society was revealed, one that presented a grand, cosmic theory of human behavior and social evolution, a theory "documented" by a vast array of socioeconomic data. Marxism was essentially simple, easy to comprehend and apply. Moreover, it had the greatest validity for societies in the initial stages of modernization. It is not surprising that it took many progressive Asian intellectuals by storm, particularly since the West offered no formidable methodological competition prior to World War II.

A Typology of Asian Communist Leaders

The intellectual has been only one element in the Asian communist movement. While he has generally been very important at the leadership level, even here he is not invariably the dominant force. To appreciate the full range of communist leadership, therefore, one must go beyond the intellectual class. Additional motivations and appeals to those outlined above must also be set forth. To be sure, the appeals of Marxism-Leninism already suggested were certainly not applicable to the Asian intelligentsia alone. Many of these appeals were felt, and felt deeply, by the supporters of communism who came from other social classes. But it is necessary now to cast a wider net, one that will encompass a broader range of human motivation in connection with politics, and suggest the three basic types of leadership that have emerged within Asian communism.

The Ideologue

This type is overwhelmingly "intellectual," but its representatives do not necessarily all come from the recognized intellectual class. Whatever their socioeconomic background, they tend to combine, in equal proportions, frustration and resentment over the *status quo*, desire for rapid change, conviction of the scientific truth of Marxism, and the desire to play the role of philosopher-king. Theirs is essentially an ideological commitment to the cause, and they are most comfortable in the roles of pamphleteers, philosophers, and intellectual tutors.

These are deeply sincere, deadly serious men in whom burns an inner fire. They have, generally, a high level of integrity, dedication, and purpose. They are prepared to sacrifice and to demand sacrifice. On occasion, their commitment is broader than Marxism-Leninism—or narrower, depending upon one's interpretation. Within this group are nationalist communists who seem as much motivated by national patriotism as by fervor for the international proletariat. Indeed, in the process of intertwining nationalism and communism, some ideologues take on the qualities of Tom Paine as much as those of Nicolai Lenin. At this stage of Asian communism, we cannot be certain of the precise quotient of nationalism that will ultimately remain in communist ideology. We can only know that it will be high.

Not infrequently, the personality of the ideologue is very different from that generally associated with the radical leader. Many ideologues are introverts, soft-spoken, moderate in personal actions, and with no particular mass appeal. Indeed, they often are men who cannot operate effectively in the open arena and who seem extremely ill at ease when confronted directly with a common man. Their support comes from the hard core of inner workers. Both their words and their personality carry respect at this level because they have demonstrated devotion to the cause, skill in tactics, sensitivity to issues, and personal integrity.

The Activist

Another prominent type of communist leader is the activist. The activist is attracted to communism because it provides an outlet for his organizational skills, his leadership capacities, and his penchant for purposeful action—or possibly, for action in any form. Doctrinal niceties may be of little concern to him. He may find theory boring and intellectual discussions tedious, but association with fellow human beings in a common endeavor that combines drama, movement, and the challenge implicit in revolution is fundamentally satisfying.

Activists can come from any socioeconomic group. Often they

emerge from the ranks of the common man, but more frequently they come from the lower middle class. Most of them are natural leaders: They are strongly extroverted, possessed of a commanding personality that attracts and holds the absolute loyalty of their followers, shrewd judges of men and clever tacticians. If they were not communists, such men might well be leaders of industry or heads of democratic labor or farmer movements. Indeed, in societies where there is sufficient economic development and social mobility, the communist movement undoubtedly loses a significant number of such individuals.

The Careerist

A third type of communist leader has been drawn into the movement because of the opportunities for personal advancement which it offers. There are various kinds of careerists: the peasant lad for whom the party means an education and the chance to escape the monotonous drudgery of farm life; the worker who hopes to gain status as a member of the proletariat, the favored class; the student who sees the possibility of gaining both intellectual and political authority in a disciplined organization; the man with military inclinations who may have the chance to lead a dedicated, powerful army.

Opportunities will vary, of course, with the given party and with its size, importance, and stage of development. No matter how weak and unpromising the party, however, it offers career possibilities or hopes to certain individuals. Life as a communist may be difficult and dangerous, but if it brings some sense of career or of personal advancement, it can produce a continuing commitment even under the most trying circumstances.

The three kinds of communist leaders presented here have been depicted as pure types. In reality, most communist leaders have been drawn into the movement for a variety of reasons and are mixed types. It may still be useful, however, to attempt a portrait of the leadership of the various communist parties of Asia, using these three types as categories, indicating both dominant and subordinate types where these are present, and suggesting current trends where a change seems to be in process. In doing so, I am acutely aware of the fragmentary nature of the evidence upon which this portrait and others soon to be presented are based. Over the past ten years, I have conducted a number of interviews with Asian communist leaders, and my hypotheses are based partially upon these interviews. Various primary and secondary sources relating to Asian communism have also been utilized. Nevertheless, the generalizations advanced here must be treated only as preliminary explorations, based upon scattered data and subject to correction and refinement as our knowledge becomes more extensive.

Chart 1

DOMINANT AND SUBORDINATE TYPES OF LEADERSHIP WITHIN THE ASIAN
COMMUNIST MOVEMENT, AND CURRENT TRENDS

Note: The position of the party or group in the following columns indicates the
dominant type of leadership, a dotted line indicates a subordinate type of importance,
and a straight line indicates a significant trend.

Ideologue	*Activist*	*Careerist*

Chinese Communist Party [a]

Mongolian People's Revolutionary Party

Korean Workers' Party

Vietnamese Workers' Party

National Liberation Front of South Vietnam

Pathet Lao

(ies) [b]
Japanese Communist Party

Philippine Communist Party

Malaysian communist parties [c]

Indonesian Communist Party

Cambodian Communist Party

Thai communist parties

Burmese communist parties [d]

Indian communist parties
(pro-Moscow faction)
(pro-Peking faction)

Nepal Communist Party

Pakistan Communist Party

Ceylon communist parties (pro-Peking faction)
(pro-Moscow faction)

[a] The Chinese Communist Party has been placed midway between the two
columns because it is led by men who must be considered to represent combined
ideologue-activist types more fully than any other Asian Communist leaders.

[b] Today, the mainstream of the Japanese Communist Party is increasingly
dominated by younger, pro-Peking elements, and hence the party is moving rapidly
toward activist control, slowed only by the "objective conditions" prevailing in Japan.
Recently, however, the JCP has ousted a number of pro-Moscow dissidents, some of
whom have organized a separate party, the JCP (Voice of Japan). Both parties show
strong ideologue tendencies.

[c] The various Malaysian communist groups, seemingly in a state of imperfect
coordination at present, are not identical in this or other respects. Naturally, the
Sarawak and Chen Ping communists are led essentially by activists, whereas the
Singapore communist movement contains a certain number of ideologues, although
their number has declined in recent years.

[d] In recent years, the legal communists of Burma, connected with the National
Democratic United Front (NUF), have had a higher percentage of ideologues than
either the White Flag or Red Flag Communists, as would be expected. In a man like
Red Flag leader Thakin Soe, however, one finds a perfect ideologue-activist combination. The White Flag Communists, incidentally, are the communists recognized
internationally as the Communist Party of Burma.

Before commenting upon the implications of Chart 1, let me present certain other aspects of current Asian communist leadership in the form of comparative tables (Charts 2 and 3).

Chart 2

CURRENT SOCIOECONOMIC CLASS REPRESENTATION WITHIN THE TOP LEADERSHIP OF THE ASIAN COMMUNIST PARTIES AND COMMUNIST-CONTROLLED MOVEMENTS

	Worker	*Farmer*	*Intellectual Petit Bourgeois*	*Other Bourgeoisie*	*Military*
Chinese Communist Party	Weak-Medium	Weak-Medium	Very strong	Very weak	Very strong
Mongolian People's Revolutionary Party	Weak-Medium	Medium	Strong-Medium	Very weak	Strong-Medium
Korean Workers' Party	Weak-Medium	Weak-Medium	Strong-Medium	Very weak	Very strong
Vietnamese Workers' Party	Weak	Weak-Medium	Strong	Medium	Very strong
National Liberation Front of South Vietnam	Weak	Medium	Very strong	Medium	Very strong
Pathet Lao	Very weak	Weak	Medium	Medium	Very strong [a]
Japanese Communist Party(ies)	Medium-Strong	Very weak	Very strong	Medium	Very weak
Philippine Communist Party	Weak	Medium	Very strong	Medium	Strong [a]
Malaysian communist parties	Medium	Very weak	Strong	Strong	Strong [a]
Indonesian Communist Party	Medium-Strong	Medium	Medium-Strong	Medium	Medium-Strong
Cambodian Communist Party	Very weak	Very weak	Very strong	Strong	Very weak
Thai communist parties	Weak	Weak	Strong	Strong	Very weak
Burmese communist parties:					
National Democratic United Front	Strong	Weak	Strong	Medium	Very weak
Red Flag	Very weak	Weak	Very strong	Medium	Strong [a]
White Flag (BCP)	Weak	Medium	Very strong	Medium	Strong [a]

Chart 2 (*cont.*)

	Worker	Farmer	Intellectual Petit Bourgeois	Other Bourgeoisie	Military
Indian Communist Party(ies)	Medium	Weak	Very strong	Strong	Very weak
Nepal Communist Party	Very weak	Weak	Very strong	Strong	Weak
Pakistan Communist Party	Very weak	Very weak	Very strong	Strong	Very weak
Ceylon communist parties	Medium	Weak	Very strong	Strong	Very weak

Note: Top Leadership, as used here, refers to members and alternate members of the politburos and central committees and to those occupying positions of comparable importance. Strength is assigned on the basis of a five-term scale: Very weak, Weak, Medium, Strong, and Very strong. Strength relates to numbers and importance within the party, not to whether the representation is greater or less than the numerical proportion of the class in the society at large.

It is recognized that the separate designation, *Military,* may be challenged in terms of the other categories employed, and that some of these categories may appear vague. *Worker* covers manual workers, lower clerical workers, and those labor leaders who can truly be considered a part of the working class as distinct from the intellectuals who have taken up labor leadership. *Farmer* includes all individuals whose primary income is derived from agriculture, irrespective of status. *Intellectual Petit Bourgeois* encompasses academicians, literati, journalists, students, and other brainworkers, including the very important category of professional bureaucracy. *Other Bourgeoisie* includes entrepreneurs, merchants, and such professional men as doctors, lawyers, and engineers. *Military* covers not only professionally trained military men, but also individuals who in the course of revolutionary careers have devoted primary or substantial energy to military pursuits, men who consider themselves, by occupation or knowledge, at least partially military specialists. It is this latter group, of course, which comprises the great bulk of the *Military* category within the Asian communist movement.

Needless to say, these categories are not mutually exclusive. And if the full background of the current leaders were added, an even more mixed profile of many leaders would emerge. To take one example, Mao Tse-tung is of peasant origin and has continued throughout most of his active life to work with the rural masses. By virtue of his education and career, he also must be considered an intellectual. But much of his life was spent in military pursuits, and he prides himself on being the father of modern guerrilla warfare. He must thus be accorded full recognition under both the *Intellectual and Military* categories, and be given half-status under the *Farmer* category.

[a] These are parties in which the *Military* (almost all the nonprofessionals described in the Note to this Chart) are strong only in relation to internal party composition. In some cases, however, Chinese or North Vietnamese training programs have greatly facilitated the emergence of guerrilla leadership and, in nearly all cases, the classics on guerrilla warfare written by Mao, Giap, and others have been available for study.

Chart 3

DATE OF ESTABLISHMENT OF COMMUNIST PARTY, CURRENT GENERATION
OF LEADERSHIP, AND GENERAL AGE SPAN OF TOP LEADERS IN 1964
(TRANSITIONAL CASES INDICATED BY ARROW)

Date Party Established	First-Generation Leadership [a] (Age)	Second- and Third-Generation Leadership (Age)
1921 (1920)[b]	Chinese Communist Party (65–75) ──────────→	(50–60)
1920		Mongolian People's Revolutionary Party (40–60)
1925 (1919)[c]		Korean Workers' Party (40–55)
1930 (1925)[d]	Vietnamese Workers' Party (55–75) ──────────→	(30–50)
1961[e]	National Liberation Front of South Vietnam (30–50)	
1945[f]	Pathet Lao (40–55)	
1922	Japanese Communist Party(ies) (65–72) ──────────→	(30–55)
1930		Philippines Communist Party (45–55)
1931[g]		Malaysian communist parties (25–50)

[a] The designation *First Generation Leadership* does not necessarily refer to the first leaders of the party, but to the continued prominence of men who were a part of the party's formative period.

[b] A communist study group was organized in Shanghai in 1920, after the arrival of Gregory Voitinsky, by Ch'en Tu-hsiu.

[c] Prior to the establishment of the first Korean Communist Party in Seoul in 1925, various *émigré* groups had founded communist organizations. One, founded in Irkutsk in 1919, was named the All-Russia Korean Communist Party, and several others emerged during this period.

[d] In 1925, Nguyen Ai Quoc (Ho Chi Minh), already a communist with five years of experience in Paris, Moscow, and China, founded the Vietnam Revolutionary Youth League, a predecessor to the Vietnam Communist Party which was created in 1930. The present Vietnamese Workers' Party was launched in 1951.

[e] The National Liberation Front of South Vietnam was created in 1961, and its hard-core party, the South Vietnam National Revolutionary Party, was established in 1962.

[f] In 1945, Lao Issara was organized. The Pathet Lao, the military organization which evolved out of this group, was created in 1951. At present, the Neo Lao Hak Xat, which was legalized in 1957, is the basic party for the communists, and the Pathet Lao is its military arm.

[g] Chinese communists were in Malaya as early as 1924, and communist activity was significant in Singapore by 1927-1928. Many authorities date the founding of the Malayan Communist Party as 1930, but one official document specifies 1931. The early party was almost completely wiped out by the Japanese during World War II, and a new party emerged. The Clandestine Communist Organization in Sarawak, of

Chart 3 (*cont.*)

1920			Indonesian Communist Party	(35–53)
1945	Cambodian Communist Party	(25–40)		
1935 (*c.* 1925)[h]			Thai communist parties	(25–45)
1943 (1938-39)[i]	Burmese communist parties	(40–55)		
1928 (1921)[j]	Indian Communist Party(ies)	(60–75)	⟶	(40–60)
1949	Nepal Communist Party	(35–50)		
1928[k]			Pakistan Communist Party	(40–60)
1940 (1935)[l]	Ceylon Communist Party (Moscow faction)	(47–65)	Ceylon Communist Party (Peking faction)	(35–50)

course, is of much more recent vintage, its predecessor being the Sarawak Overseas Chinese Democratic Youth League, established in 1951.

[h] Communist activity among the Thai Chinese goes back to the era of Chinese Communist Party-Kuomintang collaboration. The precise founding date of the CCP in Thailand is unclear, and the party has undergone several basic changes. The Thai Communist Party dates its founding from 1935.

[i] While the Burmese Communist Party was officially founded in 1943, proto-communist groups, springing out of the Thakin movement and various contacts with Indian and British radicals, date back to 1938-1939.

[j] An *émigré* Indian Communist Party was organized in the Soviet Union in 1921, and there are even reports of one such party established in Tashkent in 1920. The official Indian Communist Party was founded in 1928.

[k] It is manifestly impossible to separate the early history of the Pakistan Communist Party from that of the Indian party although, in a strict sense, the Pakistan party dates only from partition.

[l] The Ceylonese Lanka Sama Samaja Party, which encompassed a wide range of socialists, including communists, was founded in 1935. In 1940, the communists were expelled and founded the United Socialist Party, which was communist in all but name. The United Socialist Party officially became the Ceylon Communist Party in 1943.

What generalizations can be drawn about Asian communist party leadership from these three charts, assuming their basic accuracy?

Types of Leadership

Ideologue leadership has predominated in the initial phases of a party's emergence and development. In weak parties this has frequently continued. As most parties have developed strength, however, and begun to vie seriously for political and military power, the trend has generally been toward activist control. Finally, among parties firmly ensconced in power, or of sufficient significance to offer major opportunities, careerist leadership has become increasingly important. Thus, the typical progression of leadership in a party, moving from its earliest development through the struggle for power and thence to control of the whole or a part of its society, is from ideologue to activist and, finally, careerist dominance.

Most Asian communist parties are moving toward activist dominance if they are not already in that category. Today, communist leaders give primary attention to party organization, cadre training, and revolutionary tactics. Indeed, it is crucial to recognize that in contemporary Asian communism, concern over organization often takes precedence over all other considerations, including those of program and policy. The present generation of communist leaders has discovered that the route to power lies more in superior organization than in appealing issues, a fact difficult for Western liberals to perceive. Making use of the many techniques now available for mobilization and commitment, they concentrate upon creating a disciplined, tightly structured, efficient machine in an otherwise loosely jointed society. Activist dominance and organizational priority are two key symbols of Asian communism today.

Class Origins of Leaders

In socioeconomic terms, Asian communist party leadership has come predominantly from what might be termed the middle class, or, as the Marxists term it, from the *bourgeoisie* and especially from the *petite bourgeoisie.* In occupational terms, a majority can be described as intellectuals, military men, or a combination of the two. Most have had some higher education, the central fact that distinguishes them from so many of their compatriots. Asian communist leaders, in short, are far closer to both traditional and other modern Asian leaders in their socioeconomic attributes than they are to the proletarian leadership projected in Marxian theory. The communist leaders share many traits with the other elements of the modernizing elite with whom they are in competition—education, status, and even a common core of values.[2] Some communist leaders, indeed, are closely related in certain respects to the more traditional segment of the modernizing elite: They come from the upper classes, and a portion of their appeal is based upon status, ethnic, or regional considerations.

This is not to deny certain significant differences nor to negate the features that make these men communists. They are individuals distinguishable, among other things, by their particular ideological convictions, by their customary political tactics and techniques, and by their very special domestic and foreign ties. In broad terms, however, contemporary Asian communist leaders have, from the beginning, been more a part of than apart from the elite of their society.

Special emphasis should be given to the importance of the military in the Asian communist movement. There has been a tendency to minimize or ignore this fact because of a partly justified belief that, since the party controls the army, political considerations are therefore paramount —and because many communist leaders can be called "military" only if that term is used somewhat loosely. In my opinion, communist leaders should be classified as military or quasi-military if they function wholly or in an important sense as military men, irrespective of their formal training and self-identification. If this view is accepted, the military component within Asian communist party leadership is, without exception, seen to be strong or very strong in those parties holding power. Even in parties not in power, wherever the tactic of guerrilla warfare is being pursued the military have naturally assumed an important role. Perhaps the most dominant single form of leadership for successful communist parties is the hyphenated intellectual-military (or military-intellectual) type. Men like Mao Tse-tung, Kim Il-sŏng, and even Ho Chi Minh can be included in this category. These men—and many others who have come to power—are old guerrilla fighters, wedded to an intellectual (or, more accurately, a quasi- or semi-intellectual) tradition.

Those Asian communist leaders who come from outside the orthodox elite classes tend to have agrarian antecedents, reflecting the fact that they emerge from overwhelmingly agrarian societies. In such cases, the normal background is that of middle or rich farmer, not that of tenant. Only the former two categories generally afford the opportunities for education, mobility, and the other attributes essential for political leadership.

Very few communist leaders currently come from the urban worker class. Even leaders who are so labeled are often intellectuals who became professional labor organizers, not true members of the proletariat. Leaders from the working class are almost entirely second-generation men, younger men not yet at the top rungs of the hierarchy. Even these are relatively few in number in most parties.

Age of Communist Leadership

Asian communist leaders in key positions, or moving into those positions, are generally second- or third-generation leaders in the age bracket from 40 to 55. This makes them somewhat younger than their competitors for power in most Asian societies. First-generation communist leaders are fading away, becoming communists emeriti, if indeed they are still alive. There are some exceptions—mainly in the newer parties—but for the most part, the veterans of the Asian communist movement are now passing from the scene. Thus, in terms of leadership, a great transitional era is currently under way.

The older generation, tending to be more strongly ideologue in type, was also generally conditioned to an international communist organization dominated by Moscow. They emerged and spent most of their active political lives in the era of monolithic world communism, when orthodoxy and heresy were pronounced in final tones from the Kremlin. Not all the older-generation leaders were totally submissive, but the strong tendency was for the more creative and independent thinkers to leave the party or be ordered out. Those who remained were either conditioned to an acceptance of Moscow directives or survived because in some fashion they had created an indigenous base of power, one not heavily dependent upon the Soviet base.

These days, and among the second generation, the activist type is more prominent. Interest in organizational work, both political and military, is high even at the grass-roots level. The international communist movement is no longer monolithic, and the new generation tends to regard Moscow with suspicion, if not hostility. It is the inspiration of Peking—the newest revolutionary model—that holds sway among this group. The quotient of nationalism is high in the current group of Asian communist leaders, however, much higher than in their predecessors. It is at least questionable whether the undeniable influence of Peking upon Asian communists can be translated into a Peking-directed Asian comintern possessed of the same monolithic qualities as the old Moscow model. As we observed earlier, the swing of the pendulum is toward adaptation rather than mechanical borrowing, toward pragmatism (i.e., doing what will work) rather than ideological purity, toward national communism rather than full-fledged internationalism. Throughout Asia, Marxism-Leninism is being consciously and unconsciously revised in accordance with these trends. Thus, the world struggle over who are the revisionists becomes all the more ironic.

Revolutionary Tactics, Party Organization, and Membership

Lenin first established the basic tactical and organizational principles that have governed communist parties in "late developing" societies, but it remained for the communist leaders of China to carry Leninist principles forward on the most successful and dramatic scale in Asia. Unlike the establishment of communist power in Mongolia and North Korea, which was primarily a product of external power, the victory of the Chinese communists was essentially the result of indigenous developments.[3] Consequently, the Chinese revolutionary model has had a major impact upon other Asian communist parties. It is a model involving not only a series of revolutionary tactics but also corresponding organizational techniques, and these two must be viewed as interactive, inseparable elements. Briefly, then, let us set forth the essentials of the Chinese model, following its developmental stages from party beginnings to the aftermath of total victory. (It will be noted that I frequently use Chinese communist language in presenting the model, so as to convey more vividly its essence. Only the parenthetical remarks, therefore, should be considered as a full effort at objectivity.)

Stage 1: Party Emergence

A premium must be placed upon the earliest possible creation of a communist party as the only legitimate organ of the proletariat. This party must be organized by the vanguard of the proletariat (i.e., intellectuals) and protected against all liquidationists, whatever travails have to be faced.

Simultaneously, the permanent party structure should be created in miniature. The party congress meets once a year or less frequently. The supreme party organ, it is composed of delegates chosen by party members. (In reality, congress delegates must be carefully selected, with due regard to regional, ethnic, and functional representation.) The congress has as its primary purpose the debate over alternative courses of action and the determination of basic party policy. (In fact, the congress serves as a sounding board and primary communications outlet for leadership, ratifying, but never making or even altering, policy.)

The central committee is established as the working committee of the congress, and generally has from 60 to 100 members chosen for their service to the party, experience, and ability. [They are chosen, also, for their absolute loyalty to the party and are often protégés of the top leader(s).] The central committee usually meets several times a year to hear reports, discuss, and on occasion debate concrete policies. (In the initial stages of the party—or in the event of a serious struggle for power or basic policy differences among top leaders—true debate may take place in the central committee, and its final decisions may have a critical influence. More usual, however, is the gradual subordination of the central committee to the primary leader(s), and its loss of any independent decision-making powers.)

In the committees appointed by the central committee, and particularly in the political committee, or politburo, resides the real power to direct the party—and, in the event of victory, the nation. The politburo normally numbers some eight to twelve men, carefully ranked and, almost without exception, the most powerful men in the party. (The politburo makes all basic decisions for the party, unless these decisions are made by one man—the party secretary-general or chairman—or a small inner clique.) A number of other executive-administrative committees are created, including a secretariat or organization committee handling organizational work, and a control committee in charge of security matters. (The key positions in all of these bodies are held by an interlocking directorate of a dozen men or less.)

This party structure, established at the outset and modeled almost precisely after the Soviet party, is permanent. Significant changes occur, however, in the actual distribution of power within this structure, particularly among the top leadership. As a general tendency, the party commences its existence with a reasonable amount of freedom of internal discussion, a freedom which extends to the central committee and may on occasion reach even as far as the party congress. Decisions have a collective quality, and criticism—at least "constructive" criticism—is permitted. The majority position, to be sure, is binding upon the minority, and the rules of "democratic centralism" always prevail: There is rank-and-file representation from the grass roots by means of successively elected bodies, and the leadership, thus legitimized, exercises its absolute authority from the top down. Nevertheless, in the formative stages, power within the party is often held more loosely and by a wider circle of men.

In time, the power circle tends to become more narrow, the decision-making process more rigid. The very structure of the communist party—and the ideology that underlies that structure—are conducive to a struggle for supremacy that must culminate in the victory of one man. The absence of any tradition of minority rights, and of any mechanism for a peaceful alternation in power, makes every contest for power a final one. Hence the struggle must be ruthless, with no holds barred. Rivals are castigated in absolute terms: "false Marxist-Leninists," "opportunists," and "traitors." When the battle is decided, purges almost inevitably follow. In the end, one man tends to emerge as supreme leader, without a serious competitor. (Rarely, this same process can take place as a natural product of party evolution.)

The formal party structure then becomes the instrument of the supreme leader and the followers whom he groups around him. It is not uncommon, however, for an element of oligarchy to persist, with the supreme leader sharing his power more or less voluntarily with two or three trusted colleagues who will never challenge his final authority. As the supreme leader ages, the pattern of power distribution may become more perfectly oligarchic, with the small group around him acquiring even greater authority. At this point, the party power structure may be similar to that before the struggle for supremacy had been decided. When the supreme leader has been seriously weakened by massive errors or by age and ill health, or when he dies, a new struggle generally occurs, making possible a temporary widening of the power circle.[4]

Stage 2: Broadening the Base of the Party

With the party launched and its permanent organizational structure established, the initial task is to develop it from a small conspiratorial coterie composed largely of intellectuals to a mass-based political organization of depth and authority.

What are the primary techniques of growth? First, it is essential to divide the society into two broad categories: the "people" and the "enemies of the people." The people are the workers, peasants, intelligentsia, and other "patriotic, national *bourgeoisie*." They represent 90 per cent of the society—and they must be wooed and won. Contradictions will exist among the people, and between the people and the party, but these can be resolved by discussion. They are not fundamental.

The enemies of the people include the feudal gentry, the big capitalists, and the reactionary political leaders—that 10 per cent of the society that must be fought and destroyed. Contradictions between enemies and the party can only be resolved by a struggle unto death. They are fundamental. (One can, moreover, slip from being "people" to "enemy of the people" by willfully opposing the party.)

Having defined the basic target, it is equally essential to define the issues that will make possible mass mobilization and commitment to the party. The basic issues are twofold: internal reforms, all of which are basically bourgeois-democratic in nature; and an appeal to nationalism, another bourgeois concept. In sum, the communist party at this stage must begin its effort to capture the bourgeois-democratic revolution by seeking to capture the very issues that are intrinsically bourgeois in character.

No element of the people is more important than the peasantry, comprising 80 per cent of the masses. To them are attuned the promises of land reform, elimination of corrupt officials and rapacious warlords, lower taxes, and a host of other benefits; to the workers, new freedoms and dramatic rises in status and living conditions; to the intellectuals and other bourgeois elements, participation in a new, noble experiment in nation-building and social justice. And to all groups, the promise of first-class citizenship in a first-class nation, rid of foreign imperialists. Indeed, the struggle to lead the nationalist movement becomes paramount—and probably decisive—in the fortunes of the party. Both the successful utilization of united front tactics and the favorable development of mass associations as front organizations are heavily dependent on the party's capacity to play upon nationalist themes.

Throughout this and the succeeding stages, however, an emphasis upon organization remains of supreme importance. Those whom the party cannot woo, it coerces. And by means of both coercion and persuasion, it seeks to build a powerful, integrated structure capable of committing members to execute orders with unquestioning obedience, and liquidating or silencing those who would interfere.

Stage 3: *Mounting the Challenge to the Ruling Party (Class)*

As the party base is extended, political and economic activities can be intensified. To the extent that bourgeois democracy does not exist, heavy pressures must be exerted upon its behalf: agitation for freedom of speech, press, and association; demands for freedom of unionization, rights for tillers, and other socioeconomic reforms. To the extent that bourgeois democracy does exist, the central tactic must be the use (and abuse) of the democratic system.

In concrete terms, this latter tactic takes two forms: (1) the simultaneous appeal for unity with, and the sustained trenchant attack upon the dominant national-bourgeois party; and (2) the coupling of legal activities with semilegal and illegal ones. At this point, it is vital to extend the party reach by joining in a united front with the more powerful, primary nationalist party, in order to combat imperialism and feudal reactionaries. At the same time, however, party integrity and independence of action must be fully protected: A constant vigil must be maintained against the threat of absorption or destruction by a superior force.

An important aspect of this tactic is the struggle to share with the national *bourgeoisie* the prestige of the central charismatic figure of the nationalist movement, the Father of the Country. To utilize and, if possible, to capture this figure is to add great impetus to the party's legitimization. Success in this effort enables the party, as the rightful successor to the great leader, to inherit the nationalist revolution upon his demise. The act of uniting with the dominant nationalist party and cultivating its leader, however, must not prejudice the task of attacking and undermining this same party and leader. Bourgeois weaknesses and crimes must constantly be drawn to the attention of the masses, and bourgeois forces must be divided, the more progressive elements being subordinated to the party and the reactionary elements being isolated and destroyed.

At this stage, it is essential that the leadership of the national democratic revolution be captured by the proletariat (i.e., the communist party) so that a continuous, uninterrupted march toward socialism can be achieved. Under no circumstances can the *bourgeoisie* be allowed to retain control of the bourgeois-democratic revolution until its completion. If that should occur, a second revolution would be necessary to complete the transition to socialism. The final stages of the bourgeois-democratic revolution must be managed by the proletariat.

To capture the bourgeois-democratic revolution, the party cannot and must not depend upon parliamentary tactics alone. No ruling class voluntarily relinquishes power. Thus, in this stage, it is essential to couple legal and illegal actions, to pursue different routes to power simultaneously, the exact admixture depending upon conditions. As the party's political and economic power develops, its potential for a truly revolutionary challenge to the ruling party grows, and it must prepare to take advantage of this fact.

Stage 4: The People's War

When conditions are ripe, or when circumstances necessitate it, the party must be prepared to shift its primary emphasis from political to military action. This does not mean the abandonment of politics, but an advance to the final, climactic stage where the decision will be determined by the outcome of military struggle, a struggle to which all political and economic resources must be directed.

Military action must follow the principles of guerrilla warfare. The red army must be built largely with peasant recruits and must find its natural habitat in the rural areas. Here it is protected against its numerical weakness, provided it is careful to cultivate the people and win them as allies. In the initial stages, it must be prepared for highly mobile warfare, striking at the enemy when and where he least expects it, making certain that it strikes in superior numbers and then fades away when the enemy musters a major force.

As these tactics succeed, it will be possible to establish a secure territorial base and create a shadow government. Party officials will now perform the necessary tasks of administration, acquiring experience in preparation for governing the entire country. Party activities also expand. There is no relaxation of politics. The cadres, greatly increased in numbers, educate and guide the people in the liberated areas. In enemy territory they operate in covert fashion, and a steady flow of recruits files out of such territory as a result of their efforts.

If the military phase goes well, the party gradually acquires a sizable portion of the country in which it reigns supreme, and it infiltrates much of the enemy's territory, operating a government-by-night, a dual administration. From its relatively self-sufficient rural bases, the party watches—and abets—increasing unrest in the urban centers and government enclaves, the product of economic chaos, administrative disorder, defeatism and low morale, and massive social dislocations. Ultimately, the cities fall like overripe fruit when the process of disintegration has run its course.

Stage 5: The Establishment of People's Democracy

With military victory comes the transition from bourgeois democracy to people's democracy, and thence ultimately to communism. First, the final stages of the bourgeois-democratic revolution must be completed under proletarian management. Land redistribution—based upon a tripartite classification of the rural classes into poor, middle, and rich—is carried out. Full freedom is announced for "the people," and swift retribution for their enemies. A series of purges against traitors and exploiters gets under way.

Chart 4 (*cont.*)

(1) Collective Leadership Dominant	(2) Some Collective Leadership but Tendency toward Small Clique Control	(3) Small Clique Control	(4) One-man Supremacy but Power Shared with Small Clique	(5) One-man Dominance
Pakistan Communist Party (?) ———→				
	Ceylon Communist Party(ies) (both factions) ———→			
			Nepal Communist Party(ies) (both factions)	

Note: This categorization warrants some explanation. In a highly organized party fitting Category 1 (*Collective Leadership Dominant*), party congress or at least central committee decisions would be of critical importance, and a maximum amount of policy initiation would take place at this level as well as via the local or regional party units. In less structured parties (probably the only parties which have ever come under this category), the entire membership has access to the decision-making process.

Category 2 is a mixed type. Membership, party congress, or central committee decisions are of significance, either consistently or sporadically, but politburo or other forms of small group control are important to the decision-making process.

In Category 3 parties, the politburo, or the dominant clique within it, plays the key role and no individual holds sustained paramount power.

Category 4 is again a mixed type. One leader is clearly *primus inter pares*, but a small group working with him plays a significant role in fashioning basic decisions.

In Category 5 parties, one leader has acquired sufficient power to make the politburo, and all other party organs, his creatures and can readily translate this will into party policy.

Chart 5

STAGES OF DEVELOPMENT OF THE VARIOUS ASIAN COMMUNIST PARTIES BASED ROUGHLY UPON THE CHINESE MODEL, AND DEGREE OF APPLICABILITY OF THAT MODEL, USING A SCALE OF 0-5 (NOT APPLICABLE TO TOTALLY APPLICABLE)

(DUAL STAGES OR TRANSITIONS INDICATED BY ARROW)

Stage 1	Stage 2	Stage 3	Stage 4	Stage 5	Degrees of Applicability
				(Mongolian People's Revolutionary Party)	2
		(South Korean) ←——————→		Korean Workers' Party	3

Chart 5 (*cont.*)

Stage 1	Stage 2	Stage 3	Stage 4	Stage 5	Degrees of Applicability
				Vietnam Workers' Party	4
		Pathet Lao			4
				National Liberation Front of South Vietnam	4
	Japanese Communist Party(ies) ⟶				1
	Philippine Communist Party ⟶				2
			Malaysian ← communist ⟶ parties		4
		Indonesian Communist Party			4
Cambodian Communist Party					4?
Thai communist parties ⟶					3
		← Burmese communist parties ⟶			4
	Indian Communist Party(ies)				3
← Nepal Communist Party ⟶					3–4
Pakistan Communist Party					3–4
	← Ceylon communist parties ⟶				3

What general themes can be drawn from the above charts?

There are no significant organizational differences among the communist parties of Asia. In each case, the party structure, established in the initial stage of party emergence, has remained basically intact and similar to the early Soviet model. As can readily be discovered, however, there is a substantial difference among current parties in the location and distribution of decision-making authority.

Among the Asian communist parties in power, two—those of North Korea and Mongolia—have recently undergone an extensive struggle for supreme power, attended by numerous purges. Kim Il-sŏng at last having won those struggles, now appears to rule his country with an iron hand, controlling all major appointments and policies. Tsedenbal's position and present role are less clear, although he appears to be dominant, powerful enough to determine all basic policy. His status, however, seems inseparably connected with Russian support.

The other two dominant parties—those of China and North Vietnam—are parties in which a supreme leader has long existed. But these supreme leaders are now aging and nearing the end of their active political careers. Increasingly, power appears to be delegated—or shared with a small group of senior leaders. And at least in North Vietnam, those senior leaders appear to be far from united. Thus, meaningful debate certainly takes place both in the North Vietnamese Politburo and Central Committee; possibly it extends to the Party Congress. Younger cadre elements, moreover, are now pushing their way up into the power structure, many of them serving as protégés—and stalking horses—for the senior men who are engaged in sharp contests for power. On a more muted basis, a similar situation may exist or be developing in China. Certainly the death or full retirement of Mao is likely to produce further alterations in the power structure of the Chinese Communist Party.

Among the other Asian communist parties, the most pronounced tendency is domination by a small clique, an inner group that may include an acknowledged leader but that in any case exercises some degree of collective power. This clique may number three or four members, it may number five or six, but it is generally smaller than the politburo, constituting merely the majority or the powerful figures therein. Small clique domination occurs under a variety of circumstances. It is most likely to exist when a final power struggle has not yet taken place and when leaders roughly equal in prestige are willing and able to work together. And even when a supreme leader has emerged or is in the process of emerging, political exigencies, personality factors, or other conditions may encourage oligarchy rather than one-man rule. A subtle combination of the two is, of course, often the most logical development at one stage.

A few cases of one-man dominance can be found among the weaker Asian communist parties, but they are unusual. One-man dominance exists currently among the Red Flag communists of Burma, and possibly in the jungle forces of Chen Peng in Malaysia, but not elsewhere. More common is some degree of truly collective leadership, which may exist as the natural product of a young party in which power relationships have not yet solidified or in parties in which there is a substantial degree of factionalism, preventing the acknowledgment of a supreme leader and causing the distribution of power on a wider scale. Under these conditions, a considerable degree of inner party democracy can exist as long as the key leaders wish to avert a major power struggle and open split.

In exploring these organizational differences, one certainly should not ignore the political culture of the society. Modes of political behavior and styles of political organization traditional in the broader cultural patterns of the society clearly help to determine the character of a party's leadership and organizational structure. The consensual, groupistic orientation of most Asian societies undoubtedly moderates monolithism in some parties. But "objective conditions"—the character of the colonial heritage, the stage of economic development, the nature of the opposition—also affect party tactics and structure. Our basic thesis, however, appears to be valid: The nature of communist ideology and organizational theory lends itself to the movement from collective to individual leadership, with the strong possibility of cyclical trends over longer periods of time.

It is clear that the communist parties of Asia have increasingly patterned their tactics after key aspects of the Chinese experience. Even where the idea was that of Lenin or some other non-Asian Marxist, it was Chinese practice which gave the idea relevance and vitality. While the Bolshevik Revolution remains a great historical event for the Asian communists, the Chinese Revolution represents the wave of the future, the source of contemporary guidance and inspiration.

Only one Asian communist party, the Mongolian People's Revolutionary Party (MPRP), continues to pay scant attention to the Chinese model. Its revolution predates the Chinese Communist Revolution by a full generation, and it continues to reflect extensive Soviet guidance. The Russians brought Mongolian communist leaders to power, and they keep them there. But in the timing of their revolution and in the external source of their power, the Mongolian communists are unique among their Asian comrades.

No doubt Mongolian nationalism, which must be directed primarily against China, is a major factor in limiting Chinese influence. It should be noted, however, that there is nothing in the present stage of Mongolian development that precludes the applicability of advanced (Stage 5) Chinese party techniques, and it is always conceivable that a pro-Chinese leader might, with Chinese assistance, topple a pro-Soviet ruler.[5]

Where does the Chinese model tend to be most useful? In general, it has greatest applicability in those societies where economic development is least advanced, where political control by "bourgeois-democratic" forces is most precarious, and where conditions are most suitable for the exploitation of the nationalist issue, preferably in the form of a "national liberation" movement. Some or all of these circumstances exist in the highest degree in Burma, Cambodia, Indonesia, Laos, Thailand, and Vietnam. There are also close ethnic and cultural bonds to China within the communist movements of Malaysia and Thailand, as a result of the strong Chinese composition of the communist parties of these two countries.[6] Thus, in these seven countries Chinese revolutionary tactics have special meaning. And it is worthy of note that, in four of these nations, the communist party has already entered Stage 4, and that in another (Indonesia), the party is progressing through Stage 3 with notable success. Only in Cambodia and Thailand, where special circumstances prevail, is the communist party at a more rudimentary level of development.

There are two other societies—Nepal and Pakistan—where, at least potentially, conditions are only slightly less propitious for the application of the Chinese model. Some of the same economic and political circumstances characteristic of the seven countries noted above exist. There is a wider cultural gap, certain facets of which may make the Chinese model more difficult to apply. At the moment, moreover, as in Cambodia and Thailand, the circumstances and stage of emergence give the communist parties of these two countries somewhat less room for maneuvering. In all four countries, for example, relatively strong leaders have followed policies of conciliation, repression, or a combination of both, in such a fashion as to prevent the communist party from moving beyond Stage 2. This situation, however, may easily prove only temporary, and we must assume that, for all of these societies, the Chinese model has potentially a relatively high level of applicability.

The Chinese model may be somewhat less relevant in India and Ceylon. The colonial histories of these societies, the circumstances of their liberation, the trends since their independence, and general cultural factors combine to render Chinese Communist Party (CCP) tactics less meaningful. Parliamentarism has a stronger hold upon the elite, a fact reflected even within the communist movements of these two societies. Utilization of the nationalist movement by the communists, moreover, will clearly be more difficult, especially in India. In addition, the political and economic intrastructure of these counthies is somewhat more highly developed, requiring different political techniques.

Nevertheless, at the grossest level, the socioeconomic character and problems of India and Ceylon are sufficiently similar to those of other underdeveloped societies to give the Chinese revolutionary model a certain appeal and validity. With the proper adaptations, it might become a serviceable instrument for the Indian and Ceylon communist parties.

North Korea is a special case. The Korean communists came to power because of Russian support, not on the basis of their own indigenous development.[7] The early stages of Chinese experience, therefore, had little meaning to North Korea. At present however, the Chinese model, as exemplified in Stage 5, is having great influence upon Pyongyang. Moreover, the earlier revolutionary tactics of the CCP are now being applied in Korean communist strategy in the South.

In Japan and the Philippines, the Chinese model appears to have distinctly limited applicability. Both societies, and particularly Japan, have gone beyond that stage of economic and political development for which the Chinese model was fashioned. In relative terms, they are "advanced" societies. Parliamentarism functions with considerable effectiveness; the nationalist issue is more difficult (although not impossible) to exploit; and economic modernization is well advanced. Notwithstanding these facts, Chinese influence upon both the Japanese and the Philippine communist parties has been growing in recent years, for reasons that will be discussed later.

In summary, the Chinese revolutionary model has had a tremendous influence upon the thinking and activity of the great majority of Asian communist leaders. Most Asian communist parties are now seeking to follow the five basic stages that characterized the Chinese Communist Revolution. They are seeking to shape their basic tactics after those laid down by Mao Tse-tung and his associates, while at the same time firmly asserting that their fundamental task is that of adapting Marxism-Leninism creatively to the realities of their own society, not the blind copying of any other revolutionary experience. In point of fact, as they interpret those realities, the Chinese model applies in most cases.

Strength and Composition of Asian Communist Parties

Having established the basic tactical and organizational lines of the Asian communist parties, let us now assess their relative strength and the socioeconomic composition of their membership (Charts 6 and 7). Once again, extreme caution must be used in reading the following charts. In many cases, the data are incomplete and uncertain; thus, the charts should be regarded as approximations, not precise tabulations.

Chart 6

RELATIVE STRENGTH OF THE ASIAN COMMUNIST PARTIES AND GROUPS

Dominant Communist Parties	Population of Nation	Party Membership	Electoral Strength (Where Relevant)	National or Regional Distribution of Strength
Chinese Communist Party	650,000,000– 700,000,000	Over 18,000,000 estimated in 1965; 17,000,000, as of July 1, 1961 (80 per cent joined after 1949; 70 per cent during First Five Year Plan); 20,000,000 cadres reported in 1963, some non-Party)	. . . .	National
Mongolian People's Revolutionary Party	1,000,000	47,000 including candidate members, in 1963 (40 per cent joined since 1947)	. . . .	National

Chart 6 (*cont.*)

Dominant Communist Parties	Population of Nation	Party Membership	Electoral Strength (Where Relevant)	National or Regional Distribution of Strength
Korean Workers' Party	10,000,000	Over 1,300,000 members and candidate members in 1964 (only 366,000 members in 1946)	. . . .	National in North (but influence in Republic of Korea negligible, as of early 1964)
Vietnamese Workers' Party	17,500,000	570,000 members in 1963 (in 1946, only 5,000–20,000 members, but no major growth since 1954)		
Strong communist parties				
Pathet Lao	2,000,000	Neo Lao Hak Xat is the primary communist instrument at present with an estimated 1,500–3,000 members. Its military arm, the Pathet Lao, has 20,000 troops, 3,000 cadres in 1965.	. . . .	Regional (about one-half of Laos, in 1964)
National Liberation Front of South Vietnam	14,800,000	35,000 hard-core troops and 60,000–90,000 part-time guerrillas in 1965; South Vietnam National Revolutionary Party, 500–600 members in 1965	. . . .	About 40 per cent Key influence in Mekong Delta, of South Vienam, as of mid-1964
Indonesian Communist Party	103,000,000	3,000,000 members and 10,000,000 – 15,000,000 front organization members claimed in 1965. Some estimates are only 2,000,000 – 2,500,000 members. (7,910 members in 1952)	Over 30 per cent Overall—approximately 10–15 per cent	Regional (mainly Java)
Indian Communist Party(ies)	465,000,000	Split into Left and Right factions in 1964; over 200,000 members in 1965, with the Left faction having a majority due to its strength in Kerala, Andhra and West Bengal. (53,000 members in 1946)	From 40 per cent in Kerala to negligible strength in Gujarat and Mysore, Madhya Pradesh	Regional (mainly Kerala, West Bengal, and Andhra Pradesh)

Chart 6 (*cont.*)

Weak Communist Parties	Population of Nation	Party Membership	Electoral Strength (Where Relevant)	National or Regional Distribution of Strength
Japanese Communist Party(ies)	96,000,000	110,000–150,000 members in 1965, with Voice of Japan faction only small minority (30,000 members in July, 1947; 200,000 in Dec., 1949; 83,000 in June, 1951)	3–5 per cent	Regional (primarily metropolitan areas, especially Kyoto, Osaka and Tokyo
Burma communist parties	22,500,000	Total of 5,000 in 1965; CPB (White Flag) 1,500 guerrilla fighters plus 2,500 supporters; BCP (Red Flag) 50–100 guerrilla fighters and 400–500 (?) supporters; Burma Workers' and Peasant Party (and other National Democratic United Front proto - communists), 5,000–10,000 in 1963, prior to being outlawed in 1964	. . . .	Regional (Rangoon and selected rural areas)
Cambodian Communist Party	6,000,000	100 hard-core members with an additional 1,000–2,000 sympathizers in leftist Pracheachon Party (1965).	. . . .	Regional (Phnom Penh)
Malaysian communist parties	11,000,000	500–600 guerrilla fighters in North Malaya plus 1,500 sympathizers; 1,000–2,000 (?) hard-core communist party members in Singapore; 100–300 hard-core communist party members in Sarawak plus 1,500–2,000 guerrilla fighters in 1965	Barisan Socialis (united front party) 35 per cent of Singapore vote	Regional (Thai-Malaysia border, Singapore, and Sarawak-Indonesian border)
Nepal Communist Party(ies)	10,000,000	3,000–4,000 members in mid-1965 plus additional sympathizers	. . . .	Regional (Kathmandu valley and Terai)

Chart 6 (*cont.*)

Weak Communist Parties	Population of Nation	Party Membership	Electoral Strength (Where Relevant)	National or Regional Distribution of Strength
Ceylon communist parties	10,650,000	Pro-Moscow faction, approximately 1,100, pro-Peking faction, 800 in 1965, with each faction having additional close supporters, possibly numbering 1,000	3–6 per cent	Regional (mainly Colombo and Southwest Ceylon)
Negligible Communist Parties				
Philippine Communist Party	30,500,000	Less than 500 active guerrilla fighters in the "People's Liberation Army," and an additional 1,500–2,000 members, mainly in Manila; also 12,000–15,000 sympathizers	. . . .	Regional (Manila and scattered areas of central Luzon)
Thai communist parties	26,000,000	Communist Party of Thailand (Thai), 200–300 members in 1963; Chinese Communist Party in Thailand, 3,000–4,000 members and supporters in 1963	. . . .	Regional (Bangkok and scattered parts of Northeast and Malaysia border)
Pakistan Communist Party	99,000,000	2,000–3,000 in East Pakistan, 300–500 (?) in West Pakistan in 1965	. . . .	Regional (East Pakistan, particularly Dacca; party in West Pakistan almost wiped out)

Chart 7

SOCIOECONOMIC DISTRIBUTION OF THE MEMBERSHIP OF THE ASIAN COMMUNIST PARTIES AND COMMUNIST-DOMINATED GROUPS

Dominant Communist Parties	Worker	Farmer	Intellectual	Other Bourgeois	Military
Chinese Communist Party	Medium–Strong	Medium–Strong	Strong	Very weak	Very strong
Mongolian People's Revolutionary Party	Medium–Strong	Medium–Strong	Strong	Very weak	Medium
Korean Workers' Party	Strong	Strong	Medium	Very weak	Very strong

Chart 7 (*cont.*)

Dominant Communist Parties	Worker	Farmer	Intellectual	Other Bourgeois	Military
Vietnam Workers' Party	Medium	Strong	Very strong	Weak	Very strong
Strong Communist Parties					
Pathet Lao	Very weak	Strong	Medium	Weak	Very strong
National Liberation Front of South Vietnam	Weak	Very strong	Medium	Medium	Strong
Indonesian Communist Party	Strong	Strong	Weak–Medium	Weak	Weak
Indian Communist Party(ies)	Medium–Strong	Weak–Medium	Strong	Medium	Weak
Weak Communist Parties					
Japanese Communist Party(ies)	Strong	Very weak	Very strong	Weak	Very weak
Burmese communist parties	Medium–Strong	Medium–Weak	Strong	Weak	Strong [a]
Cambodian Communist Party	Very weak	Very weak	Very strong	Medium	Very weak
Malaysian communist parties	Medium–Strong	Very weak	Very strong	Weak	Very strong [a]
Nepal Communist Party	Very weak	Very weak	Very strong	Medium	Very weak
Ceylon Communist Party(ies)	Strong	Weak	Very strong	Medium	Weak
Negligible Communist Parties					
Philippine Communist Party	Very weak	Strong	Strong	Very weak	Very strong [a]
Thai communist parties	Medium–Strong	Very weak	Strong	Weak	Very weak
Pakistan Communist Party	Very weak	Very weak	Very strong	Very weak	Very weak

[a] Included in this category are guerrilla fighters, whatever their previous occupations.

Accepting these charts as roughly accurate, what conclusions can we draw from them?

Almost all Asian communist parties must be regarded as highly elitist. This generalization holds for parties in power as well as for those in initial stages of development. The Korean Workers' Party alone deserves the label "mass party" on the basis of its membership and the relation of that membership to the total population of North Korea. The only other parties approaching mass status in terms of membership are those of China and Indonesia but, in both cases, party members constitute only a tiny fraction of the total adult population. Thus, even in societies where the party is dominant or strong, its members rarely constitute more than 5 per cent of the adult population, and usually much less.

Membership alone does not necessarily provide a good index of party power. The formal membership of the communist parties of India and Laos, for example, is scarcely indicative of the true political and military strength of these parties.

What Factors Make for the Strength or Weakness of a Communist Party in Asia?

A detailed answer to this question involves the type of country-by-country analysis undertaken in the succeeding sections of this volume. In general terms, the most critical factors would appear to be these: Is the party able to utilize effectively—and if possible, to capture—the nationalist movement? Is it able to develop mass foundations, particularly among the peasantry, so that it can have a broad base for military and political activities? Can it neutralize, capture, or discredit the prevailing national leader and his party? And the answers to these questions in turn may lie in even broader issues: At what stage of socioeconomic development is the particular society in this, the late twentieth century? What are the cultural legacies and ethnic divisions, and who can best utilize them? How united and how skillful are the opponents of the party? Do the party leaders exhibit organizational skills? Upon what external aid can the party count and how much external resistance must it face?

At this point, it will be sufficient to present a general profile of the strong and the weak communist party. First, the strong party almost always has a military component of significance. Among the dominant and strong communist parties of Asia, only two—those of India and Indonesia —lack this element. They alone are, or appear to be, experimenting with the peaceful route to power. But at least in the case of the Indonesian Communist Party, there is clear evidence that this is a tactical position that can be abandoned. PKI (Parte Kommunist Indonesia) leaders have had experience in guerrilla warfare; extensive attempts to infiltrate the Indonesian military have long been under way; and none of the party pronouncements in the PKI, as in other communist parties, precludes the use of force to obtain revolutionary victory, if force is necessary.

Almost all of the important communist parties of Asia also have a substantial *petit bourgeois* intellectual element in their membership, indicating the vital significance of capturing as many of the educated elite as possible. This element, to a large extent, constitutes the middle-level leadership of the society, a group commanding the respect of the masses. Once again, the Indonesian Communist Party is a partial exception, but recent indications are that the PKI is trying to increase its intellectual contingent.

Perhaps the most distinguishing feature between strong and weak communist parties in Asia, however, is the presence or absence of some mass base. And at this stage, that mass base, if existent, is likely to be peasant. Among the dominant or strong parties, all have medium to strong worker or peasant representation. These are the classes that compose the guerrilla forces or the red army; these are the classes that provide the potential for meaningful economic or political action.

The weak or negligible communist parties are generally characterized by very strong intellectual dominance, practically no mass base, and minimal military potential. As might be expected, these parties are largely divorced from reality, operating more in the fashion of intellectual debating societies and lacking any capacity for significant political, economic, or military action. And, as is usual among small, intellectual-type groups, factionalism tends to be high.

Except for those holding power, the Asian communist parties must be considered regional, not national, parties. Their primary strength, with few exceptions, is in the key metropolitan areas and selected rural districts, generally those most involved in the modernization process. The exceptions are cases where the party has been able to cultivate a remote rural area because its terrain makes it easy to defend against hostile forces or because the party has been able to exploit grievances indigenous to the area. The most notable of such exceptions are in Burma, Laos, Malaysia, and Thailand.

In the majority of cases, however, the communist parties of Asia derive their greatest opportunities from modernization and have their primary bases in urban centers. Whatever their hopes for large-scale peasant participation, most Asian parties are more dependent upon Tokyo, Osaka, Manila, Singapore, Djakarta, Bangkok, Phnom Penh, Calcutta, Dacca, Kathmandu, and Colombo.[8] Perhaps the rapid urbanization of Asia and the concomitant increase in the numbers of industrial workers will reduce the need for peasant support. There is a double-edged problem, however, which Chinese communist experience does not necessarily answer for other societies. If the cities increasingly provide a potent source of manpower for the communist party, communist urban bases will remain exceedingly vulnerable in the event of serious conflict with the government. Indeed, they will grow more vulnerable as various Asian governments achieve some measure of authority and power.

On the other hand, the difficulty of committing the peasantry to long-range, militant political action is great, especially if tight organization is important. Chinese experience notwithstanding (and the assistance provided the CCP by the circumstances of the anti-Japanese war was tremendous), most attempts to organize the peasants on behalf of communism in Asia have thus far been unsuccessful. The Chinese model proved a failure in Japan, the Philippines, Malaysia, and Burma. Only when a strong nationalist quotient could be added, as in Vietnam, has that model shown its potential strength.

Undoubtedly, Asian communism will continue to be characterized by dual tactics: the establishment of urban bases from which the political and economic tactics suitable to parliamentarism can be mounted and through which the proletariat can be recruited; and the establishment of rural bases which in normal times serve as auxiliary outposts but which, in time of emergency, become crucial to the party's survival—wellsprings of guerrilla warfare, centers of mass recruitment, and the beginnings of a territorial base.

Current Policies of the Asian Communist Parties

It remains for us to analyze the current line of Asian communist policy, searching out the dominant themes. While the various parties are at radically different stages of development and while there are a few notable exceptions to the major trends, these policies, in general, follow a consistent pattern. Here are the key policies being pursued and the basic theses that underlie them, some distinction being made between those parties which are in power and those which are struggling for control.

The Enemy

The primary enemies of the party are two: (1) world imperialism, led by the United States; and (2) the reactionary feudalist and capitalist elements at home. The most immediate and serious threat, however, comes from American imperialism; hence, this must be made the central target. If American imperialism is defeated, the domestic reactionaries will have lost their ally and source of support. They will automatically become weak and ripe for destruction.

Among the communist parties in power, this thesis is strongly espoused by all except the Mongolian People's Revolutionary Party. The parties of China, North Korea, and North Vietnam are currently following the hard line on the United States and insisting that all true Marxist-Leninists must do likewise. The attack upon American policies and motives is everywhere shrill; no interest is evidenced in any accommodation with America except on communist terms, and policy toward the United

States is a test of a party's revolutionary sincerity. At the same time, none of these parties is interested in becoming involved in a direct confrontation with a nation vastly superior in military power. Consequently, militancy is confined mainly to words—and assistance to guerrilla fighters who cannot be fully identified with the existing communist states.[9]

Among the parties not in power, the hard line toward the United States, and priority to the struggle against world imperialism is the dominant theme. In some cases, this position was reached only after an inner party struggle, but it is now the official line with very few exceptions.

The Use of Force

Whether the socialist revolution can be conducted by peaceful means or only by the ultimate use of force depends upon the attitude of the enemy. It should be assumed, however, that force will probably be necessary; consequently, the party should not be bound either ideologically or practically to a concept of peaceful revolution only.

The communist parties in power, all of whom attained their position via civil or international war, generally take a very firm position on the question of revolutionary tactics, insisting that the probabilities that force will be necessary are overwhelming, outlining the principles of guerrilla warfare as an essential revolutionary tactic, and strongly condemning the "soft" position—of the Soviet Union and various European parties—which suggests that socialism may be attained through peaceful coexistence, gradual evolution, or the structural reform of capitalism. Once again, the Mongolian party is an exception, siding with the Soviet Union on this matter, as on others.

A *strong majority of the Asian communist parties not in power* are currently committed to the assumption that they will probably have to resort to force in order to come to power. While not interested in abandoning legal tactics, they are not prepared to be bound by them. With few exceptions, their faith in the parliamentary route to socialism is very limited. Consequently, they accept guerrilla warfare as a likelihood at some stage, and they are studying closely the Chinese and Vietnamese experience.[10] Militancy and a penchant for action are rising in most parties. The party organization is increasingly a tightly disciplined one which is yet sufficiently flexible to operate at different tactical levels at the same time.

The United Front

The united front tactic is essential in order to develop a mass base and to harness both the nationalist and the reform issues to the communist cause. Even should guerrilla warfare prove necessary or desirable, there should be no abandonment of political action or the united front technique.

The Chinese, North Korean, and North Vietnamese parties continue to regard the united front technique as a valuable one, and consequently, they plan to retain it for the indefinite future. Thus, in communist China, North Korea, and North Vietnam, a multiparty facade is maintained. The multiparty system is defended theoretically on the score that all classes deserve representation and that internal contradictions between and among classes will be long-lasting. In practical terms, this policy enables the communists to have diverse channels for mass mobilization and indoctrination, to continue a broad nationalist appeal in the period of "people's democracy," and to maintain a high degree of continuity with the past—all without jeopardizing party control in the slightest.

The central myth of communism in power is summed up in the concept of the mass line: All ideas and ultimate authority derive from the people; all power to enforce those ideas and that authority lies within the party. Meanwhile, a process of experimentation continues with respect to a number of vital political issues: What is the appropriate combination of centralization and decentralization? What is the best size and character of administrative units? How many cadres can best be utilized and how can the people be caused to participate? None of these questions has been determined with finality in the present stage of Asian communist development. The broad outlines of political organization and control, however, are clear, and these will not be altered in the foreseeable future.

For the parties not in power, this is generally a period of seeking to challenge the ruling party, primarily through political action. A number of parties, however, have added military activities to political ones or are contemplating such action. Indeed, the simultaneous development of legal and illegal action—the union of parliamentary and extraparliamentary tactics—summarizes the main trend among those parties struggling for dominance in their societies.

The success of both tactics depends upon the effective creation of a mass base, the meaningful development of a united front. This in turn revolves upon the ability of the party to interact positively with all available nationalist and reformist issues. The central tactic is to connect the struggle for "national liberation" from imperialism with the struggle for the overthrow of "feudalism" and reaction at home, and then to establish a national democratic government composed of all "progressive" classes. At this point, the "bourgeois-democratic" stage of the revolution must be completed, and its proper completion requires ultimate management by the vanguard party. The Asian *bourgeoisie,* in short, cannot be trusted to effect their own revolution, particularly if the final transition to socialism is to be a peaceful one.

Thus, the parliamentary tactic requires the party to emphasize the menace of imperialism, colonialism, and neocolonialism, while at the same time espousing the full range of "bourgeois-democratic" internal reforms. Meanwhile, the extraparliamentary tactic requires the development of a strongly disciplined organization, capable of sustaining major sacrifices and able to count upon the masses sufficiently to operate a successful guerrilla struggle which initially will be against heavy numerical odds.

How to merge with the broad "progressive" forces of the society and yet maintain a totally independent, militant organization deeply committed to its own unchallenged authority is, and always has been, a central problem for the communists. United front tactics—the tactics of parliamentarism—are not proving effective for most Asian communist parties at present. The communists indeed have reason to lose faith in the ballot. In most open societies, the rate of growth of their voting strength is too slow to be comforting and, in those few societies where their gains offer considerable hope, parliamentarism itself often proves ephemeral. Then the party is forced to maneuver for power on a different basis.

Despite the emphasis upon united front tactics, moreover, the Asian communist parties have never been so isolated as they are today. Only in a few countries, such as South Vietnam and Laos, where the "national liberation" movement is nearing its full crest, and in Indonesia, where the "progressive bourgeois" forces continue to be most cooperative, do the communists have close liaison with other groups. And even where the united front tactic has had some success, new problems develop that often prove difficult to resolve. How strongly should the "national-bourgeois" forces be supported, and the national leader? Can military preparations be safely postponed, or does this jeopardize the party's future in case of a rupture? In short, the united front tactic, while useful and necessary, is not a panacea, as the whole history of the Asian communist movement so clearly indicates. At this point, however, the problem confronting the communists is generally how to achieve a united front, not how to control it.

The Two-stage Revolution

In specific terms, the political and economic programs of the Asian communist movement must be geared to the concept of a two-stage but uninterrupted revolution. In the first stage, the emphasis must be upon constitutional rights, free political participation, full civil liberties, broad social welfare measures, land reform, protection for the rights of the working class, and a mixed economy. In theoretical terms, the communist party in this stage must aid in the completion of "bourgeois democracy." In practical terms, it must seek to weaken state power, extend the libertarian aspects of the society, and mobilize the dissident elements of the community. There is a certain conflict between the progressive and the destructive elements of this program, but this can be a paradox beneficial to the party.

The second stage of the revolution, that of the transition to socialism, requires radically different policies. Now, the emphasis must be upon the sharp demarkation between "the people" and "their enemies." Under a people's dictatorship, the people are to have full freedom, their enemies no freedom. All the political policies of "people's republics" must be understood in this light. Economic policies are now geared less to social welfare and more to the total mobilization of manpower and resources for productive purposes. In theoretical terms, the communist party must act as vanguard and undisputed leader, so that an uninterrupted peaceful transition can take place from managed bourgeois democracy to socialism. In practical terms, the new stress is upon the establishment of undisputed party supremacy, the creation of a powerful, monolithic state, and the conduct of a sustained drive for economic modernization.

The communist states of Asia have established party supremacy and have gone far toward achieving formal unity. Dissidence, possibly substantial, clearly exists, but no established communist party appears to fear mass revolt. The instrumentalities of persuasion and coercion are formidable enough to make that likelihood remote. And in this era of communist nation building, no appeal is more potent than that of nationalism. The nationalist quotient in the political programs of the Asian communist states is extraordinarily high, reflecting the fact that the nationalist and the communist revolutions are reaching their peak in these societies at the same time. In the final analysis, however, the voluntary element is probably less than the coercive in these first-generation communist states, although coercion has many gradations and it is a primary purpose of the party to move from coercion to voluntarism by means of organization and education.

Even in the economic sphere, the nationalist emphasis is currently strong. Stimulated by the Sino-Soviet dispute, the Asian communist states have all enunciated a policy of developing an independent and self-sustaining economy, one not primarily dependent upon external aid—and control. Moreover, at least in China the earlier, romantic notion of walking on two legs—that is, of a simultaneous emphasis upon rapid industrial and agrarian modernization—has been modified. As is well known, agriculture has been recognized as the key to modernization and given a clear priority. The pace of the drive, moreover, has been relaxed, at least temporarily. In general, however, the primary appeal of the communist regimes is one calling for sacrifice, for Spartanism, so that the catching-up process can be completed in the shortest possible time. It would be unwise to deprecate the economic gains, particularly in the industrial sector, that have been attained under communist rule, and it would be equally unwise to minimize the costs—human and material.

The parties of the noncommunist states, almost without exception, are seeking to pursue bourgeois-democratic policies while, at the same time, preparing for their future tasks under a people's dictatorship. Today, the fundamental tactic is to insist on a united front against American imperialism, on the struggle for social reform measures, and on the realization of full democratic rights. Some of the leading parties, to be sure, have difficulty in assigning priorities: The Japanese Communist Party assigned prior emphasis to the struggle against American imperialism, rather than against monopoly capitalism, only after a fierce internal fight. The question of political versus military tactics has long plagued the parties of the Philippines, Burma, and Malaysia. The parties of Indonesia, India, Nepal, and Ceylon are constantly debating specific policies in terms of the degree of support or opposition that should be given to the national government. The broad formula outlined above, however, has now been officially accepted by almost every Asian communist party.

Stated Principles of the International Communist Movement

The international communist movement is based upon the principles outlined in the Moscow Declaration of 1957 and the Moscow Statement of 1960. The essential themes of these two documents (particularly as interpreted by Peking) can be outlined as follows:

1. All parties are independent, equal, and sovereign entities, and no external decisions can be forced upon them against their will.
2. All decisions pertaining to the international communist movement shall be reached on the basis of consultation, consensus, and unanimity.
3. The primary threat from within the communist movement is modern revisionism, a deviation which manifests itself primarily in the reluctance to support revolutionary movements, in the search for accommodation with the capitalist and imperialist forces of the world, and in the abandonment of true Marxist-Leninist principles of internal socialist development.
4. Comradely aid and assistance from one party to another, and from one communist State to another, are essential to the health of the communist movement, but such assistance should fully respect the integrity of the recipient. Big-power chauvinism and the use of aid as a means of political pressure are anti-Marxist actions.

The Sino-Soviet Dispute

As is well known, escalation of the Sino-Soviet dispute has now reached the stage where communist China appears to be in the process of establishing a *de facto* Fifth International (assuming that the Trotskyites have the right to consider theirs the fourth). The primary issues between Russia and China have been threefold: (1) the struggle over issues of organization, decision making, and leadership of the international communist movement; (2) communist revolutionary tactics in the late-twentieth-century world; and (3) the terms and conditions of comradely assistance.

Each of these issues reflects the different cultural legacy, historical background, timing of revolution, and current world status of the two major communist states. Thus, the basic differences are fundamentally expressions of differing national interests. The Chinese, from a minority position, naturally emphasize equal decision-making rights and total independence for weak and small communist parties within any supranational organization; the Russians, from a different position, emphasize the necessity for those having primary responsibility also to have certain primary rights. The Chinese, from a position of military weakness, stress the importance of unfolding the world revolution as the basic method of competing with the imperialist forces which are led by the United States; the Russians, from a position of power, emphasize the importance of nation-to-nation competition based upon peaceful coexistence and the avoidance of nuclear war. The Chinese want maximum comradely aid under conditions of full sovereignty and complete noninterference in their internal affairs; the Russians believe that they must give priority to their own internal development, and that aid produces reciprocal rights and duties. No doubt, the personality of Nikita Khrushchev exacerbated the quarrel and helped to account for some of the bitter polemics. There is no indication, however, that a mere change in leadership will solve the fundamental issues that separate the two communist giants. On the contrary, the evidence strongly suggests that despite Khrushchev's ouster, the cleavage remains a deep one.

Two of the three small communist states in Asia—North Korea and North Vietnam—are now strongly in the Chinese orbit. In recent times, their pronouncements on all or almost all of the basic issues have favored the Chinese position. Mongolia, on the other hand, remains firmly in the Soviet camp, although the MPRP has been rocked with a recent series of purges, some of which may be related to the dispute.

The Chinese position is also currently favored by the great majority of communist parties in noncommunist Asian states. Only in South Asia (the parties of India, Pakistan, Nepal, and Ceylon), is the Soviet line accepted by a majority of party leaders. In the other Asian parties—those of Japan, the Philippines, Indonesia, Malaysia, Cambodia, Laos, Thailand, and Burma—the Chinese line holds sway.

Initially, many of these parties tried desperately to establish and maintain a neutral position, thereby avoiding the internal repercussions of partisanship. At the same time, some of the Asian leaders sought to serve as mediators in the quarrel. But this tactic failed, and increasingly the parties were forced to speak out on such burning issues as Albania, Yugoslavia, Cuba, the Sino-Indian border dispute, the treaty banning above-ground tests of nuclear weapons, and certain broader issues like modern revisionism.

As was feared, debate over these issues, and the broader external pressures involved, created splits in the parties or widened splits that were already existent. The result is that most of the Asian communist parties have been factionalized. Some—such as those of India and Ceylon —have been split asunder. In others, notably those of Japan and Burma, earlier cleavages have been aggravated. Even within the dominant communist parties, the reverberations have been serious. Indeed, this fact constitutes the most basic pressure upon the Russians and Chinese to mend their breach.

Sources of the Chinese Appeal

What are the fundamental reasons for the Chinese appeal? Perhaps they can be summarized succinctly, as follows:

The Geographic and Cultural Proximity of China. The political influence of the Chinese communists extends over approximately the same area that Chinese influence historically covered in the periods of Chinese power. No small Asian communist state or party can ignore the presence and the power of this major new force.

The Identity of Chinese National Interests with Those of Most of the Other Asian Communist Parties. The CCP, as the dominant party in a backward society which is forging a modern revolution and finding its primary opponent in the United States, has much in common with the other Asian communist parties. Hence, the Chinese revolutionary model and experience constitute forms of valuable assistance.

The Combination of Chinese Diplomatic Finesse and Russian Errors. There can be little question that the Chinese, strongly ethnocentric though they may be, have been far more skillful in their public relations and diplomatic handling of Asian communists than the Soviets, who appear relatively ignorant of Asian ways, unconcerned about Asian sensitivities, and excessively bureaucratic. Personal contacts and impressions have, on balance, greatly aided the Chinese.

Concrete Material Aid and Assistance from China.   Beginning with the Korean War, the Chinese commitment to Asian communism steadily mounted. In a great variety of forms, the Chinese communists have given training, military support, and organizational funds to many if not all of the Asian parties. Meanwhile, in relative terms at least, the Russian commitment has declined and, in some areas, Soviet Russian involvement appears to be more closely associated with "national bourgeois" governments than with "comradely" parties.

Future Policies

If the Asian communist parties have inclined toward the Chinese position for these reasons, it would be wrong to assume that these parties intend to become satellites of Peking. That may in fact occur, but undoubtedly the primary objective of the Asian communist leaders is to establish the maximum independence, power, and maneuverability for their own parties and movements. The nationalist tide, as we have already observed, is running strong, not only in the CCP but in most other Asian communist parties as well. In the short run, the majority of Asian communist parties will probably continue to pursue the Chinese line, out of self-interest. But it is doubtful that Peking, even if it wishes to do so, can ever effect the type of control that Moscow once exercised via the Comintern. Chinese influence and controls will be more subtle, although not necessarily less effective, reflecting the new age of polycentrism and of separate communist nation-states.

Meanwhile, within each Asian communist party, in the future as in the past, it is likely that one fundamental difference will be that between men who are basically nationalist-communists and men who are primarily internationalist-communists. At present, the nationalist-communists are generally dominant, but it is possible that, at some future point, the internationalists may again emerge to challenge the prevailing nationalist tides. No point in the evolution of the communist movement is a more interesting one to follow.

The future of communism in Asia remains in doubt. In the past, it has taken a massive war to bring the communists to power. The first Asian communist state, Mongolia, was born in the aftermath of World War I. The communist states of China, North Korea, and North Vietnam were produced as a result of World War II. Now, some communists are seeking to expand their power on the basis of a different type of war: the national liberation movement. Their greatest chance of success appears to be in South Vietnam and Laos, with the possibility of a later chance in South Korea. Less promising, at least immediately, are the prospects in Malaysia, the Philippines, and Thailand, although the general balance of political and military power in Southeast Asia will ultimately affect basic trends in all of these nations.

Where the tactic of national liberation is premature or unsuitable, other communists are now seeking to advance via the united front. The best chance of success via this route is currently in Indonesia. In other states, the immediate prospects are not promising. Some states, notably Japan, are in reality post-Marxist societies, nations in which economic and political evolution has moved beyond the range of massive communist appeal. Certain other states have nationalist leaders capable of engaging in successful political competition with the communists.

But the two central issues, of course, remain to be answered. What major power configuration will ultimately dominate Asia? Have those backward societies which are forced by their circumstances to undergo rapid modernization a suitable alternative to communism? The future of Asian communism will be determined by the answers to these questions.

Communism in Asia: Toward a Comparative Analysis

1. Japan and the Philippines have attained a high level of national unification. The military strength of the Republic of Korea and Indonesia is appreciable. In general, however, the noncommunist states of Asia currently lack the unity, discipline, or power of their communist counterparts.

2. For example, they would pay homage to the four major concepts bequeathed by the West to the world—progress, science, industrialization, and democracy—insisting only that these concepts be defined and executed in a particular fashion.

3. This statement should be modified, since the Japanese invasion provided the springboard for communist victory; nevertheless, internal developments were critical to Chinese communist success.

4. It should be noted here that the most basic long-range struggle within a communist state may well be the struggle to establish some orderly means of leadership succession and to achieve the continued primacy of collective rather than individual leadership. It is yet too early to determine whether in their further evolution, such parties as the Communist Party of the Soviet Union and the Chinese Communist Party can attain these conditions. One can only assert that, to date, the cycle noted above has prevailed, and that current communist party structure and ideology continue for the most part to support such cycles.

5. It is impossible at present to know whether pro-Peking elements exist in the MPRP and whether recent purges were connected with the issue. It would not be surprising if such were the case.

6. As noted, there are two communist parties in Thailand: a small party composed of Thais, and a more significant Chinese Communist Party in Thailand, composed of Chinese. There is also a substantial commitment to Hanoi among the Vietnamese refugees in the Northeast, and a certain number of adherents to the Malaysian Communist Party among elements in the extremity of South Thailand where Ch'en Ping and his guerrillas operate.

7. At a more elementary level, this point would also apply to the Pathet Lao, whose position to date has been heavily dependent upon North Vietnamese support.

8. The National Liberation Front of South Vienam (NLFSV) and the Pathet Lao, of course, are exceptions, but even for them—and particularly for the NLFSV (or its hard core, the South Vietnam Revolutionary Party)—Saigon may prove to be a decisive factor.

9. Although the facts are somewhat unclear, North Vietnamese attacks upon American ships in the Gulf of Tonkin would appear to be a mysterious exception to general communist policies.

10. Japanese party leaders have spent much time studying Peking's approach, as have the leaders of Burma, Malaysia, Thailand, the Philippines, and Indonesia. The Indonesian leaders have also observed Hanoi's methods, as have comrades from the National Liberation Front of South Vietnam, the Pathet Lao, and the Cambodian Communist Party.

Selected Bibliography

Barnett, A. Doak, *Communist Strategies in Asia: A Comparative Analysis of Governments and Parties.* New York: Frederick A. Praeger, Inc., 1963.

Brimmell, J. H., *Communism in Southeast Asia: A Political Analysis.* London: Oxford University Press, 1959.

Brzezinski, Zbigniew K., *The Soviet Bloc.* Cambridge, Mass.: Harvard University Press, 1960. Revised paperback edition, New York: Frederick A. Praeger, Inc., 1961.

Hudson, G. F., Richard Lowenthal, and Roderick MacFarquhar, eds., *The Sino-Soviet Dispute.* New York: Frederick A. Praeger, Inc., 1960.

Problems of Communism, Monthly Journal.

Rose, Saul, *Socialism in Southern Asia.* London: Oxford University Press, 1959.

Trager, Frank N., ed., *Marxism in Southeast Asia: A Study of Four Countries.* Stanford, Calif.: Stanford University Press, 1959.

World Strength of the Communist Party Organizations. Washington, D.C.: Annual Publication of the Department of State.

Building a Communist Nation in China

Chalmers Johnson

No method of operation is more
characteristic of the Maoist era of Chinese Communist Party
history than the "mass line," according to which the
Party derives its policies from the ideas of the people
themselves and then leads the people on
the basis of these policies. The Chinese communists
have used the mass line as both a long-term
strategy and a short-term tactic. The greatest guarantee of
eventual success in any enterprise is believed to be the
support of the masses, and the day-to-day *modus operandi*
for every type of chore is: "Learn from the masses, unite with
the masses." "The mass line is the basic line of the
Party and this line must be followed at all

times, by all departments, and for all types of work. During the period of the revolutionary wars, the Party in all its work used the method of integrating the efforts of the leadership and the masses." [1]

The last sentence of the above quotation suggests that the revolutionary period is an important key to understanding Chinese communist organizational methods. The so-called mass line was developed at that time, and it lies at the heart of Mao Tse-tung's theories of revolutionary war. Western scholars have devoted much attention to the mass line as it exists in the thought of Mao Tse-tung; [2] however, they have done little toward evaluating the relative significance of various pronouncements by Mao and relating these to their concrete historical context. I believe that in order to understand the viability and the logic of the mass line one must explore the influence of military victory on the leadership of the Party. The persistence of the mass line reveals the continuity of Mao's methods as leader of the Revolutionary War and as leader of the struggle for economic growth.

The experiences of the revolutionary period between 1927 and 1949 have served as an endless source of precedents and examples for the communist leadership since their coming to power. In devising methods for reaching its goals for economic growth and political development, the Party has turned again and again for inspiration to the policies used in Yenan and earlier. Let us begin, therefore, by looking at the Party's pre-1949 revolutionary strategy. There are three overriding aspects of this strategy that have made it so influential: (1) the same leadership that guided the revolutionary struggle for power has guided the revolutionary struggle in power; (2) the revolutionary strategy of the Chinese Communist Party (CCP) is a domestic product, not a Russian import; and (3) this strategy produced a stupendous military victory against overwhelming odds.

The Guerrilla Heritage

After the Kuomintang-Communist Party rupture of 1927, the few communists who remained began to reexamine the history of their movement, to evaluate their mistakes, and to develop a strategy that might lead them to victory. It was Mao Tse-tung and the group of mutinous military officers who joined him in 1927 and 1928 who ultimately perfected a winning strategy. Their theory of revolution did not come fully into being as early as 1928, but neither is it entirely a modern, retrospective rationalization. The period between 1927 and 1936 was one of experimentation and development. By the time the Sino-Japanese War began, the Party thought it understood the techniques of making a revolution in China; and, from 1937 on, it drove to eventual success in accordance with its wartime conception. The victory of 1949 served to lend an unimpeachable authority to the ideas and techniques that Mao had developed in the early Yenan period.

What were the problems connected with making a revolution in China, as Mao and his associates gradually began to perceive them after 1927? First, the Comintern-dictated policy of placing major reliance on a united front with bourgeois forces was clearly wrong. After 1927, the Chinese communists used the united front as a _tactic_ but never again as a fundamental strategy. In a more profound sense, Mao's Party redefined the idea of united front to mean union with the masses, but it never again placed basic trust in the original idea of joint operations with a rival elite group.

The rejection of the Comintern's united front strategy was implicitly a rejection of Leninism, since it was Lenin's _Left Wing Communism: An Infantile Disorder,_ presented as a guide to the Second Congress of the Comintern in 1920, that had laid down the united front as international communist policy for making revolutions. Mao and his associates did not reject Lenin, however; they incorporated and transcended his ideas. What they did reject was Soviet leadership of the Chinese Revolution. One lesson of 1927 was that China's revolution would have to be made by _Chinese_ leadership; no revolution was ever likely to succeed so long as the Chinese Communist Party was merely the agent of Russian foreign policy. The new Chinese attitude did not necessarily imply hostility to Stalin, but it did imply independence.

The second major conclusion that Mao and his group drew from their experiences in 1927 was that military force would play a central role in China. Chiang had temporarily managed to crush the communists because he had an army; Mao eventually won by forging a better army. In Shanghai in April, 1927, in Canton in December, 1927, and in Ch'angsha in July, 1930, the Chinese communists learned that unarmed masses or weak armies cannot stand up to professional armies. The choice the Party faced was to wait in preparation for a windfall that might destroy Chiang's forces or to devise methods that would overcome them frontally. Mao chose the latter course.

Strategy of the People's War

The Maoist strategy of revolution is basically one that supplies an answer to the question: How does an objectively weaker military force vanquish an objectively superior, professionally trained military force at the command of the _status quo_ power? Mao's answer—probably his most lasting contribution to communist theory—is what he calls "people's war." This doctrine of revolution via people's war can be divided into five main principles.

Mobilization of a Sustaining Population.   On January 27, 1934, Mao
stated, "Revolutionary war is a war of the masses; it can be carried out
only by means of mass mobilization and by relying on the masses." [3] On
May 4, 1939, he reiterated, "What is the lesson of the revolution in the
last fifty or more years? Fundamentally it is a lesson of 'arousing
the masses of the people.' . . . All must know that only by mobilizing the
broad masses of workers and peasants, who constitute 90 per cent of the
country's population, can we defeat imperialism and feudalism." [4] In
a directly military context, he asserted, "Because guerrilla warfare basically derives from the masses and is supported by them, it can neither
exist nor flourish if it separates itself from their sympathies and cooperation." [5] Even his enemy, the army of the Kuomintang, conceded, "Mao
believes that the true source of strength to sustain a war lies with the
people; war can be won only with the support of the mass of the population." [6] Thus, Mao Tse-tung's answer to the technical superiority of the
Kuomintang armies was the mobilization of a totally hostile population
against them.

It is easy to speak of mobilizing an entire population, but it is a
difficult thing to carry out in practice. What is needed is a broad ideological appeal that will gain the revolutionary party the support of the
masses without alienating any significant segment of those masses. The
Chinese communists tried two such appeals during the Maoist period
of their Revolution: First, during the Kiangsi Soviet period, they promised
land reform to the poor peasants of south-central China; then, after 1937,
they appealed to Chinese nationalism in launching resistance to the
Japanese invasion.

The first appeal met with a favorable response, but it encountered
several major difficulties. It was attractive only to the poorer segments
of rural society and therefore did not produce the overwhelming mass
support required for guerrilla operations. Nor was the appeal to land
reform exclusive with the communists. Probably most important, reformed
areas could not be consolidated over an area sufficiently wide to prevent
their encirclement by Kuomintang troops. As Benjamin Schwartz has
observed, "the fragmentized nature of the Chinese countryside did not
make for the spread of political contagion beyond the area immediately
affected." [7] In 1934, despite several brilliant military victories by Mao's
forces, the Kuomintang armies overwhelmed the communist-controlled
areas. The communists retreated to the northwest where, after 1937, they
successfully made their second appeal: to the nationalism of the rural
population, awakened by the Japanese invasion.

Organization of the Mobilized Population.   After discovering the
key to the support of the people, the Party had to organize them. In
Mao's strategy, organization complements mobilization. The Party and

its military cadre organized the people into mass associations, which then provided military support as well as giving the masses a sense of political participation. One of the major functions of Party organization was to provide the people with political and practical education; mass associations also served to isolate persons who did not support the mass movement. The final stage of organization was the creation of territorial bases. As the bases expanded and were consolidated, they became a regular guerrilla infrastructure, supplying the communist troops with food, refuge, training centers, and sources of manpower. These communist rural enclaves also weakened the *status quo* power by removing land from its control.

Creation of a Large, Party-led Revolutionary Army. Having organized a mass movement and set up a rebel infrastructure, the Party began to recruit a revolutionary army. This army was built around and trained by the nucleus of Red Army veterans from the Kiangsi Soviet. It was characterized by an extreme emphasis on discipline and on maintaining friendly relations with the local population. Good civil-military relations, or *chün-min kuan-hsi*, were not so much a sign of the Party's humanitarianism as they were an integral part of its revolutionary strategy. Since the Party's army was pitted against an objectively more powerful force, it had to employ guerrilla tactics, and it had to have the support of the population militarily (i.e., actively) as well as logistically (i.e., passively). The people provided the troops with intelligence, labor, guides, recruits, and material supplies, and they served as a defending militia when the formal army was fighting outside the bases.

In order to guarantee the closest cooperation between the guerrilla army and the sustaining population, Mao devised his "three disciplinary rules" and "eight points of attention." [8] The Red Army first enforced them in 1928, and the People's Liberation Army (PLA) reissued them on October 10, 1947. Today the PLA and the militia still teach and demand from their troops "good three–eight style." Although some professional military officers would like to eliminate the guerrilla quality from China's armed forces, the persistence of such ideology into the present is a sign of the Party's faith in its earlier methods.

The three disciplinary rules were: (1) Obey orders in all your actions; (2) Don't take a single needle or a piece of thread from the masses; and (3) Turn in everything captured. The eight points of attention were: (1) Speak politely; (2) Pay fairly for what you buy; (3) Return everything you borrow; (4) Pay for anything you damage; (5) Don't hit or swear at people; (6) Don't damage crops; (7) Don't take liberties with women; and (8) Don't ill-treat captives. [9]

Since May, 1960, the three disciplinary rules have been redefined as follows: (1) Correctly grasp the trend of politics; (2) Endure difficulties and practice thrift; and (3) Respect shrewd and positive strategies. The eight points of attention have been reduced to an eight-character phrase calling for unity, dedication, austerity, and activity (i.e., *t'uan-chieh, chin-chang, yen-su, huo-fa*).[10]

Guerrilla Tactics. Mao Tse-tung's writings on military subjects reveal his basic belief that in China (and, today, elsewhere) there was no path to revolution other than armed struggle. He advocated waging guerrilla warfare against the army of the enemy in order to wear it down to the level at which it could be defeated. His tactics all display two characteristics: (1) They are intended to create battle situations in which a weaker force may defeat a stronger force; and (2) The implementation of these tactics depends upon the existence and functioning of a mass guerrilla infrastructure. With the support of the population, the relatively weaker communist forces could have prior knowledge of the enemy's strength, could set ambushes, could fight only at times and places of their own choosing, and could avoid enemy mop-ups.

Mao's basic military proposition is simple: to concentrate a temporarily superior force in order to guarantee the success of every pitched battle and to avoid all evenly matched or unfavorable contests. "Our strategy is to pit one against ten, while our tactic is to pit ten against one—this is one of the fundamental principles on which we beat the enemy." [11] From this slogan, endlessly repeated and elaborated from 1936 to the present, have come the famous beliefs that all enemies are "paper tigers," that all popularly supported revolutions are invincible, and even a good deal of the Chinese theory of "contradictions."

The Stages of Protracted War. In order to make his strategy of revolution work, Mao insisted that the revolutionaries commit themselves to a long struggle. Guerrilla fighting, as seen by Mao, had one specific purpose: to weaken the enemy via a protracted war of attrition. In 1948, as parity between the rebel and defending armies approached, the guerrilla armies went over to larger and larger mobile campaigns of encirclement and destruction. Finally, in the last stages of the war, the Chinese communist forces reverted to positional warfare in order to complete their revolutionary conquest. In an authoritative exegesis of Mao's military thought, Ch'en Po-ta explains:

> Guerrilla warfare does not have the capability of deciding the outcome of a war. Final victory has to be won by means of regular warfare. However, the regular warfare phase in the Chinese revolutionary war was the outgrowth of the long period of irregular guerrilla warfare. . . . From little to big, from weak to strong—that is the general law of the expansion of revolutionary strength.[12]

These five principles constitute the essence of Mao's strategy of a people's war. In its fully developed form, the theory includes several other techniques—for example, psychological warfare, favorable treatment of prisoners of war (in order to demoralize the enemy's rank and file), and tactical use of a united front. However, the five principles listed here form the basis for all of Mao's other military-political axioms.

The Influence of the Strategy of the People's War

The influence of this strategy on contemporary Chinese communist practice cannot be exaggerated. The men who devised it—Mao, Liu, Lin Piao, Chu Teh, and others—conceived it as early as December, 1936.[13] To them it reflected the lessons of their Kiangsi campaigns, and it constituted the blueprint which they followed to final victory. That victory —which not even Stalin believed to be possible in the post-World War II period [14]—was the most important revolutionary achievement of the twentieth century after the Bolshevik Revolution. A guerrilla army crippled and then annihilated the forces of one of World War II's "Big Five" —an army that was backed with lavish financial, material, and technical assistance from the United States. The men who led this revolution are the same men who have ruled China for 15 years. Mao Tse-tung, once a guerrilla leader in south-central China, is now Chairman of the Communist Party; Liu Shao-ch'i, once political commissar of the New Fourth Army, is now Chairman of the People's Republic; Teng Hsiao-p'ing, once political commissar of the 129th Division, is now Secretary-General of the Communist Party; Ch'en Yi, former commander of the New Fourth Army, is now Minister of Foreign Affairs; Li Hsien-nien, who fought as a guerrilla commander in central China, is the present Minister of Finance; P'eng Chen, who led the government in the Chin-Ch'a-Chi base, is now a member of the Political Bureau; and this list could be extended indefinitely.

The communist victory in China was not the only evidence the CCP had that its strategy was a genuine contribution to communist theory of revolution. Comparable developments in Indochina, Algeria, and elsewhere suggested that the strategy was something more than the application of Leninism to China. Thus, the Chinese communists began to argue for the relevance of their revolution as a model, and they began to venerate Mao Tse-tung as a military genius. As early as November 16, 1949, Liu Shao-ch'i stated:

> It is necessary to set up wherever and whenever possible a national army which is led by the Communist Party and which is powerful and skillful in fighting the enemies. It is necessary to set up the bases on which the liberation army relies for its activities and to make the mass struggles in the enemy-controlled areas and the armed struggles coordinate with each other. Armed struggle is the main form of struggle for the national liberation efforts of many colonies and semi-colonies.[15]

Fourteen years later the Chinese communists are still advocating the same strategy.[16] There are several problems connected with it, however, that the communists have faced only obliquely. For example, they themselves were never able to obtain the mass following upon which the strategy depends until the Japanese invasion had occurred. They know that the Japanese invasion created the social conditions upon which they built their revolution, but as "scientific socialists" they cannot advocate mobilizing a population by deliberately provoked invasions. Classical Marxism leads them to maintain that the working masses are always mobilized, although their own experiences in Kiangsi do not support that belief. Nevertheless, in occasional flashes of candor they do concede that war has been the midwife of communist revolutions. In his celebrated "On the Correct Handling of Contradictions among the People," Mao wrote:

> The first world war was followed by the birth of the Soviet Union with a population of 200 million. The second world war was followed by the emergence of the socialist camp with a combined population of 900 million. If the imperialists should insist on launching a third world war, it is certain that several hundred million more will turn to socialism; then there will not be much room left in the world for the imperialists, while it is quite likely that the whole superstructure of imperialism will utterly collapse.[17]

Another difficulty of the strategy is that the wartime appeal used by the Chinese Communist Party in order to gain the support of the masses was nationalism (as it was for the rebels in Indochina, Algeria, and elsewhere). Mao has recently suggested that there is nothing incompatible between nationalism and Marxism-Leninism. In his August, 1963, statement on the racial protest movement in the United States, he made the significant comment: "In the final analysis, a national struggle is a question of class struggle." [18] His basis for making this surprising leap is his concept of the masses or the people, and his belief that the people want revolution. They require leadership, and the party—as the vanguard of the proletariat—is uniquely equipped to provide that leadership. But there has been a shift of emphasis away from both Marx's concept of the proletarian class and Lenin's concept of the vanguard party. Both concepts persist in Chinese communist ideology, but they overlay and serve a more basic category of social analysis—namely, the people. Slowly but perceptibly, the populist stream of Maoist ideology is displacing traditional elements of communist theory. Contradictions, antagonistic and nonantagonistic, now exist within the ranks of the people. President Kennedy's successor, we are told, is anticommunist, antilabor, and antipeople.[19] Kuwabara Toshiji, a Japanese authority on Maoism, believes that the paper tiger theory epitomizes Mao's revolutionary optimism and that its roots lie in Mao's belief in the "almighty people." [20]

It has been recognized that the Chinese communist theory of revolution is of great relevance to both CCP history and contemporary Chinese foreign policy. However, its relevance to domestic policy and to post-1949 Chinese communist ideology is equally great. The leaders of the Party did not forget, after the war, that the mobilized and organized masses of China had already accomplished one miracle: They had defeated the Kuomintang armies. If they could do that, the leaders argued, perhaps they could also overcome economic obstacles that, objectively speaking, China was not ready to overcome. Mobilization and organization—or, in the language of the mass line, "from the masses and to the masses"— therefore live on in China in a nonmilitary setting. The Party's faith in the masses, properly mobilized and organized on the old guerrilla model, has produced the scarcely disguised idealism that persists even after the reversals of the Great Leap Forward.

Compare, for example, the ideas that the Chinese Party has dared to inject into the international communist controversy concerning strategy:

> Every oppressed nation and every oppressed people should above all have the revolutionary confidence, the revolutionary courage, and the revolutionary spirit to defeat imperialism and the reactionaries, otherwise there be no hope for any revolution. The only way to win victory in revolution is for the Marxist-Leninists and revolutionaries to combat resolutely every trace of weakness and capitulation, and to educate the masses of the people in the concept that "imperialism and all reactionaries are paper tigers," thereby destroying the arrogance of the enemy and enhancing the spirit of the great masses of the people so that they will have revolutionary determination and confidence, revolutionary vision and staunchness. [21]

Lack of technically competent personnel, or of earth-moving equipment, or of steel-making capacity, or of atomic weapons can all be surmounted by the mobilized and organized masses, just as were the tanks and aircraft of the Kuomintang.

The Communes and After

The strategies for economic development pursued by the Chinese communists since 1949 follow a pattern similar to the strategies of revolution adopted by the Party between 1921 and 1949. In the first period of the revolution, from 1921 to 1927, the CCP accepted the policies and orders of the Soviet Union. Similarly, in the first period of economic development, 1950 to 1957, the Party adopted the policy "Learn from the Soviet Union," and it slavishly copied the Soviet emphasis on the development of heavy industry. Soviet industrial experience proved to be as irrelevant to the realities of the Chinese economy as the united front strategy had been to the realities of Chinese politics. During the Great Leap Forward, the Chinese Communist Party again turned to domestic conditions and its own experience as guides to action. It placed the mass line in command. Liu Lan-t'ao, alternate Secretary of the Secretariat of the Party's Central Committee, stated, in 1959:

> There are persons who are determinedly opposed to placing politics in command, saying that as ideological and political work cannot yield grain or steel, this task is unable to solve any practical problem. This ideology, which tends to sever the political leadership of the Party from the practical work of the masses and political work from operational work, aims actually at weakening and even repudiating the role of the leadership of the Party. May we ask, are the tremendous over-all leap forward and the great success of the people's communalization program in rural areas in 1958 not historic miracles achieved by placing politics in command and by adhering resolutely and completely to the mass line of the Party? [22]

The Great Leap Forward was an attempt to overcome the baffling problem of lagging agricultural productivity. During the first five-year plan, industrialization had gone ahead at amazing speed and with great success. But the continuation of the program was threatened by the inability of agriculture to pay its bills—to provide food for the rapidly growing urban sector, to supply an exportable surplus in order to earn foreign exchange, and to produce the raw materials needed for light industry. The Party had neglected investment in agriculture; instead it had assumed that collectivization on the Soviet pattern, together with the alleged economies of large-scale production, would result in increased output. However, according to official statistics, food grain production rose from 182.5 million tons in 1956 (the year in which collectivization was completed) only to 185 million tons in 1957.[23] This was the smallest increase since the 1953 crop year (in official figures), and it placed the 1957 agricultural growth rate well below the average annual rate of population growth.

Faced with this situation, the communists neither abandoned the goal of industrialization nor redirected a larger share of the country's investable funds into agriculture. Instead they chose the policy of "walking on two legs," simultaneously advancing the modernized and traditional sectors of the economy. Industry continued to receive the lion's share of available development funds, while the traditional sector, i.e., agriculture and handicrafts, was to increase its output via mass line techniques.

In essence, the Great Leap Forward relied on the mobilized and organized will of the masses to overcome the enemy of stagnating agricultural productivity. Many persons have speculated on the origins of the commune idea, and it has been variously ascribed to K'ang Yu-wei's utopian thought,[24] Russian experience in the war communism period,[25] the spontaneity of the peasants themselves, a generalization throughout the society of the huge concentrations of labor used in the 1957 water conservation projects, and the personal left-tending communism of Mao Tse-tung and Liu Shao-ch'i. All or none of these may have contributed to the form the communes took. Another source undoubtedly was the wartime guerrilla bases, in which a multiple-village unit also performed diverse agricultural, manufacturing, militia, and welfare functions.

In harking back to the guerrilla bases, however, the Chinese found something more important than the form of the communes themselves. In their hour of need, with the Soviet model once again tarnished, they turned to the same source of power that had carried them to revolutionary victory—the masses. The mass line had been applied tactically in China from the day the Party came to power; in 1958, it was elevated to a strategy. Concerning the mass line prior to 1949, Liu Shao-chi has written:

> In the democratic revolutionary period, the Chinese Communist Party . . . went deep into the villages and for more than 22 years led the armed revolutionary struggle, which used the villages to encircle the cities. What the Party adopted was the mass line policy of resolutely relying on the peasants' political consciousness and organized strength, mobilizing the peasants to save themselves.[26]

In 1958, the Party did the same thing, this time for the sake of economic development. Its cadres exhorted, enticed, and drove the rural members of some 740,000 agricultural producers' cooperatives into approximately 24,000 people's communes of an average size of 5,000 households each. A movement that originally was to take five or six years was completed in about six weeks. Amid a blaze of catechismic propaganda slogans—such as the "three red flags" (i.e., the general line of socialist construction, the Great Leap Forward, and the people's communes); "three bitter years of struggle"; "overtake Great Britain"; "close cropping —deep plowing"; "red and expert"; and "politics in command"—the peasantry allegedly "marched into battle" against nature, determined to overcome her.[27]

Mao's revolutionary strategy and the mass line on which it is based had been battle-tested and proved sound. If the Party were to use them successfully in analogous situations, however, it could not violate the inner logic of the mass line. In other words, mobilization was not something that the Party alone could supply. Whereas the Japanese invasion of 1937 had genuinely mobilized the population, in 1958 the Party cadres themselves were in a position much like that of the Japanese invaders. In the fall and winter of 1958 to 1959, the Party discovered that organization without mobilization does not work. If the communes did not provoke open hostility (which they certainly did in some areas), at the very least they provoked a slow-down. The mess-hall communism of the early months guaranteed food and lodging to the entire rural population regardless of how hard or how little a person worked. The consequent destruction of all incentives resulted in less production, although this fact was at first disguised by the natural bumper harvest of 1958. When the weather turned unfavorable, the weaknesses of the communes were exposed in their most glaring light—incipient starvation.

The Party has consistently blamed the food shortages of 1959 to 1962 on the worst natural disasters in a hundred years and, more recently, on the withdrawal by Russia of technical assistance. Today we know, from an unimpeachable source, that the people themselves blamed the communes. The *Bulletin of Activities* of the People's Liberation Army General Political Department, a secret, or *chi-mi,* Army periodical recently made available by the U.S. State Department to scholars in the West, documents the extent of popular dissatisfaction during the crisis period.[28] On January 1, 1961, General Hsiao Hua, Director of the PLA's General Cadres Department, told a conference of political commissars:

> Because of this year's great disasters in agriculture, difficulties exist in food supply. . . . Our troops consist of peasants and workers wearing uniforms. When certain localities are troubled by agricultural crises, it is bound to be reflected among the troops. Because of these economic difficulties, political problems have greatly increased in the military units.[29]

He and other military leaders stated that "rebellious elements" existed in the Army, and he acknowledged that "destructive activities by counter-revolutionaries" in the countryside were affecting the morale of the Army's rank and file.

After an inspection trip in Honan and Shantung during late 1960, Wang Tung-hsing, a Party member and a Vice-Governor of Kiangsi province, reported that some soldiers were skeptical about the three red flags. Several men told him that, "because Mao Tse-tung is in Peking, he does not know the realities of peasant life. That is why he sends food to the cities." Another soldier thought that the distribution of food was unfair and that the Party was giving priority to industrial workers.[30] The *Bulletin of Activities* contains extensive reports on mail censorship by Army censors. One company censor found that 79.8 per cent of all the letters received by soldiers in his company contained unfavorable and discouraging news of the food crisis at home.[31] Soldiers given home leave returned to their units depressed, and more ideological problems existed among those soldiers who had been visited at the Army camp by their families.[32] General Lo Jui-ch'ing, Chief of the General Staff, arrived in Kunming on January 20, 1961, to make a personal investigation of the situation. After inspecting army units in Kunming, Chengtu, Chungking, and Wuhan, he reported alarming instances of murder, pilfering, and suicide, the presence of "destructive elements," weakness in the study of Mao's works, and wrong or obscure attitudes toward the three red flags.[33]

The General Political Department had no trouble in locating the source of these difficulties. Lo Jui-ch'ing found that the worst conditions existed in units composed predominantly of ex-peasants and that the communes were the specific object of the peasant-soldiers' resentment:

> When questioned, the soldiers gladly talked about industrial develop-
> ment, land reform, and the cooperatives. However, they avoided dis-
> cussing the people's communes or agricultural development. Evidently
> the Party's directives concerning the people's communes have not been
> well disseminated.[34]

Four months later, after an inspection trip in the Nanking area, General Hsiao reported that although the General Political Department had instituted an extensive campaign of indoctrination, lack of confidence in the people's communes still persisted.[35]

The Party responded to this situation by dispersing all potentially rebellious units and by launching a renewed propaganda drive in order to educate wavering soldiers. During 1960 and 1961, the Army undertook the "2-remembrances and 3-inspections" movement (i.e., *liang-i san-ch'a*), the "four-good company" movement (i.e., *ssu-hao chung-tui*), and the "five-good soldiers" movement (i.e., *wu-hao chang-shih*). The two remembrances were of class difficulties and of national difficulties; the three things to inspect were one's viewpoint, one's fighting spirit, and one's work. The four-good company movement consisted of good political ideology, good military training, good "three-eight style," and good personal discipline. The five-good soldiers movement consisted of good political thought, good productive labor, good results of study, good military and political activities, and good organization and discipline.[36]

However, the Party could not dissipate the hostility of the peasants themselves by relying solely on propaganda and indoctrination. Faced with imminent disaster for its program, and possibly for its own authority, the Party retreated. It began progressively to dismantle the communes and to turn its undivided attention to the agricultural problems that the communes had failed to solve.

The reform of the communes and the development of the present agriculture-as-foundation policy took three years. The transition began at the eighth plenum of the Eighth CCP Central Committee in August, 1959, and it ended with the formal elaboration of new economic guidelines at the Party's tenth plenum in September, 1962. During this period, extensive and fundamental changes were made—changes that were and still are loaded with theoretical implications. Basically, the reforms can be summarized under three general categories: production team autonomy, the reopening of the cadre-peasant dialogue, and the policy that "agriculture is the foundation of the economy while industry is the guide" (*i nung-yeh wei chi-ch'u i kung-yeh wei chu-tao*).

The average size of a commune is 4,756 households, whereas the average size of a production team is 20 to 40 households. Prior to mid-1959, responsibility for agricultural production was vested in the commune administrative committee and its numerous departments and subcommittees. The commune administrative committee compensated the members of the commune for their labor in accordance with two systems of payment: fixed monthly wages of six or eight different grades; and payment in kind, in the form of free meals, housing, and so forth. These forms of remuneration and labor organization lacked incentives, since the various actual work groups simply followed the orders of the commune management committee. Neither the soundness of these orders, nor the industry of the commune members, nor the speed with which tasks were accomplished could affect the members' wages or payments in kind.

As a result of peasant opposition, Communist Party doubts, and the food crisis of 1960, the Party decentralized, by stages, the original form of commune organization. In August, 1959, at the eighth plenum of the Central Committee, the Party instituted the so-called "three-level" organizational pattern for communes; and it specified that ownership of land rested at the brigade level. The brigade is an intermediate level of organization between the commune and the production team. It corresponds in size to the old higher agricultural producers' cooperative (i.e., 100 to 200 households), just as the production team of 20 to 40 households corresponds to an earlier form of collectivization, the lower agricultural producers' cooperative.

The eighth plenum resolution declared that "the right of ownership at the level of the production brigade is basic, and the right of ownership at the commune level is partial." [37] What this statement meant, in practical terms, was that the brigade became the basic accounting unit and the brigade cadres became the basic decision-making group. The brigade henceforth determined its own crop arrangements, targets, and costs; and the cadres of the commune government could not interfere with brigade decisions. The commune became, in effect, a purchasing and supplying agent for the brigades under its jurisdiction.

The purpose of this reform was to reintroduce differential rewards for well-organized, hard-working brigades and to penalize less competently managed units. Shortly after the devolution of authority to the brigades, the Party also changed the form of labor compensation. It introduced the system of "three guarantees and one reward" (*san-pao i-chiang*).[38] Under this system, the brigade and the commune concluded an agreement specifying the brigade's output, costs, and manpower requirements for a specific production period. If the brigade exceeded its guaranteed output, it was paid a reward; if it fell short of its guaranteed output, it had to pay a penalty. In effect, poorly administered brigades paid well-run units in recognition of their accomplishments.

Beginning in the autumn of 1960, the Party further decentralized the communes by lowering the level of decision making to that of the production team. On January 1, 1962, the *People's Daily* officially announced that the production team was the basic unit of economic accounting within the three-level ownership system. The team, which corresponds to a village or a part of a village, is much closer to the precommunist form of agricultural management than either the brigade or the commune. Two reasons for lowering the basic accounting unit to the level of from 20 to 40 households were the need to recapture the knowledge and experience of older peasants and the desire to bring the three-guarantees-and-one-reward incentive system closer to the actual agricultural producers. Numerous reports indicate that the brigade cadres often ignored the *expertise* of experienced farmers when issuing orders to teams under their control and that production suffered as a consequence. Today a production team concludes contracts for agricultural deliveries with the commune via the brigade. If it exceeds its guarantees, it is rewarded accordingly; if it falls below, the members of the team must pay a penalty. The livelihood of production team members depends upon their contracts, their ability to produce a surplus, and the productive activities they engage in as a sideline.

There were several other features to agricultural reform. For example, private plots of land were restored to commune members; rural fairs, or markets for the sale of privately produced goods, were once again permitted; and huge numbers of ex-peasants who had gravitated to the cities were ordered to return to the countryside. Undoubtedly many of these policies are temporary. Even the granting of economic autonomy to a group as small as the production team was a pragmatic response to the agricultural crisis. Team independence cannot be regarded as a permanent feature of Chinese economic organization:

> The system of collective ownership at three levels with the production team as the foundation conforms to the present level of the peasants' consciousness and will tend to raise it. The system is the best school for

conducting socialist education among the peasants, and it will remain for a fairly long time.[39]

The restoration of local control and rewards for hard, creative work helped to increase production in 1962 and 1963. Natural calamities had damaged crops in 1959, 1960, and 1961. Still, the rise in food grain output during 1962 and 1963, to the level of 1957, cannot be explained solely by changes in the weather.[40] The removal of the counterproductive features of the early communes and the encouragement of team initiative halted China's so-called descending economic spiral. One of the most intriguing questions concerning the reforms is why team-level production should be greater than brigade-level production. The three-guarantees-and-one-reward incentive system, plus the greatly expanded size of the private sector, are certainly prime causes; however, Western scholars suspect that the success of the production team may rest on old village and clan loyalties. The teams happen to approximate the size of a small village or part of a village.[41]

Post-crisis Leadership Problems

Despite China's recent recovery of economic viability, there is considerable evidence that the peasants experienced a major loss of faith in the Party's ability to lead. During the crisis period the communist press reported that peasants were resurrecting geomancy and that rural secret societies were reappearing.[42] These items suggest that the Chinese peasantry, faced with starvation as a result of following the Party's leadership, reverted to traditional methods and forms of organization. More serious for the Party was the damage inflicted on the mass line. The cadres, instead of operating "from the masses and to the masses," simply herded the people into communes regardless of popular opinion. In its retreat from the communes, the Party blamed the cadres, taking the greatest precaution to avoid criticizing either the top leadership or the formal policies. Nevertheless, the cadres are the Party's representatives at the level of actual contact with the people, and the Party cannot discredit them for long without weakening its own ability to rule.

Leadership of the Chinese command economy has always rested on a small body (that is, small in relation to the population) of dedicated supervisors, foremen, team leaders, and functionaries known collectively in China as cadres, or *kan-pu*. Estimates of the number of cadres vary greatly, but the probable figure is around 20 million, a few million more than the membership of the Communist Party.[43] These men and women may or may not be Party members, but if they are not they have usually demonstrated their progressive political inclinations as Communist Youth League members, in school, or as Army veterans. Speaking of the size of the Communist Party itself, Liu Shao-ch'i noted, on July 1, 1961, the fortieth anniversary of its founding, that it then had approximately 17 million members. Of these, 80 per cent had joined after 1949, and 70 per cent had joined during the first five-year plan, from 1953 to 1957. In other words, only about 20 per cent of the communist elite in China can be considered hardened revolutionaries. An absolute shortage of cadres has persisted since the establishment of the regime, and many of the present 20 million cadres are deficient in ability by the communists' own standards.[44]

Although the cadres are technically nothing more than the sergeants of the Party, the minor functionaries who carry out orders as best they understand them, it is clear that they were not entirely blameless in the failure of the communes. They were the men who, in the autumn of 1958, carried the Party's propaganda about the "entrance into communism" so far as to confiscate even the bedding and the cooking utensils of the peasantry. They were the men who stubbornly pursued the policies of close planting and deep plowing without consulting old peasants who had farmed the same land for decades. Needless to say, they were following orders; but on the basis of recently published reports it appears as if the cadres were indeed tending to become a bureaucratic stratum or a new class. It is this tendency—the genuine divorce of the cadres from the masses—that present Party policies are aimed at eradicating.

The Party hopes to rehabilitate the cadres' reputation by getting them out of commune and brigade offices and putting them to work in the fields. A movement for cadre physical labor began during the summer of 1963 and is continuing at the present time. During July, 1963, the *People's Daily* devoted most of its editorials to cadre labor, and a whole double issue of *Red Flag* [45] was given over to the subject. One article complained that:

> . . . some of the hsien [i.e., county] and commune cadres, particularly the leading cadres, are always busy convening and attending meetings, listening to reports, preparing charts, and reading documents at their offices the whole year around. They are unable to mix with the broad masses, to conduct investigations, and to give personal guidance in work.[46]

According to the Party, the cadres must perform manual labor because "participation by the cadres, particularly at basic levels . . . shows the people that Party cadres are ordinary laboring people, not magistrates sitting above them." [47]

The Party is certain that part of the problem lies in the tendency of cadres to become "big shots." "Some brigade and production team cadres, and even some older Party members and cadres, say to themselves, 'We are now cadres. If we ever again take part in physical labor together with commune members, it will not be in keeping with our status.' " [48] The Party's answer to these pretensions is work in the fields, often unpleasant or demeaning work, so that the cadres may set an example for the people. Manure collection, for instance, has occupied a prominent place in the communist press's discussions of cadre labor: "Have we not heard many basic level workers say, 'How can I complain when the secretary of the hsien Party committee also carries manure?' " [49] A former middle-school student, who in 1961 had returned (or been sent) to the Nankuo commune in Szechwan province, complained to the editor of *China Youth News* that he had been ridiculed by his production team for collecting manure. To his question, "Is manure collection by a young intellectual 'retrogressive'?" the editor replied:

> Your problem illustrates the fact that for several thousand years physical labor was despised by the exploiting class and that their old viewpoint, according to which scholars could not cultivate fields, is still not completely eradicated. Now scholars go to the rural areas to cultivate fields. Their purpose is to alter the people's way of thinking and to change their customs.[50]

A more authoritative reason for the cadre labor movement was given in the *People's Daily*:

> It is a revolution in leadership style and working methods, aimed at revising the bureaucratic practices left behind by organs of the old society. It is a revolution in the bureaucracy aimed at preventing and overcoming the erosive effects of bureaucracy and safeguarding the purity of our Party and state organs.[51]

The virulence of this campaign indicates that the Party's surrender to localism during the food crisis was only temporary. As the economy begins to respond to team autonomy and clear-cut incentives, the Party is trying to recapture control of it (although as yet without curtailing economic decision making at the team level). The movement for cadre labor also reveals that the leadership still considers the mass line a sacred method of political guidance. For cadres to lead the people by working among them is a basic proposition of the mass line. We do not know with any degree of accuracy the extent to which the Party lost influence during the food crisis, nor do we know the degree to which control is now maintained by coercion. But it is clear that the Party is at least attempting to reestablish the popular mandate that it enjoyed in 1957.

The New Strategy of Economic Development

While the mass line continues to function as a tactic of communist leadership, it has been abandoned as a strategy for achieving a new Great Leap Forward. The strategy of economic development in China today is addressed squarely and realistically to the primary national problem: how to increase agricultural productivity. The communists no longer believe that this problem can be overcome merely by mobilizing the will of the masses. They have learned that it will require a patient application of capital, technology, education, and rational planning.

In May, 1958, the Party described its "general line of socialist construction" as "the achievement of more, quicker, better, and more economical results in building socialism." This line produced the Great Leap Forward. On June 30, 1961, Liu Shao-ch'i announced that the Party's goal was "the development of our national economy in a planned and proportionate way." [52] Between 1961 and 1963, Party organs, national congresses, special conferences, and the political and technical press flooded the country with information on the detailed meaning of the phrase "planned and proportionate development."

The first major change was that investment in heavy industry for its own sake was abandoned. Instead, modern industry was made the servant of agricultural development. Since the ninth plenum of the Central Committee in January, 1961, capital construction continues only in the coal mining, timber, chemical fertilizer, agricultural machinery, and transportation sectors.[53] At the same time, direct investment in and extension of credit to agriculture was begun. The Party delivered a definitive statement of its pro-agricultural economic policy at the Central Committee's tenth plenum in September, 1962:

> We must mobilize and centralize the power of the Party and the country to sustain our agriculture and the collective economy of the people's communes. We must make available the necessary materials, technology, finance, leadership, and personnel organization; and we must enforce technological reform in agriculture by stages, according to local conditions.[54]

Technological reform, as specified by the tenth plenum and other conferences, includes mechanization, electrification, water conservation, and the application of chemistry to agriculture. The new course for industry and the transformation of agriculture are known in China today under the slogan: "Agriculture is the foundation and industry is the guide."

Mechanization, electrification, water conservation, and a greater use of chemical fertilizers are all intended to produce an increase in per-mou output (one mou equals one-sixth of an acre). In order to calculate mechanization, Chinese planners have established a measure for tractors called a "standard unit." One standard unit is a 15-horsepower machine capable of working 1,500 mou (i.e., 100 hectares) of land for a full range of jobs—plowing, harrowing, cultivating, and harvesting.[55] If only plowing is mechanized, one standard unit can be responsible for about 3,000 mou. A single Red East tractor, the type manufactured at the Loyang heavy tractor plant, is equivalent to 2.4 standard units and can thus plow about 7,000 mou of land. At the present time, China possesses a total of about 100,000 standard units (possibly no more than 40,000 to 50,000 actual machines), capable of working about one-tenth of its arable land.[56] It needs 1,000,000 standard units.

Rural electrification and water control are complementary, since electricity provides the power that operates the irrigation pumps which deliver or drain off water. Genuine progress has been made in both of these areas. What is unusual is that Party statistics compare the present situation today with 1957 instead of with the preliberation period; in other words, the communists are not trying to disguise the fact that they paid almost no attention to agriculture until the Great Leap Forward. Beween 1957 and 1962, 70,000 kilometers of high-tension lines were constructed. Some 1,000 hsien and municipalities now have electricity, and the volume of electricity used by agriculture in 1962 was 13.8 times what it was in 1957. Fifty per cent of the rice crop area in the Yangtze delta is served by electricity, as are 4,000,000 mou of the Pearl River delta.[57] Peasants have been quoted as saying, "Water wheels are no longer turned by stepping on the pedals; just flick a switch." The new electric pumps are nicknamed "iron dragons."

The Chinese communists claim to have installed electric pumping equipment equal to 1,600,000 kilowatts—a figure 23 times greater than that of 1957, but still woefully small for China's approximately 100 million hectares of arable land.[58] The water and electricity situation in the Pearl River delta is illustrative, however, of the transformation taking place. This area experienced its "worst drought in 60 years" during early 1963; but as a result of some 3,000 meters of high-tension lines and several large-scale water conservation projects constructed in recent years, no serious damage occurred. The communes contributed the funds and the manpower for modernizing this region. An official of the Department of Water Conservation and Electric Power of Kwangtung province recently asserted:

> There was no drastic change in the countenance of Kwangtung's water conservancy facilities until the Great Leap Forward of 1958. . . . During the last six years a total of one billion worker-days were put into conservation projects by a huge construction army composed mainly of peasants but augmented by cadres, officers and men of the Liberation Army, industrial workers, urban inhabitants, and students. This huge army has moved a total of 1.3 billion cubic meters of earth.[59]

China has two big chemical fertilizer plants, one at Dairen and the other at Lanchow, supplemented by several smaller units, such as the one at Nanking.[60] Their present output does not even come close to meeting China's needs. An English economic research group estimates that

1960 production was 1.9 million tons and that China's total requirements are about 20 to 25 million tons.[61] Okazaki Kaheita, a Japanese authority, believes that China's fertilizer needs are around 15 million tons, if Chinese farmers are to use it at the same rate Japanese farmers do. However, he estimates that China's production is only 1 million tons. According to a different Japanese study, deliveries of fertilizer by the chemical industry, during the first two months of 1963, were 100 per cent greater than in the same period in 1961.[62] Nevertheless, China must import some fertilizer while continuing to invest in her own chemical industry, if agricultural output is to be raised rapidly.

The agricultural situation in 1964 suggests that the Chinese have made a sound *beginning* toward the scientific development of agriculture. From the point of view of the mechanics of economic development, this beginning actually appears to owe a good deal to the communes. As many transitional societies other than China illustrate, economic development does not come about solely as a result of investment. It is the product of a receptive social environment, determined leadership, technical competence, and money. The communes contributed to economic growth primarily through their influence on the social environment: They cleared away much of the old "social rubble" that stood in the way of agricultural growth. For example, the communes rationalized the distribution of land more efficiently than any system had for decades. Even in the higher agricultural producers' cooperatives, the plots of land actually worked by each cooperative were determined by titles issued at the time of land reform (i.e., 1951 to 1952). Often discontiguous and of unequal value, this land could not profit from water conservation until it had been combined into the communes and redistributed to the production teams. As the director of the Eight-One Commune in Nanch'ang hsien, Kiangsi, put it:

> In the cooperative period we wanted to plant more double-season rice in order to increase our grain output, but we did not dare do so because our manpower was small and the farms of the different cooperatives intersected one another, making it impossible to open irrigation ditches systematically. We felt the manpower shortage even more when we wanted to build large water conservation works against severe floods and droughts.[63]

The communes could also afford to purchase and maintain agricultural machinery. Each standard unit costs 15,000 yuan, and the average production team has neither sufficient funds with which to buy a tractor nor enough land on which profitably to use it. On the other hand, it can certainly benefit from commune tractor stations and from commune-wide electric power grids. The head of the Eight-One Commune observed:

In the period of individual operation, one household owned several parcels of land of perhaps ten mou each; therefore it was impossible to employ such machines [tractors and electric water pumps]. In the cooperative period, when the area of land cultivated was bigger and one or two tractors were sufficient, maintenance and repair of machinery became a problem because it was impractical to establish a maintenance and repair plant for just one or two tractors.[64]

Today his commune has six tractors, and there is a trend to state tractor stations of 40 standard units that lease equipment to several communes.[65]

In analytical terms, the history of the communes illustrates a phenomenon encountered in all developing systems. An elite group directing the rapid modernization of a backward society has to meet two different demands—demands which can easily become antagonistic. On the one hand, it must create a social environment conducive to long-range economic growth; on the other hand, it must meet the short-term needs of the society for food, clothing, defense, and welfare. However, social engineering to meet the first demand may create a short-term crisis so severe as to threaten the day-to-day operation of the system. This is what happened in China during the second five-year plan. Now that the crisis has been weathered successfully, the people may be beginning to appreciate some of the benefits of rural reorganization. The commune is also an improved unit of local political administration over the hsien, previously the lowest effective unit of national government. There were 24,000 communes at the end of 1958, whereas the number of hsien in 1958 was 1,882. Clearly, the central government has come much closer to the agricultural producer.

Although the Party made many mistakes in devising its strategies of development, it has now reached a point where some of the most painful initial social engineering is behind it. Effective centralized control over the entire territory has been achieved. The problems of bureaucratic proliferation have been met frontally in the *hsia-fang* movement, which was begun in 1956. (*Hsia-fang*, i.e., "downward transfer," involves the decentralization of the cadre class and the reallocation of the city population to the rural areas. Although the least studied in the West of all Chinese communist policies, it probably has greater political and social significance than any other reform.) [66] The educational system has been sweepingly reformed. Even birth control is no longer regarded dogmatically as a form of neo-Malthusianism.[67] In short, a social environment receptive to economic growth has been created, and the Party has finally brought its own ideas concerning that growth into coherence with the realities of Chinese agriculture. Money is now the major requirement.

Current Chinese financial policies reflect the same pragmatism that has informed the development of the pro-agriculture strategy. The leaders admit candidly that funds cannot be secured from external sources and that China must rely primarily on its own savings.[68] Recognition of their internal isolation has enabled some Chinese economists to begin conceptualizing more clearly than in the past where internal savings come from. Chart 1 is one Chinese economist's subdivision of the components of Chinese national income.

Chart 1

NATIONAL INCOME

Accumulation	*Consumption*
Sources:	By social groups:
State accumulation	State administrative expenses
Collective accumulation	Defense expenses
Uses:	Culture, education, and public health
Capital investment in agriculture, light	Social insurance and relief
industry, and heavy industry	By individuals:
Nonproductive capital construction	Income of workers
(state administration, defense,	Income of peasants
schools, hospitals, theaters, etc.)	Income of intellectuals
Social reserve fund and liquidity	Income of capitalists

There is nothing startling about these categories from the point of view of descriptive economics. What is unusual in the Chinese communists' theorizing is that they no longer regard this structure as an artificial barrier to progress, one that political enthusiasm alone can demolish. Today they are willing to work within this framework; and although they express the various ratios by the value-laden term "contradictions," the policy guidelines that emerge from this type of analysis are generally conducive to steady growth. Chiang Hsüeh-mo, the economist who constructed the above chart, concludes:

> The contradiction between accumulation and consumption reflects the contradiction between national construction and the improvement of the people's living conditions; that is, it reflects the contradiction between the long-range interests and the immediate interests of the people and between collective interests and personal interests. . . . An increase in accumulation must be based on the uninterrupted development of production and on an appropriate and steady rise in the people's living standards. The enthusiasm and creative power of the masses are decisive factors in socialist construction. To insure the enthusiasm of the masses at this stage it is necessary on the one hand for the Party to proceed with careful, complex ideological and political work in order to raise the socialist awakening of the masses, and on the other hand to spur and consolidate labor enthusiasm by means of certain material incentives.[69]

The Party's recognition of these components of growth has contributed one essential quality to their development that was conspicuous by its absence during the first decade—balance. The need for balance is being stressed in various slogans: e.g., "Over-all plans and proper arrangements" and "The whole country like a chess board."

One practical consequence of the Party's interest in financial matters is a new emphasis on tax accounting and tax collecting. Tax-collecting cadres have been specially exempted from the cadre labor program, and an article from the *Ta Kung Pao* of October, 1963, throws some light on the problems they are supposed to be solving instead:

> There are some comrades who maintain that since both state enterprises and taxes belong to the state, what taxes are omitted by the enterprises will be transferred to their profit and eventually paid up to the treasury. There is therefore thought to be no great need for tax supervision.[70]

What is wrong with this reasoning, according to the Party, is that taxes are fixed while profits vary with costs. If tax funds are included as profit, it becomes impossible to judge the efficiency of an enterprise and to make "over-all plans and proper arrangements." The recent crackdown on tax administration has revealed abuses such as juggled ledgers and cases of collectors settling disputes (i.e., "contradictions") on the spot by increasing or refunding taxes.

On the agricultural front itself, the government has adopted two measures to finance mechanization. It has developed a movement of team-level savings, and it has vastly increased the credit available to rural productive units. Teams are being urged to increase their own investable surplus by means of a four-point program: (1) increased production on the basis of present resources; (2) the development of subsidiary production (forestry, animal husbandry, and so forth); (3) the maintenance of strict economy over nonproductive expenditures; and (4) the correct management of the ratios between accumulation, short-term production expenses, and consumption.[71]

In order to help teams increase production, the state is making it possible for the more efficient communes to buy machines on credit. There are at present two main forms of farm credit: loans from state banks, and loans from credit cooperatives. The credit cooperatives, which administer mutual-aid funds at the commune level, make short-term loans (no longer than a year) solely to meet team needs for seed, implements, liquidity, and so forth. It is the long-term state bank loans that have been greatly expanded. "Since 1962, Chinese state banks have sponsored long-term farm loans by using the special loan funds established by the national financial budget."[72] We do not know the exact size of this program, but it may have run as high as two billion yuan during 1963.

The average loan is reported to be between 1,000 and 5,000 yuan.[73] A secondary reason for the expanded loan program may be the central government's desire to control the autonomous teams through financial supervision, just as taxation has been used to control the rural markets. The rural savings program plus expanded state credit constitute the basic means for financing technological reform. As usual, they are expressed in a slogan: "Rely primarily on oneself and secondarily on state support." [74]

Communist China today offers an example of a late-developing agricultural society that has attained—through bitter trial and error—a comparatively clear understanding of the elements of economic growth within its own economic geography. The tenth plenum estimated that mechanization will require 20 to 25 years to complete; actually it will probably take until the end of the century. And mechanization alone will not raise agricultural output; a trained corps of scientific agronomists is as necessary as more tractors to long-term success. Nevertheless, with its present policy of developing agriculture to the level that it can support an industrial establishment, China has a fighting chance of emerging from the transitional status that it occupies along with a majority of the world's peoples. The attainment of an understanding of how to develop their economy may well be the greatest achievement of the Chinese leaders since 1949. The ever-present danger is that impatience may again lead them to take foolhardy shortcuts toward their ultimate goal. The Chinese communists were lucky with the Great Leap Forward; another such experiment could be fatal.

The Sino-Soviet Dispute

The last great stronghold of the mass line is the People's Liberation Army. Chinese communist military strategy remains wedded to the belief that the support of the masses is the single most important element in offense or defense, and the Chinese Army is trained, organized, and equipped as if it were a giant guerrilla force. By official pronouncement, the atomic bomb is a paper tiger or, as the Army recently put it, "the spiritual A-bomb is more important than the material one." [75] The Chinese communists do not ignore military weapons, but they believe that the technical qualities of an army are secondary to its morale, determination, and popular backing. In short, they conceive of the military arts as an adjunct to the political arts, and they explicitly reject what they call "narrow military professionalism." The Minister of Defense, Lin Piao, laid down official Chinese military policy shortly after he replaced the discredited professional, P'eng Te-huai:

At the present stage of building a modernized army, when the technical equipment of our army is being constantly improved and the mastery of technique and the raising of the technical level of our army have become more important than ever before, is the human factor still of decisive significance? Some comrades take the view that modern warfare differs from warfare in the past, that since weapons and equipment available to our army in the past were inferior we had to emphasize dependence on man, on his bravery and wisdom, in order to win victories. They say that modern warfare is a war of technique, of steel and machinery, and that in the face of these things, man's role has to be relegated to a secondary place. . . . Contrary to these people, we believe that while equipment and technique are important, the human factor is even more so.[76]

Why is it that the Chinese communists cling so tenaciously to the mass line in their theory of military organization? As we have seen earlier, part of the answer lies in the influence of their revolutionary heritage. The Chinese communists do not distinguish between a military and a political sphere, between war and revolution, because in their own revolutionary experience both categories were equated. They have powerful reasons for believing that these distinctions are false, and within and outside of the communist bloc they advocate that revolutionary wars on the Chinese model are the true path to communism. However, this is only half the reason for the persistence of the mass line in military affairs.

Although the Chinese communist theory of revolution is one of the major causes of the Sino-Soviet dispute, the dispute itself perpetuates the mass line in the Army because China no longer has access to modern military equipment. In advocating the mass line, the military is in part making a virtue out of a necessity. In July, 1960, the dispute caused the Soviet Union to withdraw some 1,300 experts from China, crippling such enterprises as the Ch'angch'un automobile factory and the Sanmenhsia hydroelectric project (intended to produce the power for making fissionable materials). Coinciding with the failure of the Great Leap Forward, the dispute halted China's industrial growth. Since China is a predominantly agricultural country, its isolation from the Soviet Union does not necessarily spell its economic doom; however, Chinese inability to acquire modern weapons and spare parts from the Soviet Union has had a great impact on the People's Liberation Army. The Army's air force (chiefly MiG-17 fighter-interceptors and Il-28, Tu-2, and Tu-4 bombers) is obsolete, and its ground-force equipment, virtually all of Russian specification, is greatly in need of replenishment. Guns and explosives, previously purchased from Czechoslovakia, are today unavailable.[77] Hence the chief asset of the 2.5 million-man PLA is its manpower, and the continuing strength of the mass line is explained partly by the fact that China has no other choice.

In 1959, several of China's high-ranking military leaders came to this same conclusion, and they argued against the dispute with Russia precisely because it would weaken China's defenses. In the summer of 1959, Marshal P'eng Te-huai clashed severely with Mao Tse-tung over a broad range of military and political issues; it was the most serious dispute among the old revolutionary leaders since the ouster of Chang Kuo-t'ao, 20 years earlier. P'eng first joined Mao in 1928, and he had served ten years as the first Minister of Defense when he was forced to resign. The People's Liberation Army accused P'eng and his chief of staff, Huang K'o-ch'eng, who was ousted at the same time, of advancing military principles at variance with Mao's ideology (i.e., the mass line strategy).[78] It seems certain, however, that military ideology was only one aspect of the disagreement between P'eng and the Maoist faction.

At the center of their dispute was the Sino-Soviet estrangement and China's decision to proceed with its development independent of the Soviet Union. P'eng and Huang appear to have favored maintaining the alliance with Russia at all costs, and they may even have entered into a Kremlin-inspired conspiracy to overturn the Chinese Political Bureau. Mao and his associates successfully turned aside P'eng's challenge, and the simmering dispute with Russia developed into the open antagonism of 1963 and after. In early 1963, Foreign Minister Ch'en Yi told a visiting Japanese delegation:

> We have thought about the ideological dispute with Russia for three years. We knew that we would be attacked for our stand and that some would criticize us as being adventurous. We even ran the risk of nuclear assault by American imperialism. However, we have to defend Marxism-Leninism. We must preserve the interests of the people of the entire world even though the Chinese people have to make temporary sacrifices. We determined to endure self-sacrifice for the sake of internationalism.[79]

The Chinese communists have cited four specific causes for the schism. The first was the failure of Russia to support China against India. In February, 1963, the Chinese wrote:

> How did these differences come to be exposed before the enemy? Thorez and other comrades allege that the differences were brought into the open with the Chinese Communist Party's publication of the pamphlet *Long Live Leninism!* in all languages in the summer of 1960. The truth is that the internal differences among the fraternal parties were first brought into the open not in the summer of 1960, but on the eve of the Camp David talks in September 1959—on September 9, 1959, to be exact. On that day a socialist country, turning a deaf ear to China's repeated explanations of the true situation and to China's advice, hastily issued a statement on a Sino-Indian border incident through its official news agency. Making no distinction between right and wrong, the state-

ment expressed "regret" over the border clash and in reality condemned China's correct stand. . . . Here is the first instance in history in which a socialist country, instead of condemning the armed provocations of the reactionaries of a capitalist country, condemned another fraternal socialist country when it was confronted with such armed provocation.[80]

Needless to say, Russian neutrality in the Sino-Indian border war of 1962 poured more gasoline on this particular fire.

A second reason for the dispute was Russia's refusal to support China's atomic weapons program without at the same time controlling it. On September 6, 1963, the *People's Daily* wrote:

In 1958 [the time of the Quemoy crisis] the leadership of the CPSU [Communist Party of the Soviet Union] put forward unreasonable demands to bring China under Soviet military control. These unreasonable demands were rightly and firmly rejected by the Chinese government. Not long afterward, in June 1959, the Soviet government unilaterally tore up the agreement on new technology for national defense concluded between China and the Soviet Union in October 1957, and refused to provide China with a sample of an atomic bomb and technical data concerning its manufacture.[81]

Here, certainly, is one of the major causes of Sino-Russian antagonism. At the same time, it enables us to see in a new light Chinese statements that the atomic bomb is a paper tiger. Atomic weapons were inconsequential to the Chinese partly because they did not have any. During 1963, they adamantly opposed the Russo-British-United States test-ban treaty (they called it the "tripartite pact," recalling an earlier treaty of that name), but they also insisted that they would acquire atomic weapons in the future with or without foreign assistance.[82] In October, 1964, China finally revealed how propagandistic its earlier pronouncements on atomic weapons had been. Responding to intelligence disclosures by the United States and Canada, China informed selected foreign powers that it had been developing its own nuclear weapons since at least 1960, and, on October 16, it conducted its first atomic explosion.

The third specific cause of friction mentioned by the Chinese is anti-Chinese subversion undertaken by Russian officials in China proper and in Sinkiang. In 1963, Japanese visitors in China were told about anti-Party activities conducted by Russian consuls in Shanghai and Nanking during 1961, and Sinkiang remains the most critical arena of direct state-to-state confrontation:

In April and May, 1962, the leaders of the CPSU used their organs and personnel in Sinkiang, China, to carry out large-scale subversive activities in the Ili region and enticed and coerced several tens of thousands of

Chinese citizens into going to the Soviet Union. . . . To this day this incident remains unsettled.[83]

Sinkiang, like the other two causes of the dispute, has no connection with China's avowed mission of preserving the ideological purity of Marxism-Leninism; however, communist ideology and differences concerning the right to interpret that ideology have contributed to the dispute. In fact, a difference over ideology appears to have been the first concrete source of grievance—the catalyst that led the two partners to see each other first as competitors and then as antagonists. In September, 1963, the Chinese Communist Party Central Committee wrote:

> The open letter of the Central Committee of the CPSU spreads the notion that the differences in the international communist movement were started by the three articles which we published in April 1960 under the title of *Long Live Leninism!* This is a big lie. . . . To be specific, it began with the 20th Congress of the CPSU in 1956. . . . The criticism of Stalin at the 20th Congress of the CPSU was wrong both in principle and in method.[84]

The Chinese communists had not, of course, suffered at Stalin's hands as the Russians and east Europeans had, and they were better able to appreciate Stalin's methods because from 1956 to 1958 their own industrial development appeared to be paralleling the Soviet Union's first five-year plan. Possibly most important, the Chinese communists resented the ideological crudity of de-Stalinization as undertaken by Khrushchev. The Chinese believed that the "cult of personality" was too shallow an explanation for Stalin's excesses, and they insisted that Stalin's errors be viewed within the over-all distinction between "antagonistic" and "nonantagonistic" contradictions. In their opinion, even if Stalin had been a problem (nonantagonistic) for Soviet society, he had been effective against imperialism (i.e., an antagonistic contradiction)—and this should not be forgotten.

The fact that the Sino-Soviet dispute partly concerns Marxist-Leninist ideology poses difficult problems for the detached observer who wants to assess the function of ideology in the independent communist nations. In my opinion, communist ideology in China functions as the ideological rationale for its revolutionary national development. Human beings do not undertake revolutionary sacrifices lightly; they require an intellectual expression of the greatness and justness of their actions. To this end, virulent nationalist movements have always found it opportune to incorporate transnational values in order to help motivate their communicants. It should be remarked that, in characterizing the Chinese revolution as "nationalist," we are using nationalism as an analytical concept. "Communism," in this usage, is a descriptive category. Thus there is nothing incompatible between the terms "nationalist" and "communist" any more than there is between "totalitarian" and "fascist." [85]

Clearly, the Chinese people have worked harder and made greater sacrifices since 1949 than can be comprehended solely in terms of coercive or manipulative goads. Communist ideology provides the intellectual justification for Party direction of the Chinese Revolution, and it underwrites "scientifically" the inevitability of revolutionary success. Maoism bolsters the Chinese in their attempt at rapid economic growth much as the emperor myth did in late Meiji Japan or classical liberalism in the industrializing West.

The ideological form that the Sino-Soviet dispute has taken in certain of its phases has damaged the functional value of Marxism as an integrative myth and a work ethic for both sides. Although communist ideology functions as a national myth in the independent communist states, its functioning is impaired if its universal, scientific pretensions become untenable. Maoism may be the concrete application to China of scientific socialism, but the Sino-Soviet dispute or the charge made throughout China in 1963 that the Russian Communist Party was then led by a "psalm-singing, incense-burning" modern revisionist is damaging to scientific socialism. When the Chinese Party tells the masses that the Russians have betrayed Leninism, what do the masses think of the claims for Maoism? Coming at the same time as the failure of the Great Leap Forward, the Sino-Soviet dispute cannot have strengthened the Party's claim to infallibility. If de-Stalinization had irreversible effects within the Soviet Union, the Sino-Soviet dispute is producing comparable changes in China and in the worldwide communist movement.

The reorientation of China's development strategy, the Sino-Soviet dispute, and the decline of the mass line, all mark a major turning point for Asian and world communism. China's new diplomatic initiatives in north Africa, France, and Japan during early 1964 are clearly intended to break its Russian- and American-imposed isolation. We do not yet know how successful these new ventures will be, nor can we be certain that they signify a change in Chinese foreign policy as sweeping as the one in agricultural policy. Moreover, the Chinese communist leaders are old; soon a new and unfamiliar directorate will take up the reins. Will those who follow the guerrilla leaders abandon the mass line once and for all? Will the Chinese cultural antipathy to birth control frustrate any and all economic development strategies? Will the Sino-Soviet dispute lead to something more serious than a *détente*? In C. P. Snow's *The Affair*, one of his dons inquires rhetorically over brandy, "How can China avoid becoming the dominant power on earth?" The answer to this question will come from the Chinese people themselves; we who observe the Chinese Revolution cannot supply it.

Building a Communist Nation in China

1. "Keng-hao ti yün-yung 'san-chieh-ho' ti ling-tao fang-fa" (Make Better Use of the '3-in-1' Method of Leadership"), *Jen-min jih-pao,* February 11, 1963, p. 1.
2. See John Lewis, *Leadership in Communist China* (Ithaca, N.Y.: Cornell University Press, 1963); and Stuart Schram, *The Political Thought of Mao Tse-tung* (New York: Frederick A. Praeger, Inc., 1963).
3. *Mao Tse-tung hsüan-chi* (Peking, 1961), I, 131
4. Mao Tse-tung, *Selected Works* (New York: International Publishers, 1954), Vol. 3, 16.
5. Mao Tse-tung, *On Guerrilla Warfare,* trans. S. Griffith (New York: Frederick A. Praeger, Inc., 1961), p. 44.
6. Republic of China, Department of National Defense, Intelligence Bureau, *Mao-fei Tse-tung chün-chih ssu-hsiang yen-chiu (A Study of Mao Tse-tung's Military Thinking)* (T'aipei, December, 1960), p. 6.
7. *Chinese Communism and the Rise of Mao* (Cambridge, Mass.: Harvard University Press, 1958), p. 101.
8. See Shanghai *Chieh-fang jih-pao,* June 9, 1962.
9. *Selected Works of Mao Tse-tung* (Peking: Foreign Language Press, 1961), IV, 155-56.
10. For an excellent study of recent military ideology, see Ch'ü Lu-chih, "Chūkyōgun naibu no fuan na chōkō" ("Symptoms of Unrest within the Chinese Communist Army"), *Tairiku mondai* (Tokyo), No. 135 (April, 1963), 70-77.
11. Mao Tse-tung, *Selected Works* (New York: International Publishers, 1954), I, 239. Also see *Mao-fei Tse-tung chün-shih ssu-hsiang yen-chiu,* p. 11 and *passim.*
12. "Study the Thought of Comrade Mao Tse-tung concerning People's War," *Hsüeh-hsi Mao Tse-tung ssu-hsiang* (Study the Thought of Mao Tse-tung) (Hong Kong, 1961), II, 80. For a more complete discussion of the theory of people's war, see my *Revolution and the Social System* (Stanford, Calif.: Hoover Institution Studies No. 3, 1964); and "Annex: Military Doctrine," in Ralph Powell, *Politico-Military Relationships in Communist China* (Washington, D.C.: U.S. Department of State, External Research Staff, Bureau of Intelligence and Research, October, 1963), pp. 18-21.
13. See "Strategic Problems of China's Revolutionary War" (December, 1936), in Mao Tse-tung, *Selected Works* (New York, 1954), I, 175-253.
14. Vladimir Dedijer, *Tito* (New York: Simon and Schuster, 1953), p. 322. See the discussion of this point by Robert North, "Two Revolutionary Models: Russian and Chinese," in *Communist Strategies in Asia,* ed. A. Doak Barnett (New York: Frederick A. Praeger, Inc., 1963), pp. 42-43.
15. Speech at Trade Union Conference af Asian and Australasian Countries (New China News Agency, Peking, November 23, 1949).
16. See Kao Ko, "The Victorious Road of National Liberation War," *Jen-min jih-pao,* June 3, 1963, reprinted in *Peking Review,* No. 46 (November 15, 1963), pp. 6-14. See also *Selected Military Writings of Mao Tse-tung.* Peking: Foreign Languages Press, 1963, an English edition of a volume published by the Chinese communists which brings together all of Mao's works on people's war.
17. February 27, 1957. Text in Center for International Affairs and the East Asian Research Center, Harvard University, *Communist China: 1955-1959, Policy*

Documents with Analysis (Cambridge, Mass.: Harvard University Press, 1962), p. 292.

18. "Chairman Mao Tse-tung's Statement Calling upon the People of the World to Unite to Oppose Racial Discrimination by U.S. Imperialism and Support the American Negroes in Their Struggle against Racial Discrimination," August 8, 1963. Printed in *Peking Review*, No. 33 (August 16, 1963), p. 7.

19. *Jen-min jih-pao*, November 24, 1963, p. 3.

20. "Mō Taku-tō no shisō to senryaku" ("The Ideology and Strategy of Mao Tse-tung"), *Chūō kōron*, March, 1963, pp. 124-25. For a similar analysis, see Professor Nomura Kōichi, "Mō Taku-tō shuseki" ("Chairman Mao Tse-tung"), *Chūō kōron*, September, 1963, pp. 55-61.

21. "The Differences between Comrade Togliatti and Us," *Jen-min jih-pao*, December 31, 1962.

22. "The Chinese Communist Party Is the Supreme Commander of the Chinese People in Building Socialism," *Jen-min jih-pao*, September 28, 1959.

23. See *Current Scene: Developments in Mainland China* (Hong Kong), II, No. 27 (January 15, 1964), 4.

24. See letter to the *New York Times* of Professor Huang Yen-yu, formerly of Lingnan University, Canton, dated December 30, 1958. Cf. *The One-world Philosophy of K'ang Yu-wei*, trans. L. G. Thompson (London: George Allen & Unwin, 1958).

25. The most thorough comparison of the Chinese communes with Russian collectives is Fukushima Masao, *Jinmin kōsha no kenkyū* (*A Study of the People's Communes*) (Tokyo, 1960).

26. *The Victory of Marxism-Leninism in China* (Peking, 1959), quoted by R. A. Scalapino, "The Foreign Policy of the People's Republic of China," in *Foreign Policies in a World of Change*, C. Black and K. Thompson, eds. (New York, 1963), p. 556. Concerning the adoption of the mass line as the basic strategy of the Great Leap Forward, see Miyashita Tadao, "Chūkyō ni okeru shakaishugi kensetsu no riron" ("The Theory of Socialist Construction in Communist China") in Nihon Gaisei Gakkai (Japanese Foreign Policy Association) *Chūkyō seiken no genjō bunseki* (*Contemporary Analysis of the Chinese Communist Regime*) (Tokyo, 1961), pp. 35ff.

27. "Tui-t'ien hsüan-chan" ("to declare war against heaven"). For this and many other military metaphors used in the Great Leap Forward slogans, see T. A. Hsia, *Metaphor, Myth, Ritual and the People's Commune*. Studies in Chinese Communist Terminology: No. 7 (Berkeley, Calif.: Center for Chinese Studies, 1961).

28. Chung-kuo jen-min chieh-fang chün, tsung cheng chih-pu, *Kung-tso t'ung-hsün*, No. 1 (January 1, 1961) through No. 30 (August 26, 1961), except for No. 9 (February). For information on the origin and availability of these documents, see *Newsletter of the Association for Asian Studies*, IX, No. 2 (December, 1963), 28-29.

29. *Kung-tso t'ung-hsün*, No. 1, p. 7; Ralph Powell, *Politico-Military Relationships in Communist China*, p. 14.

30. *Kung-tso t'ung-hsün*, No. 1, pp. 12-13.

31. On censors, see *ibid.*, No. 1, p. 14; No. 7, p. 18.

32. On home leave and visitors, see *ibid.*, No. 1, p. 14; No. 7, p. 18; No. 22, p. 7.

33. *Ibid.*, No. 7, p. 18; No. 11, p. 2.

34. *Ibid.*, No. 11, p. 3.

35. *Ibid.*, No. 22, p. 9.

36. Ch'ü Lu-chih, "Chūkyōgun naibu no fuan na chōkō," *Tairiku mondai*, No. 135 (April, 1963), pp. 70-77; Powell, *Politico-Military Relationships in Communist China*.

37. *Communist China: 1955-1959* (Cambridge, Mass.: Harvard University Press, 1962), p. 537. (Translation slightly altered.)

38. See "Hold Fast to the System of Three Guarantees and One Reward and Strive Constantly to Improve It," *Jen-min jih-pao*, December 29, 1960.

39. Li Chien-heng, "On the Long Duration of the System of Collective Ownership," *Ta Kung Pao*, July 30, 1962 (U.S. Consulate General, Hong Kong, *Survey of China Mainland Press* [SCMP] 2808).

40. See Michael Freeberne, "The Role of Natural Calamities in Communist China," *Current Scene*, II, No. 25 (Hong Kong, December 23, 1963).

41. Cf. John Lewis, "The Leadership Doctrine of the Chinese Communist Party: The Lesson of the People's Commune," *Asian Survey*, III, No. 10 (Berkeley, Calif., October, 1963), pp. 457-64; and H. F. Schurmann, "Peking's Recognition of Crisis," *Problems of Communism*, X, No. 5 (Washington, D.C., September-October, 1961), pp. 5-14.

42. See the discussion on "brotherhood organizations" formed in Shantung, Peking, *Kung-jen jih-pao*, September 4, 1963. Cf. "Red China Fights Rise in Occultism," *New York Times*, Western ed., November 8, 1962, p. 8.

43. *Jen-min jih-pao*, July 4, 1963, p. 2; *Jen-min jih-pao*, August 29, 1963; *Three-Monthly Economic Review*, No. 43 (London, September, 1963), p. 2.

44. See James R. Townsend, "Democratic Management in the Rural Communes," *China Quarterly*, No. 16 (London, October-December 1963), p. 149.

45. No. 13-14 (July 10, 1963).

46. "Create Favorable Conditions for Rural Party Branch Secretaries to Take Part in Labor," *Jen-min jih-pao*, July 21, 1963. Translation published by U.S. Department of Commerce, Office of Technical Services, Joint Publications Research Service (JPRS) No. 21, 515.

47. *Hung-ch'i*, No. 13-14 (July 10, 1963), (JPRS, No. 21, 795).

48. "Teaching by Words and Deeds," *Jen-min jih-pao*, July 29, 1963 (JPRS, No. 21, 515).

49. *Ibid.*

50. *Chung-kuo ch'ing-nien pao*, October 15, 1963, p. 2.

51. *Jen-min jih-pao*, July 21, 1963.

52. *Communist China: 1961* (Hong Kong: Union Research Institute, December, 1962), I, 6-7.

53. *China News Analysis* (Hong Kong), Nos. 409, 490.

54. Quoted in Liang Hsiu-feng, "An Exploratory Study of the Essentials of Chinese Agriculture and Steps Toward Its Technological Reform," *Ching-chi yen-chiu (Economic Research)*, No. 9 (Peking, September, 1963), pp. 18-22.

55. See Yang P'ei-hsin, "The Question of Funds in the Agricultural Modernization Process," *Ching-chi yen-chiu*, No. 6 (June, 1963), pp. 10-19; and Chūgoku Kenkyū-sho (China Research Institute), *Shin Chūgoku nenkan (New China Yearbook)* (Tokyo, 1963), pp. 62, 157.

56. Liao Lu-yen, Minister of Agriculture, "Collectivization of Agriculture in China," *Peking Review*, No. 44 (November 1, 1963), p. 13.

57. Wang Wen, "Electricity for Rural Use," *Kung-jen jih-pao* (Peking), September 24, 1963, p. 2 (JPRS, No. 21, 854).

58. *Ibid.;* also Liao Lu-yen, *op. cit.*

59. "Water Conservancy in Kwangtung," *Yang-ch'eng wan-pao* (Canton), May 25, 1963, p. 1.

60. See the annotated compilation of all major factories, thermal-electric and hydro-electric power stations, and coal and other mines repaired or constructed in China between 1953 and December, 1960, in *Chūkyō seiken no genjō bunseki*, pp. 269-306.

61. Economist Intelligence Unit, *Three-Monthly Economic Review, Annual Supplement* (London, June, 1962), p. 3.

62. Okazaki, *Shisō* (Tokyo), June, 1963, p. 114; "Chūkyō no kodō ("The Pulse of Communist China"), *Gaikō jihō* (*Review of Diplomacy*) (Tokyo), May-June, 1963, pp. 38-39. Also see "Concentrate the Strength of the Whole Party and the Whole Nation on Aiding Agriculture," *Jen-min jih-pao,* October 22, 1962, reprinted in *Peking Review,* No. 46 (November 16, 1962), pp. 13-14, 19.

63. Wan Shao-ho, "Five Years of the 'Eight-One' Commune," *Hung-ch'i,* No. 21 (1963), pp. 23-27 (JPRS, No. 22, 177). For a recent description of other communes, see Hoashi Kei, "Chūgoku no tabi" ("Journey in China"), *Gaikō jihō,* September- October 1963, pp. 65-73.

64. Wan Shao-ho, *ibid.*

65. Yang P'ei-hsin, *Ching-chi yen-chiu,* No. 6 (1963).

66. For a preliminary analysis, see T. A. Hsia, *A Terminological Study of the Hsia-Fang Movement,* Studies in Chinese Communist Terminology, No. 10, Center for Chinese Studies (Berkeley, Calif.: 1963).

67. The Chinese emphasize planned childbirth rather than restriction of childbirth. Many forums have been held in Shanghai, particularly on Women's Day (March 8) to publicize the advantages of planned childbirth. See Shanghai *Chieh-fang jih-pao,* March 5, 1963; and Shanghai *Hsin-min wan-pao,* March 7, 1963. Cf. *Bungei shunjū* (Tokyo), September, 1963, pp. 69-73, on present trends in birth control in China.

68. Yang P'ei-hsin, *Ching-chi yen-chiu,* No. 6 (1963).

69. Chiang Hsüeh-mo, "Some Questions in Relation to Accumulation and Consumption," Shanghai *Wen-hui pao,* November 25, 1962.

70. See P'eng Wei-ts'ai and Wang Hsüan-hui, "The Problem of Tax Supervision in State Enterprises," *Ta· Kung Pao,* October 10, 1963, p. 3; and "Firmly Grasp the Collection of Industrial and Business Taxes and Profits," *Ta Kung Pao,* October 6, 1963, p. 1 (JPRS, No. 21, 931).

71. Yang P'ei-hsin, *Ching-chi yen-chiu,* No. 6 (1963).

72. Hu Li-chiao, "Effective Financial Management of Farm Village Helps Collective Economy," *Jen-min jih-pao,* July 11, 1963 (JPRS, No. 21, 515).

73. Economist Intelligence Unit, *Three-Monthly Economic Review,* No. 40 (November, 1962), p. 4; *Communist China: 1961* (Hong Kong: Union Research Institute) I, 118-19; and *Gaikō jihō,* May-June, 1963, p. 39.

74. Yang P'ei-hsin, *Ching-chi yen-chiu,* No. 6 (1963).

75. Quoted in Powell, *Politico-Military Relationships,* p. 19.

76. "March Ahead under the Red Flag of the Party's General Line and Mao Tse-tung's Military Thinking," NCNA, September 29, 1959.

77. Economist Intelligence Unit, *Three-Monthly Economic Review,* No. 40, p. 10.

78. Powell, *Politico-Military Relationships,* p. 5.

79. Reported by Kurota Hidetoshi, "Chū-So ronsōka no Chūgoku no hyōjō" ("The Face of China After the Sino-Soviet Dispute"), *Ekonomisuto* (Tokyo), August 6, 1963, pp. 36-39.

80. "Whence the Differences? A Reply to Thorez and Other Comrades," *Jen-min jih-pao,* February 27, 1963 (*Peking Review,* No. 9, March 1, 1963, p. 10).

81. "The Origin and Development of the Differences Between the Leadership of the CPSU and Ourselves," *Jen-min jih-pao,* September 6, 1963 (*Peking Review,* No. 37, September 13, 1963, p. 12).

82. Ch'en Yi's interview with visiting Japanese newsmen, October, 1963. Reported in the *New York Times,* Western ed., October 29, 1963, p. 1.

83. *Peking Review,* No. 37 (September 13, 1963), p. 18.

84. *Ibid.,* p. 7.

85. For a more complete discussion of this problem, see my *Peasant Nationalism and Communist Power* (Stanford, Calif.: Stanford University Press, 1962), Chaps. 1 and 7.

Selected Bibliography

Barnett, A. Doak, *Communist China and Asia: Challenge to American Policy.* New York: Vintage Books, Inc., 1960. (Paperback ed.)

————, *Communist China in Perspective.* New York: Frederick A. Praeger, Inc., 1962. (Paperback ed.)

Boorman, Howard L., Alexander Eckstein, Philip Mosely, and Benjamin Schwartz, *Moscow-Peking Axis: Strengths and Strains.* New York: Harper & Row, Publishers, Inc., 1957.

Eckstein, Alexander, *The National Income of Communist China.* New York: Free Press of Glencoe, Inc., 1961.

Floyd, David, *Mao Against Khrushchev.* New York: Frederick A. Praeger, Inc., 1963. (Paperback ed.)

Hughes, T. J., and D. E. T. Luard, *The Economic Development of Communist China, 1949-1960* (2nd ed.). London: Oxford University Press, 1961.

Johnson, Chalmers A., *Peasant Nationalism and Communist Power: The Emergence of Revolutionary China, 1937-1945.* Stanford, Calif.: Stanford University Press, 1962.

Lewis, John W., *Leadership in Communist China.* Ithaca, N.Y.: Cornell University Press, 1963.

————, *Major Doctrines of Communist China.* New York: W. W. Norton & Company, Inc., 1964. (Paperback ed.)

Li, Choh-ming, *Economic Development of Communist China: An Appraisal of the First Five Years of Industrialization.* Berkeley, Calif.: University of California Press, 1959.

Lifton, Robert J., *Thought Reform and the Psychology of Totalism.* New York: W. W. Norton & Company, Inc., 1961. (Paperback ed.)

London, Kurt, ed., *Unity and Contradiction: Major Aspects of Sino-Soviet Relations.* New York: Frederick A. Praeger, Inc., 1962.

MacFarquhar, Roderick, *The Hundred Flowers Campaign and the Chinese Intellectuals.* New York: Frederick A. Praeger, Inc., 1960.

Mu, Fu-sheng, *The Wilting of the Hundred Flowers: The Chinese Intelligentsia under Mao.* New York: Frederick A. Praeger, Inc., 1962. (Paperback ed.)

Schram, Stuart, *The Political Thought of Mao Tse-tung.* New York: Frederick A. Praeger, Inc., 1963. (Paperback ed.)

Snow, Edgar, *The Other Side of the River: Red China Today.* New York: Random House, 1962.

Yang, C. K., *A Chinese Village in Early Communist Transition.* Cambridge, Mass.: The Technology Press of the Massachusetts Institute of Technology, 1959.

Zagoria, Donald S., *The Sino-Soviet Conflict: 1959-1961.* Princeton, N.J.: Princeton University Press, 1962.

Mongolia

The First Communist State in Asia

M. T. Haggard

The Soviet-oriented Communist Party of
Mongolia has ruled Mongolia since 1921. The Mongolian communists
today have firm control of the country, having eliminated
other power centers—including the Tibetan-Buddhist
religious hierarchy—by the early 1940's.
Sufficient economic progress has been made in
the past 15 years, primarily through large-scale
material and technical assistance from the Soviet Union,
to make the Mongolians more tolerant of those
aspects of socialization which have brought
about unwanted changes in the traditional Mongol way of life.
The Soviet Army enabled Mongolian communists to gain
control of Mongolia, and the Soviet Union

has been the guarantor of the present Mongolian state since its inception. Soviet military assistance was important in the squelching of a widespread rebellion in Mongolia in 1932 and, in 1939, Soviet troops prevented the Japanese from adding Mongolia to their list of mainland conquests. In 1950, Soviet pressure resulted in Chinese communist agreement to guarantee the independent status of the Mongolian People's Republic (MPR).

The Party and government structures established in Mongolia were patterned after those in the Soviet Union. In writing their constitutions, the Mongolians have lifted articles, sometimes whole chapters, out of Soviet constitutions, with very little change.

The present head of both the Party and government, Y. Tsedenbal, owes his position to the backing of Moscow, and the MPR under his direction has adhered closely to Soviet policies. Tsedenbal regained the top Party position in 1958, with Khrushchev's backing, and in 1959 purged 6 members of the Politburo. Purges in 1962 and 1963 removed two Politburo members who aspired to replace Tsedenbal and who were also accused of overstressing Mongolian nationalism at the expense of close U.S.S.R.-MPR ties. There is no evidence that these men were pro-Chinese; however, the possibility remains that they might have encouraged the Chinese as a means of giving the MPR more leverage in its relationship with the Soviet Union.

A new purge in December, 1964, expelled from the Party three members of the Central Committee who were charged with "anti-party factional activities." The latest shakeup indicates that the pro-Soviet group still has not eliminated nationalists and other opponents of its policies from the upper levels of the Party. This continuing instability is in sharp contrast to the relative stability of the top leadership of the other Asian Communist countries. It is probable that the Soviet leadership changes, coupled with the Chinese nuclear explosion, increased the strength of the nationalist forces. Existing discontent is not due to any serious questioning of the Mongolian-Soviet relationship, but to Tsedenbal's unquestioning support of Soviet policies and to the resulting friction with the Chinese. The present pro-Soviet ruling group will probably maintain its position, however, as long as it has strong Soviet support, and there is no indication that this support has weakened.

On major issues of dispute between Communist China and the Soviet Union, the MPR has without qualification backed the Soviet Union. However, Soviet policy frequently coincides with the professed goals of the MPR. The peaceful coexistence theme, for example, is in line with what the Mongolians consider to be their own interest. A major aspect of Mongolian foreign policy since the end of World War II has been the desire to expand contacts with all nations, and following

Soviet policy is obviously more likely to contribute to the success of this Mongolian goal. The Mongolians have no ax to grind, as do the North Koreans and the North Vietnamese.

One of the major reasons for the MPR's firm pro-Soviet alignment, however, is its heavy dependence on Soviet economic assistance. More than three-quarters of all outside assistance for the development of agriculture and industry has come from the Soviet Union. The Soviet Union is scheduled to provide over one-third of the total capital investment for the third five-year plan (1961 to 1965). Total aid received and promised, about $900 per capita, makes Mongolia the most aided country, per capita, either inside or outside the communist bloc.

There is another factor of critical importance: While many Mongolians are not completely happy with the present arrangement with the Soviet Union, they do not have the same antipathy toward the Russians as they have for the Chinese. The memories of centuries of Chinese domination are not pleasant ones, and there is no desire to see such domination reinstituted. Russian control has been more subtle.

The Mongolian People's Revolutionary Party

The official history of the Mongolian People's Revolutionary Party (MPRP) states that it was founded by the merger of two secret revolutionary groups, one led by Sukhe-Bator and the other by Choybalsan. These men are celebrated as the leaders of the 1921 Revolution, though it is probable that their role has been magnified in recent years by Mongolian and Russian historians.

Shortly after the Bolshevik Revolution, the Chinese moved into control of large parts of Mongolia. For a time, Mongolia was a battlefield, with White Russians and Chinese vying for control. However, partisan groups of Mongols were coming into being, mainly in the northeastern districts bordering the Soviet Union. These groups, purportedly led by Sukhe-Bator and Choybalsan, met near Kiakhta, in Soviet territory close to the Mongolian frontier, in March, 1921, and held the First Congress of the MPRP. The Congress created a Provisional Revolutionary Government (PRG) and a People's Revolutionary Army (PRA). It also decided to ask the U.S.S.R. for assistance in removing both Chinese and White Russians from Mongolia. The PRA, backed by the Soviet Army, subsequently moved south and took Urga in July, 1921. In the following months, the remaining White Russian troops were liquidated or were driven out of the country.

The MPRP, after it had been established in Mongolia with Soviet assistance, was paraded before the world as a purely national movement, independent of the U.S.S.R. In effect, however, the Soviet Union had restored the old Tsarist protectorate over Mongolia. The U.S.S.R.'s role in the establishment of an independent Mongol state was obviously one in which protection of Soviet borders and advancement of the Russian national interest was of primary concern. Soviet troops and advisers remained in Mongolia, and the Red Army did not leave until 1925, when the MPRP was firmly in power.

During the first three years of its life, the Party was cautious in its internal policy, since a difficult diplomatic war was being waged between the Soviet Union and China over Mongolia's status. As long as that was not definitely determined, it was considered necessary to keep the Living Buddha of Urga as the nominal head of the state, which had been proclaimed a constitutional monarchy. After three years of negotiations, the Chinese government finally concluded that it did not have the power to restore its control in Mongolia; in the treaty of 1924, the Chinese recognized the dominant Soviet position in Mongolia, though nominal Chinese sovereignty was continued.

On the death of the Living Buddha in 1924, the MPRP decided not to install a successor, and the Party Central Committee passed a resolution establishing the Mongolian People's Republic. The first constitution of the MPR, drafted with Soviet assistance, was patterned after the 1918 constitution of the Russian Soviet Federated Socialist Republic (R.S.F.S.R.), and the structure of the MPR's government, to a large extent, paralleled the governmental system of the U.S.S.R.

The left group in the MPRP gradually increased its strength, and it gained control of the Party at the Seventh Party Congress in 1928. Elated by their success in defeating the rightists, the leftists now argued that Mongolia could proceed directly to socialism. They attacked on every front, aiming at the liquidation of the nobility and the religious hierarchy. These policies led to open rebellion, which was quelled only with Soviet military assistance. Not only did the rural herdsmen participate actively in this rebellion, but even members of the Party and its Youth League, as well as some detachments of the Mongolian People's Army, engaged in it.

The Party later claimed that the leftist leadership "violated the Leninist principle of mass leadership and pursued a policy of separating the Party from the masses, and in so doing alienated a sizable segment of the rural population." [1] The Party also asserts that the Japanese took advantage of the discontent to organize subversive work which was in part responsible for open rebellion. The official record states that Stalin himself advised the end of the "left deviation," and, in June, 1932, a plenum of the Central Committee of the Party so decided. The Party now adopted a more gradual, sophisticated approach, placing emphasis on persuasion and education.

Until the 1932 Central Committee plenum, Choybalsan had been only one of the important figures in the MPRP. After the plenum, however, he was clearly in the ascendancy, and he became more and more the symbol of increasingly close cooperation with the Soviet Union. By the time of the Ninth Party Congress, in 1934, the Choybalsan group was in firm control.[2]

The period of absolute control of Mongolia by Marshal Choybalsan has been compared to the Stalinist period in the U.S.S.R. This comparison is particularly apt with respect to the arbitrary nature of police rule. Choybalsan quickly moved to eliminate all opposing centers of power, the Lamaist hierarchy and what remained of the nobility being major targets. With these groups removed, Choybalsan's police moved on others, and an atmosphere of fear developed. Little was done to bring the police under tighter control until his death in 1952.

Some information on Choybalsan's role in this period has become available as the Mongolian leadership has followed the Soviet Union in carrying out a de-Stalinization program. Mongolian leaders have accused Choybalsan of fostering a personality cult, of abusing his authority as Party leader, of glorifying Stalin, of overrating his own contribution to Mongolian history, and of underrating the "deeds and efforts of the Party and the people." [3] The de-Choybalsanization campaign in Mongolia resulted in the removal of his name from the state university, from the industrial combine in Ulan Bator, and from a province in eastern Mongolia.[4] The tomb of Sukhe-Bator and Choybalsan in Ulan Bator, however, remains undisturbed. Tsedenbal has been particularly sensitive to overzealous attacks upon Choybalsan, and one of the principal charges made against high-ranking Party members removed in 1959 and 1962 was that they had used the campaign against Choybalsan to further their own careers. Some of these purged members apparently had hoped to link Tsedenbal to the personality cult charges made against Choybalsan, since Tsedenbal had been Choybalsan's protégé since the 1940's.

Tsedenbal has been the first ranking member of the Party Secretariat since 1940, except for a four-year period from 1954 to 1958 when D. Damba was First Secretary of the Party. Tsedenbal apparently did not have the power to maintain control of the Party after Choybalsan's death in 1952. According to the official record, Tsedenbal was replaced as First Secretary "at his own request, because of his heavy duties." [5] This was also the period before Khrushchev had consolidated his position of power in the Soviet Union and when the principle of collective leadership was being stressed in the U.S.S.R. and other countries in the communist bloc. The Damba group remained in the ascendancy until mid-1958 and, in late 1957 and early 1958, appeared to be winning. At a plenum of the Central Committee of the Party held in November, 1958, however,

Tsedenbal replaced Damba as First Secretary of the Party. At the next plenum of the Central Committee, in March, 1959, Damba and his associates were expelled from their Party posts.

Damba was officially charged with "lack of principle and dishonesty before the Party, stupid idealist-political backwardness, conservatism and inertia, egotism and faulty self-criticism." [6] He was criticized for allowing feudal elements to slow down the development of socialism. He was also charged with perverting the campaign against the cult of personality into a personal grab for power.[7]

Attempts have been made to prove that Damba was pro-Chinese and that Tsedenbal's triumph represented a victory for the Soviet faction in the MPRP. It is true that Chinese influence increased considerably during the period when Damba headed the Party, but there is no evidence that the Damba faction was pro-Chinese. Damba apparently wanted to slow down the pace of the changes which were taking place in Mongolian life as a result of the predominant Soviet influence in Mongolian policy making.

The pro-Damba faction of the Party, including three full members and two candidate members of the Politburo, was removed at this time. These Politburo members were charged with being "unfit in ideological and political work and unworthy in personal character." The Chairman of the Party Control Commission was also removed, charged with "having failed to cope with the work" of his office.[8]

The most notable instances of factionalism in the Party since 1959 have involved the cases of D. Tomor-Ochir and L. Tsend. Tomor-Ochir was removed from the Politburo and the Secretariat in July, 1960, was reinstated in January, 1962, and was again removed from these posts in September, 1962. Tsend, the Second Secretary of the Party, was removed from all Party and government positions in December, 1963. Both Tomor-Ochir and Tsend apparently had made bids to replace Tsedenbal as leader of the Mongolian Party and state, and their removal was in part the result of a pure struggle for power. They were perhaps more nationalistic than Tsedenbal, and Tsedenbal used this weapon against them in convincing Soviet leaders that they were a danger both to his leadership and to the continuance of the Soviet Union's dominant position.

Tomor-Ochir was charged with using the campaign against the cult of personality to further his own ambitions—that is, by trying to connect the members of the Central Committee and Politburo with the errors made by Choybalsan. He was also accused of trying to disseminate the view, in his position as director of the Institute of Party History, "that only his leadership in Party affairs would develop the Marxist-Leninist character of the MPRP."

Tomor-Ochir was further charged with trying to revise or annul a number of Central Committee decisions condemning nationalism. It was asserted that he had supported his nationalist views by seeking to elevate the role of Genghis Khan. *Unen* stated that Tomor-Ochir's nationalist views were really aimed at the relationship between the MPR and the U.S.S.R., and called such views "a feature which unfortunately has become too widespread in our country." [9] He was also condemned for taking a "dogmatic view with regard to Marxist-Leninist theory," implying some sympathy for the Chinese communist doctrinal position. Tomor-Ochir's goal, stated *Unen*, was to replace the internationalist leadership of the Central Committee of the Party with a nationalist one.

Tsend was removed for similar reasons. The charges indicated that he had made a stronger bid than Tomor-Ochir to replace Tsedenbal, but it took Tsedenbal a bit longer to isolate Tsend and undercut his position. Tsend was charged with attempting to move into Tsedenbal's position permanently in the second half of 1961, when Tsedenbal was in the Soviet Union recovering from injuries sustained in an accident. Tsend was also accused of promoting nationalism and attempting to weaken the relationship between the MPR and the U.S.S.R. He was linked with Tomor-Ochir in the campaign to promote nationalism and glorify Genghis Khan.

The Central Committee also listed, in great detail, Tsend's deficiencies in carrying out his responsibilities as Second Secretary. The charge stated that, since early 1962, "he has not done anything and has not shown any initiative in the industrial, construction, trade, transport, and communications fields." He was also accused of interfering with the work of the State Planning Commission and the Construction and Economic Commission. Apparently, Tsend was made the scapegoat for the failure of the 1963 construction plan. The charges listed above also imply that he may have objected to the increasing role of CEMA in Mongolian economic planning and the resulting decrease in Mongolian control over its internal affairs.

Tsend was replaced on the Politburo by S. Lubsan, MPR ambassador to the Soviet Union since 1960. Lubsan has since been named a First Deputy Chairman of the Council of Ministers. It is possible that Lubsan's advancement to high rank in the Party and government can be attributed to Soviet pressures. Discussions during Tsedenbal's long visit to the U.S.S.R., from mid-July to mid-September, 1963, may have been related to the ultimate decision to purge Tsend and promote Lubsan.

In 1964 the ruling group moved to tighten its control of the Party, attempting to isolate followers of Tsend and those who might question the wisdom of Party policy which had resulted in abject dependence on the Soviet Union and in the rapid deterioration in relations with Peking. The resolution of the December, 1963, plenum called on all Party organs to resist any manifestation of nationalism capable of weakening

U.S.S.R.-MPR ties and to "wage an implacable struggle against the penetration into our midst of an ideology which is alien to Marxism-Leninism." The resolution called on all Party organs to suppress any attempts to weaken Party discipline or to "violate the norms of democratic centralism and collective leadership." [10]

In late December, in the first plenum held since the removal of Tsend, three Central Committee members were expelled from the Party for "anti-party factional activities." These opponents of Tsedenbal were tagged with the usual nationalist label and it is probable that they had questioned the MPR's slavish backing of Soviet policies. It is probable also that those purged had protested other aspects of Tsedenbal's dictatorial rule: Tsedenbal admitted that they criticized his iron-fisted rule of "democratic centralism" as a survival of the Stalinist era. Tsedenbal claimed that nationalist elements continued to operate "clandestinely" in Mongolia.

The dissension in the Party appears to have been directly responsible for a trip to Mongolia in January and February of 1965 by A. N. Shelepin, member of the Presidium and Secretary of the Central Committee of the CPSU. Just how successful Shelepin was in smoothing over the friction is not known; it was announced, however, at the conclusion of his trip that the U.S.S.R. had decided to give "new, large economic aid" to Mongolia.

Party Structure

Party organization and operation follow the Leninist pattern established in the Soviet Union, with its emphasis on control from the top by a small elite. Ultimately, force backs up this control, but in more recent years the Party has relied more on persuasion and education. And the Party is now able to point to some accomplishments, which serves as a means of weakening any possible trouble centers.

The supreme organ of the Party, according to the Party statutes, is the Party Congress. In practice, the Congress automatically approves decisions already made by the small executive bodies of the Party. The Congress remains, however, one of the regime's major forums for disseminating its views to the rank and file and, indirectly, to the Mongolian people. After each Congress, Party meetings are held throughout Mongolia to ensure rapid dissemination of current policies.

During the early years of the Party, before one-man rule became the pattern, there was often real discussion of major points of policy. Party congresses met about once a year until the Eighth Congress, in 1930. The next four years, during which the Party had to quell a rebellion, were very turbulent, but by 1934 Choybalsan was emerging as the strong man. Beginning with the Ninth Party Congress in 1934, the Party

Congress lost its importance as a center of power. Now, the congresses are called by the Party leaders; they are shows, under the tight control of the Politburo.

To conduct Party work between congresses, the Party Congress elects a Central Committee which ordinarily holds plenums every six months. This Central Committee, a more important body than the Congress, is also controlled by Tsedenbal and his followers. More than two-thirds of the members of the Council of Ministers, the most important government body, are members of the Central Committee. Important Party decisions between congresses are usually announced at plenary sessions of the Central Committee.

According to the Party statutes, the Central Committee "directs the activities of central state and public organizations through Party members working in them." The Central Committee "directs all Party work," establishes Party organizations as needed, and controls the use of Party members and Party funds. The Central Committee organizes a Politburo to handle political work, a Secretariat to handle organizational work and other work of an executive-administrative character for the Party, and a Central Control Commission to check on the execution of Party decisions. No other details are given on the work of the Politburo or the Secretariat, though one other article of the Party constitution does give a breakdown of departments of the Central Committee. These departments are under the direct control of the Secretariat.[11]

The election of the Central Committee by the Congress is, in effect, a formal approval of a list already selected by the Politburo. Most members are Party and government leaders or important local Party officials. It is probable that most of the members of the Central Committee are there as protégés of one or another of the ruling groups. Plenums of the Central Committee are used by Party leaders to get local reaction to Party-government policies and to maintain close contact with officials in the provinces. Plenum meetings, like meetings of the Congress, are carefully controlled by the Politburo and usually consist of the presentation of decisions already made by the ruling group. The plenums are used to announce important policy statements and are also usually the medium for official notification of purges or shake-ups in the high command.

A totalitarian society requires unified decisions by one person or, at most, by a handful of people. Hence it is not surprising that the ultimate decision-making power in the MPR resides in the Politburo. The Politburo, though theoretically selected by the Central Committee, has selected its new members in recent years on the basis of their loyalty to Tsedenbal and their pro-Soviet views.

Tsedenbal reduced the size of the Politburo when he consolidated his control, presumably to reduce the circle of those in power and thereby make it easier to maintain direct control. Prior to 1959, there were nine members and five candidate members of the Politburo. Tsedenbal reduced this number to seven members and two candidate members, and it has remained at this level.[12]

The Politburo meets frequently, probably one or more times a week. Very little is known about its organization and working practices. It is likely that very close contact is maintained with the working departments of the Central Committee and that major questions of importance are funneled through these departments and the Secretariat for presentation to the Politburo.

The most important body in Mongolia for preparing plans and proposing policy is the Secretariat of the Central Committee. It ranks second only to the Politburo in the making of decisions. All five secretaries are also members of the Politburo, enabling the pro-Soviet group to maintain close control over the agencies which implement policy. While the Politburo is concerned with executive decisions, the Secretariat is the supreme administrative agency of the Party.

Though the secretaries are formally elected by the Central Committee in plenary session, this is merely an automatic approval of individuals already selected by the top leadership. The number of secretaries dropped from six to four when Tsedenbal regained control, but a fifth was added in 1964. Since 1959, the only changes in the Secretariat have been associated with the removal, reinstatement, and subsequent removal of Tomor-Ochir as a secretary, the purge of Tsend in 1963, and the addition of Molomjamts in 1964.

We have no information about the actual division of responsibility among the secretaries, but previous work assignments of the five members give some idea as to how duties are parceled out. Tsedenbal is concerned with the general operation of the Party and government, both in foreign and domestic affairs, and he is not likely to be tied down by any specific administrative functions within the Secretariat. The Second Secretary exercises general supervision over the Secretariat and the departments of the Central Committee. L. Tsend was the Second Secretary from 1959, when he replaced Damba, until his own removal in December, 1963. N. Jagbaral was named to the Secretariat following Tsend's removal, but he has not been identified specifically as the new Second Secretary. Jagbaral is an agricultural specialist and presumably is concerned with Party activities in the livestock raising and farming sectors of the economy. Molomjamts was responsible for coordination of CEMA activities in Mongolia prior to his election to the Secretariat and probably has a similar responsibility on the Secretariat.

The other two secretaries are in charge of Party work and agitation and propaganda. T. Dugersuren is believed to fit the first category, which apparently includes some supervision over economic development. B. Lhamsuren has been active in Party and mass organization work of a propaganda character and is probably handling the agitation-propaganda function. He has been head of the Higher and Specialized Secondary Education Committee and probably has the education department under his supervision. He was recently relieved of his duties as deputy chairman of the Council of Ministers, ostensibly to give him more time for Party work.

One agency of the Central Committee that is likely to assume increasing importance is the Party Control Committee. The powers accorded to this committee by the Party statutes are considerable and include checking on the execution of decisions of the Central Committee. The Control Committee probes into the lives of Party functionaries and members to see if their politics and their behavior is satisfactory. Tsedenbal's report to the sixth plenum of the Central Committee in December, 1964, severely criticized the Control Committee for its failure to carry out directives of the Party; some of the onus for internal Party difficulties was thereby transferred to the Control Committee. There were some mitigating circumstances, however, according to Tsedenbal: he claimed that some organizations of the Party, the Youth League, and the trade unions "placed obstacles" that hampered the Control Committee in its work.

Tsedenbal indicated that the role of the Control Committee would be enlarged both in the field of general Party control and in economic development. He admonished the Control Committee to "examine the activities" of any persons expected to be in league with those Central Committee members expelled in December, 1964: Tsedenbal claimed that those purged had opposed the "strengthening of state, party, and public control as well as party and state discipline." Tsedenbal indicated that part of the problem lay in the lack of coordination between the Party Control Committee and the State Control Commission.

Party organization below the national level includes the *aymag* (provincial) and primary Party organizations. The structure of Party organizations at these levels is roughly the same as at the national level. National Party concern with local Party operation has become more pronounced in recent years, particularly since Tsedenbal's speech to the Fourteenth Party Congress in 1961, in which he stated:

> In the struggle for successful solution of the problems of economic and cultural development and of the communist education of the workers, the role of local party organizations and of each individual party member is increasing to an immense degree. Thus the obligations of leading party organs is that of improving on a daily basis the leadership of local party

organizations, raising the level of their work, and expanding their influence among the masses. It is necessary to provide constant party control over the fulfillment of the production plans of each industrial enterprise, state farm, agricultural collective, and other economic organization, making widespread use of the right to control administrative activities.[13]

Executive bodies of Party cells have been reproved for their failure to carry through decisions of the Fourteenth Party Congress, for not keeping a constant check on the performance of tasks assigned to individual Party members or to groups of Party members. Cell leaders have been criticized for making changes in the leadership of local enterprises too frequently. Criticism alone apparently did not produce the results desired and, in 1963, the MPRP made several changes in cell organization and administration to enable the primary Party organizations to cope with the increased duties and responsibilities assigned to them. The cell secretary now has an assistant, a deputy chairman, to help him in his work. Further, the basic salaries of all cell secretaries were raised 40 per cent in 1963.[14]

Membership of the Party

The MPRP remains a small elite, comprising less than 5 per cent of the total population. By the end of 1964, there were over 47,000 members and candidate members in a population of over 1,000,000. The Party has grown only gradually in recent years, indicating an effort to keep it small enough to permit rigid enforcement of discipline and to maintain relatively high standards.

The Party has, in line with decisions of the Thirteenth and Fourteenth Party Congresses, "considerably increased the requirements on applications for Party membership." Tsedenbal, in 1961, criticized local Party organizations for not examining more closely the qualifications of each potential recruit. The Party must grow, he noted, but only "on the basis of the best members of the working class, of advanced people in industry, agriculture, and other branches of the nation's economy who by their concrete actions have shown boundless devotion to Party affairs." He stated that increased demands would be made on each member of the Party and that "a number of persons were excluded from the ranks of the Party who were undeserving of membership." [15]

Official Party membership reached 43,902, including 2,077 candidate members, in April, 1961. The following table indicates the growth of membership in the Party: [16]

1920:	160	1928:	15,000	1940:	13,000
1924:	4,700	1930:	30,000	1947:	28,000
1925:	7,600	1932:	42,000	1954:	32,000
1926:	11,600	1934:	8,000	1956:	40,000
1927:	14,000	1939:	9,000	1957:	43,000

Though the educational level of the average Party member is lower than that of members of the Communist Party of the Soviet Union (CPSU), it is significantly higher than the educational level of all adult Mongolians. In 1960, for example, the Party claimed that all Party members were literate, whereas the over-all literacy rate in Mongolia was approximately 80 per cent. According to the Party, approximately 9 per cent of Party members had higher education, 27 per cent had secondary education, 19 per cent had elementary education, and 44 per cent had no formal education but were literate. This contrasts sharply with 1925, when 50 per cent of the Party members were illiterate.

The occupational composition of the membership of the Party has generally been broken down into three groups: workers; rural workers; and staff workers, sometimes referred to as intelligentsia. The percentage of workers rose from 7, in 1950, to 26, in 1961, indicating both the superior role granted to the workers by communist philosophy and the expansion of industry in Mongolia. On the other hand, the rural herdsmen and other agricultural workers, who still constitute over 60 per cent of the total population, comprise only 25 per cent of the total Party membership. This is a sharp drop from 1934, when 60 per cent of the Party's members came from the agricultural sector, and from 1950, when 40 per cent came from the agricultural sector. The third category, the staff worker, constituted, in 1961, about one-half the total membership.

The position of women in the Party has improved gradually. By 1961, women comprised 18 per cent of the Party membership, over 17 per cent of the delegates to the Fourteenth Party Congress were women, and 5 per cent of the members of the new Central Committee were women. But women headed only 41 of the 1,274 Party cells in 1961, about 3 per cent of the total.

There has been no apparent discrimination against minority groups in the recruiting of new Party members. Party membership is approximately proportional to the total population. In 1960 the Kazakhs, for example, constituted about 4 per cent of the total population and about 3.9 per cent of the Party.

Instruments of the MPRP

The major instruments of the MPRP in controlling all of Mongolia, in addition to the formal government organization, are the mass organizations, particularly the youth organizations and the trade unions, and the propaganda machinery.

The Party-controlled mass organizations have the major function of rallying public opinion behind the national policies and programs desired by the Party leadership, and they are actually the foundation for much of the control exercised by the regime over the populace.

These organizations also provide the regime with at least some indication of the public temper, as well as with a means of surveillance.

Mongolian youth organizations are expected to supply recruits for the Party and to train men and women for work in all phases of the government and the economy. The Revsomol, the Party's major auxiliary, and the Young Pioneers are closely modeled after the Komsomol and Pioneer organizations of the Soviet Union.

Probably the most important mass organization, next to the youth groups, is the Central Council of Trade Unions (CCTU). The CCTU not only has control and propaganda functions, but also performs duties ordinarily carried out by government. The importance of the trade unions has increased as the MPR has placed more stress on industrialization and has given the trade unions the task of administering the government's social insurance program. A major reorganization of the CCTU, in August and September, 1963, was aimed at bringing all workers, of whatever category, into one of the national trade unions. These unions include: (1) agricultural workers; (2) industrial workers; (3) trade and transport workers; (4) construction workers; and (5) cultural-educational workers.[17]

In 1960, the MPRP established a new mass organization, the Mongolian Society for the Dissemination of Scientific Knowledge, to facilitate nationwide dissemination of the Party propaganda line. This society, directed by the Chairman of the Propaganda and Agitation Department of the Central Committee of the MPRP, theoretically encompasses the whole of the intelligentsia of Mongolia. Intelligentsia, in this sense, includes scientists, writers, artists, engineers, technicians, teachers, physicians, Party workers, workers in state and social organizations, and "the leading workers of industry."

In addition, national conferences of ideological and propaganda workers were held in 1961 and 1963. The first conference was critical of propaganda work in the rural areas, primarily because of the continuing passive resistance to collectivization, and it called for intensification of propaganda work in these areas. At the second conference, in January, 1963, Tsedenbal and other Party leaders emphasized the necessity of tying propaganda work in with the everyday problems of economic development. Propagandists were instructed to publicize the achievements of outstanding workers and to publicize local production goals and their relationship to national goals.

Governmental Machinery of the MPR

The constitution of the MPR and the government which it describes are, as in other communist states, merely one part of the over-all control system maintained by the MPRP. The notion that a constitution serves to establish boundaries, beyond which the governing authority cannot go, has no validity in a communist state. The constitution itself is considered to be subordinate to the dictatorship of the proletariat, which Lenin once described as "rule that is unrestricted by any laws." The MPRP's supreme position in Mongolia is clearly stated in the preamble to the 1960 constitution:

> The leading and guiding force of society and state in the MPR is the Mongolian People's Revolutionary Party, directed in its activity by the scientific theories of Marxism-Leninism.[18]

The constitution describes the Great People's *Hural* (the Mongolian legislative body) as the "supreme authority" in the MPR. It rests at the top of a pyramidal hierarchy of *hurals* which are, in almost every respect, identical to the soviets in the U.S.S.R. In practice, the Great People's *Hural* has little power; whatever power exists in the governmental structure is largely exercised by the Council of Ministers and, to a lesser extent, by the Presidium of the Great People's *Hural*. But these executive bodies of the *Hural* are merely transmitting points for the small executive bodies of the Party, particularly the Politburo and the Secretariat. The top Party men also occupy the top government posts. For example, the Chairman of the Council of Ministers is Y. Tsedenbal, who is also the First Secretary of the MPRP; the Chairman of the Presidium of the Great People's *Hural* is J. Sambu, member of the Politburo of the MPRP; both of the first deputy chairmen and the two ranking deputy chairmen of the Council of Ministers are all members of the Politburo.

Provincial and local government organization is similar to that of central government bodies. The major difference in the Party-government relationship at this level seems to be that Party organizations outside of Ulan Bator have a greater tendency to bypass the government machinery in carrying out Party-government directives from the national level. The communists claim that an important feature of the provincial and local government setup is the holding of joint meetings of local Party functionaries and members of the executive committees of the local *hurals*, but even this arrangement implies Party control of policy and administration at the local level. National Party officials frequently complain that local Party leaders, particularly at the *somon* (i.e., county) level, run their areas as if they were private fiefs, without consulting local government officials and, in fact, replacing these officials arbitrarily as they see fit.

The Defense Establishment

The armed forces are an instrument of the Party, directly controlled by a special military department of the Central Committee. There have been no indications of a separate military viewpoint in Mongolia, and the armed forces are responsive to Party orders. Party control is facilitated by the high percentage of Party members, over 90 per cent, in the officer corps. The present Minister of People's Army Affairs is a member of the Central Committee of the Party.

Though Mongolia's military establishment is large in proportion to the total population, it would be incapable of any effective resistance to invading forces from either Communist China or the U.S.S.R. Mongolian leaders have recognized the impossibility of a military defense of the country, and rely on their military assistance agreement with the Soviet Union to maintain the Mongolian state as an independent entity.

Because of the labor shortage in Mongolia, the armed forces are used extensively in construction work and in agriculture and industry. At a military conference in February, 1963, Tsedenbal declared that, as Mongolian frontiers were not in danger of aggression, army activities were to be focused primarily on supporting the economy. Army construction units were used in the construction of the new industrial city at Darhan, in 1963 and 1964.

The Judicial System ✗

The operation of the Mongol judicial system is to be understood only in terms of the Marxist-Leninist conception of law and of the judicial function. Law has not been conceived of as embodying, or as being based on, any abstract ideas of justice. Rather, law is considered the expression of the will of the dominant class, which is represented in Mongolia by the MPRP. The courts and the prosecutors work hand in hand with the regular and secret police in order to maintain the Party in power. The purpose of the judicial system is to protect the dictatorship of the proletariat from "various feudal and capitalist elements."

The recent emphasis on socialist legality has not brought about any change in the functions of the courts. On the contrary, Party leaders have been loud in their denunciation of the judicial system for failing to bring about proper respect for law. The criticism of the courts and of the prosecutor system has even extended to a direct listing of the deficiencies of the Party cells in the Supreme Court and in the Office of the Public Prosecutor. An editorial in *Unen*, in January, 1962, stated that these Party cells had "failed to coordinate the Party ideological and organizational work with the functions of their office, and have failed to produce a noticeable improvement in the work of these organs." [19]

The Development of Domestic Policy
The Struggle With the Lamaist Hierarchy

The initial attempt to eliminate the power of the monasteries and the Tibetan Buddhist religious hierarchy in the period from 1929 to

1932 was a complete failure. Rebellion broke out, and Soviet armored cars and planes were necessary to restore order. The policies toward the monasteries were relaxed immediately following the rebellion, but this resulted in a sharp rise in the number of monasteries and lamas. This type of situation presented an effective barrier to any program of socialization the Party hoped to introduce, and the Party adopted more subtle means of depriving the monasteries of their strength.

The building of new monasteries was forbidden, searches for reincarnations were prohibited, monasteries were forbidden to interfere in political and social affairs or to take upon themselves judicial or administrative functions, to enroll as lamas minors and persons eligible for military service, and to set one monastery in a position subordinate to another. Despite some resistance, these policies were effective. The number of monks in the monasteries dropped sharply and, by 1940, the Lamaist hierarchy no longer presented a major problem to the Party. Theoretically, religious activity is still permitted in Mongolia, and the state allows two small monasteries to continue religious services. These monasteries are maintained largely for the benefit of Buddhist visitors from south and southeast Asia.

There is considerable evidence, however, that the Buddhist religion retains some support in the rural areas and, as the quotation below shows, Party media still devote space to denunciation of "religious peddlers":

> Religion is one of the more harmful survivals of the past. Quite a few of our people are unable to rid themselves of primitive concepts due to the influence of religion over a long period of time. Certain elements deceive people in poorly organized areas. Treacherous elements hold religious ceremonies of disciples. They receive gifts and donations for their services. Wherever the disciples of these religious groups are assigned, most of them present obstacles to our work.[20]

The Collectivization of the Rural Herdsmen

The attempt to collectivize the rural herdsmen, carried out at the same time as the attempt to break the power of the monasteries, was a disastrous failure. The herdsmen were not prepared for the change and they forcibly resisted the seizure of their livestock. The total number of livestock, 21,950,000 head in 1929, dropped by over 7,000,000 in the period from 1929 to 1932. Large numbers of livestock were slaughtered by embittered herdsmen, and thousands of others were lost through neglect and improper care.

The Party did not deviate from its goal of collectivization, but it did adopt a more gradual, sophisticated approach which emphasized persuasion and education.

In 1958 and 1959, a stepped-up campaign apparently was successful, and the government claimed that 99.6 per cent of all rural herdsmen were organized into collectives and state farms by the end of 1959. There is reason to believe, however, that in many areas the collective organization is a paper one, maintaining only loose control over individual herdsmen. Only 78 per cent of all livestock was state-owned in 1960; the rest were privately owned by members of the collectives.

The collectivization of the rural areas has been a factor in Mongolia's failure to increase the number of livestock. Party leaders at first refused to admit that a reduction in the number of livestock had occurred in 1959 and 1960. Livestock, in 1960, was originally claimed to number 23,000,000 head,[21] but this figure was subsequently revised downward to less than 21,000,000.[22] At the beginning of 1964, it was still less than 22,000,000.

Party leaders have listed other reasons for the drop in the number of livestock: adverse climatic conditions; incorrect organizational activities; water shortage; and so forth. High export commitments to the U.S.S.R. have also been a factor, but, beginning in 1963, the U.S.S.R. agreed to a cut in meat imports from Mongolia, as a means of assisting the Mongolians to reach livestock production goals and to prevent further depletion of their breeding stock.

Extremely heavy snowfall in most areas of Mongolia in the first part of 1964 caused considerable loss of livestock, with consequent adverse effects on agricultural and industrial plan goals. These losses would have been considerably reduced if the fodder storage and animal shelter construction programs had been carried out successfully. So far as is known, a scapegoat for this disaster has not been designated.

Full-scale Economic Planning

Long-range detailed economic planning did not get under way until 1948, but it has since developed to such an extent that, by 1965, the Mongolians were working out plans for 1970, 1975, and 1980. Since 1962, Mongolia has maintained close liaison with other CEMA nations in working out its long-range development plans.

Mongolian planning has had, as its primary aim, the development of the pastoral economy, but more recent plans have also stressed industrial development and farming. A major goal of the planners has been to settle the nomadic herdsmen in permanent locations, both to tighten control and to diversify the economy sufficiently to eliminate its extreme reliance on livestock raising. The goal of the third five-year plan (1961 to 1965) was to reach the stage at which industrial production would exceed agricultural production.

CEMA emphasis on national economic specialization probably means that the MPR will remain a supplier of raw materials to other countries in the communist bloc—in particular, a supplier of meat and other animal products. The increased role of the CEMA in MPR economic planning means even less independence for Mongolia in deciding the future course of its economic development.

Educational Policies

The educational program of the regime has been one of its major successes. The literacy rate has risen from less than 1 per cent, in 1921, to approximately 80 per cent, in 1963. The state educational system was a major weapon in the fight to destroy the power of the Tibetan Buddhist religious hierarchy, and it has continued to be used to weaken the traditional Mongol values and to replace these values with those more in conformity with Marxism.

A major reorganization of the educational system to take seven years to accomplish, was begun in 1961, in line with the changes made in the Soviet Union and other communist countries, as a means of ensuring a steady supply of skilled manpower for all sectors of the economy. The new system combines studies with practical labor in the secondary schools. The seven-year schools are being replaced with eight-year schools, and the graduates of these schools are either to continue their studies in eleven-year schools or receive a complete secondary education in evening schools while working full time. Separate technical and specialized secondary schools are to train skilled manpower for industry.[23]

Mongolia's International Position

The MPR's Stand on Major Issues

The MPR followed the lead of the Soviet Union in its early attacks on the leadership of the Albanian Communist Party and in its indirect attacks on the Chinese Communist Party (CCP). But the early, mild references to the CCP have become progressively more bitter. The MPR endorsed the denunciation of the Albanian leadership at the Twenty-second Congress of the Communist Party of the Soviet Union (CPSU) in 1961. In early 1962, Tsedenbal stated, "We cannot agree with the reservations on this question which, for instance, the delegation of the Chinese Communist Party made at the Soviet Twenty-second Party Congress." [24]

The speech made by Tsedenbal at a Peking rally at the time of the signing of the Sino-Mongolian border agreement (December 26, 1962) left no doubt as to where the MPR's loyalties lay. Tsedenbal was very definite in his praise of the Soviet Union's policy of peaceful coexistence and in his expressions of approval of Soviet action during the Cuban crisis. In early 1963, Tsedenbal reiterated Mongolian support of the Soviet Union in the Cuban crisis, and this time he directly attacked the Chinese People's Republic (CPR) for its "irresponsible and arrogant attitude." [25] The government of the MPR endorsed the 1963 nuclear test-ban agreement without reservation, and berated the Chinese communists for denouncing it.

Subsequent attacks on the Chinese leadership in 1963 and 1964 resulted in a steady deterioration of relations between Peking and Ulan Bator. The MPR heartily endorsed the Suslov report to a plenum of the CPSU Central Committee in February 1964, which was extremely critical of the Chinese. Ulan Bator backed the Soviet call for a communist summit conference and a preparatory meeting to arrange the conference. Mongolia strongly supported the Soviet Union's right to participate in the Second Afro-Asian Conference held in Algiers in June 1965.

A major attack was made by Tsedenbal on the Chinese "self-reliance" policy in the lead article in the September 1964 issue of *World Marxist Review*. Tsedenbal presented a general defense of CEMA and of the benefits to be derived from "division of labor under socialism" and coordination of economic plans. Tsedenbal defended Mongolia's economic dependence on the Soviet Union, claiming that acceptance of extensive Soviet aid was in the best interests of Mongolia and had "helped to strengthen the sovereignty of our country." [26]

Mongolia's strident anti-Chinese stance reached a new peak in September with abusive attacks on the CPR and on Mao Tse-tung for lingering Chinese territorial designs on Mongolia. The Soviet Union seized on statements made by Mao Tse-tung to a group of visiting Japanese in July 1964, in which he stated that he had asked Soviet leaders in 1954 to restore Mongolian independence and to make a general attack on Chinese territorial aspirations in East Asia. Moscow implied that Mao had asked for the incorporation of the MPR into Communist China, and claimed that Khrushchev "naturally refused to discuss this question."

Ulan Bator followed up this Soviet lead by not only denouncing Chinese designs on Mongolia but by showering abuse on Mao. Mao, the Mongolians claimed, had "exposed himself" for what he was, and the "malicious intentions" of the Chinese leaders who "have long dreamed of making the MPR an outlying region under Chinese power" were now obvious. Ulan Bator claimed that Chinese designs on the MPR gave evidence of the racist and expansionist aims of Chinese policy. Mongolian fears of Chinese domination were spelled out in the criticism of Chinese policy toward minority groups, with the Mongolian statement claiming that Chinese control would force "our people to share the lot of the Inner Mongolians." The Mongolians warned the Chinese that "we have a friend who stands on guard with us in the defense of the interests of our country."

These charges coincided with a report, by a Yugoslav news agency, of a concentration of Chinese troops along the Mongolian border. An increase in military strength along the border could be a reflection of Chinese concern with Soviet "defense" measures in areas adjacent to the Sino-Soviet border and uneasiness as to Moscow's motives in "escalating" its polemical attack against so-called Chinese territorial aspirations in Asia. The strengthening of border defense could also be part of a new effort by Peking to prevent Mongolians in the Inner Mongolian Autonomous Region (IMAR) from fleeing into the MPR.

Mongolia's heavy propaganda barrage against Communist China and CCP leaders stopped abruptly after the Soviet leadership shake-up in October, 1964. The Mongolian radio and press were extremely cautious in their references to the purge in the Soviet Union. There was no criticism of Khrushchev. This silence reflected the equivocation of Brezhnev and Kosygin, who themselves took a soft line pending consolidation of their own position. The Mongolians continued to echo Soviet foreign policy statements, but without direct reference to the Chinese. In view of Mongolia's exposed position, many Mongolian leaders probably would welcome a suspension of the polemic.

Tsedenbal did not comment publicly on the removal of Khrushchev. Tsedenbal had maintained a close relationship with Khrushchev, and any hasty condemnation of the fallen leader could have provided ammunition for those "nationalists" in Mongolia who were unhappy with the satellite relationship with the Soviet Union. Tsedenbal's conferences with Brezhnev and Kosygin after the purge resulted in a new Soviet aid agreement, an indication that his relations with Moscow remained essentially unchanged. Tsedenbal was in the midst of a tour of East European countries when the purge occurred, and the fact that he continued the tour without interruption would indicate that he was not worried about his position in Mongolia. Tsedenbal returned to Moscow before and after trips to Hungary and Poland and may have served as an emissary to explain the policies of Brezhnev and Kosygin to the Hungarian and Polish leadership.[27]

Mongolian Nationalism

History and geography combine to place Mongolia between two powerful neighbors who threaten its existence as an independent political entity and who also threaten the traditional Mongol culture. Mongols have, in the twentieth century, reacted to this threat with nationalist movements aimed primarily at the formation of an independent Mongolian state. The establishment of the MPR in part answered this desire, but it did not fulfill the desires of the pan-Mongolists, who favored the union of all Mongolia into a "Greater Mongolia."[28]

There are over three million Mongols living in Asia, and approximately two million of these live in Communist China and the Soviet Union. Over one-and-three-quarter million Mongols live in Communist China (mostly in the Inner Mongolian Autonomous Region, IMAR) and over a quarter-million Mongols live in the U.S.S.R. (mostly in the Buryat Autonomous Republic, formerly called the Buryat-Mongol Autonomous Republic). Non-Mongol immigration into these areas has steadily decreased the strength of pan-Mongolism, however. In the IMAR, the Chinese now constitute well over 80 per cent of the population; in the Buryat Autonomous Republic, about 70 per cent of the population consists of Russians and Ukrainians.

The MPRP has exploited Mongolian nationalism for its own purposes, but has also been quite critical of those who have excited a feeling of nationalism in Mongols at the expense of "proletarian internationalism." The Party leadership of course subscribes to the communist theme of the international fraternity of the working classes, but its position on Mongolian nationalism has been determined by the Soviet Union's extreme sensitivity on the subject.

The purge of Tomor-Ochir, as we have noted, was ascribed in part to his nationalist passions and to his idealization of the role of Genghis Khan in Mongolian, Russian, and Chinese history. Tomor-Ochir was responsible for staging the 1962 celebrations of the eight-hundredth anniversary of the birth of Genghis Khan. In the Soviet Union there was no commemoration of the anniversary, but the Chinese publicized the celebrations taking place in the MPR and organized a festival in the IMAR. The Chinese, apparently willing to forget their own humiliation at the hands of Genghis Khan, seized the opportunity to stir up trouble between the Russians and the Mongolians.

That nationalist feeling is still strong in Mongolia is evidenced by this and other incidents, but the Party leadership has been critical of many of the older intellectuals who have tended to glorify the Mongolian past. Professor B. Rinchen, a member of the Academy of Sciences, has been severely criticized for his opposition to the changes taking place in Mongol society and for his attempts to popularize the past.

Relations with Communist Countries

Relations with the U.S.S.R. The MPR has been, since 1921, a satellite of the Soviet Union. Of necessity, relations have not been those of equal partners; the Soviet Union has been at times heavy-handed in its attitude toward the MPR. However, the relationship has not been without substantial benefits for the MPR.

After World War II, when China recognized the independence of the MPR, the Soviet Union and Mongolia concluded an agreement which has formed the basis for subsequent U.S.S.R.-MPR relations. This 1946 Treaty of Friendship and Mutual Assistance in effect guarantees to Mongolia Soviet assistance against outside attack.[29]

Agreements between the U.S.S.R. and MPR since that time have been largely concerned with economic and cultural assistance and co-operation. A statement made by Bulganin and Tsedenbal in Moscow (in May, 1957) noted that, between 1947 and 1957, the U.S.S.R. had extended credits of 900 million rubles to the MPR, that it had agreed to make a 200-million-ruble loan for the period from 1958 to 1960; and that property and material valued at over 100 million rubles had been provided as outright gifts. The credits for the period from 1958 to 1960 were used primarily for the expansion of land under cultivation and the further development of livestock raising.[30]

Soviet assistance during the third five-year plan, in the form of long-term credits, will amount to one-third of the capital investment for the whole plan. The U.S.S.R. is to assist in the construction of the fuel and power engineering complex being built in the Darhan area. Extensive Soviet assistance is also being received in the reclamation of virgin land.[31]

At least four new Soviet aid agreements were announced in 1964, with the first two coming on the heels of the winter losses. Under the first agreement, the Soviet Union granted additional credits for new construction in the Darhan complex and for housing construction in Ulan Bator. A protocol also outlined Soviet assistance to areas of Mongolia which were hardest hit by snowstorm. Soviet engineering, technical, and construction workers were scheduled to participate in the projects listed. The second agreement granted new credits totaling 140 million tugriks and listed new construction projects to be undertaken by the Soviet Union. These projects were designed to "overcome the temporary difficulties" facing the Mongolian economy.

A third agreement in early October granted the MPR credits to pay for extra goods to be imported by the end of the year. A communiqué stated that "important industrial and consumer goods" would be shipped to the MPR under the credit. A fourth agreement resulted from Tsedenbal's talks with the new Soviet leaders in late October, in which the Soviet Union agreed to render even more assistance to help Mongolia fulfill its 1965 economic plan.

Soviet benevolence toward the MPR has not been without compensations for the U.S.S.R., however. Mongolia has been forced to yield to Soviet pressure in accepting the incorporation of the Tannu Tuva area into the U.S.S.R. In 1921, after Chinese troops were driven out, Tannu Tuva, formerly known as Urianghai, was occupied by the Soviet Union. In 1924, residents of the area declared for affiliation with the

MPR, but Soviet troops successfully put down the rebellion. The U.S.S.R. did make one concession, returning to the MPR a small area west of Khobsogol, but the Tannu Tuva area still comprised about 66,000 square miles. In 1926, the MPR reluctantly recognized the independence of Tannu Tuva. Intensive colonization by Russians, and the introduction of a national Tuvanic written language, tightened the Russian hold on the area.[32]

In 1944, the U.S.S.R. incorporated Tannu Tuva as an autonomous region and, in 1961, the area became an autonomous republic of the U.S.S.R. In 1958, Mongolia reportedly was forced to cede to the U.S.S.R. a small area, adjacent to Tannu Tuva, in which mineral deposits had been discovered.

Relations with Communist China.   Mongol policies toward Communist China have been conditioned by memories of past injustices inflicted by previous Chinese governments and by fear that the Chinese might regain control. The strong pro-Soviet policies of the Tsedenbal government, which have included bitter criticism of the Chinese Communist leadership, resulted in a steady deterioration of relations between Ulan Bator and Peking in 1963 and 1964.

Communist China comes off a poor second to the Soviet Union in any analysis of its aid and trade relationships with the MPR. Assistance given by the U.S.S.R., already described, has been about four times as great as that given by the CPR, and approximately the same ratio holds true for trade. This ratio is widening, as a result of a steady drop in the level of Chinese assistance and with the removal of Chinese workers in 1964.

Statements from Ulan Bator and Peking over the removal of the Chinese labor force were conflicting. The Chinese claimed that the workers were returned home at the request of the Mongolians, but Ulan Bator denied this, claiming that the workers were leaving because their contracts had expired. The indications are that the Mongolians let the contracts lapse probably because of Soviet pressure, because the Soviets had agreed to replace the workers and because the Mongolians themselves were disturbed over the incidents involving the Chinese and Mongolians and because of the danger of such a "fifth column" in case relations became even more strained. At any rate, between April and July nearly all the remaining 6,000 workers returned to China.[33] There are apparently a few Chinese technicians and workers remaining to finish projects already begun by the Chinese.

One factor contributing to strained official relations has been the propaganda activities of the Chinese embassy in Ulan Bator. The MPR in May 1964 delivered a note to the Chinese embassy claiming that propaganda activities of the embassy dealing with the "mistaken views of the CCP leaders on the major problem of our time" constituted a direct interference in the internal affairs of the MPR. The note demanded that the distribution of propaganda material be stopped immediately. The note stressed that this was the fourth such protest against Chinese propaganda activities, the previous ones being delivered in June, July, and September of 1963.

Three incidents between Mongolians and Chinese occurred in Ulan Bator in 1963 and 1964. In the first, in December 1963, the "showcase of the embassy of the CPR containing Chinese propaganda material was smashed." [34] In the second incident, a Yugoslav press service reported (in March 1964) that a dispute over wages by Chinese workers resulted in 15 Mongolians and Chinese being hospitalized. In July, during a cycling meet, tempers flared, with the Mongolians claiming that several Chinese beat a Mongolian spectator unconscious. Militiamen reportedly "dragged" the Chinese to the CPR embassy. The last two incidents resulted in formal protests to the Chinese embassy.

Even with the current fragile status of Mongolian-Chinese relations, both sides apparently want to continue relations at a level higher than might be suggested by the strident tone of Mongolian propaganda prior to the Khrushchev purge. For example, the Mongolians sent one of their top-ranking men, S. Lubsan, to attend Chinese national day ceremonies on October 1. Further, a Mongolian official stated during Chinese national day celebrations in Ulan Bator that the CPR was still helping the MPR "build industrial establishments" with long-term loans. The Chinese have also apparently put no stumbling blocks in the path of the ground survey which is working out the details of the 1962 boundary agreement.[35] And, finally, the Chinese have refrained from answering Mongolian propaganda attacks.

The 1962 boundary treaty served as another admission by Peking of the complete independence of Mongolia. The CPR had previously, in the 1950 Treaty of Friendship and Alliance with the Soviet Union, agreed to a "complete guarantee of the independence status of the Mongolian People's Republic." [36]

Relations with other Communist Countries. Because of its geographic location and relative isolation until recently, the MPR's relations with other communist countries until recently were limited. In 1948, North Korea became the first communist country, other than the Soviet Union, to establish relations with the MPR,[37] and for a time relations with North Korea were probably closer than they were with European members of the bloc. This pattern has been changing, however, under the impact of the Sino-Soviet dispute and with the greater ability of the European countries to assist Mongolia's economic development. This trend has accelerated since June, 1962, when the MPR was admitted to CEMA.[38]

The MPR is the only Asian communist country which has become a member of CEMA. Communist China, North Korea, and North Vietnam remain observers at CEMA meetings, not very active observers at that, and it was necessary to amend the CEMA statutes to allow the admission of a non-European state. Policy planners in the MPR view CEMA membership as a means of stepping up material and technical assistance from the European communist bloc countries. A CEMA meeting held in Ulan Bator in October, 1963, and attended by representatives of the U.S.S.R. and the European communist countries, discussed Mongolian development plans for the period from 1963 to 1980 and explored the assistance CEMA countries might give to help Mongolia fulfill the 1980 plan.

In mid-1963, a CEMA agricultural committee visited Mongolia to advise the MPR on the development of animal husbandry and to assist the Mongolians to eliminate crippling livestock diseases. They also advised on the "need to try to mechanize completely" most aspects of animal husbandry. The MPR expects CEMA assistance to replace the revenue formerly derived from the CPR imports and exports shipped through Mongolia. CEMA assistance is expected in the building of factories to process animal products, including meat, leather, and wool. Further, CEMA assistance is to be utilized for development of Mongolian mineral production, including lead, gold, and feldspar. The CEMA Permanent Commission on Geology, meeting in Ulan Bator in October, 1963, elected the chief of the MPR Geological Survey as its chairman.[39]

Major assistance to the MPR from the European communist countries, prior to and during the third five-year plan, has come from Czechoslovakia and East Germany, and significant assistance has also come from Poland and Hungary.

Mongolian cultural relationships with the European communist countries have increased noticeably in recent years. Delegations, including some of Mongolia's foremost literary and artistic figures, have attended youth, peace, and similar festivals in Prague, East Berlin, and other communist cities. The MPR has student-exchange programs with some of the east European communist countries and also has exchanged Youth League and Young Pioneer groups.

Mongolia and the Noncommunist World

A major aim of the MPR, since the end of World War II, has been to extend worldwide contacts. The MPR has a number of reasons for pursuing this goal: to gain more leverage in its relationship with the

Soviet Union; to disprove the charges, made in 1946 and thereafter, that the MPR was not an independent state; to increase Mongolian foreign trade; to receive technical and material assistance; and to carry on cultural and educational exchanges.

Mongolian propaganda, aimed at all the new, underdeveloped countries, has emphasized that the Mongolian techniques of economic development could profitably be used by any nation facing the problems the MPR has faced. At the Fourteenth Party Congress, for example, Tsedenbal stressed the importance of the Soviet-Mongolian relationship in the success of Mongolian policy, implying that underdeveloped countries could benefit from a similar relationship:

> The fraternal relations between the MPR and the U.S.S.R. are based on the great principles of proletarian internationalism and are models of the equality and mutual assistance between large and small states.
>
> The MPR's experience in this field, in noncapitalistic development, has a very great international significance especially now that the backward peoples of Asia and Africa have been liberated from the imperialist yoke and the problem of forms and methods of reorganization of their socio-economic life and the course of their future development are becoming even more urgent.
>
> Soviet assistance created favorable conditions for liberation of the Mongolian economy from the domination of foreign capital and for development of Mongolia's economy in an orderly manner.[40]

An article in *Namiin Amidral*, entitled "Under the Invincible Banner of Leninism," expanded on the advantages of socialism constructed with Soviet assistance:

> The fact that the MPRP closely tied the fate of the Mongolian people with the people of the Soviet Union, leading power of all progressive mankind, has proved to be a vital factor in gaining freedom for the Mongolian people and in building socialism in our country.
>
> That the MPR has managed to bypass capitalism and is marching toward socialism with the help of a victorious proletarian country is a bright example for the world to see. Comrade Khrushchev has pointed out that Lenin's teachings about bypassing the stage of capitalism have been realized by Kazakhstan and by the MPR.
>
> The success of the Mongolian people and their historical example has a tremendous international significance at this time when the national liberation movement is spreading throughout the world and when a considerable number of independent countries have come into being.
>
> Some of the new and young nations are learning from our experience and methods, especially in the need to deal effective blows against domestic reactionary elements and the foreign imperialist forces that

nourish them, the need for increasing the volume of capital investment by the state into industry, for developing various forms of collectivization in agriculture, the need for putting the ruling power into democratic hands and for attracting the masses into the business of governing the country.[41]

India was the first noncommunist country to establish relations with Mongolia, in 1955, and it was followed by 18 other noncommunist countries by the end of 1964. The MPR has extended unreciprocated recognition to a number of other countries, primarily the new states in Africa. Except for Cuba, the MPR did not have relations with any country in the western hemisphere until Canada recognized it in January, 1964.

The MPR has exchanged economic and cultural missions with Japan since 1959, but formal recognition has not yet taken place. Japan and Mongolia discussed the establishment of diplomatic relations in mid-1961, at about the same time negotiations were being carried on between the MPR and the U.S. Japanese-Mongolian trade remains at a low level.

Diplomatic relations were not established with a noncommunist European nation until January, 1963, when the MPR and the United Kingdom agreed to exchange ambassadors. Subsequently, Austria, Finland, Switzerland, and Sweden have established relations with the MPR.

Mongolia has long been interested in establishing relations with the United States, believing that U.S. recognition would immediately open the door to expansion of contacts with the noncommunist world. Officially however, from 1945 to 1961, the U.S. questioned whether the MPR possessed the attributes of sovereignty, and direct government-to-government relations were therefore not considered. The U.S. explored the possibility of establishing diplomatic relations with the MPR in mid-1961, but the question has not been considered since that time. Mongolian leaders still indicate, however, that the MPR desires to establish relations but that the U.S. will have to take the initiative.

In an interview in December, 1961, L. Tsend stated that only U.S. policy, not Mongolian, prevented the establishment of relations. Tsend stated that the MPR hoped to benefit from American scientific and technical know-how, to develop trade, and to carry out cultural and artistic exchanges. Tsend also stated that the MPR was interested in advanced American techniques, particularly in the raising of livestock.[42]

Membership in the United Nations

Mongolia's campaign for more international contacts was climaxed in the fall of 1961, when the MPR was admitted into the United Nations. Mongolia had attempted as early as 1946 to gain U.N. membership, but the opposition of the United States, and later of Nationalist China, prevented her admission until an arrangement pairing the admission of Mongolia and Mauretania was worked out between the U.S.S.R. and the noncommunist countries. Nine of the Security Council's eleven members voted in favor of the MPR. The United States officially abstained, and Nationalist China took no part in the voting.[43]

Prospects

The present close relations between the U.S.S.R. and the MPR probably will continue. The internal political situation in Mongolia will continue to be heavily influenced by developments in the Soviet Union and Communist China. Instability in the CPSU will likely be reflected in the MPRP. If the present ruling group maintains the confidence of the new Soviet leadership and the present level of Soviet assistance continues, this pro-Soviet group is likely to remain in power. The 1962, 1963, and 1964 purges indicate, however, that the pro-Soviet leadership still has not eliminated "nationalists" and other opponents of its policies from the upper levels of the Party.

The steady deterioration in Mongolian-Chinese relations and the consequent reduction in Chinese assistance has made Mongolia even more dependent on the U.S.S.R. and other CEMA countries. Mongolian desire to increase noncommunist contacts, particularly its desire to establish relations with the United States, as a means of improving the MPR's bargaining position with the Soviet Union and as a possible new source of technical and material assistance, is likely to continue. The U.S.S.R. probably will continue to encourage Mongolian activity in international organizations and in noncommunist countries because of Moscow's desire to exploit the Soviet-Mongolian relationship in its own foreign policy.

Mongolia: The First Communist State in Asia

1. Kh. Choybalsan, "Great History of the Mongol People," *Bolshevik*, No. 13, 1951. (*Soviet Press Translations*, V, No. 20, November 15, 1951, p. 618.)
2. Owen Lattimore, *Nationalism and Revolution in Mongolia* (New York: Oxford University Press, Inc., 1955), pp. 73-74.
3. *Unen* (*Truth*), Ulan Bator, March 29, 1962, pp. 8-14; February 1, 1962, pp. 3-4. Translation published by U.S. Department of Commerce, Office of Technical Service, Joint Publications Research Service [JPRS], in *Translations from Unen: No. 18,* JPRS No. 13,226.
4. *Unen*, February 25, 1962; March 22, 1962 (JPRS, No. 13,226).
5. *Izvestia*, November 26, 1954 (*Current Digest of the Soviet Press*, VI, No. 48, January 12, 1955, p. 8).
6. Robert M. Rupen, "Outer Mongolia: 1957-1960," *Pacific Affairs*, XXXIII (June, 1960), 141-42.

7. *Namiin Amidral (Party Life)*, Ulan Bator, June, 1959.

8. *Pravda*, April 1, 1959 (*Current Digest of the Soviet Press*, XI, No. 13, April 29, 1959, p. 21).

9. *Unen*, October 18, 1962.

10. The resolution was not published until June 1964. The Mongolians candidly state that the resolution, which was largely a polemic directed against the Chinese, was not published in December because public polemics "had been discontinued at that time. So the MPRP Central Committee considered it advisable to refrain from publishing the resolution at that time."

11. Washington University, Far Eastern and Russian Institute, *Mongolian People's Republic*, Human Relations Area File, 1956, 3 Vols. (Subcontractor's Monograph HRAF-39, Wash-1). Vol. III, pp. Pol. 48-50.

12. Full members of the Politburo at the beginning of 1965 were: T. Dugersuren, N. Jagbaral, S. Lubsan, D. Maydar, D. Molomjamts, J. Sambu and Y. Tsedenbal. Candidate members were: B. Lhamsuren, and N. Lubsanrabdan.

    This leadership group remains comparatively young. Tsedenbal, for example, is only 48, Lubsan is 52, and Lhamsuren is only 41. Members of the Politburo come from all sections of the country. Tsedenbal was born in northwest Mongolia, Sambu in central Mongolia, Lubsan in the southeast, and Lhamsuren in the northeast. Little data is available on the socioeconomic background of these men.

13. U.S.S.R., *XIV S'ezd Mongol'skoy Narodno-Revolutsionnoy Partiy* (Moscow: State Publishing House for Political Literature, 1962), p. 78. See also *Political and Economic Information on Mongolia*, JPRS, No. 17,335, January 28, 1963, 97-98, trans. from *Kommunist* (Moscow), No. 11 (July, 1961).

14. *Unen*, July 20, 1963, p. 1 (in *Translations on Mongolia: No. 38*, JPRS, No. 21,276, October 1, 1963, p. 25).

15. *XIV S'ezd Mongol'skoy Narodno-Revolutsionnoy Partiy*, pp. 63-64. See also JPRS, No. 17,335, 79-80.

16. Washington University, *Mongolian People's Republic*, HRAF, Vol. 2, p. 533.

17. *Hodolmor (Labor)*, Ulan Bator, September 10, 1963, p. 2; September 11, 1963, p. 2; September 14, 1963, p. 2; September 17, 1963, p. 2; September 18, 1963, p. 2 (in *Translations on Mongolia: No. 41*, JPRS, No. 21,851, November 13, 1963, pp. 61-77).

18. Mongolian People's Republic, *Konstitutsiya Mongol'skoy Narodnoy Respubliki*. Ulan Bator, Gosizdatel'stvo MNR, 1961, p. 5.

19. *Unen*, January 13, 1962.

20. *Namiin Amidral*, January, 1963.

21. Mongolian People's Republic, *Narodnoye Khozyaystvo Mongol'skoy Narodnoy Respubliki za 40 let; statisticheskiy sbornik*. Added title in English: *National Economy of the Mongolian People's Republic for 40 years: Collection of Statistics* (Ulan Bator: Gosudarstvennoye Tsentral'noye Upravleniye Soveta Ministroy MNR, 1961), p. 57.

22. Mongolian statistics continue to be unreliable. The MPR does not provide an over-all gross national product figure, simply because Mongolian planning and statistical systems are unable to provide such a figure. There has been no uniform pricing system and statistical records of all types of enterprises are spotty. The MPR, with CEMA help, is now trying to correct this deficiency.

23. *Unen*, July 7, 1961 (in *Translations from Unen: No. 15*, JPRS, No. 12,436, February 13, 1962, 40-54. Also Ulan Bator, Montsame in Russian to USSR, March 1, 1963).

24. Moscow, Tass in English to Europe, January 31, 1962.

25. *Unen*, January 9, 1963, in *Translations on International Communist Developments: No. 383*, JPRS, No. 18,025, March 8, 1963, p. 5.

26. Tsedenbal, Yumzhagiin, "Economic Co-operation of the Socialist Countries: a Vital Necessity," *World Marxist Review* (English edition of *Problems of Peace and Socialism*), VII, No. 9 (September, 1964), 2-9.

27. Tsedenbal spent nearly 3 months in the Soviet Union in 1964, visiting Moscow in April for 2 weeks to attend Khrushchev's 70th birthday celebrations and again visiting the Soviet Union for about 6 weeks in July and August on a working vacation. Tsedenbal has spent 6 to 8 weeks in the Soviet Union every summer for the past several years. He made 4 stops in Moscow in October and was again there for 2 weeks during the November 7 celebrations.

28. Robert Rupen, "Mongolian Nationalism," *Royal Central Asian Journal*, April, 1958, pp. 157-58.

29. Gerard M. Friters, *Outer Mongolia and Its International Position* (Baltimore: The Johns Hopkins Press, 1949), pp. 143-49.

30. Robert Rupen, "Outer Mongolia Since 1955," *Pacific Affairs*, XXX (December, 1957), 346.

31. Mongolian People's Republic, Information and Broadcasting Department, Mongolian Embassy in New Delhi, India, *Mongolia Today*, Vol. III, No. 7, July 1961, p. 8.

32. Friters, *Outer Mongolia and Its International Position*, pp. 130-132.

33. The biggest failure in the economy in 1963 was in the field of construction and installation, and part of this failure may have been due to the drop in Chinese aid and to the gradual drop in the number and effectiveness of Chinese workers. A Yugoslav report indicates that the productivity of the Chinese workers dropped sharply during their last several months in the MPR.

34. Belgrade, *Politika*, December 6, 1963; Belgrade, *Borba*, March 28, 1964.

35. *Peking Review*, No. 52, December 28, 1962, pp. 5-7. *Unen*, March 26, 1963, pp. 1-4.

36. HRAF, *Mongolian People's Republic*, Vol. II, p. 589.

37. Relations with other communist countries were established as follows: Albania, May 17, 1949; Communist China, October 6, 1949; East Germany, April 13, 1950; Poland, April 14, 1950; Bulgaria, April 23, 1950; Czechoslovakia, April 25, 1950; Rumania, April 29, 1950; North Vietnam, November 18, 1954; Yugoslavia, November 20, 1956; Cuba, December 7, 1960.

38. *Pravda*, June 10, 1962.

39. Budapest, *Nepszabadsag*, October 24, 1963.

40. U.S.S.R., *XIV S'ezd Mongol'skoy Narodno-Revolutsionnoy Partiy*, pp. 6-8. Also JPRS, No. 17,335, pp. 6-8.

41. JPRS, No. 19,802, *Translations on International Communist Developments No. 448*, pp. 2-10. From *Namiin Amidral*, April 1963, No. 4, pp. 3-7.

42. The *New York Times*, December 17, 1961, p. 33.

43. The *New York Times*, October 26, 1961, p. 1.

Selected Bibliography

Haggard, M. T., "Mongolia: The Uneasy Buffer," *Asian Survey*, V, No. 1 (January 1965), 18-24.

Langer, Paul F., *The Minor Asian Communist States: Outer Mongolia, North Korea and North Vietnam.* Santa Monica, Calif.: The Rand Corporation, 1964, pp. 1-18.

Lattimore, Owen, "Communism: Mongolian Brand," *The Atlantic*, CCX, No. 3 (September, 1962), 79-94.

————, *Nationalism and Revolution in Mongolia*. New York: Oxford University Press, Inc., 1955.

————, *Nomads and Commissars: Mongolia Revisited*. New York: Oxford University Press, Inc., 1962.

————, *Studies in Frontier History*. London: Oxford University Press, Inc., 1962.

Matveyeva, G. S., *Sotsialisticheskiye Preobrazovaniye v sel'skom khozyaystve Mongol'skoy Narodnoy Respubliki*. Moscow, 1960. Translated as *Socialist Transformation of Agriculture in the Mongolian People's Republic*, U.S. Department of Commerce, Office of Technical Services, Joint Publications Research Service [JPRS], No. 5, 943, October 25, 1960.

Narodnoye Khozyaystvo Mongol'skoy Respubliki za 40 let; statisticheskiy sbornik. Added title in English: *National Economy of the Mongolian People's Republic for 40 years: Collection of Statistics*. Ulan Bator: Mongolian People's Republic, 1961.

Political and Economic Information on Mongolia [includes Tsedenbal's report to the Fourteenth Party Congress]. JPRS, No. 17, 335, January 28, 1963.

Rupen, Robert A., "How the Mongolian People's Republic Is Really Ruled," *China News Analysis* (Hong Kong) May 15, 1964, No. 516.

————, "Mongolia in the Sino-Soviet Dispute," *The China Quarterly*, No. 16 (October-December, 1963), 75-85.

————, "Recent Trends in the Mongolian People's Republic," *Asian Survey*, IV, No. 4 (April, 1964), 812-820.

————, "The Mongolian People's Republic and Sino-Soviet Competition" in *Communist Strategies in Asia*, ed. A. Doak Barnett. New York: Frederick A. Praeger, Inc., 1963, pp. 262-292.

Titkov, Vasiliy Ivanovich, *Gosudarstvennyy stroy Mongol'skoy Narodnoy Respubliki*. Moscow: Gosyurizdat, 1961. Translated as *The Government of the Mongolian People's Republic*, JPRS, No. 17,456, 1963.

Tsedenbal, Yumzhagiin, "Economic Cooperation of the Socialist Countries—a Vital Necessity," *World Marxist Review* (English edition of *Problems of Peace and Socialism*), VII, No. 9 (September, 1964), 2-9.

XIV S'ezd Mongol'skoy Narodno-Revolutsionnoy Partiy (Fourteenth Congress of the Mongolian People's Revolutionary Party). Moscow: U.S.S.R. State Publishing House for Political Literature, 1962.

Stalinism in the East

Communism in North Korea

Chong-Sik Lee

The Korean Workers' Party, the parent
organization of the Democratic People's Republic of Korea,
is in firm control of North Korea. During the past
19 years of turbulence, the North Korean communist
leaders have successfully transformed
themselves from the lowly agents of the Russian
occupying forces into the undisputed rulers
of a highly disciplined and monolithic communist regime.
As they have matured in age, accumulated experience,
and consolidated their political and economic power,
the North Korean leaders have begun to manifest more and more
confidence, even arrogance, about their abilities,
and to pursue more nationalistic policies.

Origins and Development of the Party

At the end of World War II, when Korea was freed from Japanese rule, communist strength in Korea was minimal. Korea had its share of communist agitators and sympathizers between 1918 and 1945, but the Japanese police had effectively quashed any and all attempts to organize a communist movement. The 1945 Communist Revolution was imposed on North Korea from without, by the Russian forces that occupied the territory north of the thirty-eighth parallel. Today's ruling oligarchy arrived in North Korea in the months from August to October, 1945, at the tail of the Russian contingents, to assist in the tasks of occupation and perhaps to establish a communist regime of their own.

At a very early stage of the occupation of North Korea, the Russian authorities put forward Kim Il-sŏng, then a 33-year-old veteran of partisan campaigns in Manchuria, as the national hero and the most appropriate communist, and hence national, leader of Korea. Kim is believed to have retreated from Manchuria to Russian territory in the early 1940's, when conditions in Manchuria became totally hostile to his small band of partisan fighters. The Russian authorities in North Korea, whose military occupation lasted until 1948, not only placed Kim in a position of prominence, but also provided him with every opportunity to establish himself at the helm of the regime and of the newly revived communist party. Thus, the young and unknown Kim was made First Secretary of the North Korean Central Bureau of the Korean Communist Party, which placed all communists in North Korea under its control in October, 1945, and Chairman of the North Korean Provisional People's Committee in February, 1946. When the North Korean Bureau of the Communist party absorbed the New People's party headed by returnees from Yenan, China, and renamed the organization the North Korean Workers' party in July, 1946, Kim was made Vice-chairman. In September, 1948, when the Democratic People's Republic of Korea (DPRK) was established, Kim was enthroned as its premier. In June of the following year, when the North and South Korean Workers' parties merged into the Korean Workers' Party (KWP), Kim was made the Chairman and the supreme leader.[1] The South Korean Workers' Party was, in itself, an amalgamation of the communists and other leftists in South Korea. By early 1949 most of its leaders had been forced to flee to North Korea, where they subordinated themselves to Kim Il-sŏng.

Under favorable conditions, the Party organization in North Korea expanded rapidly. In July, 1946, when the North Korean Workers' Party was organized, the membership was 366,000;[2] in March, 1948, the Party strength was 700,000; and, at the end of 1952, it had reached 1,000,000.[3]

In April, 1956, at the Third Congress of the KWP, the membership was reported to be 1,164,945. As of August 1, 1961, the figure stood at 1,311,563, including 145,204 candidate members.[4] North Korea now has one of the highest proportions of party members to population among the communist countries.

The Leadership

The North Korean Premier's pattern of consolidating leadership and power is strongly in the style of Stalin. Initially, he shared power and responsibility with rival groups, but when the potential rivals exhausted their usefulness, they were purged from the Party and Kim then surrounded himself with individuals whose personal loyalty was unquestionable. The purges that led to the consolidation of Kim's power were carried out in a number of distinct stages.

The intra-Party struggles of the prewar period, when Kim Il-sŏng's personal power was not beyond challenge, were mostly aimed against the leading elements of the "domestic faction." Emasculation of this group was important at this stage for both the Russian and Yenan returnees, because the indigenous leaders possessed exceedingly strong personal control over the local organizations. This group of veteran communists, which included O Ki-sŏp, Chong Tal-hyŏn, Yi Pong-su, and Yi Chu-ha, was therefore attacked by Kim Il-sŏng as having indulged in egocentricity, individual heroism, sectarianism, local separatism, and other sins. Those who were not immediately removed from the scene were relegated to minor bureaucratic positions.

Some, indeed, of the veteran communists of the domestic faction were retained in such important positions as Vice-premier or other ministerial positions, but they, too, exhausted their usefulness by the time the truce was signed in 1953. Soon after the truce, on August 3, the Pyongyang regime indicted Yi Sung-yŏp, former Secretary of the South Korean Workers' Party and Minister of Justice, and 11 other major figures of South Korean origin, on charges of espionage for the enemy and an attempt to overthrow the regime.[5] Although Pak Hŏn-yŏng, the top man of the domestic group, who had held such important posts as that of Vice-premier and Foreign Minister, was not indicted at this time, it was intimated throughout the trial that he was the mastermind behind the group. The alleged conspirators supposedly contemplated the establishment of a new government under the premiership of Pak. Pak was subsequently indicted and sentenced to death in December, 1955.

Once the domestic faction communists were eliminated from positions of power, a struggle for power was waged between Kim Il-sŏng's personal followers and the returnees from Yenan. Some men of the so-called "Russian faction"—those Koreans born and raised in the Soviet Union, as distinguished from temporary exiles like Kim Il-sŏng—sided with men of the Yenan faction.

The open struggle between some of the Yenan faction and Kim Il-sŏng was spurred by the de-Stalinization campaign in Russia. It is evident that the Yenan group, along with Pak Ch'ang-ok, a Russian faction man who was Minister of Mechanical Industry, decided that the cult of personality should end in North Korea, just as it had in the Soviet Union. At the August 1956 plenum of the Party's Central Committee, which had been called to hear the Premier's report on his visit to the Soviet Union and eastern Europe, Yun Kong-hŭm, the Minister of Commerce and the Yenan faction leader, boldly criticized the authoritarianism of Kim and the "anti-people" nature of Kim's policies. He also attacked the cheap wages paid to workers and the cruel treatment accorded the farmers. Other renowned theoreticians, such as Ch'oe Ch'ang-ik and Pak Ch'ang-ok, supported Yun's arguments.[6] The supporters of the Premier, however, outnumbered the dissidents and branded the critics as anti-Party reactionary elements. According to one source, these three major critics were expelled from the Central Committee and stripped of their official functions, but P'eng Te-huai, the Chinese Defense Minister, and Anastas I. Mikoyan, the First Deputy Premier of the Soviet Union, intervened and secured their reinstatement to the Central Committee.[7] But Kim's opponents were soon vanquished.

The last step in the continuous process of purges was directed against the 69-year-old Kim Tu-bong, the elder statesman of the Yenan group, who had been Chairman of the Presidium of the Supreme People's Assembly since its establishment in 1948 and the first Chairman of the North Korean Workers' Party. Together with Vice-premier Pak Ui-wan, a Russian faction man, and O Ki-sŏp, the former Secretary of the North Korean Communist Party, Kim Tu-bong was alleged to have conceived of overthrowing the Party leadership.[8] With his purge in 1958, the Yenan group was virtually eliminated from the North Korean political arena.

We can better understand the characteristics of the leadership of North Korea if we examine the background of the top echelon. It must never be forgotten, of course, that Kim Il-sŏng stands alone as the supreme leader. According to the Party constitution, the supreme organ of the Party is the Party Congress, which is to be held every four years. During the intervals, an 85-member Central Committee, and particularly its 11-member Political Committee, directs and guides the affairs of the Party. Thus the power is concentrated in the Political Committee, which is headed by Kim Il-sŏng. The background and positions of the other ten members of the Political Committee are as follows:

Ch'oe Yong-gŏn: Vice-chairman of the Central Committee; Chairman of the Presidium of the Supreme People's Assembly. Veteran of partisan campaigns in Manchuria.

Kim Il: Vice-chairman of the Central Committee; first Vice-premier of the DPRK. Veteran of partisan campaigns in Manchuria and a company commander under Kim Il-sŏng.

Pak kum-ch'ŏl: Vice-chairman of the Central Committee; Vice-chairman of the Supreme People's Assembly. Served as a liaison man between Kim Il-sŏng in Manchuria and the small underground movement in the Kapsan area near the Manchurian-Korean border from 1936 to 1938.

Kim Kwang-hyŏp: Vice-premier of the DPRK; Army general. Veteran of partisan campaigns in Manchuria under Kim Il-sŏng.

Kim Ch'ang-man: Vice-chairman of the Central Committee; Vice-premier of the DPRK. Former follower of a nationalist-communist, Kim Won-bong; headed the Propaganda Section of the Korean Independence League at Yenan. The sole member of Yenan origin.

Pak Chŏng-ae: Vice-chairman of the Presidium of the Supreme People's Assembly. Former Minister of Agriculture; imprisoned by the Japanese for communist activities within Korea. Domestic faction origin. The only woman in the Political Committee.

Nam Il: Vice-premier of the DPRK. Former Chief of Staff of the Army; former Foreign Minister. Believed to have been born and educated in the Soviet Union.

Chŏng Il-yong: Vice-premier and Minister of Electrical and Coal Industries. Russian origin.

Yi Hyo-sun: Vice-chairman of the Central Committee and member of the Presidium of the Supreme People's Assembly.

Yi Chong-ok: Vice-chairman of the Central Committee. Former First Vice-premier.

It is evident from the above list that individuals who had close personal connections with Kim Il-sŏng in the preliberation era predominate in the Political Committee. Kim Il, the number-two man of North Korea, Pak Kum-ch'ŏl, and Kim Kwang-hyŏp were all under the direct command of Kim Il-sŏng in Manchuria. Although Ch'oe Yong-gŏn also has a partisan record in Manchuria, his area of operation was in northern Manchuria while that of Kim was in the southeast. This partly explains the fact that Ch'oe is heading the Supreme People's Assembly, the post vacated by the Yenan group's Kim Tu-bong. We must assume that Kim Ch'ang-man (of Yenan origin), Pak Chŏng-ae (of domestic origin), and

Nam Il (of Russian origin) carefully avoided close alliance with their former colleagues, primarily by exhibiting unquestionable allegiance to the supreme leader, and thereby survived the series of purges. Did they also play some role in the downfall of their old colleagues?

In theory, the Political Committee is the embodiment of collective leadership, a principle to which the North Korean leaders pay homage. When the cry of the cult of personality was raised in North Korea after Khrushchev launched his de-Stalinization campaign in 1956, apologists for Kim Il-sŏng claimed that collective leadership had always been practiced in North Korea and that the cult of personality had never existed. If anything, the theoreticians argued, individual heroism, the root of the cult of personality, had been found only among the Premier's opponents who wished to advance individual interests above those of the Party by attacking the Party leadership.

In spite of these apologists, however, the cult of personality reigns unchallenged in North Korea today, far beyond the degree to which it is practiced in Communist China. Huge portraits of Kim still hang in front of public buildings, and gigantic characters proclaiming "Long Live Marshal Kim Il-sŏng" have been erected over the most prominent buildings. Publications eulogizing the revolutionary past of the Premier are issued *ad infinitum*. Monuments, museums, and parks are erected in every North Korean locality where Kim set foot before 1945. Histories are rewritten to castigate or ignore all the communist activities of the preliberation era except those of the Kim Il-sŏng group. The activities of the Yenan group in China, for example, are not even mentioned in the official histories published after 1958.

The Emphasis on Nationalism

The outstanding characteristic of the post-Korean War policies of the Pyongyang regime is the emphasis on nationalism. This has been reflected in its economic, political, and foreign policies as well as in its historiography. While it is difficult to offer definite explanations for the intensified emphasis on nationalism, it is possible to speculate on the motives.

It should be recalled that the Russian-armed North Korean forces almost succeeded in conquering the entire peninsula in the summer of 1950. Only the air superiority of the United States prevented the communist troops from overrunning the Pusan perimeter south of the Naktong River before the Inchon landing in September. Is it not reasonable to assume that the leaders in Pyongyang requested air coverage by the Soviet air force in the critical summer months? This, of course, would have necessitated the overt participation of the Soviet Union in the Korean War which, in spite of Pyongyang's insistence, Moscow strove to avoid. We can draw a striking parallel with the invasion of the Bay of Pigs.

Later in the same year, MacArthur's landing in Inchon reversed the situation. The northern advance of the United Nations forces almost drove the communist forces out of Korea. It is reasonable to assume that the desperate North Korean leaders requested immediate Soviet intervention during their catastrophic retreat. In the winter of 1950, direct Soviet intervention, beyond verbal denunciation of the United States, seemed to be essential—but the Soviet Union was not willing to risk a major war to save the North Koreans. It needs to be emphasized that North Korea was definitely within the Russian sphere, not the Chinese, in 1950.

Chinese intervention in October did alter the situation on the Korean War front, but the North Korean communists must have had some nerve-wracking moments. What if the Chinese communists had not been able to rescue North Korea? Would the Soviet Union have intervened then? Would the Soviet Union risk dangers in the future to aid its fraternal parties in a moment of extreme need?

It is reasonable to assume that the North Korean leaders were compelled to sacrifice their control of the war and to swallow their pride in accepting the Chinese "volunteers" who came to the rescue. Evidence suggests that the North Korean communists were not always in harmony with the Chinese, and one may suspect that the differences were rarely settled in favor of the Korean position. Thus, the Korean communists had ample reasons to loathe their weaknesses—military, political, and economic.

As soon as the truce was concluded at Panmunjom on July 27, 1953, the North Korean communists set about remedying their deplorable situation. On August 5, the Premier delivered a major policy speech at the sixth plenum of the Korean Workers' Party, delineating the policies to be followed. The points stressed most strongly by Kim were the strengthening of the people's democracy and the consolidation of the "democratic base" in North Korea. Kim argued that this would certainly contribute to "peaceful unification" and independence.

Stress on Industrial Development

Undoubtedly, the situation in North Korea was difficult in 1953. Destruction of industrial facilities had been almost complete,[9] the food shortage was severe, and consumer goods were scarce. For these reasons, some of the leaders reportedly advocated a balanced recovery and development program designed to alleviate the immediate difficulties of the populace. This group of leaders, including Ch'oe Ch'ang-ik and Pak Ch'ang-ok, evidently envisaged a program to loosen the wartime control of the economy, import more food and consumer goods, and at the same time carry forth a moderate industrial recovery program.[10] The Soviet advisers evidently favored this moderate course.

But the party's dominant group, including the Premier, emphatically rejected the moderate proposals. The sufferings of the masses were evidently the least of the leadership's concern. While praising the "patriotic mobilization of the people which greatly contributed to the attainment of victory in the war," Kim Il-sŏng admonished against any relaxation of pressure. "We must appeal to the patriotic dedication of the masses to develop mass labor mobilization in the effort to reconstruct the war-torn industrial enterprises and the educational and cultural facilities." [11]

The plan adopted in North Korea was a modified version of the industrialization policy of the Communist Party of the U.S.S.R. under Stalin. The formula, acclaimed by North Korean theoreticians as original and creative, called for the "priority development of heavy industry together with the simultaneous development of light industry and agriculture." The rapid reconstruction and development program was to be carried out through successive stages of: (1) a preparatory period of from six months to a year; (2) a three-year plan from 1954 through 1956; and (3) a five-year plan from 1957 through 1961. A seven-year plan, for 1961 through 1967, was adopted later.

The simultaneous-development program meant, in practice, concentrated capital investment in heavy industry and a minimum allocation of capital to light industry and to agriculture. Living standards of the masses were kept to the lowest level of subsistence, even by Korean standards. Production of consumer goods received little attention until 1958, and even the farmers were allowed to consume only a fraction of their agricultural products. Collectivized agriculture became an auxiliary to industry, with the farmers obliged to supply both food and industrial raw materials, at the same time as they provided most of the capital for industrial development through compulsory savings. Agriculture was completely collectivized through the agricultural cooperative system, the process being completed in 1958.

In his speech to the sixth plenum, in 1953, the Premier assigned priority to the following industries: steel mills; machinery production; ship construction; mining; electrical generation; chemical fertilizers; petroleum; construction materials; and cement. Textile mills and food-processing factories received only brief mention. The responsibility for production and distribution of sundry daily necessities was relegated to the provincial committees, which in reality meant the postponement of action in these fields. As Kim Il-sŏng admitted five years later, in June, 1958, even the discussion of enlarging the production of daily necessities was meaningless before that time. It was impossible, said Kim, "to raise the problem of the food-processing industry before the problem of food shortage was solved. Both food processing and the production of daily necessities required certain foundations [i.e., heavy industry]." [12]

In statistical terms, 39.9 billion won or 49.5 per cent of the total capital investment of 80.6 billion won (price standard of January 1, 1950), were allocated to industry during the three-year plan of 1954 through 1956; of this sum, 81.8 per cent was invested in heavy industry. During the five-year plan of 1957 through 1961, 55 per cent of the total capital investment of 147 billion won was allocated to industry; of this, 83 per cent was for heavy industry. [13]

Kim Il-sŏng stated, at the sixth plenum of the Party in 1953, that one of the reasons why the economic reconstruction and development was possible was the "trustworthy support and assistance granted by the Soviet Union, the Chinese people and various fraternal peoples." The total amount of aid received between the end of the war and April, 1963, is reported to be equivalent to 550 million U.S. dollars. [14] But, according to North Korean sources, three-fourths of all foreign aid was spent on the acquisition of the means of production (heavy and light industries), only one-quarter going to agriculture and consumer goods. [15]

Although North Korea continues to receive some aid and loans from other communist countries, the plans succeeding the initial three-year plan have had to be financed mainly by internal savings. [16] In order to finance its ambitious industrial development after 1956, it was necessary for the Pyongyang regime to enforce compulsory savings averaging 25 per cent of the national income. [17] According to communist sources, this ratio of savings was even higher than those enforced in the Soviet Union and Communist China in comparable periods of their history. [18] It is easy to perceive that the North Korean leaders demanded the utmost sacrifice and perseverance from the populace.

There is no doubt that North Korea has made significant economic gains during the postwar era. According to official reports, North Korea had successfully shed all residues of the distorted colonial economy by 1958. It is now, in communist parlance, an industrial-agricultural society. In 1960, 71 per cent of the total production was industrial and only 21 per cent was agricultural. [19] This is a marked change from 1949, when industry represented only 47 per cent of national income. Table 1 shows the production in some sectors of North Korean economy in 1963 and 1960, as compared with 1946.

Table 1

PRODUCTION OUTPUT VOLUME OF INDUSTRIAL GOODS

	Production in 1963	Production in 1960	1960 Increase over 1946
Electric power	11,766,000,000	9,139,000,000 [a]	2.3 times
Coal	14,040,000	10,620,000 [b]	8.4
Pig iron and granulated iron	1,159,000	872,000 [b]	285
Steel	1,022,000	641,000 [b]	127.2
Chemical fertilizers	853,000	561,000 [b]	3.6
Cement	2,530,000	2,285,000 [b]	22.2
Fabrics	Not given	189,000,000 [c]	72

Source: *Democratic People's Republic of Korea,* 1961, pp. 20-21 and Statistical Board Release, January 17, 1964.
[a] Kilowatt hours
[b] Tons
[c] Yards

Independence and Self-reliance

These changes in the economy were immediately reflected in the North Korean communists' pattern of indoctrination and justification for their policies. Until the three-year plan was completed in 1957, and while North Korea was predominantly dependent upon foreign aid, the communists justified their policies on the ground that the accelerated economic development contributed to the consolidation of a democratic base in North Korea. Thus, Kim Il-sŏng argued in 1954:

> When we effectively bring about economic construction and improve the people's livelihood in the Northern part [of Korea] and make it a great paradise, no power can suppress the revolutionary forces of the South Korean people, who will long for the Northern part and oppose the reactionary regime in South Korea. [Economic resources of the north] would also enable us to solve easily the problems of the South Korean people's livelihood when the unification of the fatherland has been achieved.[20]

As the economic condition improved in North Korea and the international situation changed, North Korean writers began to place more emphasis on an "independent and self-reliant economy" as an essential aspect of the party's economic program. Although the phrase was not totally new in the North Korean context,[21] it did not come to the forefront until about 1957. It is interesting to note that the Chinese communists also began to stress this same theme about this time. By 1961, articles on the independent and self-reliant economy predominated in the Party's theoretical organ, *Kŭlloja,* replacing the former theme of the consolidation of democratic base.

The new stress on independence and self-reliance, of course, did not come about accidentally. As the initial efforts for reconstruction were completed, foreign aid was drastically reduced. Soviet aid was not forthcoming, and the Chinese did not have enough to offer much assistance. Improvement in the economy also produced more respect and prestige for North Korea among the communist countries,[22] and the conflict within the international communist camp provided an opportunity for the North Koreans to speak more freely of independence. The simultaneous adoption of the identical theme by the Chinese and the North Koreans also suggests the possibility of Chinese influence. In any event, the North Korean communists were gaining more self-confidence and self-respect. Kim Il-sŏng's statement of January, 1958, was remarkably straightforward:

> In times before, if we wanted more irrigation, we needed to buy pumps, transformers, generators, and electric motors. So, we were not able to decide on the matter by ourselves but had to ask the people who offered to provide the materials. *But we now have the right to speak and decide by ourselves.* [*Emphasis supplied.*] [23]

The emphasis on a self-reliant economy was preceded by intense indoctrination in "things Korean." In April, 1955, the Premier admonished the Party members for not knowing Korean history and events connected with their own country. Party members were simply memorizing the principles of Marxism, he complained, and were not able to apply these principles. Further, on December 28, 1955, he delivered a major speech on ideological education stressing the need for "firmly establishing *chuch'e*" (i.e., a theme). He argued that there was an urgent need to consider seriously why the ideological activities of the past had fallen into dogmatism and formalism and why the propagandists and agitators had not been able to probe various problems deeply. The Party workers, according to Kim, had not been creative, and had only copied and memorized the ideas of others.[24]

"What should be the *chuch'e*, or theme?" (In other words, what should be the principal criterion in emulating others?) To answer this question, the Premier posed another: "What are we doing?"

> We are engaged in none other than the Korean revolution. The Korean revolution is the theme of our party's ideological activities. Therefore, all ideological activities must be adapted to the interest of the Korean revolution. The purpose of our study of the histories of the Communist Party of the U.S.S.R. and the Chinese revolution, or the general principles of Marxism-Leninism, is entirely for the correct execution of our revolution.[25]

According to the Premier, North Korea's adulation of the Soviet Union was extreme. In the walls of the People's Army's recuperation centers hung pictures of Siberian fields. In the "democratic propaganda rooms" in the countryside hung pictorial charts of Russia's five-year plan, but none of North Korea's three-year plan. There were photographs of "factories of foreign nations," but none of Korean factories. Elementary schools displayed portraits of Mayakovsky and Pushkin, but none of Korean heroes.

The Premier was also emphatic in denouncing those who advocated blind imitation of the Soviet policies. For instance, he attacked Pak Yong-bin, then the head of the Organization and Guidance Department of the Central Committee, who had proposed that the Korean Party should remove its strong anti-American slogans because the Soviet Union was relaxing her stand against the United States. The Premier charged that this kind of advocacy not only had no common ground with revolutionary creativity, but also would paralyze "our people's revolutionary awareness." Kim ostensibly supported the "Soviet people's efforts for relaxing international tension," but argued that North Korea's "struggle against American imperialists" was in harmony with Soviet policy. Although the Premier did not elaborate on what appeared to be a unity of opposites, his implicit argument was that the strong stand taken by North Korea would soften the American imperialists and hence contribute to peace. It is worth remembering that these statements were made at the end of 1955.

In stressing the need for more study of things Korean and for a new patriotism for Korea, Kim also evoked the concept of the unity of patriotism and internationalism. To love Korea, said Kim, was to love the Soviet Union and the socialist camp. To love the Soviet Union and the socialist camp was to love Korea. That was because, according to Kim, there were no national boundaries in the great tasks of the working class of the world.

Naturally, Kim Il-sŏng's speeches on ideological or doctrinal education were also devoted to attacks upon the so-called sectarian elements of the Yenan, domestic, and Russian factions. During the war, said the Premier, "Hŏ Ka-i, Kim Chae-uk, and Pak Il-u had argued uselessly over the method of political activities in the army. Those from the Soviet Union wanted to follow the Russian way and those from China wanted to follow the Chinese way." Of course, the "Party Central [i.e., Kim Il-sŏng himself] decided that the Party should learn from both the Soviet Union and China and create methods best suited to our country's actual conditions." [26]

Kim's admonitions were well heeded by the Party's historians and propagandists, whose works on Korean history have rapidly multiplied. These writers can be grouped into three categories: (1) historians exalting the glories of ancient Korea and the virtues of the progressive scholars of seventeenth- and eighteenth-century Korea; [27] (2) pseudo-historians and propagandists apotheosizing the revolutionary past of Kim Il-sŏng; and (3) economists and propagandists praising, in greatly exaggerated form, the accomplishments of the regime. The tasks of these writers vary, but all are united in glorification of the fatherland, and those who deal with modern material are united in exaltation of the Premier.

Peaceful Unification of Korea

Nationalism has been an important theme of the communist leaders —not only for the North Korean masses, but for the anticommunist South Koreans as well. As has been noted, the peaceful unification of the fatherland was presented in North Korea as the primary justification for the frantic development of heavy industry. North Korea is to serve as the democratic base for a united Korea.

Like other policies adopted in North Korea during the postwar period, the principle of peaceful unification is not totally new. It should be recalled that the Pyongyang regime had issued strong appeals for negotiations for peaceful unification just a week before launching the attack on South Korea on June 25, 1950. The appeals were issued by the Fatherland Unification Democratic Front, the organization established to "promote the unification movement." The Fatherland Front, however, is an apparatus of the regime for mobilizing all noncommunist democratic forces in North and South Korea. Ostensibly, it is a united front of all the political parties and groups throughout Korea. The Pyongyang regime, which still adheres to the notion of a people's democracy, maintains the skeleton of a number of noncommunist parties and groups for this purpose, including the *Choson Minjudang* (i.e., the Korean Democratic Party) and the *Ch'ŏndogyo Ch'ŏng-u-dang* (i.e., the Ch'ŏndogyo Youth Fraternal Party). These parties and groups are still represented in the Supreme People's Assembly, although they are believed to have almost no members.

The advocacy of peaceful unification was accepted credulously by some, both in North and South Korea, before the war. The renewed appeal after the war, however, was received with universal skepticism even in North Korea. The communist leader spoke on this point in November, 1954:

> Some people think that peaceful unification is impossible and hence regard our current appeal as nothing but a formality. Even among our party members there are those who think this way.[28]

In order to convince his subordinates that the slogan was more than an expression of vague hopes and formality, Kim treated some of the difficult theoretical problems that revealed potential areas of conflict with the positions taken by the Soviet Union, notably the question of peaceful coexistence and American imperialism.

Kim Il-sŏng asserted that there were some who extended the policy of peaceful coexistence of the two world camps into Korea and wrongly concluded that the two separate Koreas could coexist. And there were others, he said, who did not attach any hope to unification because of the obstruction posed by the American imperialists. Kim made it known that he was in complete agreement with the principle of peaceful coexistence. In fact, he said, the principle was "absolutely correct," but impossible to apply to Korea:

> . . . the idea that Korea could be separated into Northern and Southern parts and that the parts should coexist with each other is very dangerous; it is a view obstructing our efforts for unification. Those holding this view would relegate the *responsibility of revolution in South Korea* to the South Korean people and relieve of the people in North Korea the *responsibility of liberating* South Korea. This is nothing more than a justification for the division of the Fatherland and for perpetuation of the division. [*Emphasis supplied.*] [29]

The Premier conceded that the peaceful unification of the fatherland would not be accomplished in a short period because of the United States. "We cannot lightly treat the power of the American imperialists," said Kim. But the United States "would not be able to avoid the eventual destruction [destined] by the law of historical development." Kim was, of course, not going to sit idly and wait for the historical law to take its natural course: "[Our] task lies in the quickening of the process of destruction through our struggle." When this has been accomplished, argued the Premier, "even if the American imperialists strove to support the Syngman Rhee clique, we could not be restrained from attaining the great task of unifying the Fatherland." One must conclude that the policy of peaceful unification is indeed a long-range one.

With these justifications, the North Korean regime aimed an intensive propaganda campaign toward South Korea. It should be remembered that, although no North Korean publications can be obtained by the ordinary citizenry of South Korea, North Korean broadcasts are readily audible there. Basically, the North Korean aims have been to alienate the South Korean masses from the United States, to establish the North Korean communists as the true patriots, and to organize, when possible, communist sympathizers in South Korea. The communist leaders seem to be aware that orthodox communist themes have little appeal in South Korea. Only through nationalist appeals, they seem to have concluded, can the South Korean people be approached.

The Pyongyang regime's basic formula for peaceful unification has not changed since 1954, when Nam Il, then Foreign Minister, presented the North Korean position at the Geneva conference. Nam advocated the establishment of an all-Korean commission, the membership to be selected by the Supreme People's Assembly of the North Korean regime and the National Assembly of South Korea. The commission would be charged with the responsibility of making necessary preparations for a free general election and of taking "urgent measures for the economic and cultural *rapprochement* of North and South Korea." [30] Some of the later proposals would endow this commission with more power. It would, for instance, head a confederation of the two Koreas and be invested with the authority to decide on matters related to foreign affairs and national defense.[31]

As in the period before the Korean War, the Pyongyang regime continues to insist, as a prerequisite for negotiation, that all foreign troops (i.e., United States forces) must be withdrawn from Korea and that all military alliances must be dissolved. The argument is that the fate of Korea must be decided by the Koreans themselves, without the interference of outsiders. In the same vein, the North Korean regime refuses to submit to a nationwide general election supervised by the United Nations. Since more than two-thirds of the population now resides in South Korea, and since most of these are probably adamant opponents of communism, the communists could not hope to win a majority in a truly free election.

The North Korean propaganda mechanism has sought to exploit every available opportunity to create a favorable image of the Pyongyang regime in the minds of the South Korean masses. The regime has also sought to gain propaganda advantages by proposing limited intercourse between the two parts of Korea. For instance, it advocated exchange visits of "cultural and commercial personnel." It also offered to enter into "economic exchange and cooperation in order to salvage the economic catastrophe of South Korea." In addition, it advocated the exchange of mail between the two parts of Korea. It even offered, in 1963 and 1964, to provide rice to relieve the South Korean population from hunger despite a continuing food shortage within its own territory.

It would be difficult to determine the impact of these proposals and propaganda in South Korea. It can be said, however, that the intensive campaign placed the regime in Seoul on the defensive and that it increased the desire of some segments of the South Korean population to open limited contacts with the north. The Pyongyang regime evidently believes that these desires can be nurtured so as to become, eventually, a strong anti-American force.

It is highly unlikely, however, that any significant segment of the

South Korean population is looking north for an alternative to its present situation, arduous though it may be. For this hostility, the communists have largely themselves to blame. Their inhumane behavior during the Korean War distilled deep and irreparable antagonism toward communism among the South Korean masses. This fact alone would make it difficult for the Pyongyang regime to organize a revolutionary base in South Korea or to promote guerrilla operations. The goal of peaceful unification is still a communist dream.

Pyongyang in the Sino-Soviet Dispute

The growing intensification of the cold war within the international communist camp has placed the Pyongyang regime in a serious dilemma. This is because the steadily worsening rift forced the North Korean communists to choose between the two contending powers at a time when North Korea could ill afford to alienate either. Moreover, various historical, geographical, and other factors made it very difficult for the Pyonyang regime to choose one side and reject the other.

For example, the North Korean Premier and most of his cohorts owed their power and position to the Soviet Union. Although Kim Il-sŏng, in his early revolutionary days, operated in Manchuria along with Chinese communists, it was the Soviet military command that nurtured his power in North Korea after 1945. In the initial period, Kim had to struggle against the returnees from Yenan, the group that had very close contacts with the Chinese communist leadership. Furthermore, it was the Soviet Union that armed and trained the North Korean Army, police, and Party. Until the Korean War, North Korea was unquestionably a Russian satellite.

Geography, on the other hand, places Korea closer to China. Although North Korea shares a few miles of border with the Soviet far east, it shares a long border with Manchuria, the industrial heartland of China. And historically, China had held suzerain rights over Korea; the Middle Kingdom long had a keen interest in Korean affairs. Thus, the dispatch of Chinese volunteers in 1950 was, in certain respects, a traditional gesture. So if the Pyongyang regime owed to the Soviet Union its creation, it owed to China its survival.

Despite North Korean claims that it has attained a balanced and self-reliant economy, the support of both the Soviet Union and Communist China is vital if the country is to develop its scientific, military, and industrial facilities. The antagonism of either of the powers would weaken Pyongyang's defenses and slacken its over-all technological and economic development.

Neutralism

These factors compelled the North Korean leaders, initially, to choose the policy of neutralism or nonalignment in the internecine conflict. Before 1961, when the dispute was being carried on without either side making public charges against the other, Pyongyang constantly reiterated the necessity of unity within the communist bloc, simultaneously eulogizing both the Soviet Union and Communist China. On questions that divided the two, Pyongyang took a nebulous and middle-of-the-road attitude obviously aimed at placating the disputants. North Korea adopted an obscure position on the question of peaceful coexistence and the revolutionary struggle, as we have already mentioned. The issues of de-Stalinization and of the communes were met in similar fashion.

Although the Chinese Communist party took up the issue of de-Stalinization immediately after Khrushchev's secret speech, by publishing, on April 5, 1956, an article in *Jen-min jih-pao* that stressed the necessity of learning from Stalin's achievements as well as from his weaknesses, the Pyongyang regime did not mention Stalin's name for some years thereafter. *Minju Chosŏn*, the organ of the government, reprinted in its April 3, 1956, issue a *Pravda* article, "Why the Cult of Personality Does Not Have Any Relationship with Marxism-Leninism," without comment. The article did not mention Stalin by name and did not suggest that the dead hero had been disgraced. In the ensuing months, North Korean publications attacked the hero worshipers within the party and praised "adherence to the principle of collective leadership by our party's Central Committee headed by Comrade Kim Il-sŏng." [32] As has been suggested above, the poisoned edge of the ideological sword was directed against Ch'oe Ch'ang-ik and others, the very critics of the cult of personality centering around Kim. This emphasis upon the principle of collective leadership obviously satisfied Moscow. The policy was also one which would have been satisfactory to Peking because Pyongyang did not attack Stalin personally. Even after the Twenty-second CPSU Party Congress in November, 1961, Kim Il-sŏng did not choose to denounce Stalin. "The name of Stalin is well known among the Communists and the people of the entire world," said Kim. But, he continued, "The Soviet Communist Party members should know him better than anyone else. The problem of how to evaluate Stalin's activities in the U.S.S.R. belongs to the category of intra-Party problems of the CPSU." [33]

This clever neutralism can also be observed with regard to the issue of agrarian collectivization. As is well known, North Korea's agricultural collectivization program closely paralleled China's, in timing and in methods. Thus, the experimental stage was launched in August, 1953; a full-scale collectivization was begun in November, 1954; and the movement was completed by August, 1958, when there were 13,309 cooperatives averaging 80 households each. In October, 1958, after the Chinese adopted the commune system, the Pyongyang regime announced the merger of small cooperatives into larger agrarian administrative units quite similar to the Chinese communes. Instead of 13,309 cooperatives, there would be only 3,843, each consisting of 300, rather than 80, households. The average acreage of a cooperative would be 500 *chŏngbo* (i.e., 1,225 acres) rather than 130 *chŏngbo*.[34]

Clearly, North Korean collectivization was modeled after Chinese. The North Korean communists, however, seem to have exercised enough prudence to avoid offending their Russian comrades. For instance, Pyongyang retained the term "cooperative," even though the Chinese adopted the term "commune" in July, 1958. Nor was any claim made in North Korean publications that the *ri* cooperatives were the "practical road of transition to communism." [35] Thus the North Korean communists could justify their agrarian policy merely as an extension of the Soviet Union's experience with "higher type cooperatives" or something similar to the giant cooperatives formed in 1958 in Bulgaria. No clear-cut explanations have been offered by Pyongyang.

Pyongyang Leans Toward Peking

However, as Sino-Soviet relations worsened after the Twenty-second CPSU Congress in October and November, 1961, and as various foreign policy issues became critical, the North Korean leaders began to adopt more distinct policies. For example, North Korea refused to follow the Russian line in denouncing the Albanian Workers' Party and its leader, Hoxha. On November 8, 1961, on the occasion of the twentieth anniversary of the founding of the Albanian Party, the North Korean leaders sent a warm congratulatory message praising its achievements and its leadership. At the enlarged plenum of the Central Committee of the Korean Workers' Party on November 28, 1961, Kim Il-sŏng reiterated the urgency of maintaining the unity and solidarity of a socialist camp that would include the Albanian Party. He further underscored the importance of proletarian internationalism, emphasizing the equality of each party and the principle of noninterference in the internal affairs of other parties. Again, on November 28, on the occasion of the seventeenth anniversary of the liberation of Albania, Pyongyang sent a eulogistic congratulatory message. The North Korean position on Albania has not changed since.

On other foreign policy issues that intensified the schism, such as the Sino-Indian dispute and the Cuban crisis, North Korea stood firmly behind the Chinese. The Nehru government was condemned as an aggressor and as a reactionary force working with the American imperialists. On the Cuban issue, the Pyongyang leaders denounced the appeasement of American imperialism as futile, and they urged all friends of peace and socialism to stand firm and to force the American imperialists to "take their bloodstained hands off Cuba at once."

On the more explosive issue of revisionism, the North Korean communists have taken a very consistent attitude since 1956. Although the March, 1956, issue of the Party's theoretical organ, *Kŭlloja*, faithfully reproduced Khrushchev's speech at the Twentieth CPSU Congress, in which he praised Yugoslavia's display of "creative Marxism" and stressed the necessity for strengthening cooperation with Yugoslavia,[36] international revisionists were indirectly attacked after the August plenum of the Korean Workers' Party's Central Committee for having aided the cause of the anti-Party, Ch'oe Ch'ang-ik's clique. The January, 1957, issue of the same journal printed an article that attacked "some elements that consciously or unconsciously serve the imperialist forces by wearing the mask of a friend of Communism yet strive to split the ranks of international Communism and revise Marxism-Leninism." This was followed by two more virulent articles in February and June, 1958. Regarding the Yugoslav Ljubljana Program (March, 1958), *Kŭlloja* carried translations of two derogatory articles in the Moscow publication, *Kommunist*.

This hostile attitude toward Yugoslavia continued after the Soviet Union had begun to woo Tito in an effort to bring Yugoslavia back into the communist camp. In 1962, even while the Soviets and Tito were exchanging visits in Belgrade and Moscow, the organs of Pyongyang were blatantly attacking Tito as a subversive traitor to the international communist movement and a faithful lackey of American imperialism. On June 23, 1963, Chairmen Liu Shao-chi and Ch'oe Yong-gŏn issued a joint statement in Peking expressing complete agreement on:

> . . . the question of further consolidating and developing relations of friendship, unity and mutual assistance and cooperation between the two Parties and the two countries and on important questions concerning the current international situation and the international communist movement.

Their joint statement on revisionism is worth quoting at length:

> The modern revisionists emasculate the revolutionary essence of Marxism-Leninism, paralyze the revolutionary will of the working class and working people, meet the needs of imperialism and the reactionaries of various countries, and undermine the unity of the socialist camp and the revolutionary struggles of all peoples. They do not themselves oppose imperialism, and forbid others to oppose imperialism. They do not want revolution themselves and forbid others to make revolution. Both sides stressed that the struggle against modern revisionism has an important

bearing on the future of the revolutionary cause of the proletariat and working people of the world as well as the destiny of mankind . . .[37]

These overt deviations of Pyongyang from the Moscow policy line could not be ignored by the Russians for long. According to the *Peking Review* of December, 1962, the Czechoslovakians and others attacked the North Koreans at the Twelfth Congress of the Czechoslovak Communist Party (December 4 to 8) for opposing "baseless charges" against the Chinese. Further, at the Sixth Congress of the East German Communist Party, held in Berlin in January, 1963, the North Koreans were treated as complete outcasts. The Pyongyang radio (January 29) was outraged:

> The Congress of the German Socialist Unity Party did not give the delegates of our party any opportunity to deliver a congratulatory speech on one or another pretext while giving the floor even to the revisionist Tito group of Yugoslavia.

What was worse, from the North Korean viewpoint, was that the Yugoslavian delegate was allowed to abuse the Chinese and that the Congress applauded when he did so.

Evidently these disciplinary measures, and other tactics, designed to bring the North Korean Party into the Soviet fold, failed. Indeed, throughout 1964 and early 1965, the Pyongyang regime issued a series of virulent attacks against the revisionist camp, which amounted to a declaration of war upon Khrushchev and his successors. Nor is there any indication yet that the Kosgyin visit of early 1965 altered Kim's total identification with Peking.

North Korean Motivations

What are the factors that drew the North Korean communists closer to the Chinese? Is the shift in the North Korean attitude a temporary phenomenon, or are there any deep-rooted causes for it?

An editorial in *Nodong Shinmun* (*Labor News*), the official organ of the Korean Workers' Party, on October 28, 1963, explained the factors involved in remarkably blunt fashion and suggested that the North Korean communists' discontent with the Soviet Union has been brewing for a number of years. First of all, the editorial was emphatic in stressing the necessity of recognizing the changing nature of international communism. The editorial admitted that the Soviet Union had been the only base for world revolution and that its support and protection was therefore a "holy and internationalistic action." Today's socialist camp, however, encompasses 13 states. It was impossible, in this situation, that one big power could represent the socialist camp and dictate the course of world revolution:

No matter how large or how developed a nation may be, the power of that nation cannot replace that of the entire socialist camp, nor can it play the role of the entire socialist camp.

The editorial urged, instead, that the equality of fraternal parties should be respected and that the notion of hierarchical order should be eliminated from the socialist camp. It was no longer possible or desirable for any one nation to order and control others from the center. No pressure should be exerted in interparty relations, and the anachronistic notions of "backward Asia" and "superior and inferior peoples" should be discarded. Decisions of one party's congresses should not be imposed on others as "common programs," and economic assistance should not be used as a means of controlling the internal politics of other parties.

The editorial presented a number of specific examples of Soviet interference in the domestic politics and policies of North Korea. The Soviet Union had "attempted to force 'the anti-cult-of-personality movement' upon other parties, and attempted to interfere with domestic politics of the fraternal parties and nations through that slogan," whereas it was "absolutely not permissible to carry out activities to overthrow the leadership of fraternal parties and nations." Here the editorial seemed to be referring to the attempt by Ch'oe Ch'ang-ik and others to overthrow the leadership of Kim Il-sŏng in 1956, after the de-Stalinization campaign was launched in the Soviet Union; evidently the Soviet Union was directly implicated in the unsuccessful attempt. A close parallel can be drawn between this situation and the purge of Marshal P'eng Te-huai in Communist China.

The editorial also stated that "in the past some comrades neither understood nor supported our party's policies on socialist construction." Without understanding the conditions in other countries, these comrades had disparaged the policies of the North Korean party by characterizing the five-year plan as "illusion," asserting that there was no need to construct a machine-production industry, and claiming that the speed of agricultural "cooperativization" was too rapid and that North Korean agriculture could not be organized into cooperatives because of the lack of agricultural machinery.

The editorial also charged that "some people who have been accustomed to interfere with other nations' domestic politics" not only had ignored the achievements of the fraternal parties, but had always suspected the fraternal parties and strained their eyes to see whether the fraternal parties observed their instructions and closely followed their experience. These people, the editorial continued, unilaterally demanded that other parties publish and broadcast the decisions of a certain party, and attempted to supervise instruction in a certain party's history and even a certain nation's language. The interference extended even over the showing of movies of certain nations. In short, the Soviet Union displayed big-power chauvinism and ignored the principle of equality and mutual respect among the parties. There was, in fact, no difference between the past actions of the Soviet Union and what the editorial called the relationship between imperialistic nations.

This tirade against the Soviet Union also discussed the opposition of "some people" to North Korea's emphasis on heavy industry, which began in 1953, and to its attempt to construct an independent national economy. The editorial argued against the idea of a "united economy of the socialist states," the philosophy behind the Comecon (Council of Mutual Economic Assistance), which it regarded as an attempt to eliminate the economic independence of various states. The policy of the division of labor would reduce various countries to annexes to one or two nations and would have them serve the interest of those nations. The editorial concluded by discussing the necessity of supporting the revolutionary struggles of all the people of the world and by stressing the need to oppose revisionism.

Roots of North Korean Behavior

The events of the postwar period and the statements issued by the North Korean regime thus permit us to indicate some of the basic factors in recent North Korean behavior. First, North Korea's maturity of power and progressive assertion of independence should be emphasized. Maturity of power did not in itself dictate a given position for North Korea, but the Pyongyang regime's sense of independence has been heightened by joining the side of the Chinese and thereby rejecting the Soviet Union, which had exercised overlordship in Korea before the Korean War. This factor is valid only so long as the Chinese recognize and respect the independence and equality of North Korea in future relations, but there are many indications that the Chinese are acting with great sophistication.

Closely connected with this factor are the similarities in the problems encountered by two countries and in the timing of their revolutions. Both the Chinese and Korean communists could accept without qualification Sun Yat-sen's famous words, "The revolution has not yet succeeded." The Chinese still have Formosa, and the North Koreans still have South Korea, to liberate. In the opinions of both the Chinese and Korean communists, the American imperialists alone obstruct the task of unification of their respective countries. It must indeed vex the communists in Peking and Pyongyang that the revisionists do not themselves oppose imperialism and that they discourage others from doing so.

Up to the present, Western scholars have not paid sufficient attention to the probability that the events surrounding the Korean War played an important role in shaping Sino-Soviet relations. The possibility of North Korea's disappointment over the Soviet Union's unwillingness to commit itself fully to the war has already been discussed. It has also been suggested, elsewhere, that at the time of the truce negotiations, the Chinese may have wanted to bargain with the United States on the Formosa question and that they failed to get full Soviet support on the matter, at the United Nations and elsewhere. Did the Chinese request Russian assistance in 1950, and again in 1956, to compel the withdrawal of the United States Seventh Fleet from the Formosan strait? In any event, the Chinese and North Korean communists share common animosities and complaints against the United States, and neither the Formosa question nor Korean unification is aided by the Soviet Union's policy of appeasement.

The similarities in the timing of revolutions also create similar attitudes toward economic development. It is natural for Communist China and North Korea to desire rapid economic development and to anticipate generous aid from the Soviet Union. The withdrawal of Soviet technicians from China in 1960 was, of course, a direct affront to the Chinese, a heavy blow that they will never forgive. And the withdrawal of Russian technicians from China certainly had relevance to North Korea, where economic sanctions could also be applied. North Koreans may also have been disappointed by the limited amount of Soviet aid in the postwar era, particularly after 1957. North Korea's stress on independence, self-reliance, and on the equality of the parties (issues that concern Albania as well as North Korea) must be seen in this light.

In the current dispute, one must not lightly dismiss factors of personality. Although with modifications, Khrushchev attempted to play the role of Stalin in international communism when neither his qualifications nor the spirit of the times allowed him to do so. In the eyes of Asian communists, Khrushchev could not possibly have been more than one of the equal members of the international leadership. It was essential, therefore, that he consult other leaders on such matters as de-Stalinization. Nor had he any right to interfere in the internal politics of individual parties. Khrushchev's record is poor in these respects. He evidently abetted the antiparty wings of Marshal P'eng Te-huai in China and of Pak Ch'ang-ok and Ch'oe Ch'ang-ik in North Korea. At a time when both the Chinese and North Korean Parties had already passed through their adolescent stage of development, not even Stalin could have gotten away with such actions. How could Peking and Pyongyang have ignored such "imperialist" deeds when they were committed by an upstart? The crucial factor here is not the proportional power and strength of respective countries and parties; it is fundamentally a question of pride, honor, dignity, and emotion—the force of nationalism.

Conclusions

North Korea has made considerable strides in the postwar era, both in the economic and the political spheres, although many problems are yet to be solved. These strides, however, have cost heavily in terms of individual dignity and human rights. This is a Stalinist era for some ten million North Koreans. Throughout this period, the communist leaders have strongly emphasized nationalism, both in internal and foreign policies. In the foreseeable future, North Korean communists are likely to continue these policies, demanding increased recognition in the international communist camp. The North Korean communists' sense of self-importance has been growing rapidly with time, and they have shown increased arrogance both at home and abroad. Posterity may record that, in the early 1960's, the leaders of the Korean Workers' Party, dizzy with success, were still facing problems—both domestic and foreign—that rendered their long-range position precarious.

Stalinism in the East: Communism in North Korea

1. For details of the pre-1950 period, see my article "Politics in North Korea: Pre-Korean War Stage," *China Quarterly*, No. 14 (April-June, 1963), pp. 3-16.
2. *Kin Nichisei Senshū* (Selected Works of Kim Il-sŏng) (Kyoto, 1952), III, 48.
3. Kaigai jijō chōsasho (ed.), *Chōsen yōran* (*Summary Facts on Korea*) (Tokyo, 1960), p. 141.
4. Korean Central News Agency, *Chosŏn Chungang Nyongam* (*Korean Central Almanac*) (Pyongyang, 1962), p. 46.
5. For the indictment and sentencing of the 12 men, see *Chosŏn munje yŏngu* (*Researches on the Korean Problem*), No. 8, August, 1953 (Tokyo). Also *Nodong Shinmun* (*Workers' Daily*) (Pyongyang), August 8, 1953.
6. Kim Ch'ang-sun, *Puk Han siponyŏn-sa* (*Fifteen-year History of North Korea*), (Seoul, 1961), pp. 155-157.
7. *Ibid.*, p. 157. Also see Glenn D. Paige and Dong Jun Lee, "The Postwar Politics of Communist Korea," *China Quarterly*, No. 14 (April-June, 1963), p. 22. Dong Jun Lee was in North Korea until February, 1959, as a reporter for *Pravda*.
8. *Kim Il-sŏng sŏnjip* (*Selected Works of Kim Il-song*), Pyongyang, 1960, V, 392. In his speech of March 3, 1958, the Premier admitted that there was no actual proof of participation by Kim, Pak, or O in a conspiracy for "an antirevolutionary riot," but they had allegedly "expressed to each other" the desire to overthrow the Party and eliminate the Party leadership.
9. Electrical generation in 1953 was reduced to 36 per cent of the 1949 level; fuel production, including coal, to 11 per cent; chemical industry to 22 per cent. The following industries were completely demolished: iron ore, pig iron, steel, lead, copper, electric motor, transformer, coke, sulfuric acid, chemical fertilizer, carbide, caustic soda, and cement. Democratic People's Republic of Korea, Academy of Science, *Chosŏn T'ongsa* (*Outline History of Korea*) (Hak-u sobang reprint ed., Tokyo, 1959), III, 285.
10. Cf. *Kim Il-sŏng sŏnjip*, V, 145, 147, 280-282.

11. *Ibid.,* IV, 39.
12. "On Enlarging the Production of People's Consumer Goods and Improving the Merchandise Circulation," June 7, 1958, *ibid.,* V, 518.
13. Cho Chae-sŏn, *Chosŏn minjujuui inmin konghwaguk sahoe kyŏngje jedo (The Socio-Economic System in the Democratic People's Republic of Korea)* (Pyongyang, 1958), pp. 35-36.
14. *Minju Chosŏn (Democratic Korea),* (Pyongyang), April 24, 1963.
15. Yi Sok-sim, "Construction of Independent National Economy in Our Country," *Kŭlloja (The Worker)* (Pyongyang), November, 1962 (No. 19), p. 14.
16. Cho Chae-sŏn, *op, cit.,* p. 36.
17. An Kwang-jŭp, "Our Party's Over-all Policies in Post-War Socialist Construction of the Economy," Kim Il-sŏng taehak, *8.15 haebang 15 chunyon kinyom nommunjip (Essays Commemorating the 15th Anniversary of the Liberation)* (Pyongyang, 1960), p. 32.
18. The ratio of savings in the Soviet Union in 1926 and 1927 was 16 to 17 per cent, although it was raised in 1932, the last year of the first five-year plan, to 27 per cent. In China, the national savings in 1952 were 15.7 per cent, but were raised to 22.8 per cent in 1956, the last year of the first five-year plan. *Ibid.*
19. Ministry of Foreign Affairs, D.P.R.K., *Democratic People's Republic of Korea* (Pyongyang, 1961), p. 20.
20. "On Our Party's Policy for the Future Development of Agricultural Management," November 3, 1954, *Kim Il-sŏng sŏnjip,* IV, 194.
21. For example, see the April, 1955 "Thesis on the Characteristics and the Tasks of Our Revolution," *ibid.,* IV, 206.
22. Kim Il-sŏng stated on September 20, 1957, that "The heroic struggle of the Korean people has heightened the international position of our country to an unprecedented level." *Ibid.,* V, 161.
23. "For the Future Development of Light Industry," January 29, 1958, *ibid.,* V, 284.
24. "On Eradicating Dogmatism and Formalism from Ideological Activities and Firmly Establishing *chuch'e,*" *ibid.,* IV, 325.
25. *Ibid.,* p. 326.
26. *Ibid.,* pp. 336-337.
27. These progressive scholars, known as the *silhak* (practical-learning) group, stressed, in order to restore the glory of Korea, the necessity of learning practical matters and things Korean, as against studying metaphysics.
28. "On Our Party's Policies for the Future Development of Agricultural Management," November 3, 1954, *ibid.,* IV, 188-189.
29. *Ibid.,* p. 189.
30. For the initial proposal of Nam Il, on April 27, see U.S. Dept. of State, *The Korean Problem at the Geneva Conference,* April 26-June 15, 1954, Dept. of State Publication No. 5609, Washington, D.C., 1954, pp. 39-40. For Minister Pyun's counter proposal see pp. 123-124.
31. See the speech of Ch'oe Yong-gon, the Chairman of the Presidium of the Supreme People's Assembly, "For the Further Promotion of Peaceful Unification of the Country," Supplement to *Korea News* (Pyongyang), No. 33 (1960), p. 24.
32. See for example Ho Il-hun's article, "Various Problems in the Correct Fulfillment of the Principle of Collective Leadership," *Kŭlloja (The Worker),* December, 1956, pp. 92-102.
33. For the text of Kim's speech at the Enlarged Plenum of the Fourth Central Committee of the party see *Nodong Shinmun,* November 28, 1961.
34. For details see my article, "The 'Socialist Revolution' in the North Korean Countryside," *Asian Survey,* II, No. 8 (October, 1962), 9-22.

35. *Cf. Peking Review,* September 16, 1958, p. 23.
36. *Kŭlloja,* March, 1956, pp. 50-53.
37. See "Joint Statement of President Choe Yong Kun and Chairman Liu Shao-chi," Supplement to *Korea Today* (Pyongyang), No. 7, 1963.
38. The opening assault came at the beginning of 1964: "Those steadfast Marxist-Leninists unjustly expelled from certain parties cannot but unite themselves and form new communist organizations in the interests of the revolution. Their action is entirely justified." *Minju Chosŏn,* January 28, 1964.

Selected Bibliography

Facts About Korea. Pyongyang: Foreign Languages Publishing House, 1961.

For Korea's Peaceful Unification. Pyongyang: Foreign Languages Publishing House, 1961.

Korea Today. (Monthly magazine, published by the Foreign Languages Publishing House, Pyongyang.)

Paige, Glenn D., "North Korea and the Emulation of Russian and Chinese Behavior," in *Communist Strategies in Asia,* ed. A. Doak Barnett. New York: Frederick A. Praeger, Inc., 1963, pp. 228-61.

Rudolph, Philip, *North Korea's Political and Economic Structure.* New York: Institute of Pacific Relations, 1959.

Scalapino, Robert A., ed., *North Korea Today.* New York: Frederick A. Praeger, Inc., 1963. (Reprint of articles published in *China Quarterly,* April-June, 1963.)

U.S. Department of State, *North Korea: A Case Study in the Techniques of Takeover.* Washington, D.C.: Government Printing Office, 1961.

North Vietnam

A Qualified Pro-Chinese Position *

John C. Donnell

The Democratic Republic of Vietnam (DRV)
has consolidated its political authority and undertaken ambitious
industrialization and agricultural collectivization
programs since its defeat of the French in 1954. On the
other hand, it has been plagued by food shortages,
a continuing lack of enthusiasm for farm
collectivization and under-par achievements
in its industrial sector.
Furthermore, it is committed to the direction and
support of a protracted "war of liberation"
in South Vietnam, a war involving great potential hazards
to its own people and economic plant in view of a
possible widening or escalation of the war

by the United States, as well as potentially great political and economic rewards if the war should bring national reunification on Hanoi's terms. The northern government's reactions to all of these problems are inter-meshed with its policies for coping with severe pressure from China and the U.S.S.R. for a clear-cut commitment to one side in the bloc dispute.

The DRV borrowed heavily from Chinese Communist experience during the first years of peace and reconstruction following the French withdrawal. Even then, though, important elements of Soviet influence were still visible in its political stance. But in 1962 the DRV became even more overtly sympathetic to the Chinese line and then swung even more markedly toward the Chinese position beginning in March, 1963.

A year later, the DRV was counted in the Chinese camp—some observers believed it had passed the point of no return—but it still qualified its criticism of the U.S.S.R. and attempted to demonstrate some of the remarkable skill it had shown earlier in straddling the widening gulf between Peking and Moscow.

The *Lao Dong* Party has recently been charged with a Chinese-style mass indoctrination campaign to strengthen the people's determination to meet persistent domestic problems and new threats of an extension of the southern war to the north. Let us turn now to the *Lao Dong* and its role in the Vietnamese Revolution.

Historical Development of the Vietnamese Workers' Party

The *Dang Lao Dong Viet Nam,* or Vietnamese Workers' Party, suc-cessor to the old Indochinese Communist Party, claimed in early 1963 to have a membership of 570,000, a little over 3 per cent of the North Viet-namese population of approximately 17 million at that time. The continuity of leadership has remained remarkably stable, enabling the Party to surmount leadership crises without any important purges in its top ranks for many years. A very brief recapitulation of the Party's de-velopment will be useful.

In 1930, Ho Chi Minh, or Nguyen Ai Quoc, as he was then known, succeeded in fusing three existing squabbling communist groups, and the new Vietnamese organization was redesignated the Indochinese Com-munist Party. It was dissolved in November, 1945, as a tactic to preserve unity among, and communist control over, the many noncommunist na-tionalists backing the Vietminh fight for independence. From the time of its formal dissolution until the advent of the *Lao Dong* in March, 1951, communist organization and indoctrination were maintained through Marxist study groups.

The Vietminh—that is, the *Viet Nam Doc-Lap Dong Minh,* or

Vietnam Independence League—carried the banner of the war against French colonialism. It is generally believed to have been founded, again by Ho, in Kwangsi, China, in May, 1941. In February, 1951, over three years before the end of the war, the Vietminh was absorbed into a United Vietnam Nationalist Front or *Lien Viet* (i.e., *Mat-Tran Lien-Hiep Quoc Dan Viet-Nam*), but the communist component of its membership was consolidated in the new *Lao Dong* party which appeared the following month. The *Lien Viet* front had been launched in May, 1946, as a broad base of support for the revolution, and it included mass organizations not only for youth and women, but also for noncommunist parties, such as the Democratic and Socialist Parties, and for Buddhist and Catholic groups. This front was absorbed, in turn, in the still broader Fatherland Front (i.e., *Mat-Tran To-Quoc*) which emerged in September, 1955, and which was calculated to appeal also to southerners disaffected with the Ngo Dinh Diem regime. It urged reunification via a transitional stage of collaboration between sovereign northern and southern governments, but it never was regarded in the south as anything more than a tactical arm of Hanoi. Although it still is in existence, it has been eclipsed by the Hanoi-dominated National Liberation Front of South Vietnam (NLFSV), which has become prominently identified with the goal of reunification.

Socioeconomic Composition of the Lao Dong

Party membership has been recruited largely from the *petite bourgeoisie*, a fact blamed by the leadership for ideological shallowness whenever policy disputes arise. A 1953 *Cominform Journal* article stated that, of 1,855 key posts in the Party, only one-fifth to one-sixth were held by persons of peasant origin, and only one-twelfth by persons from workers' families. The rest were held by intellectuals or men from bourgeois families.[1]

The *Lao Dong* has clearly experienced great difficulty in its attempt to broaden its base of support among workers and even more among peasants. It had a small membership in 1946, reported later by Hanoi to have been only 5,000 (but said by the August 1952 *Cominform Journal* article to have been 20,000). The Party underwent a purge in 1950 and 1951, but expanded rapidly following its reconstitution as a mass communist party so that by independence, in 1954, it totaled 400,000. Not long afterward, however, widespread peasant dissatisfaction culminating in the peasant revolts in central Vietnam decreased the rate of growth. By early 1963, the total still was only 570,000.[2]

The 1956 peasant uprisings were sparked by harsh land-reform measures which owed considerable inspiration to the DRV's Chinese advisers. The *Lao Dong* was eventually obliged to soften these decrees, and the Party Secretary-General, Truong Chinh, stepped down, offering self-criticism to placate internal critics. The Army, largely of peasant origin itself, had remained steadfast even to the extent of crushing some peasant groups in pitched battles. But the experience shook Army leaders, who for some time remained critical of the Party for having lost touch with the peasants to such a serious extent.

The Party never really made amends to the hundreds of thousands of peasants and other survivors reportedly victimized by the land reform measures. It apparently decided to concentrate on building its strength in urban areas among workers and intellectuals, as well as in the Army, and to count on a longer-range development of proletarian consciousness among the peasantry.

The lack of "class comprehension" among the recent and youthful additions to the ranks of industrial workers has been noted in Party statements. In 1961, "young workers accounted for about 60 per cent of the total number and even 80 per cent in some areas," so that less than 40 per cent of the proletariat was composed of the comparatively class-conscious old-time workers or displaced farmers who had become industrial laborers during the period of French domination.[3]

Party leaders call regularly for heavier recruitment among youth and women.[4] The Lao Dong periodically has admitted its weakness among the ethnic minorities who live in the highlands which comprise three-fourths of the land area of the north. Thinness of Party membership is to be expected in remote areas, but a March, 1962, statement claimed that 35 per cent of the highland communities lacked Party cells.

Lax direction of Party cells comes in for continuing criticism. In early 1962, one Party spokesman criticized comrades in "some regions" for failing to convene any meetings for six months at a time or any criticism sessions for two years.[5] The most astonishingly candid critique of Party weaknesses in recent times was published in the Party journal in March, 1963, in which it was openly admitted that the Party had been seriously damaged over the past few years by a slackness of security precautions, so that bourgeois groups, "anti-Bolsheviks," and enemy agents had "succeeded in infiltrating leading organs to carry out sabotage."[6]

It said also that "U.S.-Diem agents" had penetrated "our own state organizations and recruited agents on construction sites, state farms, enterprises, . . . government organs, armed units and, particularly, in leading organs and important bases . . ." This resulted in the destruction of "some basic party organs" and "leading organs" as well as "the arrest or death of some cadres." The impression given here was that this anti-Party activity had occurred mostly in the past. More recently, however, during an "ordinary investigation conducted in the party's ranks, a number of persons were unmasked who falsely claimed to be party members and who attended party meetings or fulfilled party tasks for years." The role of "U.S.-Diem agents" in this picture is obviously emphasized to dramatize the external threat and to gloss over more routine organizational failings to cope with political apathy and flagging cadre morale in some areas. But the threat of infiltration has obviously caused growing concern as the DRV's own involvement in the Viet-Cong insurgency in the South has increased. In a wider context, such criticism represents a more routine weapon in intra-party struggle and it laid the political foundation for the later announcement of a sweeping ideological national vigilance against modern revisionism, as will be shown later.

Party Leadership and Factions

The striking tradition of political unity among Vietnamese communist leaders, possibly surpassing that of the Chinese communists, has been a factor of inestimable strength to the Vietnamese movement. True, contention between pro-Soviet and pro-Chinese factions has continued over the years and at times has been bitter. But even so, the antagonists' public statements have carefully blurred the identity of their targets and thus obscured the picture available to Party outsiders of the opposing line-ups and the men in the middle.

The *Lao Dong* Central Committee appears to have about 100 members, although the only officially revealed membership list, of 1960, named only 71. Forty-three are full members and the others are alternates.[7] The Politburo has 11 regular members, including President Ho Chi Minh (but not the aging figurehead, Vice-president Ton Duc Thang), and two alternates who serve ex officio from their top posts in the security appartus. The 11 full members are the following:

Ho Chi Minh: Chairman of the *Lao Dong* Central Committee; President of the DRV.

Le Duan: First Secretary of the Party; chief of the Vietminh resistance in South Vietnam from 1949 to 1951.

Truong Chinh: former Secretary-General of the *Lao Dong;* Chairman of the National Assembly Standing Committee; Chairman of the Nguyen Ai Quoc Training School for Party cadres.

Pham Van Dong: Premier.

Vo Nguyen Giap: Minister of Defense; Commander of the Vietnamese People's Army; a Vice-premier.

Le Duc Tho: chief of the Vietminh resistance in South Vietnam from 1951 to 1954, after clashing with Le Duan, the earlier chief.

Nguyen Duy Trinh: a Vice-premier.

Nguyen Chi Thanh: a high-ranking general and head of the Political Department of the Army until 1961; then divested of military rank and assigned to direct the agricultural collectivization movement.

Pham Hung: a Vice-premier.

Le Thanh Nghi: head of the Industrial Board under the Premier's office.

Hoang Van Hoan: specialist in international affairs and diplomacy.

Ho always has been the moderator of factional tension, although he himself has been regarded as friendly to the Soviet Union ever since his original training there in the early 1920's. He has had the political sagacity to plot an independent Vietnamese course between the Sino-Soviet antagonists whenever possible, and he has done much to dampen factional conflict within the *Lao Dong*. He even attempted strenuously to mediate between Mao and Khrushchev, as at the 1960 Congress of the 81 Communist Parties in Moscow. At this writing, Ho is 75 and has spells of poor health. Although he still appears frequently in public, his participation in important diplomatic trips abroad and the enunciation of important policy statements in his own right has declined.

Le Duan, a founding member of the Indochinese Communist Party, has risen rapidly in Party councils since 1951, when he was relieved of his command of the Vietminh resistance in the south and replaced by Le Duc Tho, and particularly since 1957. He has traveled abroad, as member and leader of DRV delegations to important conferences, and he led the early 1964 delegation to Moscow (with stops in Peking) on the ticklish business of seeking increased material support from the Soviets while the DRV was taking a pro-Chinese line in the dispute within the communist bloc. His policy statements have been accorded the prominence due a very powerful Party leader. His speeches veered progressively toward the Chinese line in 1963 and 1964, but he has been careful to give the Soviet Union its due for earlier revolutionary inspiration and for diplomatic and economic assistance to the DRV, and he has continued to express continuing hope for Sino-Soviet solidarity and to direct moderate pleas to Moscow to see the error of its modern revisionism. Le Duan and Le Duc Tho are known to have retained a mutual antagonism from their earlier clash in the south, but the implications of this to the rift in the communist bloc are not clear.

Truong Chinh (an alias meaning "long march"), the Party's leading ideologist and the leader of its pro-Chinese faction, developed a strong following in the Party during his lengthy tenure as Secretary-General from 1941 to 1956. Later he developed his new post of Chairman of the Standing Committee of the National Assembly into one of new authority. Chinh is believed to enjoy the support of Politburo members Nguyen

Duy Trinh and Nguyen Chi Thanh. Thanh's removal from the Army, in 1961, probably occurred because he had challenged the authority of Giap. In 1963, Thanh appeared to have recouped a good deal of his former power, judging from the prominence given his militant speeches and articles.

General Vo Nguyen Giap, the brilliant soldier who heads the pro-Soviet faction of the Party, retains the strong affection of the people of the north as the hero of Dien Bien Phu, but his political fortunes within the Party undoubtedly have suffered during the DRV movement toward the Chinese position. He and Truong Chinh, once close collaborators, are arch foes. However, statements by Giap are now carried by the DRV press and radio endorsing the Party line that "modern revisionism" is the "main danger at present."

Premier Pham Van Dong is a diligent administrator identified mainly with carrying out policy for Ho, apparently including Ho's balancing of Party factions. He does not have a personal following in the Party, but is evidently respected by others who do.

Economic Development of North Vietnam

The basic and constant propaganda theme of the DRV is that "the common task of the Vietnam revolution is to build socialism in the North and simultaneously to carry out the national democratic revolution in the South in order to achieve peaceful reunification of the country . . ." The theme appears in numerous variations, some putting less and some more stress on the role of the north as an ideological and material base of the revolutionary effort in the south than does the above quotation, which is from a speech made by Le Duan in December, 1963.

The DRV and her allies in the communist bloc have been determined to make North Vietnam a showcase for communist developmental methods in southeast Asia and have placed typical emphasis on industrialization. Thus the first five-year plan for 1961 through 1965 (which follows a preliminary three-year plan) "sharply reflect[s] our Party's line concerning . . . particularly heavy industry." This has aroused some dissent within the Party and also has given rise to certain large projects of showpiece value, which apparently cannot always be defended on rigorous economic grounds. In the five-year plan, capital investment in industry is to increase from 36 per cent of the total to about 49 per cent, about 80 per cent of the latter in production goods. The investment in agriculture is to be "almost doubled" to 28 per cent. Total food production is to rise by 32 per cent, but most of the increase will be secondary crops: corn; sweet potatoes; beans; manioc; and so forth. The potential increase in rice production is leveling off, even with wider use of fertilizer and multiple cropping, and the recent campaign to move one million Vietnamese from the delta to the sparsely populated highlands can enlarge only the cultivation of nonrice crops.

Industrial production is supposed to increase annually by 20 per cent, and agriculture by 10 per cent, but the norms for 1963, a year of calamitous weather, had to be cut to 17 per cent and 6.4 per cent. An average annual food increase of 6.4 per cent is not large, considering the present low rates of consumption and the fact that little of the increase will be in rice, which is greatly preferred over the secondary foods. There is to be a similarly modest increase, 6.7 per cent, in other consumer goods.

These goals appear even less generous in light of the average annual increase in the population. The rate, based on the 1960 census, is claimed by the regime to be 3.5 per cent, but is probably around 3 per cent. Birth control is advocated by the regime, generally on the grounds of its benefits to mothers and children. The idea that it can be a solution to the food problem is skirted.

The DRV has a spotty record of economic attainment. Rice production, at the end of the preliminary three-year plan in 1960, was about 50 per cent below target, and five-year plan goals have not become noticeably easier to achieve. In 1963, industrial output rose a claimed 6.5 per cent, far short of the original goal of 13 per cent and even of the revised target of 7.9 per cent. The totals for rice and all other food production, moreover, dropped about 13 per cent below the 1962 level. Consequently, per capita food production was apparently the lowest since the war ended in 1954.[8]

Le Duan said, in April, 1962, that a peasant's average monthly income was about ten *dong*, or about 34 U.S. dollars per year. Workers averaged 27 to 100 *dong*, he said (the equivalent of $92 to $340 per year), but still suffered more shortages than peasants—a fact, he added ruefully, which the peasants often did not understand.[9] The regular monthly rice ration is supposed to be 15 to 18 kilograms (33 to 40 pounds) per person, depending on his age, physical condition, and so forth, but the ration is decreased when harvests are poor.

Economic Aid from Other Communist Countries

Chinese economic aid has outweighed that of the Soviet Union and its European satellites, though it may not have accounted for two-thirds of all aid, as sometimes reported. The total, from 1955 to 1963, was something over one billion dollars. The Chinese have favored outright grants, while the Russians have stressed long-term credits. Soviet aid has been significant in providing funds and technical assistance for over-all industrial planning. This inevitably has reflected to some extent Moscow's CEMA-based philosophy of economic integration of the communist bloc and specialized production by its members (the DRV is not a member of CEMA, the Council for Economic Mutual Assistance). Although this principle has been bitterly attacked by the Chinese, and although there have recently been more frequent echoes in DRV statements of the Chinese theme of self-sufficiency, Soviet assistance to the DRV could hardly have been condemned by any but the most fanatically pro-Chinese elements of the *Lao Dong*, since Hanoi is in such great need of any help it can get toward industrialization. Soviet aid apparently was reduced after the DRV's refusal to sign the test-ban treaty, but the extent of the reduction apparently has been less than originally supposed.

Soviet and European satellite aid has included credits for agriculture and mining, but it also has ranged through more advanced types of assistance to the economic infrastructure, e.g., electric power and communications facilities and machinery for heavy industry. Earlier Chinese programs provided basic construction materials for irrigation and transportation systems and for light industry. Peking has provided more technicians than the Soviet bloc—over 5,000 Chinese were said by Ho Chi Minh to have come to Vietnam by May, 1963—but many of them have been merely skilled laborers on road construction, for example. More recently, China has committed a large amount of its aid to the large Thai Nguyen industrial complex of plants producing pig iron (eventually steel) and allied products.

Impressive as the Thai Nguyen plant has appeared to the Vietnamese and to foreign observers, it appears to have been undertaken without sufficient preliminary research (the Chinese evidently decided to sponsor it during their own Great Leap Forward) and its economic viability will be limited primarily by the absence of coking coal in the DRV and the great cost of importing it. The high-quality anthracite which is plentiful there is mixed with other types of coal to produce substitutes, but these still cause eventual clogging by slag which can be removed only by periodically shutting down and dismantling the blast furnaces.

Collectivization Problems

The DRV's agrarian program has been in trouble for years because of popular resistance or apathy toward the vaunted benefits of collectivization and the frequently deplored lack of technical and administrative skills to carry it out effectively. The DRV has followed China in the progression from labor exchange teams of 30 or 40 members to lower-, then higher-level cooperatives, and finally to state farms, but it has not attempted to introduce communes. The emphasis on consolidation of the cooperatives during 1962 to 1964 added 2 per cent to the number of farmers involved in cooperatives, bringing the total to 87 per cent. Of the almost 30,000 cooperatives, one-third are of the more fully socialistic, "higher" type. By early 1964, over 10,500 of these comprised entire hamlets and 208 consisted of entire villages,[10] but the average cooperative in early 1963 was said to have 85 members. State farms were introduced in late 1955, and by 1962 there were 55, the majority being operated by the Army.[11]

Some of the highest ranking members of the Party, including Ho himself, have visited cooperatives to encourage greater effort and, in the process, have made some exceedingly candid remarks about recent difficulties. Le Duan, in a November, 1962, visit to Nghe An (where peasant outbreaks occurred in 1956) acknowledged that, the previous year, the peasants had complained to him about being compelled to join. He responded frankly with the collectivist rationale for the gradual erasure of the private plots distributed earlier: "We all know that, following the completion of land reforms, agriculture in the North, with very low average per capita cultivated acreage, was divided and barely self-sufficient. Such agriculture cannot satisfy the needs of socialist industrialization . . ."

The highlands which cover three-quarters of North Vietnam have posed special problems for the cooperative campaign and for the five-year plan goal of moving a million lowland Vietnamese to half a million hectares of new farmland there (this goal was whittled down to 450,000 hectares in 1963). The earliest groups of settlers were relocated in existing communities of ethnic minority peoples, but this caused considerable friction. Later migrant groups were assigned to separate areas, but, because these were not often provided with the favorable terrain and soil features of the sites already occupied, the result was greater hardship and lower production. By the fall of 1963, only about 50 per cent of the land reclamation and 17 per cent of the manpower adjustment (i.e., resettlement) goals had been achieved.[12]

Poor leadership and organization by government cadres have figured prominently in the weaknesses of the collectivization program. The regime admitted, for example, that: "In analyzing the cases of cooperatives which had to close down in early 1963, we have noted that the main cause was mostly that of Party commissioners who gave up their leadership." [13]

To combat these weaknesses, the Party launched a movement for the improvement of cooperative management and for strengthening state leadership in agriculture during the final two years of the 1961-through-1965 plan. It decided to assign a large force of administrative cadres to a relatively small percentage of cooperatives to devise a simple but more effective planning and management routine during the first 18 months and, then, during the final 18 months, to spread the new techniques to the rest of the cooperatives.[14]

The thorny question of farm production incentives drew conflicting recommendations from Party spokesmen in 1963, reflecting the debates in Party councils between the gradualists and the anti-revisionists on Vietnam's ideological position in the dispute among the communist countries and on domestic policies consistent with that position. Proponents of the hard line publicized instances of poor performance and failure in cooperatives where private cultivation and incentive payments were said to have gradually eroded the collectivist spirit.

The Party's great concern over the food problem comes to light in all manner of official utterances.[15] It produces continual exhortations to cadres and peasants not only to work harder but to improve state and party discipline and to deepen ideological understanding down to the level of the hamlet. Such statements indicate confidence in the regime's capacity to overcome difficulties but, at the same time, they reflect a tone of near desperation in prodding farmers to exert their utmost. An Agricultural Ministry report of January, 1964, told farmers of the crucial importance of getting the winter-spring crop started on schedule and urged, "If necessary, we can work day and night." [16]

Despite collectivization difficulties and the particularly low farm yields for 1963, and despite routine failures to achieve overly ambitious industrial norms, however, the DRV economy cannot be assumed to be on the point of collapse. Rather, it appears to be a moderately going concern claiming with some justification to have brought the people a measure of economic stability. And it has moved steadily forward in building the industrial plant it considers so vital to national power and prestige.

The DRV in the Sino-Soviet Split:
A Qualified Pro-Chinese Position

Before tracing the DRV's accelerated movement toward the Chinese camp in early 1963, we must emphasize to the reader that Hanoi has been directing and supporting the Viet-Cong insurgency in South Vietnam since its inception and that it has also been supporting the Pathet Lao in Laos. Therefore, it regards the issues in the Sino-Soviet split as crucial to its own security and development, not in an abstract ideological sense but with a critical eye to their applicability to DRV goals of building the socialist base in the North and winning the war in the South. The U.S.S.R. obviously is more easily able to afford substantial economic and industrial assistance, but Soviet arguments for peaceful coexistence with the noncommunist world and for evolutionary means of advancing the communist cause are far less attractive to Hanoi than the Chinese willingness to back a militant "liberation" campaign in South

Vietnam and furnish ideological justification and support for such campaigns in the international political arena. Threats by American and South Vietnamese spokesmen to extend the war to the North have heightened the anxiety with which Hanoi perceives these issues and increased intra-Party factional conflict over means to meet such threats. They also have generated additional demands by Hanoi on its bloc partners for material and diplomatic support for the Southern campaign.

Thus the *Lao Dong* has not come to its clearer endorsement of the Chinese line suddenly. As P. J. Honey points out, Hanoi's statements on peaceful coexistence, since the latter half of 1959, have had to reconcile this concept with the violent activities of its cadres in the South and have described peaceful coexistence as "a form of class struggle between socialism and capitalism." [17]

The DRV followed Moscow's earlier lead in the reconciliation with Tito but it renewed its original condemnation of Titoist revisionism when Tito published his Draft Program in 1958. Shortly thereafter, the Vietnamese press carried parts of a Peking editorial condemning Tito under the title "Modern Revisionism Must Be Criticized." It has continued the attack periodically ever since, and from early 1963 its fervor has matched that of the Chinese.

The independence of Hanoi's policy toward Albania has been comparable. The DRV has never supported Soviet attacks on Albania. Ho Chi Minh and others, however, have generally sought to avoid offending the U.S.S.R. over the issue, and they have intimated to the Chinese their disapproval of the unconditional Chinese support for Albanian aggressiveness in the split. This has been the basic DRV position on Albania since 1961, and both the communist giants have seen fit to let it stand.[18]

The North Vietnamese communist concern with national liberation struggles, and specifically with the Viet-Cong insurgency in South Vietnam, goes back to the long fight for independence from French colonialism. In 1960, however, the *Lao Dong* leadership signaled a new stage of its direct involvement and an acceleration of the southern campaign via the statements of Ho Chi Minh in 1959, of General Vo Nguyen Giap in early 1960, and of various leaders, including Ho and Le Duan, at the Third Party Congress in September, 1960. In December, the National Liberation Front of South Vietnam (NLFSV), a typical communist front, was formed in the south to rally the support of intellectuals and bourgeois nationalists as well as of peasants, workers, and former resistance fighters or Vietminh. A year later, the People's Revolutionary Party of South Vietnam emerged to assume the role of elite vanguard of the National Liberation Front. The PRPSV, which is the approximate equivalent in the South of the *Lao Dong* in the North, operates from headquarters called Central Office, South Vietnam (COSVN). Both COSVN and the headquarters of the National Liberation Front are located in or near northern Tay Ninh Province which borders on Cambodia.

In 1961, Hanoi continued to accelerate the flow southward of ex-Vietminh resistants who had been regrouped in the North in 1954-1955 and in that year the Viet-Cong scored striking successes. But in 1962 there was a reversal in the tide of war due to large-scale United States assistance to the Ngo Dinh Diem government. By early 1963, DRV spokesmen, including General Giap, had shed some of the optimism of their 1962 analyses of the war, and certain DRV statements to NFLSV cadres indicated that Hanoi preferred a consolidation of gains rather than attempts to expand the military effort at that time.[19]

More forthright acknowledgment of DRV direction of the war appeared in this period:

> The U.S.—Diemists . . . are well aware that North Vietnam is the firm base for the Southern revolution and the point on which it leans, and that our party is the steady and experienced vanguard unit of the working class and people and is the brain and factor that decides all victories of the revolution.[20]

Before going on to the events immediately precipitating the DRV's sharp turn toward China, let us note its position on the critical issues in the immediately preceding period. Peking had failed to get Hanoi support against Moscow at the 1960 Bucharest Conference but, as time went on, various events tended to bring the North Vietnamese and Chinese closer together. Let us examine some recent ones.

A long-pending issue before the tripartite International Control Commission charged with investigating and reporting violations of the 1954 Geneva Accords was resolved by an ICC condemnation of the DRV in June, 1962, for subversion in South Vietnam in the form of men and munitions sent from the North. The Indians long had refused to go along with the Canadians in voting against the Polish members of the Commission on this question; and well before the new charges against Hanoi were published, Hanoi, already informed of the Indian change of heart, had become furious with the Indians. This reinforced the DRV's sympathy toward the Chinese in the Sino-Indian border affair and the DRV subsequently gave a strong endorsement to Chinese policy in the Himalayas.

Even more important, Soviet policy in Laos had brought a military air supply channel through Hanoi to Kong Le but Hanoi saw this favorable situation end with the new Geneva Accords which formally ended the Lao conflict in July, 1962. Thus, the Soviets, after lending such direct support to the Lao insurgents, had led the communist negotiators at Geneva in the quest for a formula to guarantee a "neutral, sovereign and independent" Laos. Hanoi undoubtedly could foresee that the new state of affairs would permit continued DRV troop infiltration into Laos and thence on into South Vietnam. But even so, Hanoi may well have concluded that the settlement represented a final degree of Soviet willingness at that time to assist the Vietnamese "national liberation" struggle which left something to be desired in comparison with the Chinese potential for continued support of a more militant line toward South Vietnam.

In late 1962, Hanoi managed to express support for both the Soviet withdrawal of missiles from Cuba and the demands in Castro's "five points." The DRV last published strong evidence of political sympathy for the U.S.S.R. at the end of 1962, but the extent to which the DRV had already endorsed key elements of the Chinese line is shown in the following passages from an article in the November issue of the Party journal, *Hoc Tap*. Peaceful coexistence was attacked on the basis that: "The transition to socialism is not a spontaneous . . . phenomenon but is the result of a fierce class struggle between the socialist and capitalist systems and . . . of socialist and national liberation revolutions . . ." Revisionism was labeled "the principal danger at present," and dogmatism and sectarianism were called only secondary dangers. But it took a line on the Soviet role in bloc defense which was to become a casualty of the test-ban treaty polemics the next summer: "War is no longer predestined, is no longer unavoidable. The force protecting the world peace is now formed by the socialist countries, of which the U.S.S.R. is the core. . . ."

The temporary expressions of favor toward Moscow came in connection with the visits, in December, 1962, and January, 1963, of two Soviet delegations—General Batov's military group and members of the Supreme Soviet—and of Czech President Novotny who, with Ho Chi Minh, wrote a final communiqué with certain obvious pro-Soviet overtones. The Chinese showed their dissatisfaction with this state of affairs by ignoring the February 3rd anniversary of the founding of the *Lao Dong*. This, together with a deterioration of Sino-Soviet relations at the East German Party Congress in January—to a point where both antagonists appeared determined to widen the rift inexorably—seems to have shocked the DRV Politburo into remedial action. A statement was drafted appealing to the communist bloc nations for unity and recommending, specifically, an end to recriminations, a world conference of communist parties, and the acknowledgment of major responsibility for the meeting by the Soviet Union and China. The DRV Politburo revealed that it had made the first two proposals in letters to communist parties in January, 1962. It repeated its determination to continue playing the strongest possible role in the quest for unity. The statement was careful to pay roughly equal compliments to both the Soviets and Chinese, although it still called the Communist Party of the Soviet Union (CPSU) "the vanguard of the international Communist movement."

This statement was the first official DRV acknowledgment of the seriousness of the communist split. It served to heighten political and factional tensions at various levels, within and outside the Party, to such a point that Vo Nguyen Giap, known by the Vietnamese as leader of the pro-Soviet faction, released an article apparently intended to confirm that the Politburo statement had truly expressed the sentiments of unity within the leadership.[21]

Starting the Final Turn toward China: March, 1963

As Honey points out, Chinese news media ignored major events in North Vietnam, during the first few months of 1963, to an extent which indicated displeasure, probably over the General Batov and President Novotny visits. Hanoi's final turn toward China at this juncture was evidently made to conciliate her giant neighbor.[22] The most visible turning point came in a number of major speeches and editorials around the anniversary of Karl Marx's death on March 14. Politburo members Le Duan and Nguyen Chi Thanh spoke. Curiously, Duan's speech was not published until April, but then it was carried in full by the *People's Daily* and broadcast by the Peking radio.[23] This speech mirrored yet another facet of the Chinese line, attacking Soviet aid to bourgeois nationalist regimes (such as the United Arab Republic) on the grounds that a nationalist country's advance along the socialist path required the existence of "a strong Marxist-Leninist party." Nguyen Chi Thanh's speech spelled out past "leftist" as well as "rightist" tendencies within the *Lao Dong* in an analysis which echoed Chinese views but was still careful to laud both Soviet and Chinese revolutionary contributions in passages explicitly dealing with the two.

This spate of pro-Chinese statements paved the way for an even more concrete demonstration of DRV support for the Chinese ideological position, in the form of an invitation to ranking Chinese leaders to make a state visit to Hanoi. The occasion would inevitably bring new Chinese pressure on the DRV for an ever clearer alignment in the dispute, but the Vietnamese evidently considered this an acceptable price to pay for the reconciliation. The Chinese attitude toward the DRV did warm considerably at this juncture, as evidenced by Peking's publication, in mid-April, of important DRV documents and statements it had earlier failed to note.

In late April, Pham Van Dong helped pave the way for the Chinese arrival by a speech to the National Assembly in which he repeated DRV agreement with the policies of the Chinese People's Republic (CPR) on the Sino-Indian border conflict, Taiwan, and UN membership.

The six-day visit by CPR Chairman Liu Shao-ch'i and Vice-premier Ch'en Yi, which began on May 10, was the occasion of great fanfare for Sino-Vietnamese amity. It brought aggressive, but still veiled, anti-Soviet statements from the Chinese. The DRV backed some, but not all, of these, since the Vietnamese hewed to the line set down by Pham Van Dong in his April speech. Liu made two major speeches, one at a mass rally and the other at the Party's Nguyen Ai Quoc School for cadres. He attacked Khrushchev's modern revisionism on grounds of crucial importance to his hosts: "whether the people of the world should carry out revolution or not, and whether the proletarian parties should lead the world's people in revolution or not." The second speech, particularly, was a fiery one which frankly avowed that the fight against revisionism would be "protracted and complicated." [24]

The joint communiqué [25] issued by Ho and Liu at the end of the visit revealed that certain tensions remained unresolved. The DRV went along with the Chinese attack on revisionism as the "main danger" (and the Yugoslav version of revisionism was overtly excoriated), but a paragraph also explained why "it is also necessary to combat dogmatism." The principles of "unity," "independence and equality," and "unanimity" were held to govern relations and policy decisions within the communist bloc, clearly a pro-Chinese position since the Soviets had substituted "a single view" for "unanimity" in their reporting of the *Lao Dong* Politburo statement of January. Both sides desired "the development of nuclear superiority by the socialist countries"—the plural form here anticipating the DRV's later rejection of the Soviet Union's test-ban treaty argument that it could furnish single-handedly whatever nuclear capability might be required for the defense of countries in the communist bloc.

Liu's line on support of the war in South Vietnam was significant because it remained essentially the Chinese position into early 1964, when the Vietnamese tried to secure more specific guarantees. The communiqué said:

> The Chinese people firmly support the heroic South Vietnamese people's just and patriotic struggle against U.S. imperialism and the Ngo . . . clique, and regard this struggle as a brilliant example for the oppressed nations and peoples . . . fighting for liberation.

President Ho *alone* was described in the communiqué as holding that the Soviet Union and Chinese parties, as "the two biggest," bear the greatest responsibility in the international communist movement and that the unity [of these two] is the pillar of the unity of the socialist camp . . ." And only Ho was cited as believing that, through the efforts of the two big parties, along with the others, unity would be strengthened.

In their editorial comment on the visit, the Chinese stressed the importance of national liberation struggles so heavily as to give the impression that the DRV had agreed with the sharp opposition expressed by

Liu to Soviet interpretations of peaceful coexistence. The actual treatment given these two key concepts in the communiqué was as follows: "[Socialist countries] must strive for peaceful co-existence with countries having different social systems on the basis of the Five Principles, and must support the revolutionary struggles of all oppressed nations and peoples." The DRV did not come around to the bellicose Chinese position until July, when an unsigned article in the Party journal (described below) took a harshly militant stance on revolutionary struggle.

A most striking contrast to the outpouring of pro-Chinese sentiment during the Liu visit was presented one week after Liu's departure, in a newspaper article by Vice-president Ton Duc Thang. The occasion was the thirteenth anniversary of the founding of the Vietnam-U.S.S.R. Friendship Association, and the title was of particular poignance, given the situation: "May Vietnam-U.S.S.R. Friendship Last Forever." The article injected a wishful implication into Soviet policy when it thanked the U.S.S.R. for supporting the South Vietnamese people's struggle and then went on to pledge that the DRV would stand with the U.S.S.R., China, and other socialist countries to struggle for the success of the national liberation movement.

In May, however, there appeared another in the series of militant statements by Nguyen Chi Thanh, the authoritative tone and subject range of which indicated that Thanh had regained considerable power in the Party during its shift toward the Chinese position. In these pronouncements, Thanh was to press his earlier demand for ideological struggle, making only passing references to the secondary leftist dangers of dogmatism and sectarianism. Thanh spoke during his inspection of the military and political institute of the Army, especially warning "middle- and high-ranking officers" against any slackening of revolutionary militancy, any tendency toward softness and corruption. The Vietnamese Revolution, which had been plagued internally by *"petit-bourgeois* ideology" and "right passivity," "cannot stop halfway," Thanh said. "It calls for a radical change in the political and economic countenance, in ideology, and in outdated customs and traditions." Ideological training must be carried out "with persistent militancy," to raise the theoretical horizons of the proletariat, to push the "struggle against reactionary forces at home," and to aid in the suppression of "the counter-revolutionaries in the northern part of our country." As might be imagined, Peking found this speech to its liking.[26]

The DRV's muted treatment of the July Sino-Soviet talks in Moscow reflected its desire to minimize the ugly fact of disunity, as well as its determination to maintain what degree of independence it could, even while its radio and press coverage of these events clearly showed its decreased optimism that the talks could succeed. On July 3, Radio

Hanoi and the newspapers summarized parts of the CPSU June 21 resolution and the CCP July 1 declaration concerning the talks to begin on July 5, and expressed the usual hopes for unity. These news stories admitted that Sino-Soviet relations had deteriorated, but they were too brief and bland to convey a real understanding of the issues and the bitterness of the antagonists.

On July 9, Radio Hanoi began to broadcast the texts of the CPSU March 30 letter and, later, the Chinese Communist Party July 14 reply, over a series of transmissions extending more than a week and a half. But these were put on a channel which apparently is available only to a limited audience in the DRV.

Meanwhile, the negotiations for a limited nuclear test-ban treaty had served to impel the DRV even further toward the Chinese position. Official Vietnamese antagonism to the treaty emerged much more gradually than that of Chinese, again suggesting protracted intra-Party debates on the relative merits of the Chinese and Soviet lines. Hanoi had supported a Soviet Union initiative toward unilateral action to stop nuclear testing in the spring of 1958,[27] but six years later the Soviet role in test-ban negotiations appeared much more threatening.

A further leftward impulse in the *Lao Dong* line was registered in the unsigned July, 1963, *Hoc Tap* article noted earlier, which adopted the Chinese rationale for class struggle and "just wars," including wars for national liberation. This article, "The Renegade Tito Again Spews the Venom of Revisionism," decried Titoist and, implicitly, Khrushchevian peaceful coexistence, describing as an acceptable version of the doctrine one closely akin to the Peking line. It adopted also the Chinese view of the aftermath of a possible nuclear war: ". . . it would bring about extremely grave consequences," but it would result in the eradication of imperialism rather than the human race. Virulent as this commentary was, it still maintained a discreet vagueness in one brief passage which hinted that the test-ban negotiations probably were the major, or at least the latest, provocation.

In mid-July, a Hanoi newspaper said the test-ban treaty "has done nothing good for the struggle of the people of the world in upholding peace [and] . . . our government . . . assuredly will not sign it."[28]

News of the initialing of the treaty in Moscow was presented on the DRV radio on July 27, in a brief, factual announcement devoid of criticism. Three weeks later, however, the domestic radio service devoted unusual coverage to the signing of the treaty, including excerpts from the Chinese and Soviet statements of July 31, as well as a *Nhan Dan* editorial. The latter emphasized "U.S. and British imperialists'" attempts to use the test-ban negotiations to "split the socialist camp," implying that the U.S.S.R. had been a dupe of the imperialists.

In August, Hanoi identified China as the main victim: "[The treaty] restricts the socialist camp—first of all China—from rapidly increasing its defense potential." The Party journal stormed at "bourgeois nationalism, the concrete manifestations of which are big-nation chauvinism, racialism, internationalism, etc." but it did not fail to sound another veiled plea to the Soviet Union for support of national liberation struggles.[29]

In mid-August, the DRV announced its full approval of the Chinese call for a conference of all nations to discuss total nuclear disarmament. By September, an unsigned article in the Party journal defended the Chinese line on a wide range of issues, although its references to the Soviet Union still were more indirect and moderate than those of Peking.[30]

General Hoang Van Thai, Deputy Chief of Staff, advanced the pro-Peking trend in a September *Hoc Tap* article by backtracking from a thesis he had propounded in an article almost three years before. Now he stressed the decisive role in war of men rather than weapons, including nuclear ones. Earlier he had written, "Either we shall progress to acquire new techniques [and weapons] or we shall be exterminated," although he did include a weak statement on the importance of man's role. Thai now decried "weaponism," "the idea that whoever possesses the most numerous and strongest weapons will win," as the guiding principle of modern revisionists, who were "relying on their nuclear arsenal to revise the fundamental principles of Marxist-Leninism concerning class struggle."

A Truong Chinh speech to the Party's cadre school contained a fascinating analysis of the Vietnamese Revolution. Originally delivered in April, 1963, on "A Number of Problems concerning the August Revolution," it was published (in *Hoc Tap*) only in September. The apparent reason for the delay would seem to lie in the distinctive aspects of the Vietnamese Revolution, which Chinh claimed contrasted with both the Soviet and Chinese models, and in his urging that new methods—implied to be uniquely Vietnamese—must be found to cope with new situations.

In discussing the Vietminh's changed forms of struggle against the Japanese toward the end of World War II, Chinh said, "It was erroneous to stick fast to the old forms when the situation had changed." He urged the use of peaceful means when possible, but said it is "chiefly forceful means to seize power that count." And then he added, with remarkable candor, "We must at times provoke internal war or external war to eliminate the oppressors and exploiters from within or without, to establish a revolutionary dictatorship . . . and to build a new society."

The Vietnamese Revolution differed from its Soviet and Chinese counterparts in that the revolutionary impulse could flow from rural to urban areas or vice versa, or it could even become manifest simultaneously in rural and urban areas. Chinh said flatly that any truly deep and broad revolution of the masses "cannot be achieved without the association of rural uprisings with city uprisings," but he acknowledged that in a backward, colonial country, "the people's revolution to seize power must, in general, be carried out first in rural areas and later extended to the urban center . . ." The conventional Maoist sequence (not labeled as such, but undoubtedly easily recognized) occurred widely in north and north-central Vietnam, he said. However, the Revolution had "begun in the provincial cities and ended in the districts and villages" of "15 of the 21 provinces of South Vietnam . . . [and] seven provinces in South Central Vietnam." And "In eight other provinces in Central and South Vietnam, the uprising broke out the same day in villages and districts." Chinh made no attempt to minimize the contrast between these events and the Soviet and Chinese experiences. He commented that, while the Chinese movement from rural to urban areas had required 22 years for completion, the Vietnamese, because of "favorable conditions . . . did not have to move mechanically from villages to districts to provinces."

Although this analysis identified the Vietnamese Revolution more closely with the Chinese model than the Soviet, its insistence upon the uniqueness of the Vietnamese model was particularly interesting, coming from the man widely known as the leader of the pro-Chinese faction of the *Lao Dong*. Parts of the piece are puzzling, and indicate that deletions and revisions were probably made before publication.

However, it does furnish additional evidence that DRV leaders are responding to peculiarly Vietnamese political pressures and not exclusively to demands for ideological commitment to either the Soviets or Chinese.

Even as Party leaders sharpened their demands for a vigorous ideological campaign to reindoctrinate the Party and people, the Party journal in August carried a curiously contrary argument against "overly abstract, 'bookish'" applications of Marxist-Leninist doctrine to agricultural problems, and espousing a "practical" approach. The writer praised cadres in a successful Hung Yen provincial cooperativization campaign who did not apply the epithet "capitalist" to people striving to "accumulate and improve their private property," because "To overcome capitalist tendencies is not to stop the working people short of a good life."

The writer said that, in Vietnam,

> . . . where developed capitalism was never obtained, . . . certain comrades emphasize class struggle [and] the destruction of the exploiting class without realizing that socialism is at the same time an evolution from small-scale to large-scale production.

Similarly, he said,

> Many cadres, . . . excessively fearful of a spontaneous generation of capitalist spirit [refused to follow the government policy of allowing] each family a certain amount of land for private cultivation . . . forgetting that a small acreage well regulated by party decrees can never turn a peasant into a capitalist.

Thus, they unwittingly "nipped the peasants' incentive to produce, lowered the peasants' living standards, and impeded the cooperative movement."

This writer also turned his fire on "a number of comrades" who overemphasized industry at the expense of agriculture. Another departure from the Party's developing fervor against the *petit-bourgeois* mentality of the masses appeared in his insistence that a leader "must pay attention to the mass opinion because the mass not only informs us on many matters, but also has imaginative solutions . . . [and] carries out the ideas of the leader." [31]

Another *Hoc Tap* article, as late as September, 1963, urged the following approach to gain peasant support for the cooperative movement: "To take part in the campaign is to enrich yourself and your country." (An earlier Council of Ministers' resolution favored the payment of incentive prices as high as. 50 per cent above the regular prices for overquota food deliveries to the state.) [32]

These views clashed head-on with those which Nguyen Chi Thanh and two other writers expressed in Party journal articles in October. One of these stated flatly that so long as private property or "an individual plot of land" continued to be used for subsidiary family economy, there would continue to be "selfish and spontaneous petty bourgeois trends." The tone of most of the article was consonant with the Chinese line, but, again, the U.S.S.R. was chided only indirectly on the most crucial issue: To make the "great work of the October Revolution . . . successful all over the world . . . we must more actively support the revolutionary movement and the international liberation movement throughout the world."

Internal conflicts within the Party over issues in the Sino-Soviet dispute were acknowledged in this October issue of the Party journal to an unprecedented extent, but the accusations of political heresy and inconstancy remained so veiled they offered few hints as to the identity of the targets or the size of any uncommitted group between the pro-Soviet and pro-Chinese factions. One writer said:

> There are many comrades who have not affirmed their class standpoint or reacted quickly . . . [and] were not fully vigilant when faced with the views and arguments set forth by revisionism and right-opportunism.

Vague concepts about life, man, humanity, the new, etc., having no clear class content, dazzled the eyes of a number of comrades, thus preventing them from realizing these are only a copy of bourgeois views . . .

Even leading cadres in certain places hold subjective views . . . They maintain that the greatest problem at the present time is to concentrate our strength on leading the economy [and that ideological training is sufficient].[33]

Nguyen Chi Thanh's article on "Improvement of Our Proletarian Stand and Ideology" in the same issue was a scathing condemnation of revisionism. Thanh repeatedly assailed "a small number of comrades" for the error of failing to understand "the nature of imperialism through the complicated events occurring recently throughout the world." Some "do not trust the correct fighting methods adopted by the southern people" and "even tremble before the fierce struggle in South Vietnam."

Thanh confirmed that these deviationists had challenged a whole range of policies: Some had "even distrusted the party's line . . . [and] wished to reduce the rate of industrialization . . . to produce more consumer goods." In agriculture, these deviationists had "harbored doubts" about production achievements "and the superiority of agricultural cooperatives." Some had even maintained that private management was better than that of the cooperatives, "that the organization of cooperatives occurred too early, [and] that they were forced upon the peasants . . ."

Thanh censured two currently popular Vietnamese novels, *Coming of Age* and *Raising the Siege,* for bourgeois viewpoints. *Raising the Siege* follows a Vietnamese soldier's quest for meaning in the ugliness of war. Thanh accused the author of planting in his hero a bourgeois interpretation of a political commissar's counsel, so that the soldier comes to accept as his goal merely the "struggle to end war, devastation, slavery, and misery." Thanh insisted the writer should have seen that "revolutionary and just wars do deserve praise" and are the source of the combatant's glory.

Coming of Age had been condemned roundly by Hanoi newspapers and in an article on "Art and Ideology" in the Party journal two months earlier, for expressing what must have been some of the frankest criticism of life in the communist North since the Nhan Van-Giai Pham literary purge of 1956. The novel, dealing with the period from 1956 to 1960, was denounced for portraying a "disorderly and complex society, without describing socialist accomplishments." It allegedly depicted such events as workers' protests, including one before the Premier's office, workers threatening cadres with bodily harm, and workers beating an assistant manager, destroying machinery, and being lazy absentees.

The reviewer also detected an element of Titoist revisionism in "the idea of workers managing themselves."

The Central Committee's Ninth Session: Still Greater Militancy

The pro-Chinese faction pressed its Party dominance still further during the Ninth Session of the Central Committee in December, 1963, but there were signs of continuing factional strife and urgent efforts to restore Sino-Soviet unity. The still tense stiuation within the Party was indicated by the following facts: a communiqué on the December deliberations was not issued until January 20; an editorial published prominently the next day in all daily newspapers expressed even greater militancy; and a long speech given by Le Duan near the end of the meeting was published only in February. And, most significantly, a Truong Chinh speech described in Duan's report as recapitulating the debate and introducing the draft resolution was withheld indefinitely from release, as was the resolution itself.[34]

All three of the available documents portrayed a world riven by increasingly fierce class conflict and stressed the role of national liberation struggles. The need for Sino-Soviet unity was emphasized plainly and, again, hope was expressed for a world conference of communist parties. Only the communiqué condemned dogmatism and sectarianism, and it did this only once, although it repeatedly attacked rightist errors. Even so, it thanked the U.S.S.R. for its contributions to international communism and its aid to the DRV. Then, in sharp contrast to Chinese polemics, it said:

> Our party draws a clear political distinction between the Tito revisionist clique, . . . and people within the international communist movement who commit the error of revisionism or right-wing opportunism. Our attitude with regard to the Tito revisionist clique is to expose it consistently, and with regard to the mistaken people within the international communist movement, to struggle for the sake of unity.

The Le Duan speech was notable for its slanting of Marx's writing to point up the role of the peasantry in proletarian revolution, its stress on elements of Lenin's work emphasizing the revolutionary role of the peasantry, on Stalin's strict "carrying out and developing" of these ideas (e.g., "Stalin made great contributions to the Chinese revolution") and, finally, the work of the Chinese communists: "It is the CCP headed by Comrade Mao Tse-tung which has carried out most satisfactorily the instructions of the great Lenin." And, again, "As Lenin once said that the strategy of the Russian revolution was a model for all Communists the world over, nowadays we can also say that the strategy of the Chinese revolution is a model for many Communists in Asia, Africa, and Latin America."

Duan claimed that "only by constant attacks from the peoples of the world can the imperialists be prevented from waging war. Only by weakening them daily is their capacity to wage war reduced daily and the possibility of protecting peace increased daily . . ."

On political deviation at home, Duan said that "a few of our party members, the majority of whom are intellectuals," believed that the *Lao Dong*, "a small party born in a former colony with a backward agriculture and a low cultural level . . . can hardly understand Marxist-Leninist science and complex international problems." He flayed this along with other varieties of "opportunism." Near the end of his long speech he set forth four Party tasks, three of which concerned the deepening of cadres' and Party members' grasp of the Party line and its stand against revisionism. The other was a call to increase Party discipline and tighten its organization, from the basic cell on up. Duan appeared to plead with his audience: "We must be very vigilant before modern revisionism. It is a terrible calamity for the revolutionary movement because, if it succeeds in infiltrating our party, it will be able to destroy the revolutionary spirit of our party and people . . ."

The same themes were repeated in a "decision" on ideological goals released by the Politburo, evidently in early March. But this claimed that the Party had been "able to strengthen the confidence of a large number of cadres, party members, and people in the party's leadership in internal as well as external activities, stabilize their thinking in the face of difficulties at home and abroad, and to develop the revolutionary spirit, the spirit of struggling heroically, the idea of self-reliance . . ." Parts of this statement ring with an apparent applicability to the Hanoi direction of cadres in South Vietnam.

A "three anti-, three pro-" administrative reform campaign begun earlier now gained increasing momentum. It opposed "corruption, waste, and red tape" and encouraged "a sense of responsibility, the strengthening of management in finance and economy and the improvement of technical knowledge."

Meanwhile, DRV involvement in the Viet-Cong insurgency had become more overt. As we have already noted, Truong Chinh commented in an April 1963 speech that, to eliminate oppressors and establish a revolutionary dictatorship, "We must at times provoke internal war or external war . . ." A few days later, the National Assembly set up a Reunification Committee to advise the Assembly and its Standing Committee (whose chairman is Truong Chinh) on reunification problems.

A series of campaigns were organized in the North, during the summer of 1963, to whip up domestic and foreign support for the campaign in South Vietnam. These included an emulation movement which recalled how Ho had told the National Assembly that he could not eat nor sleep in peace and would continue to decline the nation's highest decoration, which had been proffered him, as long as the country was partitioned and the southern compatriots were suffering. He said:

> Each ton of coal, each machine, each quintal of food . . . we produce or economize will help speed up socialist construction in North Vietnam, constitute support to the South Vietnamese people's valiant struggle, and contribute to . . . the peaceful reunification of our country.

A "Week of Struggle against U.S. Aggression in South Vietnam" overlapped the celebration of Vietnam Day on July 20, commemorating the ninth anniversary of the Geneva agreements. North-South Brotherhood Libraries were organized in the provinces and countless rallies and speeches hammered home these themes.

In September, the National Assembly Standing Committee headed by Truong Chinh issued an appeal to the southern Vietnamese to support the NLFSV. It warned the people of the north to be vigilant in countermeasures "to crush all U.S.-Diemist schemes to sabotage North Vietnam" and to "turn hatred into deeds" useful in building socialism in the north as "a strong basis for the struggle for the country's reunification."

In October, the International Trade Union Committee for Solidarity with the Workers and People of South Vietnam was organized in Hanoi at a conference attended by delegates representing "31 countries and trade union organizations." A resolution of this conference followed the usual pattern of DRV demands: the immediate end of "U.S. aggression and intervention" in South Vietnam; the withdrawal of U.S. military personnel and war material; and "the settlement of the internal affairs of Vietnam by the Vietnamese people themselves on the basis of the 1954 Geneva Agreements." [35]

In December, a half-million people massed at a rally in Hanoi, led by several Politburo members, to open a "Week of Struggle against the U.S. Imperialists and their Henchmen, to Increase Production and to Support the South Vietnam People." [36]

The Le Duan Mission to Moscow

The increasing consonance of the *Lao Dong* line with the Chinese evidently had brought a curtailment of Soviet aid, as we noted earlier, and the DRV sent a delegation headed by Le Duan to Moscow to confer with Soviet leaders on issues undoubtedly including aid, from January 31 to February 10, 1964. The delegation traveled via Peking, but no news was released concerning that part of the trip except that the group received an "enthusiastic welcome" there.

Politburo members Le Duc Tho and Hoang Van Hoan (as well as

To Huu and Nguyen Van Kinh) accompanied Duan and held "many meetings" with CPSU officials, including Suslov, and one long meeting with Khrushchev, according to the short communiqué released in Hanoi only on February 15. On obviously the thorniest issue of the consultations, a DRV request for a firmer Soviet commitment of support for the war in South Vietnam, the communiqué merely said, "The CPSU delegation declares its resolute support for the just struggle of the Vietnamese people against the . . . acts of the United States imperialists in South Vietnam . . ." This resembled the vague language of the Soviet delegation's pledge of support for the southern campaign at the October meeting of international trade union delegates in Hanoi.

A *Nhan Dan* editorial delineated Hanoi's dissatisfaction with the Soviet position more sharply than the communiqué. It first cited "opposition to modern revisionism" as the basis for strengthening the unity "of all revolutionary and progressive forces in the world." Only the editorial mentioned revisionism; neither it nor the communiqué referred to dogmatism. And only the editorial said specifically that the *Lao Dong* considered the strengthening of solidarity with the U.S.S.R. and with China to be an important task.

The editorial dealt with the DRV position toward the U.S.S.R. in language that would strike the Chinese as double-talk but which actually described its diplomatic straddle explicity: "Our party and people constantly proceed from the standpoint of defending the purity of Marxist-Leninism to consolidate and develop the relations with the Soviet Union as well as to support all the efforts made by the Soviet people in Communist construction." But the key statement of the piece, one evidently summarizing the DRV's reaction to the whole venture, came after the description of the Soviet pledge to the struggle in the South and said: "We clearly see that, *transformed into practical deeds*, this statement will be a valuable contribution not only to the revolutionary cause of our people but also to the national liberation movement in the world as a whole." [Emphasis supplied.]

The DRV and the War in South Vietnam

What are Hanoi's present political and war aims in South Vietnam and how far does she count on her communist-bloc allies for support? The strategy of Hanoi (and of the NLFSV) for attaining a so-called independent, peaceful, and neutral South Vietnam has varied over the past few years. During much of 1962, the DRV called for consultations by the Geneva cochairmen to prepare an international conference on South Vietnam, and it carried similar appeals from the NLFSV in its radio and press outlets. At times there has been a Hanoi-backed NLFSV demand for a neutral zone consisting of South Vietnam, Cambodia, and Laos. A Laotian type of coalition government has been urged as a solution, and even after the deterioration of the Laotian situation the idea of a South Vietnamese political coalition of all people opposed to U.S. intervention and its "lackeys" has remained central.

When the Johnson Administration hinted, in February, 1964, at greater U.S. involvement in the war in South Vietnam and the possibility of South Vietnamese raids into the north. Hanoi had just published its 1964 prognosis of the southern campaign. This February *Hoc Tap* article speculated that the United States was "determined to test its strength for some years" but it thought "the eventual use of tactical nuclear weapons by the United States . . . may be unlikely" because such weapons did not lend themselves well to "the recent close fighting" in which friendly troops could be killed with the enemy.

If the United States should attempt to prosecute the war in the South by attacking North Vietnam, the article said, "they would have to cope not only with North Vietnam, but also with China or eventually with the socialist camp as a whole." And if the United States "used tactical or strategic nuclear weapons, that might directly lead to retaliation with the same weapons."

Subsequent press reports from Peking and Moscow showed, however, that Hanoi had tried to lead its allies further than they were willing to go, at least in public declarations. A *Tass* statement affirmed full support for the Liberation Front cause, but it actually said only that the Soviet Union could not remain indifferent to indications of increasing conflict. It made no direct reference to North Vietnam and it did not specify the type of support it might lend.

China reacted with a caution reminiscent of its vague statement on defense assistance in the Ho-Liu communiqué of May 16, 1963. This had contained emotional assurances of moral support but no concrete guarantees. Nor did it hint at any offer of the kind of joint defense effort the Chinese had offered the Vietnamese in connection with Marshal Yeh Chien-ying's visit to Hanoi in December, 1961.[37] Now the Peking reportage of the *Hoc Tap* article went so far as to omit all references to possible attacks on North Vietnam and the threat of Chinese intervention.[38] Shortly after, China continued its call to revolutionary action in other areas in emulation of the Viet-Cong, but it still refrained from acknowledging any U.S. threat to attack North Vietnam and suggested only indirectly that such action would be dangerous.[39]

Although Hanoi has long harped on the theme of growing sentiment in South Vietnam, and abroad, for a neutral South Vietnam, it has rejected with scorn the idea of neutralizing all of Vietnam. As a Hanoi broadcast of February 12, 1964, put it, "Why did Johnson raise the question of neutralizing both zones of Vietnam [when] he knows too well that our people will never accept the neutralization of North Vietnam?"

Occasionally the DRV has even deigned to use the United Nations to pressure the United States to cease its intervention in South Vietnam and to respect the Geneva agreements, even though Hanoi has consistently deprecated the world body as an imperialist tool and even though there is no bond of legal obligation between it and the Geneva signatories as a group. But in October, 1963, the regime loudly protested that the UN was violating the sovereignty of the South Vietnamese people when it prepared to send a mission to Saigon to investigate alleged discrimination against the Buddhists. It held that the Geneva agreements covered such matters and that the UN mission was therefore illegal.

This statement also mentioned, but only in passing, an argument that the northern regime has made more aggressively elsewhere—that is, that the Southern Republic "is but an administrative organ of South Vietnam." Hanoi has been seconding the NLFSV's claim to be the "legitimate representative of the South Vietnamese people" since 1962, although the Front, in fact, up to 1965, enjoyed only moral support, not formal diplomatic recognition, from communist-bloc and certain neutralist nations. Its Liberation News Agency operated only in Cuba, Algeria, East Germany, and Czechoslovakia.[40]

It is difficult to tell whether the NLFSV may have exerted pressure on the DRV in favor of either antagonist in the Sino-Soviet dispute, though the Front occasionally has hinted at its dissatisfaction with the rate of assistance supplied from the North and beyond. In view of the war situation in which the NLFSV operates, it would seem likely to favor the pro-Chinese line and to pressure Hanoi to follow it. Occasionally the Front actually has acted with a dash of autonomy from the DRV, but only in matters of support for the war effort in the South, judging from the scanty evidence available.[41]

The Chinese have shown more enthusiasm for the Front as, for example, when a Front delegation went abroad in 1963 to seek diplomatic and other assistance. In Peking, Mao himself received the delegation (as did the highest ranking leaders of Korea, Indonesia, and Cuba), whereas in Moscow it was met only by a Secretary of the Central Party Committee.[42]

An authoritative article on DRV policy in the southern campaign, in the February, 1964, issue of Hoc Tap not only inclined toward the older, cautious view that "the war must be long [and] hard," but added that it also must be "self-supporting." To some extent, "self-supporting" is used here to deliberately obscure the magnitude of the DRV's role in the venture.

It is impossible to estimate the amount of material assistance that the DRV, China, and the Soviet Union have furnished the NLFSV in tactical and strategic direction and in cadres and material. As the international trade union group in Hanoi made preparations in October to mark the December 20 founding date of the NLFSV as an international event, Ho Chi Minh told the conferees that great moral and material aid might be required from their nations. But the only material assistance that Hanoi has admitted sending south is limited amounts of medical equipment and supplies, and most of this is attributed to foreign donors. The first of such shipments was described in a news account on February 7, 1963, which said that some of it had been donated by the East Germans, implying that the DRV itself had furnished the rest. A clandestine Front broadcast from South Vietnam in January, 1964, said that the Soviet Union had sent the first half of a 100,000-ruble medical shipment, following a decision of October, 1963; later Hanoi broadcasts said that Mongolian trade unions had given 75 cases of medicine and that Albania had given clothes, blankets, and medicines.

Conclusion

Hanoi appears determined to retain a degree of independence in the quarrel within the communist bloc, despite its long swing toward the Chinese position and the increased authority of the pro-Chinese faction in the *Lao Dong*. The implications of this for future leadership of the Party and state are difficult to assess. There are some obvious changes, such as Nguyen Chi Thanh's restored prominence, but the roles of other leading figures in the two factions and in any possible middle group remain unclear. As we noted earlier, Ho Chi Minh's name is still invoked as the highest authority in party statements but younger men, particularly Le Duan, are assuming some of the authority that once accrued to him uniquely. Truong Chinh, leader of the pro-Chinese faction, has been very busy and his activities have been reported prominently in the press. He may possibly have regained as much power as he held in the early years of the regime.

Le Duan's role is problematical, since it is not clear whether he has led the trend toward China or whether he has been pulled along, but it is probable that Duan is respected by his Politburo colleagues for his capacity to respond to Chinese pressure by integrating the most workable Chinese policies into DRV policy while still maintaining political communication with the U.S.S.R. Meanwhile, there have been no overt signs of a purge of the pro-Soviet faction, and Vo Nguyen Giap, for example, goes along with the anti-revisionist line, at least publicly.

Hanoi's attempts to maintain a degree of independence doubtless will be rendered more difficult by its increasing dependence on Chinese material assistance. Soviet cuts in aid following the DRV refusal to sign the test-ban treaty may have been substantial, although Hanoi has gone to some pains to show its people and the outside world that some Soviet technicians are still carrying out assistance programs in Vietnam. On September 1, 1963, there was a reception in Hanoi for foreign technicians working in the DRV; still later in 1963, Soviet science and health delegations arrived in Hanoi to provide training; and the inauguration, in January, 1964, of the first operational phase of an industrial power plant at Uong Bi, which the U.S.S.R. had supplied with "all equipment and raw materials" and the guidance of 30 "elite technicians" was a well-publicized event.

Any reduction in foreign aid could not help but hurt the DRV, which has its own commitments to furnish a certain amount of military assistance to insurgents in South Vietnam and Laos, and would bring further hardship to the Vietnamese people who have lived on short rations for years. The Chinese may have agreed to supply any quantity of aid cut off by the Soviets. Given the rudimentary level of North Vietnamese economic development, this might not prove an unduly heavy burden for the Chinese.

Is the DRV likely to be allowed by China and the U.S.S.R. to retain the degree of independence it desires? For the foreseeable future, at least, it probably will be. The Soviets already have demonstrated their inability to keep Hanoi in line. The Chinese, whose ideological line is basically much more compatible with Hanoi's own long-range interest in reunifying Vietnam, are in a much better geographical, political, and economic position to influence Hanoi in various ways, particularly if it is true that they may have taken on the responsibility to furnish aid dropped by the Soviets. But while the Chinese may well be able to continue to influence DRV policies, they will not necessarily be able to dictate policy to Hanoi.

There are three major points to remember. First, Chinese economic aid probably has only limited political leverage on the Vietnamese communist leadership. Although North Vietnamese economic gains have fallen below desired levels and the Vietnamese people may not enjoy living standards they had been promised, they are not, by all accounts, suffering seriously from malnutrition, nor do they appear to be actively disaffected with the regime. The complete cessation of Chinese assistance probably would not cause the regime's economic collapse.

The Vietnamese communists undoubtedly would make further concessions to prevent the withdrawal of Chinese aid, but this may never be demanded of them because of a second decisive factor. This is Hanoi's great value to Peking in its present political and military role. The modicum of independence retained by Hanoi centers around its refusal to condemn the Soviet Union unequivocally and to follow the Chinese line that pro-Chinese factions in other communist parties should split off from these parties if they cannot control pro-Soviet elements within them. But on the crucial issue of national liberation struggles, Hanoi is, in fact, Peking's star performer, at some sacrifice and considerably greater immediate risk to itself than to its bloc partners. Lastly, the age-old antagonism of the Vietnamese to foreign rule, particularly by the Chinese, still persists, as is evidenced at least in part by Hanoi's frequent propaganda emphasis on the difference between the former Chinese "feudalists" and the new breed, the communists. However, if Hanoi should have to call on Peking for emergency assistance, or if the war were extended beyond its presents limits, China's leverage on the DRV would probably increase and so would the influence of the pro-Chinese within the *Lao Dong.*

In any event, Hanoi is not likely to diminish the aggressiveness of its policies toward South Vietnam. In 1954 it was the Chinese who caused the Vietnamese communists to shift from war to more peaceful tactics, mainly on the assumption that the fragile southern government could not long survive. And there must have been an at least implicit understanding with the Chinese that the DRV eventually would have another chance to take the South by more forceful means if political struggle did not suffice. The DRV is now availing itself of that deferred opportunity. It wants the South with its rice, it wants to eliminate its southern rival, the Republic of Vietnam, and it wants reunification on its own terms.

North Vietnam: A Qualified Pro-Chinese Position

* The views expressed in this chapter are those of the author. They should not be interpreted as reflecting the views of The RAND Corporation or the official opinion or policy of any of its governmental or private research sponsors.

(Titles of articles from Vietnamese periodicals are omitted from the citations because of their frequently great length and the fact that the author's name and date of journal issue suffice for the location of the materials in question—Author.)

1. From an article in the August, 1953, issue of the *Cominform Journal* cited in Bernard B. Fall, *Le Vietminh, La République Démocratique du Viet-Nam: 1945-1960* (Paris: Armand Colin, 1960), p. 173.
2. Nguyen Huu Khai article in the Party journal *Hoc Tap* (i.e., *Studies*), March, 1963.
3. Duong Huong, article in *Hoc Tap,* September, 1963.
4. Le Duc Tho, quoted in *Tien Phong,* June 19, 1963.
5. Vu Duong, article in *Hoc Tap,* February, 1962.
6. Nguyen Khai, *ibid.,* March, 1963.
7. P. J. Honey, *Communism in North Vietnam: Its Role in the Sino-Soviet Dispute* (Cambridge, Mass.: The M.I.T. Press, 1963), p. 21.

8. These calculations are based on data announced in a Hanoi domestic broadcast in Vietnamese on January 31, 1964.

9. This speech was serially published by *Nhan Dan* on July 13 to 15, 1962. The exchange rate used here is 3.53 *dong* to the U.S. dollar. Other exchange rates used by Vietnamese and foreign (including some American) sources range from 1.2 to 4 *dong* to the dollar.

10. Vietnam News Agency, editor's note introducing a Hanoi English-language broadcast of January 15, 1964.

11. Hanoi Vietnamese language broadcast, March 5, 1963; and Bernard B. Fall, *The Two Vietnams* (New York: Frederick A. Praeger, Inc., 1963), p. 161.

12. Nguyen Duong Tam, article in *Hoc Tap*, September, 1963.

13. Truong Ngoc, article in *Hoc Tap*, October, 1963.

14. Hanoi broadcast in Vietnamese, March 10, 1963.

15. Vu Quang Tiet, article in *Hoc Tap*, August, 1963.

16. *Nhan Dan*, January 7, 1964.

17. *Nhan Dan*, December 7, 1960, cited in P. J. Honey, *Communism in North Vietnam*, pp. 89ff. Also see pp. 40ff., where Honey describes the DRV's reactions to Sino-Soviet pressures from the 1950's through May, 1963. As he shows, the pro-Soviet and pro-Chinese factions in the *Lao Dong* Party were successively dominant in the earlier period, as follows: 1954 to 1956, pro-Chinese dominance; 1957, policy swing toward the Soviet Union, with the pro-Chinese faction resisting strongly in the autumn; 1958, balance restored between the two factions; 1960, pro-Soviet tendencies apparent in deliberations of the *Lao Dong* Third Congress in September; in November, singular effort by Ho to restore Sino-Soviet differences at the meeting of the 81 Communist Parties in Moscow; 1961, attempt by the *Lao Dong* to maintain cordial relations with both sides as Chinese pressure increased.

18. *Ibid.*, pp. 61 and *passim*, especially pp. 107 and 113. Recent DRV statements have been less guarded in their praise of Hoxha, e.g., in a Hanoi Radio broadcast in English, November 29, 1963.

19. See Minh Tranh, article in *Hoc Tap*, March, 1963.

20. Nguyen Khai, article in *Hoc Tap*, March, 1963.

21. Vietnam News Agency, February 21, 1963.

22. Honey, *Communism in North Vietnam*, pp. 152ff.

23. Le Duan, article in *Hoc Tap*, April, 1963. This speech was broadcast by New China News Agency (NCNA) on April 15 and published in full by *People's Daily* on April 16, 1963.

24. NCNA, May 15, 1963.

25. *Ibid.*, May 16, 1963.

26. The text was published in the Vietnamese Army newspaper, *Bao Quan Doi Nhan Dan*, May 25, 1963, and broadcast by Radio Peking in English on June 8.

27. Honey, *Communism in North Vietnam*, p. 59.

28. *Tien Phong*, July 14, 1963.

29. Hung Son, article in *Hoc Tap*, August, 1963.

30. Unsigned article in *Hoc Tap*, September, 1963.

31. Le Trung Viet, "Positive Leadership," *Hoc Tap*, August, 1963.

32. Nguyen Duong Tam, article in *Hoc Tap*, September, 1963; Hanoi domestic broadcast in Vietnamese, April 26, 1963.

33. Hoang Minh, article in *Hoc Tap*, October, 1963.

34. The communiqué was carried on Radio Hanoi's International Service in English on January 20, and the editorial was broadcast on the same channel the next day. Le Duan's speech was published in the February *Hoc Tap*. Neither the

Truong Chinh speech nor the resolution have been published as of this writing (January, 1965).

35. Hanoi English-language broadcast, October 24, 1963.
36. *Ibid.*, December 15, 1963.
37. NCNA, December 21, 1961.
38. NCNA release published in *People's Daily*, February 28, 1964.
39. *People's Daily*, March 4, 1964.
40. Pham Van Dong, article in *Bratislava Pravda* on February 25, 1963; Hanoi English-language broadcasts of December 28, 1963, and January 16, 1964.
41. Honey, *Communism in North Vietnam*, pp. 111, 112, cites two instances of this in 1961 and 1962. Occasional Front broadcasts reveal an enthusiasm for the Chinese which may be somewhat less restrained than similar programs from Hanoi, e.g., the NLFSV statement on the fourteenth anniversary of the CPR on October 1, 1963.
42. Hanoi English broadcast, December 28, 1963.

Selected Bibliography

Burchett, Wilfred G., *North of the 17th Parallel* (2nd ed.). Hanoi: Privately published, 1957.
Fall, Bernard B., *Le Viet-Minh: 1945-1960.* Paris: Armand Colin, 1960.
————, *The Two Vietnams: A Political and Military Analysis.* New York: Frederick A. Praeger, Inc., 1963.
Hoang Van Chi, *From Colonialism to Communism.* New York: Frederick A. Praeger, Inc., 1964.
Honey, P. J., *Communism in North Vietnam: Its Role in the Sino-Soviet Dispute.* Cambridge, Mass.: The M.I.T. Press, 1963.
————, ed., *North Vietnam Today: Profile of a Communist Satellite.* New York: Frederick A. Praeger, Inc., 1962.
Tanham, George K., *Communist Revolutionary Warfare.* New York: Frederick A. Praeger, Inc., 1962.
Tongas, Gerard, *J'ai vécu dans l'enfer communiste au Nord Vietnam et j'ai choisi la liberté.* Paris: Les Nouvelles Editions Debresse, 1961.
Trager, Frank N., ed., *Marxism in Southeast Asia.* Stanford, Calif.: Stanford University Press, 1959.

The Pathet Lao

A "Liberation" Party

Bernard B. Fall

In large measure, the Laotian communist
movement appears to be based not on the ethnic Laotian
lowlanders but on many of the minorities of Laos—Thai, Meo,
and Malayo-Indonesian [i.e., *Kha*, Lao for slave] peoples.
Whether this situation is the result of
deliberate decisions by the Laotian communist
leadership or their Vietnamese sponsors or whether
it arose out of the natural circumstances that the bulk of
the Laotian territory under communist control is located in
minority areas, is not clear at present.
In any case, the ethnic composition of the
Pathet Lao adds a complex and fascinating factor
to the study of this movement.

Origins

Throughout the entire period of French colonial domination, Laos constituted a political and administrative backwater. There was only a single *lycée* in Vientiane which dispensed a full French high-school education. Only 14,700 Laotians had attended French-type primary schools by 1945, and less than 100 (mostly from noble families) had received an advanced Western education. Such an education usually began for Laotians with the equivalent of junior college studies in neighboring north Vietnam which, during the colonial period, housed at Hanoi the only full-fledged university then existing in Indochina. This explains why quite a few of Laos' senior leaders, regardless of political hue, speak Vietnamese and have a particular affinity for Hanoi as a center of culture. Some, notably Prince Souphanouvong, the titular leader of the Pathet Lao, also found Vietnamese wives there. A very few—the most notable examples were perhaps Prince Souvanna Phouma and Prince Souphanouvong—went on from Hanoi to a full college education or even graduate work in France.

It is, therefore, not surprising that political consciousness should have reached the Laotians via Hanoi or France. This was particularly true of the communist movement. Until the creation of the specifically Vietnamese *Dang Lao Dong* (Workers' Party) on March 6, 1951, there existed only an Indochinese Communist Party (ICP) created in January, 1930, which supposedly also included Laotian and Cambodian elements. As early as 1936, it was known that the ICP's Central Committee included a Laotian member, Kham Seng.[1]

Kham Seng allegedly was a relative of a tribal leader, Kommadam (or Komadome), from the southern Laotian Boloven plateau who had been killed by the French colonial forces at the end of the extremely bloody Boloven uprising of 1936 and 1937. The Boloven had been in an almost permanent state of insurgency against the French since 1910, and tribesmen from the area eventually provided, as will be seen, an impressive number of guerrilla and political leaders to the Pathet Lao—just as the neighboring Lao lowland area, Savannakhet and Paksé, was to provide Veintiane with a goodly number of right-wing politicians: Prince Boun Oum, Katay Sasorith, and Generals Kou Abhay and Siho, among others. Prince Boun Oum allegedly participated in the French repression of the Boloven revolt, since the Boloven were located on the territory of his principality of Champassak. This overlay of ancient ethnic hatreds, beyond doubt, plays a certain role today in the relationships between the right-wing Laotians and their Pathet Lao opponents.

Nevertheless, the most important Laotian left-wing leader was an ethnic Lao lowlander of princely origin, Souphanouvong. The youngest of twenty sons of Prince Boun Khong of Vientiane, who had several wives, Souphanouvong stood little chance of acquiring a position of great importance within the feudal structure of his country. His eldest half-brother was Prince Phetsarat. Prince Souvanna Phouma was somewhere in between. Phetsarat, who had obtained an engineering degree abroad with a specialty in printing machinery and who, as Viceroy of the Kingdom of Luang-Prabang, resided at Vientiane,[2] advised Souvanna and Souphanouvong to study abroad and thus acquire knowledge which would permit them to rise to high posts within the colonial administration.

Both princes, after *lycée* studies at the Albert Sarraut *lycée* in Hanoi,[3] went to highly competitive French engineering schools and did extremely well. Souvanna took a triple engineering degree in marine, electrical, and construction engineering. Souphanouvong took a civil-engineering degree at the well-known *École des Ponts et Chaussées* in Paris.

It was during his stay in France that Souphanouvong became interested in left-wing politics. The year was 1937. France was ruled by the Popular Front, and French universities seethed with sympathizers for the Spanish Republic in its fight against Franco and his Nazi and fascist supporters. According to communist sources, Souphanouvong took the unusual course, for a man of his background, of working during college vacations. As a dock laborer in Le Havre and Bordeaux, he came to know the French working class and its problems and "was caught up in the spirit of the great days of the Popular Front."[4]

Upon his return to the Far East in 1939, Souphanouvong was appointed to the Public Works Department of the French colonial government (Souvanna Phouma went into the civil administration of Indochina), married a Vietnamese girl from Hanoi who is said to have been a committed communist even then, and began to build roads and bridges throughout north Vietnam and Laos. That job not only put him in everyday touch with a great number of local inhabitants—Lao uplanders, lowland Laotians, and Vietnamese—but also gave him intimate knowledge of the topography and local resources of his own country. It was to stand him in good stead later, during his guerrilla days. To this day, a certain type of bridge with round culverts is known in Laos as "pont Souphanouvong."[5]

When Japan occupied Indochina in 1941, Souphanouvong, as well as other Laotians, Cambodians, and Vietnamese throughout the peninsula saw the moment ripe for shaking off French colonial rule. Whether myth or not, another communist source asserts that Souphanouvong met Vietnamese communist leader Ho Chi Minh in south China and asked him for advice as to what to do next. Ho's answer allegedly was: "Seize power from the colonialists." [6] Souphanouvong supposedly heeded the advice and returned to Vientiane, where he began to organize young members of the *bourgeoisie* into an anti-French resistance group. He failed, however, to make extensive contacts with upland chieftains, and this proved to be a serious error.

On March 9, 1945, the Japanese overthrew whatever remained of the French colonial administration in Indochina and invited the rulers of Cambodia, Laos, and Vietnam to proclaim their countries' independence under Japanese aegis. King Sihanouk and Emperor Bao-Dai took advantage of the offer. King Sisavang Vong of Laos refused at first, arguing that "independence under duress" would be just as politically meaningless as independence under colonialism itself. But the King relented when the Japanese arrested his heir (now King) Savang Vatthana and held him prisoner in Saigon, and Laos was formally proclaimed to be independent on April 8, 1945.

Prince Phetsarat, who, as Viceroy, had assumed the function of prime minister, set up a provisional Laotian government in Vientiane and created, on August 18, 1945 (three days after Japan's surrender), a *Lao Issara* (i.e., Free Laos) committee which became the nucleus of a Laotian political party. Both of his well-known brothers and other members of the Vientiane upper classes joined the new group. However, the arrival of French paratroop teams,[7] dropped into Laos along with British teams from Force 136, brought a clash between the King and Phetsarat: The King felt that he had been right in not accepting independence from the now-defeated Japanese and he dismissed the Viceroy from his post on October 10, 1945.

That dismissal brought about a miniature revolution in Vientiane. A People's Committee formed in that city proclaimed a new revolutionary government under Khammao, an old civil servant, on October 12, and dismissed King Sisavang Vong from the Laotian throne on October 20. Souvanna Phouma took the post of Minister of Public Works— a rather unimportant post for someone of his background—while his younger brother Souphanouvong cumulated the key posts of Minister of Defense and of Foreign Affairs and was appointed commander of the Laotian Army.[8] Katay Sasorith, a Laotian southerner of humble (and partly hill-tribe) origin, whose father owned a *bistro* in Paksé, became Minister of Finance. Nhouy Abhay, Laos' only Bachelor of Letters, became Minister of Education. This situation already contained the makings of a typical Laotian crisis: the King isolated in Luang-Prabang; a government in Vientiane representing little else but itself and made up of the traditional elite; and the bulk of the country at the mercy of whoever wanted to seize it.

The seizing was done by the French. Backing up the returning French was Prince Boun Oum of Champassak, who had withstood the Japanese invasion with a mixed Lao-French guerrilla force and who now began to march slowly north with the help of French paratroops. The political tide had turned against the Free Laotians in Vientiane, because Ho Chi Minh's Democratic Republic of Vietnam had, on March 6, 1946, arrived at a modus vivendi with France which provided for the return of French troops to North Vietnam. Souphanouvong's hastily marshaled troops were no match for the French in a pitched battle. On March 21, 1946, at Thakhek, the *Lao Issara* forces were decisively defeated. Souphanouvong himself tried to flee in a pirogue across the Mekong into Thai territory, but was caught in mid-river by a French Spitfire fighter and strafed. He was badly wounded and most of his companions were killed, but the pirogue reached Thailand and Souphanouvong was nursed back to health in Bangkok. The *Lao Issara* movement had lost the first contest with France. The Vientiane regime, with Khammao, Phetsarat, Souvanna Phouma, and Katay, fled to Thailand and, on April 23, 1946, King Sisavang was crowned King of Laos once more. On the 24th, French forces entered Vientiane. On May 13, 1946, a French paratroop force under Colonel Imfeld, which had been dropped earlier on Luang-Prabang, linked up with French troops from Vientiane and the French reconquest of lowland Laos was complete.

From Lao Issara *to Pathet Lao*

The *Lao Issara* refugees in Bangkok continued to style themselves the Laotian government-in-exile, but as the French yielded at least some of the appearances of power to a Laotian government at home, certain *Lao Issara* members began to support a compromise solution that would permit them to return home. Khammao resigned from his premiership-in-exile in favor of Phetsarat, who now called himself "Regent." But he and his brothers began to drift apart. Phetsarat adopted a sterile wait-and-see policy which was to lead to ten years wasted in exile before he returned home in 1957, to become Viceroy again but only to die a few months later. Souvanna Phouma returned to Vientiane when the *Lao Issara* government-in-exile officially declared itself dissolved on October 25, 1949, after Laos formally gained its independence from France. But Souphanouvong had already chosen a more dangerous course.

He had been in Hanoi late in 1946 and had seen Ho Chi Minh's preparations for resistance against the French. After the outbreak of the Indochina War on December 19, 1946, he had watched with great interest how the lowland Vietnamese of Ho successfully withdrew into the mountain tribal areas to keep up the fight that was to lead them eight years later to full victory over the French. Souphanouvong now began to make contacts with the anti-French tribal leaders in southern Laos. His unbending will to resist the French militarily, as well as his extreme political views, led to his expulsion from the *Lao Issara* on May 16, 1949. But Souphanouvong was no longer interested in the fate of the dying movement. He was on his way through the jungles of Laos and Vietnam, to join Ho Chi Minh's mountain redoubt at Tuyên-Quang, north of the Red River delta. The split between the nationalist and procommunist factions of Laos began at this point. It was still wide open almost 20 years later.

At Tuyên-Quang, Souphanouvong convened a congress of hardcore Laotian rebel leaders on August 13, 1950. Among those present were: Sithone Kommadam, representing the southern Kha tribes; Phai-Dang (Faydang) of the Meo; and Nouhak Phoumsavan. The congress, with the obvious encouragement of the Democratic Republic of Vietnam (DRV), proceeded to elect a new resistance government of what it called the State of Laos, or Pathet Lao. Souphanouvong was, of course, the prime minister of the new regime. Rejecting the traditional royal Laotian flag with its tricephalous elephant, the new Pathet Lao regime displayed a flag very similar to North Korea's except for a missing red star: a red field bordered by two dark-blue horizontal stripes with a white disk at its center.

A subsequent meeting held in North Vietnam in November, 1950, provided the Pathet Lao with a new political movement, the *Neo Lao Issara* (i.e., Free Laos Front) and a new political program whose tenor was bound to appeal to every Laotian: equality of all races in Laos; united struggle against the French; and abolition of unjust taxes.

While the Pathet Lao could still claim national autonomy to some extent, its subordination to the DRV and the total coordination of its operations with those of the Vietnamese communist movement soon became apparent. Between March 3 and 11, 1951, when the DRV set up its own, specifically Vietnamese, communist party (and no doubt at the same spot in the jungle), a meeting took place among Vietnamese, Laotian, and Khmer (i.e., Cambodian) communist leaders. Among those present were Ton Duc Thang (since 1960, Vice-president of the DRV); Souphanouvong; and Sieu Heng (head of the Khmer Liberation Committee). Burchett gives us a clear picture of the important results of that conference:

> It was decided to set up a Viet Nam-Khmer-Lao Alliance which called on the people of the three countries to coordinate their fight to defeat the colonialists. It was on the basis of these decisions . . . that Vietnamese volunteers later entered Cambodia and Laos to fight side by side with the Khmer Issarak forces . . . and the Pathet-Lao.[9]

The March 11, 1951, agreement must be regarded as a key step in the subsequent relations between Laos and North Vietnam, for it provides a semblance of a legal rationale for the commitment of North Vietnamese volunteers to fight on the side of the Pathet Lao, just as Chinese "people's volunteers" had fought alongside the North Koreans in Korea. Burchett does not underestimate the importance of this North Vietnamese support when he writes [10] that the "Pathet-Lao received a powerful stimulus when Vietnamese volunteers swept into Laos early in 1953."

Indeed, it was the Laotian invasion of 1953 and 1954 by North Vietnamese forces supported by elements of the Pathet Lao which provided the essential local contacts and intelligence, which finally broke the back of the French in Indochina. After all, lest it be forgotten, the battle of Dien Bien Phu was fought in order to save Laos from Vietnamese invasion. In March, 1953, the first Laotian provincial capital, Sam Neua, had fallen into Vietminh hands and had been handed over to Souphanouvong as a seat for his government. By July 20, 1954, when the first Geneva cease-fire agreement was signed, the Vietnamese communists and the Pathet Lao controlled roughly the same area as they controlled ten years later: the bulk of the Laotian uplands (i.e., two-thirds of all of Laos) with the exception of the *Plaine des Jarres*, then solidly French-held.

Nevertheless, the Pathet Lao had suffered a serious defeat at the Geneva conference. Neither Russia nor Communist China had succeeded in getting the Laotian or Cambodian rebel regimes accepted as conference participants—a privilege granted the DRV without the slightest question. As Phoui Sananikone, the Royal Laotian delegate, told the conference:

> We have said, and we repeat, that the military operations in Laos are the work of Viet-Minh troops, that is to say troops foreign to the country by race, tradition and ideology. We maintain that the so-called "free government," which by a gross misuse of language they [the North Vietnamese] misterm the "Laos Resistance Government," has been fabricated lock, stock and barrel by the foreign invaders.

The conference adopted that view, and the Pathet Lao was not heard from directly at Geneva in 1954. However, unlike Cambodia, which had won its military battle against the *Khmer Issara* and thus did not have to yield a regroupment area to them, Laos had to pay in part the price of military defeat: Two northeastern provinces, Phong Saly and Houa Phan (Sam Neua) and a connecting corridor between them were assigned as a regroupment area to the Pathet Lao forces, their capital to be in the town of Sam Neua (in Houa Phan).[11] But it was not a full-fledged victory for Souphanouvong, either. As Burchett remarks:

> Thus, in return for a promise of nation-wide elections in which the
> Pathet-Lao would take part like any other political party, the Pathet-Lao
> forces agreed to withdraw from their old resistance bases in the centre
> and the south and concentrate in the two northern provinces . . . This
> was a hard decision to make; it was especially bitter to pull out of the
> Komadome [Kommadam] country in the provinces of Attopeu and Sara-
> vane and the Bolovens Plateau. But it was accepted.[12]

According to the Final Declaration of the 1954 Geneva Conference,
a nationwide election would be held in Laos during 1955, and the political reintegration of the Pathet Lao into the Laotian nation would be
achieved on that basis. In the meantime, however, the Pathet Lao movement had acquired a permanent home base in two provinces; a recognized
de facto military force, the Pathet Lao Fighting Units (henceforth better
known by their French initials UCPL, for *Unités Combattantes Pathet-
Lao*); and the legal means for nationwide political agitation.

It was the latter gain that was to prove fatal in the long run to the
noncommunist Laotian central government.

The Pathet Lao Power Structure

Like almost all communist movements in underdeveloped countries,
the Pathet Lao consists of an extremely small communist hard-core
group and a vast united front movement covering all strata and all age
groups of the population. The core party in Laos is the *Phak Khon Ngan
Lao* (PKNL, or Laotian Labor Party) which, according to the extremely
sketchy information available,[13] was created late in 1952, in North
Vietnam, as a Laotian adjunct to the *Lao Dong*.

By 1953, it was thought to have only 17 members; Prince Souphanouvong was not its head, but merely one of its Central Committee
members; Nouhak Phousavan was thought to have been its real leader
as late as 1959. The PKNL has continued to be an elite cadre unit. Seven
years after its creation, its total known membership was 62, including 8
women. Its main job is "political preparation." It carries out no guerrilla
activities or overt sabotage of any kind, but it probably acts as a political
coordinator with the North Vietnamese and Thai communist organizations. Some of its members have at times been reported by the Thai
police as having been seen in northeastern Thailand, particularly among
the Vietnamese refugees who have lived at Mukdahan for the past 20
years. Its main job inside Laos is to direct the activities of the broad
support organizations grouped inside the Laotian Patriotic Front (i.e.,
Neo Lao Hak Xat, or NLHX), which was created on January 6, 1956.

It is probably the background existence of the PKNL which permitted the NLHX to continuously emphasize the nationalist character of

its program, as Souphanouvong himself was to explain to an East German journalist in 1959:

> We are no Communist Party, as is being asserted quite often, but members of the national liberation movement which is called Pathet-Lao abroad. Our movement called itself Neo Lao Issara, Laotian Freedom Movement. The program of that movement was national independence and peace—and that, too, is the program of the Neo Lao Hak Xat.[14]

With a solid political and military base, the Pathet Lao has rarely lost its momentum in Laos since 1955. Already, on the eve of the Bandung Conference on April 13, 1955, the Royal Laotian Government, headed then as later by Prince Souvanna Phouma, issued a long and detailed report describing the activities in violation of the 1954 agreements of the Pathet Lao and of Vietnamese people's volunteers who apparently had not departed from Laos.[15] Contrary to expectation, the administration of the two northeastern provinces had remained totally in Pathet Lao hands. Military and civilian schools in Sam Neua had begun to turn out trained cadres for further operations. In short, the Pathet Lao (PL) behaved, in the apt image of a Rand Corporation report, as if its position were, "though on a much reduced scale, similar to that of the Chinese communists in 1945 . . ." [16] That is, it was preparing itself in a remote military and political base for the showdown that was to come when all conditions for it were ripe. As a Laotian government report said at the time: "In their immense majority the NLHX cadres stand up under the stress, lower their heads under the storm, but refuse to yield." That was particularly important in those provinces which officially had been returned to Royal Laotian Government (RLG) control, but where the infiltrated PL cadres remained at their posts.

Within the regroupment areas (where they operated openly as the civil and political administration) and in the provinces under theoretical RLG control (control that was to become more and more theoretical as time went on), the Pathet Lao set up full-fledged paragovernmental structures (Chart 1). These were largely patterned on what the North Vietnamese regime had done between 1945 and 1954 and were eventually operated with a similar degree of fairly high efficiency.

The structure is based on the rule-by-committee system from the top to bottom of the scale, with a special watchdog apparatus controlling the whole structure for the benefit of the central leadership.

Chart 1

PATHET LAO ADMINISTRATIVE STRUCTURE

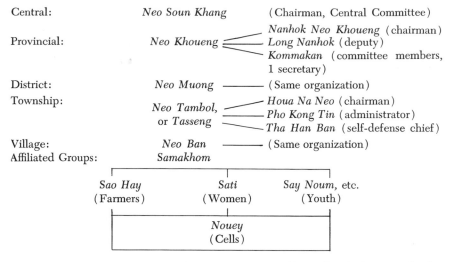

Central: *Neo Soun Khang*   (Chairman, Central Committee)

Provincial: *Neo Khoueng*   *Nanhok Neo Khoueng* (chairman)
                                                      Long Nanhok (deputy)
                                                      Kommakan (committee members,
                                                      1 secretary)

District: *Neo Muong* ———— (Same organization)

Township: *Neo Tambol,* ———— *Houa Na Neo* (chairman)
                            or *Tasseng* ———— *Pho Kong Tin* (administrator)
                                                      Tha Han Ban (self-defense chief)

Village: *Neo Ban* ———— (Same organization)
Affiliated Groups: *Samakhom*

Sao Hay   *Sati*   *Say Noum,* etc.
(Farmers)   (Women)   (Youth)

Nouey
(Cells)

The committee system shown repeats itself at all echelons, with the committee members of the higher echelons being at the same time the leaders of the lower echelons. For example, most of the *Kommakan* (i.e., committee members) of the provincial echelon will be in fact the *Nanhok Neo Muong* (presidents of subordinate district front committees), and so forth. The key echelon is that of the township (i.e., *tambol,* or *tasseng*); the best-trained communist cadres are said to operate there. Very often, the NLHX village administrative official, the *Pho Kong Tin,* is at the same time the official village head for the Royal Laotian Government. In other words, the local administration in Laos is often completely entwined with the communist underground organization. Thus has developed a system of "parallel administration" which is harder to bring under control than the more usual situation where the legal administration is under open attack.

The whole Pathet Lao administrative system is under the constant control of ubiquitous and completely secret *Kene sane* (i.e., he who sees), roving inspectors directly appointed by Nouhak who constantly report on how the regular communist administrative echelon performs. Each *kene sane* can, in turn, appoint several deputies who do not know each other and, thus, unknowingly also report on the activities and performance of their own colleagues.

Strength of the Pathet Lao

Estimates of the over-all numerical strength of the movement are widely divergent. The 1959 consensus, based on extensive surveys and interviews throughout Laos, was that there were at least 1,500 full-time armed Pathet Lao guerrillas. By 1964, there were estimated to be about 20,000 Pathet Lao troops in the country, backed up by perhaps 5,000 North Vietnamese regulars. At least 10,000 Laotians and mountaineers left Phong Saly and Houa Phan provinces for North Vietnam when they were temporarily integrated with the rest of Laos in November, 1957. Table 1 shows the estimated strength of the permanent cadres of the NLHX administrative structure in 1960. The figures are very unlikely to have been revised downward by 1965.

Table 1

NUMERICAL ARRANGEMENT OF PATHET LAO ADMINISTRATION

Lan-Xang (provinces of Luang-Prabang, Nam-Tha, and Sayaboury)	500
Vientiane (city and province)	700
Tran-Ninh (Xieng-Khouang and eastern Vientiane)	400
Central Laos (Khommouane and Savannakhet)	1,000
Southern Laos (Bassac and Attopeu)	400
	3,000

In addition, small groups of specialists are being trained abroad. Soviet and communist Chinese sources mention Laotian students in Moscow and Peking, some of whom are Meo (also, Miao) mountaineers. Their total number seems never to exceed 100, and another 100 study in North Vietnam. Recent reports speak of military specialists (a large proportion of them tribesmen from central and southern Laos) who are being trained in North Vietnamese military schools, in addition to those being trained in PL schools at Sam Neua and Khang Kay in Laos. While those figures may not seem impressive at first glance, they are sufficient —within the Laotian context of scarce and poorly trained leadership material—to tilt the balance of strength dangerously to the PL side.

By 1965, the *administrative* hold taken by the PL power structure over large areas of Laos was, in fact, more dangerous to the survival of a noncommunist Laos than the military situation, although Western observers usually blithely disregard it. As of 1965, there existed at least eleven full-fledged PL provincial administrations (out of a total of sixteen Laotian provinces), and these successfully overshadowed the legal but ineffective RLG administration. There even exists an openly known PL governor of the province of Vientiane: Say Pethrasy. Significantly, all those PL-held provinces abut directly on North Vietnam, and actual PL control limits itself to the mountainous areas for the time being. However, it is sufficiently flexible to expand or retract, according to the fortunes of the political and military situation, without losing its structural integrity.

In those provinces which PL forces do not entirely control, they nevertheless maintain base areas (i.e., *Phun Than*) composed of village groups that are solidly under the control of the NLHX or the PL forces. This does *not* mean that they no longer are accessible to Royal Army forces or even to periodic inspections by government civil servants. On the contrary: Such personnel is received politely, but with sufficient reserve to show that such visits from outsiders are unwelcome. Gifts are refused, and offers of help are turned down with the explanation, "No aid is needed. We're helping each other and can get along very well without your aid."

In a base area, communist indoctrination is continuous. The schools are communist-run. There generally exists a dispensary and at least one good radio receiver capable of listening to the Lao-language programs of Radio Hanoi and Radio Peking. Some bases have their own short-wave transmitters. Propaganda periodicals and newspapers are edited, printed, and distributed. For a time, the *Lao Hak Xat,* with a print run varying between 25,000 to 40,000 copies, was by far the largest Lao-language publication in the country.

A friendly Asian military observer who had an opportunity to tour parts of backcountry Laos in the spring of 1960 reported, upon his return, that "the Pathet Lao in hundreds of villages has almost reached the stage of political organization that enabled the Vietminh to defeat the French in Vietnam."

That, unfortunately, turned out to be no exaggeration.

The Open Contest

It is not within the scope of this study to recount in detail the incredible sequence of erroneous estimates, overoptimism, and maladministration which eventually led Laos to its parlous state in 1965. These factors alone would probably have sufficed to destroy all chances of the survival of a noncommunist Laotian state. The rising efficiency of the Pathet Lao and of its communist-bloc mentors added to the peril.

After two years of arduous negotiations, the two enemy brothers, Souvanna Phouma and Souphanouvong, finally reached a mutually acceptable agreement on November 2, 1957. It provided for the reintegration into the Laotian national fabric of the two PL-controlled provinces; the absorption into the RLG administration of PL civil servants; and the integration into the Royal Laotian Army of 1,500 UCPL officers and men. In exchange, the PL accepted RLG administrators in the northeastern provinces; the surrender of its excess military equipment; and the total departure of North Vietnamese "volunteers" and "experts." In addition, free elections were to be held in several provinces of Laos, to add 21 legislators to the 38-man National Assembly. Two cabinet posts went to the PL: Souphanouvong himself became Minister of Planning (for which, as an engineer, he was well suited) and one of his chief aides, Phoumi Vongvichit, became Minister of Religious Affairs (as which, as a pro-communist, he was expected to be able to do little harm).

Prior to the elections, which were set for May, 1958, the Pathet Lao even agreed to surrender its weapons. In a special ceremony held on February 18, 1958, at the *Plaine des Jarres,* 1,501 UCPL soldiers were officially accepted as Royal Army personnel, while another 4,284 UCPL soldiers and 1,479 dependents and civilian personnel were officially discharged. The UCPL also surrendered 4,773 weapons, including 23 machine guns, 10 automatic rifles, and 65 mortars. Since the total number of UCPL forces at that time was officially estimated at 6,199, the number of weapons surrendered, while obviously not amounting to total disarmament, was impressive.

The May, 1958, elections that followed were a farce. As one high RLG official admitted later (and without arousing the slightest ripple of indignation anywhere), corruption, as well as internal division, was rampant on the anticommunist side:

> Candidates who had been rejected for the sake of unity demanded to be reimbursed for their campaign expenses, which in some cases reached astronomical proportions: two or three hundred thousand *kip* [then about $10,000], and even more. In contrast to the pettiness and rather sordid quarrels occupying the government factions, the two opposition parties [17] had formed an alliance and were presenting a solid disciplined front.[18]

The NLHX and its neutralist ally *Santiphab* not only presented a united front; they also presented a wide range of candidates, including two princes, one woman, and one Kha mountaineer. And thus out of the 21 seats at stake, they gained 9 for the NLHX and another 4 for the *Santiphab.* That was proportionally less communist or fellow-traveling representation than, for example, existed in the French or Italian parliaments at that time. The situation appeared alarming to Washington, however, and the immediate American reaction was to throw support to Laotian civilians and military men of extreme right-wing persuasion in the hope of creating a strong government that would be able to cope with the Pathet Lao menace. That proved to be not only a miscalculation, but a fatal error.

It is, of course, fruitless second-guessing to try to assess whether Souphanouvong, if given a chance in 1958, would have preferred to obtain a strong PL position with a unified noncommunst Laotian regime and thus shake off his North Vietnamese mentors—to have taken a Tito-like position, as has sometimes been suggested—or whether, under any circumstances, he was determined to make a bid for undivided power under PL control. The fact remains that the coup-like reactions of the Vientiane government to the PL victory and its radical departure from Souvanna Phouma's neutralism (he was compelled to resign on July 22, 1958) played its part in the open clash between the RLG and the NLHX that was to follow. This writer fully shares the view of the authors of the previously cited Rand Corporation report, who appraise the outbreak of the 1959 fighting in Laos as follows:

> In retrospect it is apparent that the [right-wing] Sananikone government precipitated the final crisis that led to war in Laos; it also is apparent that while the Sananikone government knew, at the time, that it was running a serious risk of open conflict with the NLHX and its mentors in Hanoi, the pattern of Communist behavior up through mid-May [1959] had not been sufficiently belligerent to deter it.[19]

In sum, the Laotian right wing totally underestimated the Pathet Lao's intrinsic strength and its capacity for sustained resistance. Worse, Vientiane also underestimated the ability of the Pathet Lao to secure outside aid, while it overestimated its own ability to make effective use of the large-scale foreign support it had been guaranteed in advance.

After unilaterally denouncing the Geneva agreements of 1954 in February, 1959 (an often-forgotten fact is that it was the later neutralist Souvanna Phouma who had succeeded in getting the International Control Commission [ICC] to cease its activities in Laos on July 18, 1958), the Sananikone government attempted to deal militarily with the problem of integrating PL Battalions Nos. 1 and 2—the first stationed at Xieng-Ngeun near Luang-Prabang, the second at the *Plaine*. Integration had been stymied because of the dilatory tactics of the PL, which chose to interpret the November, 1957, agreements to mean that integral PL units, with their own officers, would be maintained within the Royal Army; the RLG, for obvious reasons, wished to disperse PL adherents throughout other units. Also the PL demanded a higher ratio of officers than is usually required for a two-battalion force.

On May 11, 1959, Battalion No. 2, surrounded at the *Plaine* by five government battalions, slipped through the encirclement with its women and children and reached North Vietnam unscathed. Battalion No. 1 made a pretense at submission and melted into the jungle on August 8. Prince Souphanouvong and all the other senior PL leaders, however, were arrested and jailed in Vientiane during May and July, which further confirms the view that the Pathet Lao, at least in the spring of 1959, was not bent on provoking a military showdown with the Vientiane government. As Sisouk na Champassak, who certainly is no friend of the PL, said later:

> Although the Neo Lao Hak Xat leaders in Vientiane launched the rebellion, they soon were powerless to stop it . . . Not only were they from the

beginning under surveillance and completely cut off from their troops, but with the start of guerrilla warfare, the military leaders naturally held the reins. After May 15, it was no longer Souphanouvong who led the rebellion, but men like Kayson and Cham Nien and their lieutenants.[20]

The events of May, 1959, were to have a deep influence on all subsequent events in Laos. When the Pathet Lao was deprived of its regular political leaders, who were accustomed to the rules of the political game in Vientiane,[21] the initiative fell to the PL military leaders, such as Colonel Singkapo, and Kaysone, and to their troops, largely composed of tribal mountaineers who had old scores to settle with the Laotian lowlanders. These events made the PL leadership extremely suspicious of working and negotiating in Vientiane. They felt they had been betrayed in Vientiane [22] in 1959, and hence they were not willing to make the same mistake in 1963 or 1964. This explains PL insistence, in 1963, on transferring the seat of government to Luang-Prabang (farther away from pro-Western Thailand, which is just across the river from Vientiane; and closer to the PL-held jungles), and repeated PL proposals for negotiating in neutralized areas to which all three sides would bring only a fixed number of armed men. In view of the military coup of right-wing generals Abhay and Siho on April 19, 1964, the senior PL leaders must have again congratulated themselves for not having accepted an earlier invitation of neutralist Premier Souvanna Phouma to return to Vientiane for further negotiations.

The notorious failure of the Laotian Royal Army, then 25,000 men equipped with tanks, artillery, and airplanes, to annihilate 1,501 ill-armed UCPL members burdered with women and children, destroyed Vientiane's last chance of achieving victory on its own terms. The reaction of the communist bloc (then still acting as a united force) was as swift as it was effective: North Vietnamese aid again began to flow to the Pathet Lao. Within less than three months (as this writer saw for himself, since he was in Sam Neua during this period) the two UCPL battalions had wreaked havoc throughout northern Laos. They were able to rout far larger Laotian units, which had finally begun to believe their own government's propaganda about a North Vietnamese invasion and who now fled in front of the smallest UCPL unit when the cry, "Vietminh," was raised. By August, 1959, the Sananikone government was driven to the wall and forced to ask for a United Nations investigation of the North Vietnamese invasion.

The United Nations investigation mission concluded, on November 5, 1959, that:

> The ensemble of information submitted to the Sub-Committee did not clearly establish whether there were crossings of the frontier by regular troops of the D.R.V.N.[23]

Subsequently, a combination of external factors led to a period of quiescence lasting almost a year. The United States contributed a show of strength by sending elements of the Seventh Fleet to Bangkok. The United Nations continued to make its presence felt, leaving a Security Council representative in Laos after its subcommittee departed. It may also be that the Pathet Lao did not desire to risk everything it had gained at Geneva in 1954 and in the Vientiane agreements of 1957.

But inside Laos itself, the carefree days of the past were fading with the old leaders. Viceroy Prince Phetsarat, the oldest of Laos' three princely stormy petrels, died on October 14, 1959, followed by King Sisavang Vong on October 29. Sisavang had reigned for 55 years. And Katay Don Sasorith, probably the most resourceful and energetic of Laos' pro-Western politicians, died on December 29. New, less experienced, and more radical leaders began to take the helm.[24]

The Neutralist Experiment

A new phase of the Laotian crisis began when all of the Pathet Lao leaders detained in Vientiane's maximum security prison escaped on May 22, 1960, taking with them the warders whom they had converted to the Pathet Lao cause.

This proved extremely important to the Neo Lao Hak Xat command. For Souphanouvong, even if he is no longer the real center of power, as certain sources have repeatedly asserted,[25] is nevertheless a national figure in both the traditional and the revolutionary senses. During the year of his absence, the NLHX had, on the whole, held its own, but neither Nouhak, with his hard-core PKNL, nor Phoumi Vongvichit nor Kaysone, had been able to do much more than hang on defensively to back-country strongholds. Contrary to expectations, the escaped Souphanouvong initially held back his men. For three months after his disappearance into the jungle, no one heard of him or, for that matter, of the Pathet Lao. Radio Hanoi, which had been extremely vocal on his behalf, remained silent. So did Peking.[26]

That silence was shattered by the neutralist coup of Captain Kong-Lê's 2d Paratroop Battalion, which overthrew Laos' right-wing regime in favor of a return to a neutralist policy, on August 9, 1960. Prince Souvanna Phouma, in semi-exile in France as ambassador of Laos, returned to the premiership.

The Kong-Lê coup was immediately hailed by the Central Committee of the NLHX in a communiqué:

> This uprising becomes part of the patriotic movement of the Lao people standing up to American imperialism, and proves that the tenacious struggle of the Neo Lao Hak Xat for national salvation already has produced

a powerful awakening of the national conscience among all layers of the population, up to and including the officers and men of the Royal Army.[27]

The program presented by Souvanna Phouma to the Laotian parliament on August 31, 1960, bore a marked resemblance to the NLHX platform. Its internal aims were a "policy of national union and an end to fratricidal wars among Laotians," and its external political aims were:

1. Pursuing a policy of neutrality in accord with the aspirations of the Lao people.
2. Respecting all international engagements, the [1954] Geneva Agreements included.
3. Accepting aid from any nation, providing it is not burdened with political and military conditions.
4. Establishing friendly relations with all neighboring countries, tightening already-existing relations, and seeking to establish relations with [other] peace-loving countries.

Souvanna Phouma and Kong-Lê were apparently attempting to return to the *status quo* established in the November 2, 1957, accords. But they failed to take into account the fact that the Laotian right wing, which in 1957 had had almost no external assistance, now had powerful outside supporters determined to keep in power in Vientiane a regime which was—in the words of an official commentator in Washington—"willing and able to resist communist aggression and subversion."

The resulting policy took the form of a countercoup based on right-wing forces, grouped around Prince Boun Oum of Champassak and General Phoumi Nosavan, in southern Laos, beyond the scope of this study to describe. The Pathet Lao, sensing that a military second round was about to be unleashed, in turn sought to draw the neutralist Vientiane regime to its side. In this, it was aided by the fact that the Soviet Union had openly come out in favor of Souvanna Phouma and had entered the Laotian scene in October, 1960, by appointing an ambassador to Vientiane for the first time. On October 27, Soviet economic aid to the Kong-Lê forces and Vientiane began by an airlift of supplies from Hanoi. Communist-bloc involvement in the Laotian situation, covert for 15 years, had finally come out in the open.

In a very small way, the Laotian crisis now began to resemble, not the Chinese model of 1945 (as the Rand report we have cited averred), but rather the Spanish Civil War. Outside powers on both sides began to use various Laotian factions as proxies for their own confrontation on Laotian soil. Faced with a direct military threat as the right-wing forces slowly fought their way northward along the Mekong, Souvanna Phouma met his half-brother face to face at the latter's headquarters at Sam Neua on November 18, 1960, and endorsed an accord between neutralists and the NLHX which provided for a "government of national union" including the NLHX, approved the establishment of diplomatic relations with the U.S.S.R., and expressed "satisfaction at the government's promise to accept aid from People's China and the Democratic Republic of Vietnam . . ." [28]

As in the latter days of the Spanish Civil War, polarization was taking place on both sides, with the hard-core left wing taking control of its side and, in the absence of any other effective foreign aid, becoming the major funnel for Soviet support. On December 9, 1960, as right-wing forces were approaching Vientiane, Colonel (later General) Kou Abhay, the regional military commander, defected from Souvanna Phouma to the right wing. A few days later, Souvanna Phouma fled into exile to Cambodia, and Kong-Lê and his veteran paratroops slowly withdrew northward. Thanks to the unbelievably inept Laotian right-wing military leadership, he was able to occupy the key *Plaine des Jarres* airstrips (there are three of them) on New Year's Day, 1961, and thus provide the communist bloc with an excellent logistic and military base in the heart of Laos. Soon a round-the-clock airlift from Hanoi was to provide Kong-Lê with the necessary equipment to match the right-wing military buildup. Moreover, the reopening of the vital Route 7 (closed since 1945) between North Vietnam and the *Plaine* brought Kong-Lê and his new-found Pathet Lao allies medium Soviet armor and field artillery.

Politically also, the NLHX soon proved that it had not lost its pace. A Committee for Peace, Neutrality, Concord, and National Union was set up in Vientiane in November, 1960, under the joint presidency of Souvanna Phouma and Souphanouvong, and similar local committees were established throughout the country wherever possible, thus further broadening the relatively narrow front structure of the NLHX. How effective those organizations could become in a relatively short time was shown by the Committee for Peace-Loving Youth of Vientiane. When it appeared that Souvanna Phouma was being pressured by the then President of the Laotian National Assembly, Somsanith, to negotiate with the right-wing leaders at Savannakhet, the Peace-Loving Youth, rapidly marshaled on December 2, 1960, invaded the Parliament building and compelled the legislature to cancel the session where such feelers toward the right were being debated. Souvanna Phouma, unable to withstand the pressure, yielded to the mob and all peace feelers were withdrawn. On December 12, 1960, the Pathet Lao proclaimed a general mobilization of its forces (which brought back to it all those UCPL members who had been discharged in 1958, and more). With new Soviet equipment and North Vietnamese "instructors" now freely flowing to the *Plaine*, new Pathet Lao and neutralist battalions began to appear throughout Laos.

The Kong-Lê forces, ironically, now styled themselves the "Royal legal forces," while the UCPL units retained their own separate command structure, although both forces cooperated under the unified command of Kong-Lê (later promoted directly to Major General) and Colonel Singkapo Chunamali Sikhot, a member of the Central Committee of the NLHX, as are most UCPL senior commanders.[29] Kong-Lê's title, President of the Supreme Military Council (of all the anti-Vientiane forces) had little practical effect except to further enhance the role of the NLHX and UCPL as a legal force fighting to reestablish a legal government in Laos.

By the spring of 1961, the right-wing forces had not only been almost completely defeated militarily, but they had also lost effective administrative control of nearly all of upland Laos with the exception of a few Meo strongholds faithful to such Meo right-wing leaders as Toubi Ly-Foung and Colonel (later General) Vang Pao. But right-wing and American attempts at organizing the mountain tribes in favor of Vientiane after hundreds of years of oppression, came too late to be fully effective. The Pathet Lao, whose policy of securing tribal support had been firmly established by Souphanouvong in 1946, had too great a start. The first cease-fire line established on May 2, 1961, shows an incredibly close concordance with the traditional dividing line between lowland Laotians and tribal uplanders. The disappearance of neutralist strongholds in Phong Saly and on the *Plaine* in the course of the mid-1964 Pathet Lao offensive changed little in that situation.

Outside Communist Influences

It is difficult to say at what precise point in time the Pathet Lao lost control over its own operations to become a mere pawn of the policy objectives of other communist powers interrested in the area—*if* the Pathet Lao is indeed a pawn.

To direct *anything* in Laos by remote control is, as the West has found out, not an easy game. In sheer physical terms alone, it is easier for the West to supply Laotian right-wing forces from nearby Thai railways and airstrips than it is for the communists to supply even the *Plaine des Jarres* across the whole North Vietnamese upland jungle with its washed-out roads (when they exist at all) and the monsoon climate which is notoriously inhospitable to airlifts. Thus, of sheer necessity, much must often be left to the local initiative—not only the initiative of Souphanouvong himself, but even the initiative of his own local commanders.[30] Many a group claiming to be Pathet Lao may, in reality, be little more than a Laotian version of a warlord band.

The increased severity, at least for the time being, of the Sino-

Soviet split has added to the complications of the Laotian situation. This has shown up clearly in the diverse Russian and Sino-DRV reactions to negotiations to restore the precarious neutralist regime established in the wake of the 1962 Geneva negotiations.[31] The fact that the West itself is about as badly split as the Sino-Soviet bloc (France holds a more conciliatory position than the United States and Britain) certainly does not make the situation less confused.

From 1959 to late 1960, the Soviet bloc unanimously asked for the mere reconvening and reactivation in Laos of the International Control Commission (ICC), no doubt inspired by fears that the well-armed right-wing forces would totally destroy the NLHX. As the military shoe switched to the other foot and destruction was more likely to befall the Vientiane regime, the still unified communist position was to make the granting of cease-fire conditional upon the convening of a Geneva conference that would almost rule out any chance of reestablishing a right-wing regime that could be militarily supported by the West. As Modelski was to observe, such a settlement also did:

> . . . necessarily prevent the immediate and outright victory of the Pathet-Lao faction and the Souvanna Phouma group then allied with it. Each of the great powers thus settled for less than their maximum objective.[32]

The agreement which was signed at Geneva on July 23, 1962, after a new flare-up of fighting in Laos had resulted in further large-scale defeats of the right-wing forces at Nam-Tha and Ban Houei Sai,[33] followed fairly predictable lines: A troika-type neutralist government under Souvanna Phouma was installed in Vientiane with Cabinet members of all three factions; an eventual reunification of the three armed forces and administrations was to be negotiated; all foreign military advisers (except, for a time, French) were to be withdrawn; and the ICC was restored its inspection prerogatives.

If the purpose of the agreement was merely to defuse the explosive situation in the Mekong valley for a time, then it must be considered at least a partial success. General Phoumi's right-wing forces, numbering over 50,000, were saved from utter destruction and given time to reorganize. The Pathet Lao, solidly entrenched in the northeast, began to take hold solidly of the mountainous part of the Laotian panhandle abutting on South Vietnam. And Souvanna Phouma, as he had twice before, in 1954 and 1959, began the thankless task of putting the Laotian pieces together again.

That he failed in the attempt is due in large part to factors over which he had little, if any, control and for which (locally, at least) the right was as much to blame as the Pathet Lao. Externally, the Sino-Soviet rift had great influence over the Laotian situation. In fact, it could be said that thus far (and until the Vietnam situation degenerates into a Korean type of war engulfing both north and south) Laos is the *major victim* of the Sino-Soviet rift. All sides involved can point to a long list of violations of the 1962 Geneva agreements by their adversaries —from murders of leading neutralist figures in Vientiane (probably by right-wing elements) and on the *Plaine* (probably by UCPL elements) to actual military attacks from extremists on both sides. An agreement of November 27, 1962, to set up tripartite military and police forces of equal strength was blithely disregarded by both left and right, and so was an agreement which directed the right wing to turn over its total control of Vientiane to tripartite control. Without this agreement the Pathet Lao leaders, for reasons shown earlier, felt highly reluctant to work in the city.[34] A series of gangland-style killings, such as that of Souvanna's left-leaning neutralist Foreign Minister Quinim Pholsena on April 1, 1963, in Vientiane, further drove home the point.

At the same time, the deepening Sino-Soviet split began to affect Russian supply deliveries to the neutralists, until they allegedly stopped altogether in the spring of 1964. The Russian embassy in Vientiane as much as openly admitted that it was no longer in a position to actively influence Pathet Lao actions. And Hanoi, under Chinese pressure, denied the Russians access to the roads and airports into Laos, or in any case, saw to it that Russian supplies went to the Pathet Lao faction rather than to the Souvanna and Kong-Lê forces. In fact, under attack by rebellious pro-PL neutralist forces led by Colonel Deuane, Kong-Lê lost the central *Plaine* airfield of Xieng-Khouang on April 20, 1963, thus beginning an attrition process that was to see the Kong-Lê troops completely driven off the *Plaine* about one year later.

Those attacks by the Pathet Lao, as well as the lack of Soviet spare parts and ammunition for his Russian armored vehicles, eventually drove Kong-Lê back into a position of *de facto* integration with the right-wing coup in Vientiane on April 19, 1964; polarization on the two extremes was again taking place—and this time, the process was at least implicitly encouraged by the military actions taken by the PL.

What contributed to strengthening China's and Hanoi's new preeminence in the Laotian struggle was the progressive tying-in of the PL-held regions with neighboring areas of China and North Vietnam. Red China had begun a significant road-building program linking the important Yunnan garrison town of Sze-Mao with the northern Laotian provincial capital of Phong Saly.[35] That road was completed in May, 1963. Together with Road 7 going into North Vietnam, it now gives Laos better land communications with its two communist neighbors than with its anticommunist neighbors to the south. Moreover, the conquest of the *Plaine* airfields of Xieng-Khouang, Phong-Savan, and Muong-

Phan (not to speak of smaller airstrips elsewhere) and of the key central Laotian field at Tchépone, provides the Pathet Lao with more than adequate outside communications. While it is not provable at this stage that Red China has an important stake in Laos, it is obvious that North Vietnam does: Laos abuts on 700 miles of highly vulnerable North Vietnamese border area and provides the best avenue of approach to South Vietnam. Both factors are vital in the present South Vietnamese insurgency.

Thus, North Vietnam has a stake of the most direct kind in keeping Laos divided, as long as the one faction friendly to it, the Pathet Lao, continues to be the strong military buffer which it has been since 1952. This will remain true as long as the Pathet Lao political leadership sees no chance to gain a controlling share in the nationwide political power emanating from Vientiane—and that will, in all likelihood, continue to be the case so long as there are anticommunist regimes in Thailand and South Vietnam. To them, the loss of part of the Mekong valley to a communist force would be an almost mortal blow. And it is likely that even neutral Cambodia would view such a presence at its borders with great discomfort. That the Pathet Lao could be considered as such a threat—not only as a puppet of its North Vietnamese allies, but in its own right—is perhaps best evidenced by the fact that, since the late 1950's, Thai police and intelligence keep picking up evidence of a Pathet Lao political subversive network among the Lao-speaking peoples of northeastern Thailand. How truly effective such Pathet Lao propaganda has been is unknown, but its persistence is in itself an ominous sign.[36]

Structurally, the Pathet Lao now seems well adapted to its limited offensive mission. Surely, the NLHX is not a mature communist party, even within the Asian context, but it is far from being a rabble of illiterate tribesmen, as some of its adversaries like to claim. Its leadership is battle-tested; and if Prince Souphanouvong may not be the all-powerful leader [37] of his movement (with the exception of the Chinese and Albanian leaders, one may well ask *who* is such a leader in the communist parties of today), he is nevertheless recognized by his followers as the only Laotian communist leader to have nationwide appeal. The reported creation in Hanoi of a joint operations staff for Laos and Vietnam with Chinese, North Vietnamese, and Pathet Lao "military and political officers," [38] is, if true, another indication that the Pathet Lao is more than a mere adjunct of the Vietnamese communist party.

The Pathet Lao, like other communist parties in this era, may well develop purely national objectives of its own. For the time being, in any case, it has become an important and, perhaps, critical factor in the tangled destinies of the Indochinese peninsula.

The Pathet Lao: A "Liberation" Party

1. Western transliteration of Lao is at best approximate. Kham Seng is also referred to as Kham Xang or Xang Kham.

2. Southern Laos was directly administered by France until 1941. Only with the Franco-Laotian treaty of August 29, 1941, did France recognize the King of Luang-Prabang as King of all Laos.

3. In 1965, the Albert Sarraut *lycée,* still named after a French colonial governor, was the last French educational institution operating in communist North Vietnam.

4. Wilfred G. Burchett, *Mekong Upstream* (East Berlin: Seven Seas Publishers, 1959), p. 223. Burchett has been a reporter for the British communist organ, *The Daily Worker.*

5. Another story about Souphanouvong's bridges is that many of them were built in advance of the roads between them, with the result that many of them bridge a river only to connect two pieces of equally unpassable jungle. Some people feel that this image fully applies to the political situation in Laos as well.

6. Anna Louise Strong, *Cash and Violence in Laos* (Peking: New World Press, 1961), p. 35.

7. For an account of French paratroop operations in Laos, see the largely unknown book by Major L. H. Ayrolles, *L'Indochine ne répond plus* (Saint-Brieuc: Armand Prud'homme, 1948).

8. Part of the information contained here comes from my book manuscript *Crisis in Laos* (Washington, D.C.: Public Affairs Press). In preparation.

9. Burchett, *Mekong Upstream,* pp. 89-90.

10. *Ibid.,* p. 91.

11. Article 14 of the Agreement on the Cessation of Hostilities in Laos of July 20, 1954.

12. Burchett, *Mekong Upstream,* p. 243.

13. Based on field research in Laos in 1959 under a Southeast Asia Treaty Organization (SEATO) research fellowship. SEATO is, of course, in no way responsible for the facts and opinions presented here.

14. Georg Krausz, *Von Indian bis Laos* (East Berlin: Verlag Volk und Welt, 1960), p. 327.

15. B. Fall, *Le Viet-Minh* (Paris: Armand Colin, 1960), p. 131.

16. A. M. Halpern, and H. B. Fredman, *Communist Strategy in Laos* (Santa Monica, Calif.: The Rand Corporation, 1960), p. 4.

17. The *Neo Lao Hak Xat* and the *Santiphab* (i.e., Neutrality Party). The latter was a left-leaning group under Bong Souvannavong, which later supported Souvanna Phouma again.

18. Sisouk na Champassak, *Storm Over Laos* (New York: Frederick A. Praeger, Inc., 1961), p. 62. It is worthy of note that Sisouk, until 1962 representative of his country to the UN, is a member of the Laotian right-wing faction.

19. Halpern and Fredman, *Communist Strategy in Laos,* p. 51.

20. Sisouk, *Storm Over Laos,* p. 83.

21. See the excellent studies by Joel Halpern on the *Lao Elites* (Los Angeles, Calif.: University of California, 1960), mimeographed, and his *Government, Politics, and Social Structure in Laos* (New Haven, Conn.: Yale University Southeast Asia Studies, 1964).

22. For example, Thao Khé, one of the UCPL battalion commanders, had come down to Vientiane under a safe-conduct pass. He was arrested upon arrival.

23. United Nations, Security Council, *Report of the Security Council Sub-committee under Resolution of 7 September 1959*, No. S/4236 (New York, November 5, 1959), p. 31.

24. Fall, *Crisis in Laos.*

25. For a sober analysis of that period, see Arthur J. Dommen, *Conflict in Laos: The Politics of Neutralization* (New York: Frederick A. Praeger, Inc., 1964).

26. Halpern and Fredman, *Communist Strategy in Laos;* and Chen Yi *et al., Concerning the Situation in Laos* (Peking: Foreign Languages Press, 1959).

27. Quang Minh, *Au pays du million d'éléphants* (Hanoi: Editions en langues étrangères, 1961), p. 72.

28. *Ibid.,* p. 86.

29. For example, Thao Tou (Pa Tou), Commander of the 2d UCPL Battalion, is a Meo chieftain from northern Laos, and a member of the NLHX Central Committee. Sithone Kommadam, the Boloven chieftain from southern Laos, is Vice-president of the NLHX Central Committee.

30. For example, several British officials captured by Pathet Lao forces in central Laos found the local commanders reluctant to accept Souphanouvong's orders for their release.

31. See the excellent study by George Modelski, *International Conference on the Settlement of the Laotian Question 1961-62* (Canberra: The Australian National University, 1962).

32. Modelski, *Ibid.,* p. 2.

33. Fall, "Laos: Who Broke the Cease Fire?" *The New Republic,* June 18, 1962.

34. For a brief but excellent account of the progressive degradation of Laos in 1962 and 1963, see Stuart Simmonds, "Laos: A Renewal of Crisis," *Asian Survey* (University of California), January, 1964, pp. 680-684. See also Parke Fulham, "A Million White Elephants," in *Far Eastern Economic Review* (Hong Kong), May 28, 1964, pp. 420-421.

35. Fall, "Red China's Aims in Asia," *Current History,* September, 1962, pp. 140-141.

36. Seth S. King, "Thais Report Rise in Reds' Activity," *The New York Times,* January 9, 1965.

37. The *Washington Post* (Washington, D.C.), May 30, 1964, spoke of the possibility of the creation of a PL-controlled neutralist government in which Souphanouvong would be Vice-premier and left-wing neutralist Khamsouk Kéola would be Premier. See also Fulham, *A Million White Elephants,* p. 421.

38. The *Washington Post,* May 31, 1964.

Selected Bibliography

Anon., *Der Befreiungskampf der Völker von Vietnam, Khmer and Pathet-Lao.* East Berlin: Dietz Verlag, 1954.

Ayrolles, L. H., *L'Indochine ne répond plus.* Saint-Brieuc: Armand Prud' homme, 1948.

Berval, René de, ed., *Kingdom of Laos.* Saigon: France-Asie, 1959.

Blume, Isabelle, *De la frontière du Laos à la rivière Bên Hai.* Hanoi: Editions en langues étrangères, 1961.

Burchett, Wilfred G., *Mekong Upstream: A Visit to Laos and Cambodia*. East Berlin: Seven Seas Books, 1959.

Chalermnit Press Correspondent, *Battle of Vientiane, 1960*. Bangkok: Niyomvithaya Printing Press, 1959.

Chen Yi *et al.*, *Concerning the Situation in Laos*. Peking: Foreign Languages Press, 1959.

Dommen, Arthur J., *Conflict in Laos: The Politics of Neutralization*. New York: Frederick A. Praeger, Inc., 1964.

Epstein, Israel, and Elsie Fairfax-Cholmeley, *Laos in the Mirror of Geneva*. Peking: New World Press, 1961.

Fall, Bernard B., "The International Relations of Laos," *Pacific Affairs*, XXX, No. 1 (March, 1957).

————, "The Laos Tangle," *International Journal* (Toronto), XVI, No. 2 (January, 1962).

————, *Crisis in Laos*. Washington: Public Affairs Press. (In preparation.)

French Government, *Convention générale franco-laotienne du 19 juillet 1949 et Conventions annexes du 6 février 1950*. Saigon: Imprimerie d'Extrême-Orient, 1950.

Halpern, Abraham M., and H. B. Fredman, *Communist Strategy in Laos*. Santa Monica, Calif.: The Rand Corporation, November 15, 1960.

Halpern, Joel M., *Government, Politics, and Social Structure in Laos*. New Haven, Conn.: Yale University Southeast Asia Studies, 1964.

————, *The Role of the Chinese in Laos Society*. Santa Monica, Calif.: The Rand Corporation, December 15, 1960.

Katay D. Sasority, *Le Laos*. Paris: Berger-Levrault, 1953.

Krausz, Georg, *Von Indien bis Laos*. East Berlin: Verlag Volk und Welt, 1960.

Modelski, George, *International Conference on the Settlement of the Laotian Question 1961-62*. Canberra: The Australian National University, 1962.

Okonitnikov, A. P., *Gosudarstvenyi stroi Laosa*. Moscow: Yuridicheskoi Literaturyi, 1959.

Quang Minh, *Au pays du million d'éléphants*. Hanoi: Editions en langues étrangères, 1961.

Report of the Security Council Subcommittee under Resolution of 7 September 1959. United Nations, Security Council: No. S/4236, November 5, 1959.

Sisouk No Champassak, *Storm Over Laos*. New York: Frederick A. Praeger, Inc., 1961.

Strong, Anna Louise, *Cash and Violence in Laos*. Peking: New World Press, 1961.

Zukrowski, Wojcech *et al.*, *Sous le ciel du Laos*. Hanoi: Editions en langues étrangères, 1961.

The Japanese Communist Party

Yoyogi and Its Rivals *

Hans H. Baerwald

The Japanese Communist Party (JCP) is an
anomaly. According to classical Marxist doctrine, Japan's advanced
state of industrialization, the superior organization of
her labor union movement, the early origins of the Party
itself (1922), and the extent to which
Marxist thought has penetrated Japanese
academic circles should make this
society ripe for the culmination of the processes of
historical materialism. Yet, among the 467 members
of the House of Representatives only 5 are
communists; and in the 250-seat House of Councillors,
only 4 are adherents of the JCP.[1] Although this
limited statistical evidence does not tell the whole

story, the fact remains that despite the attention lavished upon the JCP by the Japanese government, by the Allied Occupation during its later years, and by foreign observers since the peace treaty, the Party is impotent by comparison with the governing Liberal-Democratic Party and its principal opposition, the Socialist Party.

Two major factors have contributed to the JCP's powerlessness. In the 1920's, the movement floundered in a morass of seemingly endless doctrinal disputes.[2] Some of these could be attributed to extraordinarily inept direction from the Comintern, some to the fact that the movement's leadership in Japan was drawn largely from the ranks of academicians who were more concerned with theoretical correctness than with the arduous tasks of building a popular mass base and gaining power. The repressive policies of the Japanese government also weakened the movement in the prewar period. No sooner would the movement begin to have the semblance of an effective organization than the government would jail the leaders or cause them to flee into exile. Under the circumstances, the conspiratorial character of the movement began to be accepted as a constant by those who remained.

During the 1930's, the movement ceased to exist as an organized force in the politics of Japan. What remained was a leadership either in jail or in refuge abroad and a disorganized, largely underground remnant existing in an extremely hostile environment and, as a consequence, seeking external support—support to which were attached ideological strings which further alienated the movement from the mainstream of Japanese thought. It is in many respects a tribute to the persuasiveness of ideas and the tenacity of a few true believers that the movement survived at all.

The history of the JCP as an organization actively participating in Japanese politics really begins in the fall of 1945, subsequent to the defeat of Japan in World War II. On October 4 of that year, the Supreme Commander for the Allied Powers (SCAP) issued a directive to the Japanese government which abrogated all laws restricting freedom of thought and assembly. Furthermore, the same directive ordered the release of all political prisoners.[3] One month later a Congress of the Party was convened under the leadership of Tokuda Kyūichi and Shiga Yoshio, both old-timers who had spent years in prison. In January, 1946, Nosaka Sanzō[4] joined them upon his return from exile in China. During the war Nosaka had beamed propaganda broadcasts from Yenan urging his compatriots to end the war against the United States, and in these efforts had the support of the American government's Office of War In-

* Yoyogi refers to the headquarters of the Japanese Communist Party, as distinct from the location of various dissident groups.

formation. He had also indoctrinated Japanese POW's in a school set up for that purpose.

Understandably enough, the JCP welcomed the Allied Occupation as a liberating force and Nosaka proclaimed that the JCP should be a "lovable party," implying that it should not resort to tactics of violence. The Party also attempted to create a united front with the socialists, in which efforts it was rebuffed. On the question of strategy and tactics, the Party adopted the line that Japan would have to go through a two-stage revolutionary process—first, the bourgeois revolution leading to the establishment of a democratic government, which process was being sponsored by the Occupation and should be supported; second, the socialist revolution led by the JCP, concerning the consummation of which some violence might be necessary. The basic thrust of the Party's program, however, was to rely on the processes of peaceful change.

This honeymoon between the JCP and the Occupation was not to last long. A number of factors contributed to the alienation. First was the Occupation's decision to retain the Emperor, whose removal, as well as the dismantling of the Emperor institution, had long been advocated by most leaders of the Party. More important was MacArthur's decision to ban the general strike scheduled for February 1, 1947.

> Under the authority vested in me as Supreme Commander for the Allied Powers, I have informed the labor leaders, whose unions have federated for the purpose of conducting a general strike, that I will not permit the use of so deadly a weapon in the present impoverished and emaciated condition of Japan, and have accordingly directed them to desist from the furtherance of such action.[5]

The organization of this strike had represented one of the JCP's major efforts to capture control of the burgeoning trade union movement. Despite the generally adverse economic conditions then existing in Japan, and despite the growing disparity between wages and the inflationary spiral of prices, the Socialist Party and the labor leaders allied with it had been reluctant to make common cause with the JCP in organizing the strike. Their lack of eagerness was influenced by advice from general headquarters (GHQ), SCAP, that the strike would not be permitted to take place, advice which the socialists had listened to with greater care than the communists. As a consequence of the failure of this gamble, the JCP lost considerable support within the trade-union movement, and the somewhat hesitant united front that had come into existence for the purposes of the general strike disintegrated quickly.

Direct action having proved a failure, the Party returned to a program of supporting those social, economic, and political reforms sponsored by the Occupation with which it agreed, although it recognized that there was an increasingly apparent divergence of basic goals. Such a position developed in the final months of the reform era. The 1947 general elections brought to power a coalition cabinet consisting of representatives of the Socialist and Democratic Parties, initially under the Prime Ministership of socialist Katayama Tetsu and subsequently under democrat Ashida Hitoshi. In many respects, the Katayama and Ashida Cabinets were the high-water mark of the reform era under the Occupation. Toward the end of this period—the summer of 1948—there was a clear indication that the "reverse course" (so termed by the Japanese to indicate the change in emphasis of Occupation policies from reform to recovery and/or reaction) had begun.

In this instance too, a trade-union issue serves as a convenient bench mark. The controversy at hand was the denial of the right to strike on the part of ". . . persons holding a position by appointment or employment in the public service of Japan or in any instrumentality thereof. . . ." [6] At least two major trade unions—the Government Transportation Workers and Communications Workers—had their operations seriously restricted by this quasi-directive which was aimed at undermining the growing influence of communists within the ranks of trade-union leaders.

Communists were not the only ones affected by the resultant amendments in the Japanese government's Public Service Law. These amendments had to be sponsored by a Cabinet in which the socialists held at least a share of power. Furthermore, scandals involving the Cabinet besmirched the reputation of the socialists. Thus, in the election of January 23, 1949, the Communist Party's popular vote jumped from the 3.7 per cent it had obtained in the 1947 election to 9.7 per cent and, instead of electing only 4 members in the House of Representatives, as in 1947, 35 communists became members of the lower house.[7]

Neither before nor since has the JCP managed to make such a respectable showing at the polls. A substantial portion of Japan's renovationist-oriented voters had turned from support of the socialists, whose ideological commitments were presumed to have been tarnished by their participation in the Katayama and Ashida Cabinets. The implication of certain socialists, such as Nishio Suehirō (current leader of the Democratic-Socialist Party) in the Showa Denko scandals had not helped the socialist cause. The socialists' share of the popular vote plummeted downward by over 11 per cent (from 26.2 per cent in 1947 to 15.5 per cent in 1949). Instead of electing 143 members of the House of Representatives, it sent only 48 to Diet posts in 1949, a drop of nearly 100 seats. The disaster suffered by the Socialist Party in the 1949 election was matched by a substantial decline (from 121 to 69 seats in the House of Representatives) in the conservative Democratic Party and a comparable rise in the electoral fortunes of the equally conservative Liberal Party (from 131 to 264 seats).[8] The Japanese electorate appeared to be turning away from the center of the political spectrum to its extremes, and many observers feared that a polarization of politics in Japan was imminent.

The JCP's electoral triumph of January, 1949, proved to be short-lived. Within 18 months, the Party had the misfortune of being hit from two diverse directions. First there was criticism from the Cominform, and just as the Party's leadership had managed to readjust itself to the new line there came the body blow dealt in concert by the Occupation and the Japanese government. Each of these deserves brief elaboration, as they helped to determine the Party's subsequent fortunes, which have been none too good.

Of the two events, the Cominform criticism is the more inexplicable. An observer would have thought that the Party's leadership had done rather well. Here was the JCP, which had been in effective existence only for about four years, more than doubling its popular vote in 21 months and increasing its Diet representation nearly tenfold. One might suppose that such a record would have pleased Stalin, who was then still giving his less than benign direction to the international communist movement. Instead, Nosaka's tactics of having the JCP be a lovable party was assailed as "anti-democratic," "anti-socialist," and as serving "the imperialist occupiers in Japan and the enemies of independence."[9]

Nosaka recanted; in all probability, this was the price he had to pay for remaining as a major Party leader.[10] While this recantation made possible his survival, it clarified for the Japanese people the extent to which the Party's leadership was subservient to internationalist control. Substantial repercussions were felt by the Party, especially among its intellectual supporters. It is at least possible that elements less subservient to Moscow within the ranks of Party leaders wanted to use this opportunity to seize control from the mainstream leadership of Nosaka and Tokuda Kyūichi.[11] Certainly there was fierce infighting between the comparatively moderate mainstream faction and the more militant internationalists led by Shiga Yoshio and Miyamoto Kenji. Before these efforts could bear fruit, the second blow fell, this time at the Occupation's instigation.

In response to the Cominform's criticism of Nosaka, the JCP increased the intemperance of its outbursts against the Occupation and turned toward acts of violence in the achievement of its goals. As a consequence, GHQ began issuing a series of warnings to the JCP, designed to keep the Party's activities within limits acceptable to the Occupation authorities. Specifically leading up to the first warnings were a series of articles in the Party's newspaper, *Akahata* (i.e., *Red Flag*), severely criticizing the Occupation and remarks of a similar tenor made on the floor of the Diet by one of the Party's representatives.[12] General Whitney, Chief of GHQ's Government Section, made the following comments in his meeting with representatives of the JCP:

> I have summoned you to give you warning, and through you to warn your associates in the Communist Party that lying statements concerning the Occupation will not be tolerated. Your statement [by JCP Representative Sunama Ichirō in the Diet] was in direct violation of a long standing Occupation directive with which you and your fellow party members are fully familiar. Its obvious purpose is to use the legislative forum as an instrument of propaganda directed against the Occupation. The *Akahata* . . . likewise is moving steadily toward the line beyond which it cannot go without similarly violating the Occupation directive.[13]

This warning by General Whitney was reinforced by General Mac-Arthur a few months later. The JCP's leadership would not, or could not (because of pressure from the Cominform), adjust its public stance. Given the nearly limitless power of the Occupation at that time, the confrontation between the Party and SCAP moved to a predictable climax.

On June 6 and 7, 1950, General MacArthur, in two letters addressed to the then Prime Minister Yoshida Shigeru, ordered the Japanese government to purge from public office the entire Central Committee of the JCP and the editorial staff of *Akahata*.[14] Even these relatively drastic steps proved to be of little avail in halting the publication of what Occupation authorities viewed as scurrilous material. On the day after the outbreak of the Korean War, MacArthur ordered *Akahata* to suspend publication for one month and, even before the month was over, GHQ ordered the Japanese government to suppress the publication of "all Communist newspapers and all offending party-line publications of whatsoever nature."[15]

Japanese government suppression of communist publications and harassment of hard-core communists and alleged sympathizers reached prodigious proportions in the year that followed. Not only was there a systematic weeding out of suspects from government employment, but the purge made substantial inroads into the ranks of those employed in private industry. Like the purge which had been initially (i.e., in 1946 and 1947) applied to large numbers of individuals for their participation in the war effort, the red purge of 1950 and 1951 cut deeply and not always with a sense of discrimination or fair play. It need only be added that while many issues in the realm of civil liberties were raised by these actions, their full elaboration would take one very far afield.

Whatever views one may hold as to the justifiability of the actions taken by the Occupation and its agent, the Japanese government, in suppressing the JCP in 1950 and 1951, the Party has not yet recovered from the consequences. On the eve of the peace treaty between Japan and the United States, the JCP was almost where it had been at the time of Japan's surrender in the late summer of 1945. It was barely legal, and much of its leadership was barred from public office and either operating clandestinely or back in self-imposed exile.

The JCP's efforts during the 1950's were designed to help it to recover and to rebuild its shattered forces. In these tasks, it has fared none too well. Its extremely slow and painful efforts to rehabilitate itself and become an effective force can be seen from Table 1.

Table 1

ELECTORAL STRENGTH OF THE JCP [16]

House of Representatives	1952	1953	1955	1958	1960	1963
Per cent of popular vote:	2.6	1.9	2.0	2.6	2.9	4.0
Seats in House of Representatives (of 467):	0	1	2	1	3	5
House of Councillors	1953	1956	1959	1962		
Per cent of popular vote:						
National constituency	1.1	2.1	1.9	3.1		
Prefectural constituencies	0.9	3.9	3.3	4.8		
Seats in House of Councillors (of 250):						
National constituency	0	1	1	2		
Prefectural constituencies	0	1	0	1		
Total	0	2	1	3		

Despite, and very possibly also because of, the vicissitudes that have beset the JCP for most of its existence, there has been remarkable continuity in its leadership for most of its history. One of the triumvirate that resuscitated the Party in the postwar period, former Secretary General Tokuda Kyūichi, died in self-imposed exile in China subsequent to the red purge. Nosaka Sanzo, Chairman of the Party since 1955 and member of the House of Councillors since 1959, has retained his intellectual acumen despite having had to adjust to innumerable changes in Party doctrine. He remains the Party's most respected spokesman, but respected more by those outside than those within the movement. The years (he is now 73) are beginning to take their toll.

Shiga Yoshio, until the spring of 1964 second only to Nosaka in seniority, had been the Party's most elected parliamentarian, having been a member of the House of Representatives since 1946 (with the sole exception of the red purge years). A graduate of Tokyo's Imperial University, he too added intellectual luster to the Party.

Repercussions of the Sino-Soviet dispute, and the JCP's increasingly pro-Peking orientation, have since compromised him. Shiga, bolting party discipline, voted for ratification of the partial nuclear test-ban treaty in the Diet on May 20, 1964. As a consequence, the JCP Central Committee voted to remove him from all Party posts. Central Committee member Nakano Shigeharu voted against Shiga's exclusion and Kamiyama Shigeo abstained from the vote. This break in Party solidarity was the first overt split in the JCP. For their pains, Kamiyama and Nakano had their Party membership suspended, thereby further strengthening the China lobby in the JCP.

Officially, the Party's key figure is its Secretary General, Miyamoto Kenji. Another Tokyo University graduate, he joined the Party in 1931 and spent the greater part of the prewar and war periods in jail. In fact, a long jail sentence (unless one was abroad, as was Nosaka) remains one of the guarantees of loyalty to the Party, and hence a guarantee of eligibility for a position of trust within it. Miyamoto has been plagued by ill health which, in conjunction with the commonly held belief that he has leaned toward a neutral role in the Sino-Soviet dispute, has not made it possible for him to exercise the leadership that his official position would seem to entitle him to enjoy. His exact factional affiliation is a matter of some controversy: earlier reports identified him as one of the key figures in the JCP's pro-Soviet faction. It is entirely possible that, as Secretary General of the Party, he tried to play the role of middleman, thus contributing to his ambiguous status in the assessment of outside observers.

The strong man of the Secretariat, until quite recently, was Hakamada Satomi, one of the Party leaders with an authentic proletarian background. Hakamada's formal education ended with the completion of primary school, but was subsequently filled out by attendance at the University for the Toilers of the East (KUTV or *Toyo-Kinrosha-Kyosan-shugi-Daigaku*) in Vladivostok. He and Miyamoto are each said to control five members of the Central Committee's Secretariat, with the eleventh (Ii Yashirō) holding the balance of power. As long as this situation prevailed, there was a neat balance between the neutralist-oriented Miyamoto faction and the Peking-oriented Hakamada faction at the highest Party level.[17]

Close observers of the Party believe, however, that the individuals thus far mentioned, even though holding key posts, are possibly nothing more than robots being manipulated from below. To understand this possibility, it is necessary to embark on a brief examination of the Party's organizational structure.

As are other communist parties, the JCP is exceedingly well organized. The Party Central Committee (*Chuo Iinkai*) sits at the top of the pyramid. It consists of 60 members and 35 candidate members, of which about one-half (i.e., 45 to 50) are followers of Hakamada. Miyamoto's faction controls about 30, and the balance is made up of individuals who had been followers of Kasuga Shōjiro, expelled from the Party for deviationist activities just prior to the Eighth Party Congress in 1961. Sitting at the core of the Central Committee is its Presidium (*Kambukai*), the membership of which is largely interchangeable. There is also a good deal of overlapping membership between the Presidium and the Party Secretariat, which is headed by the Secretary General, Miyamoto Kenji.

Directly beneath these organizations are the various special bureaus of the Party. It is at this level that many of the power struggles (currently revolving around Hakamada and Miyamoto) are settled. Thus, for example, Hakamada is director of the Organization Bureau. One of his followers, Anzai Kuraji, controls the Personnel Bureau; another Takeuchi Shichirō, controls the Labor Union Bureau; and yet another, Sunama Ichirō (whom we noted earlier as the JCP firebrand in the Diet who was reprimanded by General Whitney) is in charge of the Young People's and Student's Bureaus. In addition, a Hakamada man, Matsumoto Saneki, is in charge of the Citizens' (*Shimin*) Bureau; Ichikawa Shoichi heads the Election Planning Bureau and Fujii Teiji is in charge of the Budget Bureau. Possibly most crucial in assessing the power of the Hakamada faction is that the chief editor of *Akahata*, Doki Tsuyoshi, and his two principal deputy editors, Hoshino Tsutomu and Ishida Seiichi, are all said to be Hakamada's followers.

Miyamoto, as Secretary General, occupies a key post, but his followers control only four of the major bureaus. Kanda Asano heads the Women's Bureau; Asakura Sumiyoshi is in charge of the Economic Research Bureau; Aoyanagi Moriyo is chief of the Legal Bureau; and Takahara Shunichi serves as director of the Education and Propaganda Bureaus. It would appear that the Hakamada faction had much the better of the bargaining that went on at the Eighth Party Congress in July, 1961, when these appointments were settled.[18]

Most observers believe that Hakamada has become the most powerful figure in the JCP. Certainly, his supporters control a substantial share of key posts. As we have noted, it is generally believed that he leans toward Peking. However, he is not the only individual who looms importantly inside what is known as the "China lobby" in the JCP.

Within the China faction, there are two groups. The first consists of a group captained by Fujii Teiji, the Budget Bureau chief, and *Akahata* editors Doki Tsuyoshi and Ishida Seiichi. They are known as the "stiff backboners" (i.e., *Sujigane Iri Toin*) and they lead about 95 hard-core members. Most of them participated in the 1951 and 1952 rash of violence sponsored by the Party and subsequently fled to China for five or six years of study. Some, if not all, may have retained their membership in the Chinese Communist Party. This belief was expressed by the Director of the First Investigation Bureau of the Public Peace Agency charged with overseeing the activities of the JCP. If this allegation is correct, it would mean that these members of the JCP are violating Party regulations, not to mention the problems that their severely divided loyalties may pose to them.

A second faction within the China lobby was led by Shida Shigeo, who also was among the leaders favoring the use of violent tactics in 1951 and 1952. He also was Miyamoto's principal rival for the post of Party Secretary General in 1958. He was purged from the Party after he lost the election, and he may well be in China at present, as his adherence to the Chinese line had been very close. In any case, he has not been seen in Japan for some time. Two of his followers, Ichikawa Shōichi and Konno Yojirō, received important Party posts in 1961, becoming Election Planning Bureau Chief and member of the Party Secretariat, respectively.

Both of these groups are collectively known as the "young officers" within the China Lobby. (The term "young officers" refers to the militants who precipitated the Japanese militarist era of the 1930's, goading their seniors into taking resolute action.) Should their stars continue to rise, there is a strong possibility that the Party will become more militant both in theory and action. Miyamoto and Hakamada can possibly be considered moderates by comparison with these young officers. Both, however, are constantly under pressure to take more extreme positions.

This elaborate Party machinery at the center sits atop a network of 46 prefectural, 271 district, and 254 local organizations. At the base of the pyramid are the cells, estimated at between 8,500 and 9,000, and in which there are probably slightly over 100,000 dues-paying, card-carrying members.[19] If the figures on Party membership are correct, and there is every reason to believe that the Japanese government is well-informed, there has been a spectacular membership increase in the past four years. In July, 1959, it was believed that Party membership had fallen to 37,000. Four years later, 102,000 was the figure most often quoted.[20] The Party had finally managed to reattain the numerical strength it had had in 1947!

The JCP is not made up exclusively of workers. At the Central Committee level, the influence of intellectuals has been noted. Over 30 per cent of the Central Committee members are university graduates, and another 25 per cent have attended either a university or an old-style high school which would have included junior college. The occupational background of most Central Committee members also is skewed in favor of professions in which some intellectual activity is a prerequisite (e.g., public service, teaching, newspaper reporting). Only one-third are classified as workers.[21] In most respects, the education and occupational background of the Central Committee is a reflection of the Party's general membership.

One occupational grouping—persons engaged in agricultural, forestry, and fishing industries—has not managed to enter the leadership in proportion to its membership. This group makes up over 11 per cent of the total membership, yet only 2 per cent of the Central Committee members are farmers and fishermen.[22] Land reform, which was accomplished under the aegis of the Occupation, did much to blunt peasant dissatisfaction. Indeed, to the extent that there is grumbling in the villages, it is by landlords who lost part of their holdings during the reform; these individuals are not likely to turn to the JCP for redress of their grievances! The one major exception to these generalizations is the predominantly rural prefecture of Nagano. Its third electoral district was the only nonurban area to elect a communist, Hayashi Hyakurō, as one of its representatives to the Diet in the 1963 general election.[23]

The JCP's electoral strength is centered in the major urban areas. Of Hayashi's four Party colleagues in the current House of Representatives, two come from Osaka, one from Kyoto, and one from Nagoya—all industrial cities in the region of west-central Japan. JCP candidates showed, in the 1963 prefectural and local elections, however, that the Party had scattered strength throughout the islands, by polling over one million votes in the elections for prefectural and major city—Yokohama, Nagoya, Osaka, Kyoto, Kobe—assemblies. (For purposes of perspective, the 1 million votes polled by the JCP must be compared to the over 20 million polled by the Liberal-Democratic Party, and the close to 9.5 million polled by the socialists.) The Party did considerably less well in the elections of executives (prefectural governors and city mayors). It would appear that Japanese voters, to the extremely limited extent that they cast their ballots for communists, might support communists running for posts within a general assembly in which their views would have to be mingled with representatives of other parties, but are leery of supporting them for positions in which they might exercise sole authority.[24]

All of these activities by the JCP require the expenditure of money. Political fund-raising is a murky area no matter what party is involved. It becomes doubly so if there is the possibility, as in the case of the JCP, that the party is involved in clandestine operations. In the view of the Special Investigation Bureau of the Japanese government's Attorney General's Office, the data in Table 2 provide some indication of the JCP's headquarters' financial resources in 1961.[25]

Table 2

JAPANESE COMMUNIST PARTY INCOME IN 1961

	Yen	Approximate Equivalent in U.S. Dollars
Party membership fees	20,700,000	$ 57,000
Income from Party enterprises such as newspaper *Akahata*	428,400,000	1,190,000
Contributions from prefectural and local Party organizations	21,000,000	57,000
Funds raised independently by Party headquarters	70,300,000	180,000
Total	540,400,000	$1,484,000

The statistics are no doubt incomplete. However, the income derived from Party-run enterprises, such as *Akahata*, is probably quite accurate, since circulation figures are readily available.

The Special Investigation Bureau found one interesting example of the manner in which the Party used an increase in *Akahata's* circulation to accomplish two purposes simultaneously. In a certain (unnamed) city hall in Kagoshima prefecture, the local Party initially induced some of the higher officials in the city government to subscribe to *Akahata*. City officials were not anxious to accede to the Party's wishes, but they hoped that by subscribing for a short time they could placate the local Party leaders, whose various demands had made the running of the city more and more difficult. Once the higher officials had been hooked, Party activists advertised this fact among the lower-ranking officials and clerks who could be easily convinced that subscribing to *Akahata* would not hurt their careers and might even be helpful. Aided by such techniques, the Sunday edition of *Akahata* jumped from 344,000 to 527,000 between June and September, 1963.[26]

Beyond these known sources—and let it be noted that the JCP periodically indicates that it has just as much trouble collecting membership dues as other political parties—there are persistent reports that the Party receives funds from abroad. Indeed, observers of the Party in Japan believe, but cannot prove, that one of the reasons for the Party's current tendency to lean toward Peking can be attributed to the larger amount of financial support it is receiving from the Chinese Communist Party than from Moscow. One known instance of Peking's financial assistance to its comrades in Japan was a contribution made, not directly to the Party but to the *Nihon Minshushugi Seinen Domei*, often referred to as the *Minseido*, the Japanese Democratic Youth League. At the time of the anti-Security Pact struggle in 1960, it is reported that the Chinese Party's Youth League's Central Committee sent 5,500,000 yen (about

$15,000) to their friends in Japan.[27] However, a single Conservative Party candidate often spends ten million yen (i.e., $28,000) just to be reelected.

The strength and influence of the JCP cannot, of course, be solely assessed on the basis of its official membership or its popular support in elections. Strenuous efforts have been undertaken by the Party either to establish subsidiary organizations or to penetrate, and ultimately to control, others already in existence. One major goal, control of the trade-union movement, has eluded the Party. To be sure, Party members have, on occasion, been able to acquire positions of leadership in one union or another (currently, the Party is believed to control the Day Workers' Union, *Zennichijirō*). However, *Sōhyō* (i.e., the General Council of Trade Unions), the largest and certainly most powerful labor union federation, has been constant in its support for the Socialist Party. Indeed, *Sōhyō's* hostility toward the JCP has been so pronounced that Japanese government observers at times believed that the JCP might try to form a separate trade union federation rather than continue in their efforts to penetrate *Sōhyō's* leadership. There is no indication as yet that the Party is taking such a drastic step.

For a time, in the late 1940's and early 1950's, the Party was reasonably successful in achieving considerable control over the major student organization, *Zengakuren*, which achieved international notoriety by playing such an important role in the movement opposing revision of the Security Pact between the United States and Japan. Even in 1960, however, the Party was only able to control the anti-main-current faction inside the student federation. The main-current leadership had been expelled by the JCP or had removed itself from Party discipline two years earlier, when the students wanted to continue to pursue tactics of violence while the senior Party, very possibly under the impact of the anti-Stalin campaign, desired a return to moderation. As of 1963, the situation inside *Zengakuren* could only be described as chaotic. It had six known factions, only one of which (*Heimin Gakuren*, or National Council of Students to safeguard Peace and Democracy) apparently has a leadership that owes its allegiance to the JCP. The other five factions, while probably remaining Marxist-oriented in their ideology, are either Trotskyite adventurers or right-wing revisionists from the Party's standpoint.[28]

More success has been achieved by the Party in controlling a more broadly based youth organization, the *Minseido*, previously alluded to in connection with a financial contribution from the Chinese Communist Party. *Minseido*, a successor to the *Kyosan Seinen Domei* (i.e., Young People's Communist League), came into existence in 1951. During the greater part of the 1950's it did not amount to very much as an organization. Beginning in 1959, the Party began to pay more attention to

Minseido, possibly because of the deviationist tendencies that were coming to the fore in *Zengakuren.* In December, 1959, *Minseido* had a reported membership of 4,000; by the fall of 1963, its membership had come close to 100,000, a target of 300,000 having been set at its Sixth National Congress in 1961.[29] At the JCP's Central Committee meeting in 1960, it was decided that *Minseido* should become *the* reservior of future Party members. It remains to be seen whether *Minseido* will fulfill its assigned role or whether, like *Zengakuren,* it too will develop factional conflicts which will limit its usefulness.

A third segment of Japanese society that the Party has tried to manipulate to its own ends is the peace movement. In this movement, by far the most popular and best-organized group has been the Japan Council for Banning Atomic and Hydrogen Bombs (i.e., *Gensuikyō*). At the last three annual worldwide rallies conducted in Hiroshima, there has been an increasingly severe clash between the Japanese Socialist Party (JSP) and the JCP for control. The Ninth World Rally, held during the first week of August, 1963, resulted in the virtual disintegration of *Gensuikyō,* a process that had begun at the rally held one year earlier. To the clash between the JCP and the JSP *Sōhyō* alliance was added the spectacle of delegates from China and the Soviet Union denouncing each other. At one point, Soviet delegates turned their backs to the podium during the course of a speech by the principal Chinese delegate.[30]

The fundamental conflict between the JCP *Gensuikyō*-ites and the JSP *Sōhyō Gensuikyō*-ites was whether the conference should sponsor a resolution condemning all tests of nuclear weapons or restrict itself to condemning those conducted by the imperialist camp. There was also the question of supporting the partial nuclear test-ban treaty signed by the United Kingdom, the Soviet Union, and the United States. On this the lines were clearly drawn, the JCP joining China in denouncing the treaty as a sham and the Japanese socialists and their labor-union allies supporting it. The events in Hiroshima underlined the deep fissure between China and the Soviet Union, as well as the fundamental divergences that existed between the JSP and JCP on this issue. This incident constituted an important lesson for participants in and observers of the rally. *Gensuikyō,* an important organization in the peace movement, may well have great difficulty in rehabilitating itself from the debacle of Hiroshima, 1963.

Ideology and Tactics

A variety of ideological controversies, with their inevitable overtones concerning strategy and tactics, contributed to slowness in rebuilding the Party in the 1950's.[31] Apparently, Khrushchev caught the JCP leaders by surprise with his denunciation of Stalin at the Twentieth Party

Congress of the Communist Party of the Soviet Union (CPSU), so that it was some years before the JCP managed to begin the task of accommodating itself to the new complexities that gradually manifested themselves in the international communist movement. The climax came just prior to the JCP eighth national conference held in July, 1961, and it produced the ouster of Kasuga Shōjirō.

Kasuga and his supporters had argued, in effect, that the JCP's principal enemy was represented by monopoly capitalism in Japan and that the coming socialist revolution would therefore be a one-stage process which could be achieved through peaceful means. (It is believed that Kasuga was strongly influenced by Togliatti's views on structural reform, which are being strongly advocated by the mainstream of Japan's Socialist Party, thereby adding to the over-all confusion.) Kasuga's opponents in the JCP won the intra-Party debate, contending that Japan's society is confronted with two enemies: American imperialism and Japanese monopoly capitalism, and that Japan, though highly developed industrially, remains among those countries that are subordinate to American imperialism. Thus a two-stage revolution is envisaged, the first being the removal of the shackles of American imperialism and only the second and later stage being the socialist revolution in Japan. Opponents of this thesis, including Kasuga, maintained that too much stress was still being placed on American imperialism as the prime enemy and that insufficient emphasis was being placed on the possibilities of a peaceful transformation of Japanese society.

Ambiguities abound in the Kasuga reformulation which, in its essentials, is a papering over of two radically different viewpoints and, at best, represents a return to the ideological posture of the JCP in the initial postwar lovable-party period. The new mainstream formula did not have sufficient support to be pressed at the Seventh National Party Congress in 1958 and might have been held up again at the Eighth had it not been for the previous departure of the Kasuga group after their failure to prevail at the Central Committee meeting in March, 1961. This Central Committee meeting settled the issue within the Party.

The defeat of Kasuga and his supporters had obvious overtones for JCP tactics. It signified that emphasis would still be given to opposing: (1) the presence of American military forces in Japan; and (2) remilitarization. In this effort the JCP has sought to create a broadly based united front, but it has been relatively unsuccessful in the last four years, as the trials and tribulations of *Gensuikyō* and events within *Sōhyō* would indicate.

The Party advocates a host of specific subsidiary policies which, in broad outline, are not too far removed from policies advocated by the socialists. The JSP, too, stands adamantly opposed to Japan's remilitarization. Socialists, too, are opposed to revision of the constitution, the revival of an oppressive police force, and the reintroduction of nationalistic propaganda in schooling. This list could be lengthened, but the main point is that the JCP has often found itself in the position of having its thunder stolen by the JSP. Relations between these two parties have been none too friendly since the anti-Security Pact campaign of 1960. More recently, the JCP has again attacked the JSP, especially Eda Saburo, leader of the JSP's mainstream faction, for being an exponent of "right-wing social democracy," "revisionism," and "petty-bourgeois opportunism." [32]

The Sino-Soviet Cleavage and the JCP

Since 1962, the many ideological and factional struggles within the JCP have been brought into sharper focus as the Party finally began grappling with the Sino-Soviet dispute. The JCP's dilemma was summed up in an interview of Shiga Yoshio.[33] He contended, as late as August, 1963, that newspaper and magazine reports of a split inside the JCP were grossly exaggerated, possibly deliberately so, by individuals (especially inside the Japanese government's security police, the Special Investigation Bureau of the Attorney General's Office) who could take satisfaction in picturing the Party as being in a state of disarray. Japan, Shiga argued, is a highly industrialized country, comparable to Italy and possibly even France in its economic development, but its geographical location is Asia. Shiga's analysis gave one the impression that the JCP was having some difficulty in determining which of these considerations should be given greater weight in the determination of Party policy.

The interview was conducted shortly after the negotiations in Moscow leading up to the partial nuclear test-ban treaty and within two weeks of the Gensuikyō's ninth rally, which had been the scene of so much confusion. When questioned on the JCP's position concerning the Moscow treaty, Shiga responded with the statement that neither he nor his Party really opposed the treaty. It was a case of wanting to alert the Japanese people to the possibility that the treaty was a sham if it did not lead to total disarmament and if it left unresolved such issues as the maintenance of military bases by the United States in Japan or having American nuclear-powered submarines call at Japanese ports. (The JCP subsequently criticized the test-ban treaty, as we shall see.)

Shiga was probably seeking to reflect the views of the Party's leadership because he was conversing with a foreigner in the presence of a member of the Party's Secretariat. In any event, he cast his vote in favor of the treaty's ratification, in contrast with the rest of his colleagues in the House of Representatives. It is possible that he was already considering this step in the late summer of 1963, though he was still observing the formalities of Party discipline.

Finally, the tenth world rally of *Gensuikyō,* the Japan Council against Atomic and Hydrogen Bombs, in the summer of 1964 proved to be two rallies rather than one. Significantly, the Russians sent delegations to both the JCP- and the JSP-dominated rallies, and their reception was far less cordial at the JCP- than at the JSP-dominated rally. Once again, the principal issue was support for or opposition to the partial nuclear test-ban treaty. It is this issue, more than any other, which has clarified who stands with whom in the competing communisms propagated by Moscow and Peking, as far as the Japanese are concerned.

Summary and Conclusion

Yoyogi, or the official JCP, has lined up squarely with the Chinese. It has done so in large measure because the China lobby has won the power struggle with the Moscow-leaning internationalist faction (i.e., *Kokusai-ha*), in the process capturing for itself Miyamoto Kenji, the Secretary General, who was one of the leaders of that faction in the early 1950's. It is, of course, possible that a new communist party, organized by Shiga and the other erstwhile internationalists, will make its formal appearance on the Japanese political stage. Such eventualities underline the dependence of Japanese communists on support, and probably direction, from abroad. It is this dependence which infuriates the younger generation of radicals, who have Marxist sympathies but are dismayed by the rigidities of their elders.

The victory of the China lobby inside the JCP was made possible not only by their greater ability and numbers. Undoubtedly, the historical, cultural, and ethnic ties between Japan and China have contributed to the pro-Peking direction taken by the JCP. These relationships, however, are not the exclusive property of the communists; allusions to them are found in the entire Japanese political spectrum.

Matsumura Kenzō, one of the senior parliamentarians in the governing Liberal-Democratic Party, has been only one of a number of conservative politicians expressing the view that Japanese foreign policy should help in breaking down the isolated position in which China finds itself in contemporary international politics.[39] Even Prime Minister Ikeda alluded to these relationships in a televised press conference on July 19, 1963. Thus, it is at least possible that the JCP's pro-Peking propensities are not necessarily based on the belief that China's ideological stance is more correct than that of the Soviet Union.

On the other hand, there is at least some evidence that more than these historic ties between Japan and China are involved in the thinking of the China lobby inside the JCP. Profound consequences would be felt in the Party's tactics and strategy should this latter group gain complete control of the Party apparatus, for it would probably mean that the Party would turn to greater reliance on direct action techniques.

In the recent past, the Party has operated within the legal confines of the political process. Its showing in the spring, 1963, prefectural and local elections indicated that it was making some gains at that level of Japanese politics. The Party also increased its share of the popular vote, from 2.93 per cent in the 1960 general election to 4.01 per cent in November, 1963, and it increased its representation in the lower House of the Diet from three to five members.

Officials in the Special Investigating Bureau of the Japanese Government charged with overseeing the JCP believe, nonetheless, that there are signs and portents of an increase in covert activities. This development seems to be connected with the increased influence of the China lobby.

It would be foolhardy to overemphasize the importance of the JCP in the contemporary context of Japanese politics. The Party remains a splinter group viewed with varying degrees of suspicion by the vast majority of the Japanese people. Even in left-wing Japanese politics, its share of popular support is only about one-tenth of that accorded to the socialists and to the Democratic-Socialist Party. The JCP's relative weakness can thus be seen in terms of the comparative strength of the socialist movement in Japan. Furthermore, the Party exists within an ordered, remarkably stable political environment, and it is confronted by a government that is extraordinarily well-informed about its activities. Thus, a series of economic, social, and political catastrophes would have to take place for the Party to become a serious contender for political power in Japan.

The Japanese Communist Party: Yoyogi and Its Rivals

1. *Sankei Shimbun,* November 23, 1963, p. 2.
2. For a comprehensive, largely pre-World War II, history of the JCP in the English language, see Rodger Swearingen and Paul Langer, *Red Flag in Japan* (Cambridge, Mass.: Harvard University Press, 1952).
3. See General Headquarters, Supreme Commander for the Allied Powers, *Report of Government Section: Political Reorientation of Japan* (Washington, D.C.: Government Printing Office, 1949), II, 463-65, for the full text of this directive.
4. Nosaka's name is often transliterated as Nozaka. According to the *furigana* beside his name in the Handbook of Members of the House of Councillors, the "s" rather than the "z" would appear to be correct. Cf. Sangiin Jimukyoku (House of Councillors Secretariat) *Sangiin Yōran (Hei) (House of Councillors Handbook [C])* Tokyo: Ōkurashō Insatsu Kyoku (Ministry of Finance Printing Office), 1962, p. 177.
5. "Statement Calling off General Strike," (January 31, 1947), in *Political Reorientation of Japan,* Vol. 2, 762.

6. General Douglas MacArthur's letter to the Prime Minister [Ashida Hitoshi] of Japan. See "Amendment of the National Public Service Law," July 22, 1948, in *Political Reorientation of Japan,* II, 581-83.

7. *Jichisho Senkyo-kyoku* (Autonomy Ministry, Election Bureau), *Kekka-Chō* (Examination Results [of House of Representatives Elections]), Tokyo, 1960, pp. 11-14.

8. *Idem.*

9. Swearingen and Langer, *Red Flag in Japan,* pp. 199ff.

10. Nosaka Sanzō, "My Self-criticism," *Zen'ei* (Tokyo: Vanguard), March, 1950.

11. This possibility was suggested to me in private conversation by an individual who was a sympathizer (though not a member) of the JCP at that time. Also see Yamabe Kentarō "*Sengo Nihon No Kyōsanshugi Undo*" ("The Postwar Japanese Communist Movement") in *Chuō Kōron* (*Central Review*), December, 1963, pp. 138-149. This issue of the magazine is devoted to "Contemporary Communism."

12. Details for this section are taken from an unpublished typescript entitled "Control of Antidemocratic Elements," prepared by Government Section, General Headquarters, Supreme Commander for the Allied Powers. The typescript bears no date, but is believed to have been written in late 1951 or very early 1952. See particularly pp. 36ff.

13. *Idem.* The Occupation directive referred to is SCAPIN 33 of 19 September 1945 among the terms of which nothing should be printed which might "disturb the public tranquility" or which constituted "false or destructive criticism of the Allied Powers."

14. *Idem.* There is reason to believe that some Occupation officials considered these actions to be too mild and recommended that the Party be outlawed. Until more of the Occupation's official records become part of the public domain, it is not possible to completely confirm this view.

15. *Idem.,* pp. 41-42.

16. *Kekka-chō,* pp. 11-14; *Sankei Shimbun,* November 23, 1963, p. 2.

17. Material for these biographies and estimates of the individuals' current status in the Party are based on interviews conducted by the author in Tokyo during the summer of 1963; also based on standard reference works such as the *Sayoku Dantai Jiten* (*Dictionary of Leftist Organizations*), Tokyo: Musashi Shobo, 1961; also see Swearingen and Langer, *Red Flag in Japan.*

18. Material based on the special edition of *Zen'ei* (*Vanguard*), September, 1961, published after the Eighth Party Congress in July, 1961; also based on Party personnel records kept by the Special Investigation Bureau of the Attorney General's Office, *Nihon Kyosanto Chuo Soshiki oyobi Yakushokuin no Hensen,* Mimeographed, July, 1963; also based on private interviews.

19. Public Security Investigation Agency, Ministry of Justice, Japan, *Current Situations in the Japan Communist Party,* 1962, pp. 133, 155.

20. *Naigai Josei Chosakai* (Domestic and Foreign Conditions Investigation Organization), *Kokunai Josei Kaisetsu* (*Comments on Domestic News*), November 15, 1963, p. 18. This magazine is published with subsidies from the Japanese government. Much of the rural membership of the Party is believed to be made up of hired hands in family enterprises.

21. Occupational Classification of Members of the Central Committee of the JCP:

Workers	32.0%
Public service employees	20.4%
School teachers	4.9%
Students	9.7%
Farmers and fishermen	1.9%
Office clerks of companies and shops	14.6%
Liberal professions	10.7%

Newspaper reporters	3.9%
Other	1.9%

Source: *Current Situations*, p. 145.

22. Occupational Classification of Party Members:

Professional Party members	2.15%
Factory workers	13.58%
General workers [a]	10.51%
Casual workers	5.27%
Public service employees	12.75%
Teachers	6.64%
Persons engaged in agricultural, forestry, and fishing industries	11.35%
Office workers	9.25%
Dealers	7.20%
Company managers	0.76%
Liberal professions	4.26%
Others	3.66%
Persons without regular occupations	4.55%
Unknown	6.52%

[a] Workers (e.g., carpenters, plasterers, and furniture makers) employed in small factories and workshops considered small and medium enterprises. Source: *Current Situations*, p. 135.

23. *Sankei Shimbun*, November 23, 1963, p. 6. Nagano, a mountainous prefecture, has a long history of radicalism.

24. Jichisho Senkyo Kyoku (Autonomy Ministry Election Bureau), *Chihō Senkyō Kekkacho: Sokuhō (Investigation of Local Election Results: Initial Report)*, Mimeographed, 1963, pp. 27-33.

25. *Current Situations*, p. 183.

26. *Kokunai Josei Kaisetsu*, November 15, 1963, pp. 9, 20. Growth in the sale of the Sunday edition of *Akahata* becomes even more spectacular if March, 1959, is taken as the starting point. At that time, sales stood at 38,000. Four and one-half years later it was 527,000, a fourteenfold increase, truly a noteworthy performance. By contrast, the daily edition has had a slower increase—from 47,000 in January, 1959, to 146,000 in September, 1963.

27. *Sayoku Dantai Jiten*, p. 63.

28. Private interview with an official of the Attorney General's Office Special Investigation Bureau on August 19, 1963. See also *Japan Times* (Tokyo), June 13, 1963, p. 12.

29. From *Kokunai Josei Kaisetsu*, p. 22.

30. Japanese Press Coverage, *Asahi, Mainichi, Yomiuri, Sankei Shimbun*, Tokyo, August 7, 8, 9, 1963.

31. The beginnings of the turn away from violence by the Party can be traced to the sixth national Party conference held in July, 1955. At this conference there was a good deal of soul-searching concerning the leftist adventurism that had played such an important role in the early 1950's. It is interesting to note that, in this instance, the JCP anticipated the changes brought about by Khrushchev's denunciation of Stalin at the Twentieth Party Congress of the CPSU in 1956. See Murakami Kanji, *Nihon Kyosanto (The Japanese Communist Party)*, Tokyo: Hobunsha, 1956, p. 183. Also see the program adopted at the eighth JCP conference (July, 1963), printed in *Zen'ei (Vanguard)*, September, 1961, pp. 97-108.

32. *Asahi Nenkan (Asahi Yearbook)* (Tokyo, 1964), p. 232.

33. Interview with Shiga Yoshio in his Diet office, August 20, 1963.

34. Material is based on Hirotsu Kyosuke, *Chūsō-Tairitsu to Nihon Kyosan-to oyobi Kakushin Jinei eno Eikyō (The Sino-Soviet Conflict and its Impact upon the JCP and the Renovationists)*, Tokyo, Mimeographed, 1963; and Naigai

Josei Chosakai (Domestic and Foreign Conditions Investigation Committee), *"Chūsō Ronsō no Gekika to Nihom Kyōsanto no Dōkō"* ("The Intensification of the Sino-Soviet Dispute Dating from October, 1961 and the JCP's Responses Thereto"), November, 1963.

35. "Let us See the Corruption of Modern Revisionists" was originally published in *Jen-min jih-pao,* September 17, 1963, when Khrushchev was attempting, with some success, to improve his relations with Tito, and was reprinted in *Akahata* three days later.

36. *Akahata,* October 8, 1963; and *Zen'ei,* December, 1963, pp. 22-27. See also Hirotsu Kyōsuke, "The Communist Party of Japan: Its Present Strength and Revolutionary Policy," *Review* (A Journal for the Study of Communism and Communist Countries), (Tokyo: Ōa Kyokai, May, 1964, pp. 35-57).

37. *Peking Review,* July 31, 1964; September 18, 1964.

38. *The New York Times,* October 4, 1964, p. 9.

39. Matsumura Kenzō, "Bridging the Gap to China," *Japan Quarterly,* XI, No. 1 (January-March, 1964), 27-31.

Selected Bibliography

American Embassy, Tokyo, *Daily Summary of the Japanese Press* and [Weekly] *Summaries of Selected Japanese Magazines.* These often contain translations of Japanese communist publications.

Government Section, General Headquarters, Supreme Commander for the Allied Forces "Control of Antidemocratic Elements." An undated typescript, believed to have been prepared in late 1951 or early 1952 as a supplement to *Political Reorientation of Japan,* Washington, D.C.: Government Printing Office, 1949.

Kublin, Hyman, *Asian Revolutionary: The Life of Sen Katayama.* Princeton, N.J.: Princeton University Press, 1964.

Langer, Paul, "Communism in Independent Japan," in *Japan between East and West,* ed. Hugh Borton. New York: Harper & Row, Publishers, 1957.

————, "Independence or Subordination: The Japanese Communist Party Between Moscow and Peking," in *Communist Strategies in Asia: A Comparative Analysis of Governments and Parties,* ed. A. Doak Barnett. New York: Frederick A. Praeger, Inc., 1963.

Public Security Investigation Agency, *Current Situations in the Japanese Communist Party.* Tokyo: Ministry of Justice, 1962.

Scalapino, Robert A., "The Left Wing in Japan," *Survey,* No. 43 (August, 1962), pp. 102-11.

Swearingen, Rodger, "Japanese Communism and the Moscow-Peking Axis," *The Annals of the American Academy of Political and Social Science,* November, 1956, pp. 63-75.

————, and Paul Langer, *Red Flag in Japan: International Communism in Action, 1919-1951.* Cambridge, Mass.: Harvard University Press, 1952.

Tsukahira, Toshio G., *The Post-war Evolution of Communist Strategy in Japan.* Cambridge, Mass.: Center for International Studies, The Technology Press of the Massachusetts Institute of Technology, 1954.

Communism
in Malaysia

A Multifront Struggle

Frances L. Starner

When Malaysia was founded in September, 1963,
the former Federation of Malaya acquired three new states and,
with them, two new fronts on which to combat communism.
Moreover, while in Malaya communism appeared no longer
to constitute an active threat to the state,
in Malaysia it challenged the government both
above and underground and, in Sarawak,
offered the reality of armed subversion. Singapore,
Sarawak, and the Thai-Malayan border area
present three different situations and three stages of
communist development. Nevertheless, among
the communist movements of southeast Asia, Malaysian
communism possesses a unique identity, which

can be attributed only in part to Malaysia's common colonial heritage.

Communism in Malaysia today is, as it has been through most of its history, an almost exclusively overseas Chinese phenomenon. Its aspirations, its occasional successes, its frustrations, and above all its limitations have generally reflected the fact that it has been essentially a movement appealing to Chinese expatriates. This is not to say that the more than four million Chinese in Malaysia show, in general, a predilection for communism; indeed, it would be erroneous to contend that the Malaysian Chinese have been united in their views either of their own interests or of the correct attitude to take toward Peking. Both for historical and political reasons, however, Marxism-Leninism established its foothold within the Chinese community; and its failure to gain permanent ground among the Malays and the Indians has reflected not so much a lack of effort on the part of Malayan communist leaders as an inability to create, except for brief periods, a basis of mutual interest with the other Malayan nationals. At times, it is true, the movement has suffered from an excessive preoccupation with issues centered on China or in the resident Chinese communities—issues with little appeal for non-Chinese. More often, it has been hampered because the interest of Malays and Indians have been regarded as competitive with, rather than complementary to, those of the Malayan Chinese.

In order to gain perspective on the current activities of the Malaysian communist movements, one must view the timing of developments in the area against this constant ethnic factor. In large part, one might conclude that communist policies in Malaysia today are a relatively direct response to the rising tide of events which culminated in Malaysian federation on September 16, 1963. Even the reaction of the Malayan communists to the Sino-Soviet quarrel is explicable in terms of the felt need for the revolutionary instrument to be used against "neo-colonialism," i.e., the threat of renewed Western domination. Here, the natural inclination of the Communist Party of Malaya to side with the "parent" Chinese party could be interpreted as simply reinforcing a position dictated by the conditions currently prevailing in Malaysia. It must be borne in mind, however, that the communist response to current events is also heavily conditioned by events of the past; in particular, the Party's ability to react to the threat of Malaysia has been severely circumscribed by its continued involvement in the war of "national liberation" launched in 1948. Communist *movements* in Malaysia, as distinguished from the Malayan Communist Party itself, are certainly less inhibited by prolonged involvement with the past. Nevertheless, the unresolved war continues to place strictures on both Party and movements, as does the rupture which occurred within the united front in Singapore in 1961.

It needs to be pointed out here that the Communist Party has always regarded Singapore as an integral part of Malaya and therefore has never distinguished, organizationally, between the two. However, since the British did separate Singapore from the peninsula for purposes of governance and since, in addition, there are important differences in the economic and social patterns of Singapore and the Malay states, the forms of Party activity in Singapore and the Federation have frequently diverged. There is, therefore, justification for talking about a movement in Singapore as distinct from that in the Federation, if one bears in mind that nominally they both serve one Party. In contrast, the Borneo states are not acknowledged by the communists—or by the Socialist Front in Singapore—as a part of the same state, even today. The communist movement there, which has assumed significant proportions only in Sarawak and only in the last five or six years, appears to be organizationally autonomous, although assisted informally by the Singapore movement. Whether a communist party of Borneo actually exists is not clear at the present time. The existence of a clandestine organization with avowed communist purposes is amply documented, however, and evidence of the intent to form a Borneo party was discovered in 1959.

A Brief History of the Communist Party of Malaya

It appears that the Indonesian communist, Tan Malaka, first brought Malaya to the attention of the Communist International. The first agent sent to work there, however, was reportedly a special representative of the Chinese Communist Party, Fu Ta Ching, who arrived in Singapore in 1925. Until the Kuomintang-Communist split in China in 1927, communist activity in Singapore and Malaya took place under the umbrella of the local Kuomintang organs (which were themselves proscribed by the colonial government at that time). Following the split in China, communist activity was not renewed among the overseas Chinese until early in 1928, when the Nanyang (i.e., South Seas) Communist Party was organized, with headquarters in Singapore, to direct activities in most of southeast Asia.[1] Two years later, the Nanyang party gave way to the Malayan Communist Party, which had jurisdiction chiefly in Malaya and Thailand. This new party was in turn virtually obliterated in 1931, as a result of police raids in Singapore which had repercussions throughout the Asian communist movement. Nevertheless, by the mid-Thirties, the Malayan Communist Party, focusing—as the Malayan movement had from the beginning—on labor action, was again a force with which to reckon. Aided by the worldwide economic depression which had drastically curtailed Malaya's export trade, communist-led unions embarked on a program of militant strike activity which seriously embarrassed the colonial government; at one point, strikers even succeeded in establishing a workers' soviet at a coal mine which they held briefly.

The Japanese conquest of Manchuria, in 1931, marked the beginning of anti-Japanese activity among the Malayan Chinese, and the communists attempted, from an early date, to capture the movement. The Party therefore had little difficulty in adjusting its aims, from 1935 onward, to conform with the Comintern's policy of a united front against imperialism. And it succeeded remarkably well in putting itself in the forefront of the anti-Japanese effort, in spite of the difficulties arising from its simultaneous anti-British activities. Significantly, it was on orders from the Chinese Communist Party that the efforts to obstruct the British war effort were abandoned, nine months *before* the Soviet Union was invaded.

Thus, when the Japanese took over Malaya, the attitude of the Malayan communists was clearly defined, and their underground forces were therefore in a position to move more decisively than other nationalist movements in the area. It is generally conceded that, in 1945, they were in a position to command the postwar settlement. Their position was without parallel in southeast Asia, but they did not choose to capitalize on the advantages they had gained during the war. The Party's failure to use these advantages to seize the governmental machinery and to block the return of the British has been the subject of much conjecture; generally it has been attributed to lack of direction from the international communist movement and to indecisive leadership.[2] Whatever the reason, the blow which might have been struck in 1945 was delayed for almost three years while the Party, able to operate above ground for the first time, returned to open activities to strengthen its base. At this time, there was a real attempt to link up with Malayan radicals to establish a multiracial party. It is true that the movement, which concealed the identity and whereabouts of its top leaders even from British liaison forces during the war, continued to maintain underground cadres and caches of arms during the brief period of its legal existence. Nonetheless, by the time the call for armed insurrections went out, the communists had lost virtually all of the tactical advantage they enjoyed in 1945, and much of the popular support as well.

When the emergency began in June, 1948, the aim of Party strategists, relying heavily upon the writings of Mao Tse-tung in this field, was to strike for a clear-cut victory and to avoid a war of attrition. In this, they seriously overestimated their own strength among the Malayan people, including the Chinese, and they seemingly underestimated the determination of the British. From the British standpoint, it was a costly campaign, involving not only the commitment of troops to treacherous jungle operations but also the resettlement of 450,000 Chinese—mostly squatters—from the edges of the jungles into new villages. This factor may have made the insurrection a success, from the point of view of the international communist movement at that time.[3] From the viewpoint of the Malayan movement, however, it can only be rated a failure, since the British had the superior resources to win a war of attrition, whereas the guerrillas of the Malayan National Liberation Army,[4] increasingly cut off from sources of supply, had not. By 1951, the Party was admitting that the terrorist tactics had failed, and was stressing the need to rebuild popular support through techniques of persuasion.

By 1955, the communists in Malaya recognized that they were about to lose the initiative they had once held in the independence struggle and upon which they counted heavily for popular support. Accordingly, the Party's Secretary General, Chen Ping, proposed a meeting with Tengku Abdul Rahman and other Malayan political leaders to negotiate an end to hostilities. The meeting, which took place at Baling in December, failed when the Tengku refused to accept the communist terms. In 1957, an attempt by Chen Ping to reopen negotiations made even less headway.

Surprisingly, the communist "war of national liberation" is still in progress. At least, the Central Committee of the Party commemorates the anniversary each year and, from time to time, proclaims to fraternal parties its continued involvement in the armed struggle for independence. The Malayan government proclaimed the end of the emergency in 1960, but it admits the continued threat of the Liberation Army from its base on the Thailand border.

The Singapore Communist Movement

Although Singapore experienced its own communist-inspired crises in the decade and a half before it joined Malaysia, it was not the scene of armed insurrection. Some Singapore communists joined the guerrillas in the Malayan jungles, but others went underground to direct anti-British activity through various front organizations. Much of the unrest which characterized Singapore in the 1950's was fomented by the organizers of "general labor unions," a device which had been utilized by communist agents for political purposes in Singapore since the 1920's. It is noteworthy here, however, that the Indians were active in the Party and in the labor front after the war for the first time. And, at the intellectual level, the Party was joined by a number of Eurasians and Europeans who functioned largely through the Anti-British League. In addition, the Chinese middle schools played a key role in communist action in the mid-

Fifties, not only serving as a training ground for new cadres but also providing the base from which antigovernment riots were launched. Finally, when 14 persons were killed in the October, 1956, riots, the elected government of Lim Yew Hock took steps to arrest the instigators and to dissolve some of the chief front organizations. In the following year, the government followed up with widespread arrests of subversives in labor organizations and in key positions in leftist parties, and on this occasion it issued a command paper detailing the techniques and the extent of communist penetration of united fronts, particularly of the People's Action Party (PAP), a radical left group.[5]

Victories for the People's Action Party at the polls in 1957 and in 1959, which carried with them the responsibilities of governing, contributed to a change in communist tactics. Undoubtedly, the overdue realization that Singapore's future was in real jeopardy was also a factor on the side of change. As indicated earlier, the communists—and most noncommunists in Singapore, also—had never recognized the island as having an existence apart from Malaya; and yet their excesses, as regards both labor and Chinese education and culture, created a real barrier to merger with the Federation. From 1957 onward, Singapore's Chinese could no longer hope to wrest favorable terms for Malayan union from the British but could only try to persuade the conservative Malay-dominated government of its wisdom. And to Kuala Lumpur, Singapore's record of extremism was anything but reassuring.

Ironically, at the same time that the PAP was achieving its greatest successes at the polls, it was not only harassed from without by police action but also divided within on questions of leadership and on ultimate aims. Its stability as a political front appears to have rested less on the compatibility of the moderate and extreme left forces who comprised it than on the demands of political expediency, and these lost much of their validity once the PAP came to power. Lee Kuan Yew, the British-educated leader of the moderate faction, owed much of his own political ascendancy to his key position in the PAP at the time when Lim Chin Siong and other leaders of the militant left were detained and hence unable to stand in the 1959 elections. After the elections, Lee fulfilled his campaign promise of forcing the release of the detained men before he would form a government, but he did not, as some observers expected, pave the way for their reentry into politics. Instead, the Lee government moved steadily toward the day in 1961 when the left wing of the PAP withdrew, taking with it a major segment of the Party's labor support, to form the new *Barisan Sosialis,* or Socialist Front. And it has been chiefly from within the *Barisan,* again freed of any responsibility for governing, that communist political action has taken place since the PAP split.

Communist Activity in Sarawak

Reportedly, some communists who fled China at the time of the 1927 purge by the Kuomintang ultimately settled in Sarawak. There is no evidence, however, that such persons engaged in overt communist activities there before the Japanese war. Moreover, in contrast with the major resistance effort of the communists in Malaya, the effort against the Japanese of the Sarawak Anti-Fascist League was relatively insignificant. The communist takeover on the Chinese mainland, however, provided the impetus for a wave of communist activity in Sarawak which, assisted by local conditions and utilizing the independence issue, has reached substantial proportions. The current movement may be dated roughly from the formation of the Sarawak Overseas Chinese Democratic Youth League, in October, 1951.

According to the colonial government, the Democratic Youth League was "poorly led by inexperienced men lacking in discipline, without direction and having insufficient knowledge of communist theory to enable them to interpret and exploit any situation arising." [6] The League participated, from its inception, in student strikes and other provocative acts against the government, with the result that an emergency was proclaimed briefly in 1952 and a number of League leaders were either deported or fled to avoid arrest. However, although the League disintegrated, a nucleus of leadership remained to become the seasoned leaders of subsequent communist groups. In 1954, the Sarawak Liberation League became the center for communist indoctrination work, apparently to be superseded, from 1956 onward, by the Sarawak Advanced Youths' Association. The latter described itself in these terms:

A mass organization of the progressive elements, that will serve and struggle for the realization of complete freedom and democracy in Sarawak. All its members must energetically study and practice the theories of Marxism-Leninism and the ideology of Mao Tse-tung, and use them for the education of the masses and for elevating, with positiveness, the level of politics and ideology of ourselves and the masses with a view to becoming one of the proletarian elements. [7]

It is not known whether a communist party of Borneo, which was in the blueprint stage in 1958 and 1959, was ever actually established, or whether its formation was inhibited by the disclosures of government intelligence forces. However, the Sarawak Advanced Youths' Association is known to be in existence today, and it is designated by the Sarawak government as the "Clandestine Communist Organization," or CCO.

It is surely no accident that the communist appeal in Sarawak was initially to the youth in the Chinese middle schools or that communism continues to gain many recruits among this group today. For at a time when the proportion of Sarawak Chinese with middle-school education is rising rapidly, Sarawak—never a land of great opportunities—has had less and less to offer the educated youth, particularly those in the Chinese language stream. As a result, there have been large numbers of middle-school graduates who were either unemployed or not suitably employed; and there have been others who remained in school beyond the usual time because of the lack of employment opportunities, and who became the nuclei of subversive activities. Among educated Chinese youth, therefore, unrest and dissatisfaction with the prospects for the future have been high. Under the circumstances, it would be surprising if some of Sarawak's young Chinese did not see an escape from their own frustrations in the successes of Communist China or pin their hopes for a brighter future on the establishment of Chinese communist hegemony in Sarawak.

As elsewhere, the communists in Sarawak also undertook to penetrate the trade unions, concentrating particularly on this field of activity in 1958 and 1959. (In Kuching, for example, the goal for 1958 was to train 100 cadres and 500 additional activists.) In August, 1961, the organization reported that the working masses had "stepped on the stage," and become the "mainstay for the direction of the socialist movement"; and the government concedes that the communists control "large and predominantly Chinese Unions" in Sarawak.

Organizational efforts among the farmers are more recent. A decade ago the communists admitted that the farmers were not ready to be organized since they did not suffer from exploitation and oppression by landlords. Equally important, the peasantry in Sarawak, described in recent documents as "narrow-minded, selfish, conservative, believing in fatalism and entertaining some other ideological defects," [8] were, by and large, not Chinese and therefore not particularly susceptible to recruitment by Chinese communists. Nevertheless, by 1960, spurred on by its successes in education, labor, and politics, the organization undertook to organize the peasants into a Farmers Association, a move which specifically received the imprimatur of Peking.[9] Although the Council Negri, or State Council, refused to register the Association on the grounds it was a communist front, and although it had negligible success among the 85 per cent of the farmers who are not Chinese, it has continued to function underground and appears to have made some headway among Chinese farmers, who have a number of genuine grievances. (The government's discriminatory policy in the allocation of lands, for instance, has been felt particularly by Chinese smallholders in rubber in the Third

Division, where population growth, declining yields, and slumping rubber prices have contributed to economic stagnation since the end of the Korean War boom.)

Politically, the communists of Sarawak launched their major effort in 1959, when they supported the effort of a number of prominent Sarawak Chinese to organize the Sarawak United People's Party (SUPP), the first political party in the colony. Although the men who organized the party were in most instances professionals and property owners, and not extremists in their political views, the communists were able to infiltrate it quite extensively by making use of their student and trade union support. Moreover, although the moderates of the SUPP (like Ong Kee Hui, who is its Chairman and the president of the Kuching City Council) have been increasingly disturbed over their inability to give direction to the Party, they have continued to cooperate with the radical left—perhaps partly in the hope that they may regain control, but also because they share its views on a number of questions affecting the Chinese community.

Strength and Organization

The Federation and the Thai Border Area

When the Malayan National Liberation Army (MNLA) found itself increasingly hard-pressed by the British military effort in 1953 and 1954, it shifted its operations northward, finally digging in along the Thai-Malayan border. Here in mountainous jungle terrain, virtually impenetrable by conventional police operations, Chen Ping and the Party secretariat established their headquarters. And it is here, on the Thai side of the boundary, that the Communist Party of Malaya (CPM) has established a "geographical terrain," an area over which the CPM exercises considerable control. Some observers, indeed, regard this region as having almost reached the stage of a "liberated area." By this move, the Party leadership secured itself and its revolutionary arm against continuous harassment by military and police forces of the Malayan government. Moreover, although the Thai and Malayan governments have mounted joint offensives from time to time to flush out the terrorist army, the MNLA's policy has been to avoid contact when possible, so that these joint operations have produced negligible results. Since the middle of 1963, indeed, it has appeared probable that even these operations would shortly cease. In the absence of evidence that the fugitive forces intend to disrupt peace and order in the country where they are domiciled, the Thailand government has adopted the view that the joint border control no longer serves a useful purpose, in spite of Malayan efforts to convince them otherwise.

In this border area, the number of known communists has remained relatively stable. According to government sources, these so-called charted terrorists number between 500 and 600 men. However, they have unquestionably built up considerable support among the Thais in the area (particularly among those of Chinese extraction), on whom they rely both for supplies and intelligence. The number of communist sympathizers therefore would appear to be several times the number of actual communists. It should be borne in mind, however, that the chief propaganda efforts of the Communist Party are directed not at the Thais, since active subversion would jeopardize the Party's base of operations, but across the border at Malaya.

If the isolation of the jungles north of the Thai border provides highly effective cover from a security standpoint, it is less than ideal as the nerve center of underground activities in the Malay states. Intelligence gathered during the emergency indicated that even at the height of communist activity in the Federation, there were delays of up to a year in the transmittal of directives from headquarters to regional commands and to the units in the field. At the present time, it would appear that the communications network has been almost completely disrupted and that local communist activity in the Federation originates in the satellite organizations or in local cells and lacks central direction. Some propaganda is, of course, disseminated from the border area, chiefly into the adjacent states. It is also known that some communications are transmitted through the regular mails, since these are not easy to check on. In the absence of sustained recruitment and indoctrination efforts within the states, however, the propaganda and study materials emanating from the border are probably no more effective and much less certain than those emanating from Communist China itself. It would, in fact, be reasonable to assume that communist organs in Malaya and Singapore currently depend far more on Peking for guidance than they do on the Party leaders along the Thai border.[10]

Communist strength in the Federation, then, is extremely scattered, with known communists and activists centered chiefly around the capital, in Penang and in urban centers in Johore, Negri Sembilan, and similar places. Some 500 persons are known to be members of the underground satellite organizations. However, since they are under close police surveillance and their contacts are closely watched, the scope of their activities is severely circumscribed and the opportunities for them to enlarge their spheres of influence are very limited. It is generally conceded that these men are engaged in watchful waiting and that they are a threat only if external conditions shift in their favor.

The Communist Party of Malaya underwent extensive reorganization shortly before, and no doubt preparatory to, the talks at Baling in 1955. Since that time there appears to have been no formal reorganization, although the constriction of the Party's effective sphere of activity has undoubtedly induced practical changes. Under the 1955 reorganization, Chen Ping was confirmed as Secretary General; a Malay, Musa Ahmad, was named Chairman; and an Indian, Balan, was named Vice-chairman. (Balan had been under detention at that time for seven years, however.) Yeong Kuo, who remained behind when the Party moved to the border, was named Vice-secretary to Chen Peng. Balan renounced communism when he was subsequently released, and Yeong Kuo was killed in 1956. Chen Ping and Musa Ahmad, however, continue to hold the same positions in the Party hierarchy today and to issue documents in the name of the Central Committee.

The Central Committee, which once had from 11 to 15 members, probably now consists of 10 or less. Whether all the Central Committee is in the border zone, or whether part of it is in China, is not known. It is highly likely, however, that Committee members with prior experience in China have returned there and serve in a liaison capacity to the People's Republic. (One Politburo member, Li On Tung, was believed to have gone to China in 1953, and several years later was reported to be back in south Thailand with Chen Ping.) The Political Bureau, which appears to be the only functioning organ of the Central Committee, certainly consists of Chen Ping and no more than two or three close associates. It is doubtful if an organization bureau exists at all; if it does, it is probably identical with the Politburo. Of two Departments of Work set up at the time of the move to the border, one, the Indian Department, no longer exists. The Department of Malay Work, however, appears to be quite active, and it is believed today to be achieving greater results among the Malays than had been achieved at any previous time in the history of the Malayan communist movement.

The Malayan National Liberation Army, which formerly consisted of 12 regiments—none of which was full regimental strength—is now reduced to 3: the Eighth, or west, regiment; the Twelfth, or central, regiment; and the Tenth, in the east. The Tenth, which was originally the Malay regiment—composed of Malays backed up by Chinese cadres —now serves as the Department of Malay Work. Chen Ping, whose rise in the communist movement during the Japanese war was attributable to his contribution as a strategist in the Malayan People's Anti-Japanese Army (MPAJA), is no doubt still Supreme Commander of the Malayan National Liberation Army. This is conjecture, however, as is much that is said about the forces operating from within Thailand.[11]

Organizationally, Malaya was formerly divided into three regions— northern, central and southern, each under the direction of a Party Bureau. With the disruption of the communist movement in the Federation, however, none of these has any significance today except the northern region, which included Penang, Perak, Kedah, and Kelantan. In recent years, this Northern Bureau has been superseded by two Border Committees—the Penang-Kedah committee, which serves the western extremity of the border, and the Kelantan-Perak committee, which functions on the eastern extremity. The propaganda function of the Party, which apparently comes under the border committees, is in the hands of Chen Tien, a close associate of Chen Ping, for whom he served as interpreter at Baling.

Singapore

The size of the communist movement in Singapore is more difficult to assess, both because conclusive evidence of communist involvement is often lacking and because the distinction between the communists and other groups with similar aims and sympathies is blurred. Communist leaders have apparently solved part of their problem of eluding the police by virtually eliminating their records and files—at least in Singapore— and as a consequence, the documents which would link specific persons to the communist network in many cases do not exist. Moreover, in the propaganda field, popular front materials have almost entirely replaced the proscribed communist publications which once constituted a significant part of the evidence of communist activity. At the same time, communism has been allied in Singapore with a number of more or less popular causes—the end of British rule, propagation of Chinese education and culture, Malayan union (as opposed to Malaysian federation), guarantees for labor and improved standards for welfare—and it would certainly serve no useful purpose to lump together all those who espouse these causes under the label of communists or even communist sympathizers. What makes the line even more difficult to draw is the presence in Singapore of large numbers of Chinese, chiefly in the Chinese language stream, who admire and take pride in the achievements of Communist China. Communism and Chinese chauvinism are not the same thing, but they are not always easy to distinguish when they serve the same causes.

Intelligence sources document a number of "known communists" on the basis of dossiers dating back many years, although in some cases they do not know either the whereabouts or the present activities of these persons. The rolls of those who have, from time to time, been detained under the Preservation of Public Security Ordinance (PPSO), give some clue to the identities of known and suspected communists, but it must be borne in mind that the government does not allege that all of these are guilty of communist activities. Rather it describes those held under preventive detention—some 200 in 1963—as communists and communist sympathizers; [12] but security agents also suggest that some roundups of leftists have been aimed at crushing the united front rather than at curbing strictly communist activity. The Malaysian Minister of Internal Security has acknowledged the existence of a "well-established network of underground [communist] cadres in Singapore." [13] These probably number no less than 250 and no more than 400; but this number would have to be multiplied several times if communist activists serving in the open front were included. (Security agencies are reluctant even to speculate on the number of persons in Singapore who could be said to deliberately and actively serve the communist cause.) How effective the Singapore and Malaysian governments have been recently in reducing communist strength in Singapore by actions directed against left-wing unions and rural associations, by purges within the Chinese schools, and by arrests of persons connected with Nanyang University and of *Barisan Sosialis* leaders remains to be seen. The Singapore underground has survived greater blows in the past, and security officials admit that it has developed a high degree of resourcefulness and flexibility in adjusting to changes in circumstances. There is already evidence that the united front may be abandoned to reduce the exposure of procommunist elements.

Organizationally, then, the Singapore movement seems to be in a state of flux. When the Southern Bureau was still functioning, Singapore was nominally under it together with Johore, but Singapore undoubtedly exercised a great deal of autonomy in Party affairs even then. The Town Committee, which directed activity in Singapore when the CPM enjoyed legal existence, was destroyed by police action about 1951. Today, the direction of the Singapore movement apparently derives from the underground, with key personnel operating from the comparative safety of the Rhio Islands and entering the city only for brief periods.[14] In recent years, those serving in the open front have generally maintained no contacts with the underground even if they once served in it; and rules against illegal printed matter have been rigidly enforced on front premises. Nevertheless, as a result of the deregistration of the radical left Singapore Association of Trades Unions and simultaneous actions taken against the *Barisan* and other components of the front, it appears that the united front itself may be superseded. By early 1964, there were indications that mass action was being abandoned and that underground satellite organizations, formed along functional lines, would be set up to direct above-ground activities in the various fields.

Sarawak

In Sarawak a third set of conditions obtains. Since few restrictions were placed on Chinese-language activities until recently, and supervision of these was slight, the precautions taken by the communists to conceal underground work were not very thorough. Even above-ground publications often advanced the Peking line. Moreover, although the Sarawak government has acted in the last several years to eradicate communist subversion, substantial quantities of communist propaganda materials and a number of documents are in circulation; these have been found in a number of instances on persons detained for questioning. Evidence of communist activity, however, has not been limited since the middle of 1963 to captured documents. Ammunition and homemade guns have been seized; and small groups of Chinese youths, hiding in huts on the jungle fringe while undergoing indoctrination, have been apprehended. Evidence has mounted also that Sarawak Chinese youths, trained in guerrilla warfare in Kalimantan, have participated in raids on border villages and in skirmishes with security forces. Apparently the government is just beginning to probe the activities of some of the subversive elements in Sarawak and to sift evidence of the relationship of the communists to other rebel groups. It is not known how many Sarawak Chinese have undergone training in Indonesia, although an Indonesian officer said in 1963 that approximately 1,600 have been trained there. The Minister of Internal Security has asserted that there are 100 "active" communists in Sarawak,[15] and this is no doubt a reasonable estimate of the youthful activists engaged in the conspiracy there at the present time. It should be observed, however, that these are not the veteran revolutionaries of the Thai border area nor the hard-core communists who have been tested in Singapore's jails. As we indicated earlier, the Sarawak communist organization apparently has no official ties with either the Malayan Communist Party or with the Communist Party of Indonesia (PKI). Unofficially, however, the Sarawak movement, which the government describes as "100 per cent Chinese," is much closer to the Chinese and Singapore communists than it is to the PKI. On questions of internal organization, there is evidence that the Sarawak communists have utilized the works of Mao Tse-tung and Liu Shao-chi on organization and strategy, some of which were used by the communists in Malaya 10 to 15 years ago.[16]

According to reports of the Sarawak government,[17] the communist organization is directed by a Central Committee which operates through four Departments of Work: namely, Labor Movement, Peasantry, Students, and Political Party. (In 1956, there were also sections for Racial Work and Literature and Culture.) As in communist organizations elsewhere, a Political Bureau and an Organization Bureau function within, and give direction to, the Central Committee. The pyramidal structure, which adheres to the principle of democratic centralism, moves upward from cells, to branches, to district committees, to area and town committees, to divisional committees, to the Central Committee at the top.

Considerable evidence has been amassed concerning the operation of the *hsueh-hsih* or study cells (which constituted a major phase of the communist program during the organizational period); the reproduction and transmission of documents and study materials; the selection, training, and recruitment of cadres; and the periodic purges, of which there have been three. There is some evidence also of the relationship between the underground and the open front; in Sarawak, unlike Singapore, a number of key individuals are known to have occupied positions at both levels. What appears not to be known, however, is who the leaders of the organization are and how they function. Although a few high-level people have been removed by detention or deportation, and the labor and political fronts have been damaged by police action, it is doubtful if the authorities have made much headway against the underground, or if they know the identities or whereabouts of the men who direct the conspiracy.

The Communist Leadership in Malaysia

In its early days, the Malayan communist movement was forced to rely on leadership from outside the area—frequently, as we have seen, with disastrous results. Later, the Party came to depend on locally trained leaders, although these were augmented from time to time by revolutionaries from China. Within Singapore and the Federation, there were two main streams from which leadership was recruited: the trade-union movement and the Chinese middle schools. Of these, the schools proved to be the more rewarding source for the top echelons of the Party; according to a Party document,[18] 60 per cent of those who have risen to Central Committee rank came to the Party by way of the student movement and this trend was only slightly less evident on the second rung of leadership. It should be observed, however, that these two streams are not mutually exclusive: A significant number of labor leaders, such as Lim Chin Siong, were not bona fide unionists but rather Party men or united front men directed into labor organization.

There was, in addition, a group within the Singapore leadership from 1950 onward, not numerous but conspicuous, who were English-educated. Most of these were non-Chinese who entered communist ranks by way of student action at the university and, frequently, also by way of the anticolonialist front organizations. These organizations, particularly the Malayan Democratic Union and the PUTERA-All Malayan Council for Joint Action, were also the source for what Malayan leadership the movement acquired. On the whole, however, the Malays, even those with radical predilections, inclined toward the Indonesian nationalist movement rather than toward the Malayan communists.[19]

There were few Malayan communist leaders, then, without some middle-school education, although the number who completed senior middle school would not seem to have been very high. (Some were expelled for their political activities before they completed their studies. These included such men as Siew Chong, who became a Politburo member and is now in China, and Chiam Chung Him, one of the top-ranking figures in the Singapore underground.) A few of those with Chinese education also had a little English education; these were found chiefly in Singapore. Most of the communist leaders attended school in the Federation or in Singapore—and some in both places—although a significant number were educated in China.

Generally the leadership had its origins in the lower middle class— that is, their parents were small shopkeepers, at least able to provide some education for their children. Chen Ping's father, for example, owned a bicycle shop in Sitiawan, and Lim Chin Siong's father has a sundries store in Singapore. A few Party officials have come from the propertied class: Wu Tien Wang, a Singapore town committee member who represented the Party at the empire communist conference in London in 1947 was a member of a proprietary family in Sitiawan,[20] and Yu Choy Yip, also a former member of the Singapore town committee and now reportedly underground in the Rhios or Indonesia, was the son of a landed proprietor, too. At the other extreme, a few Party leaders have come from extremely poor economic circumstances and have themselves been employed at very menial tasks. The parents of Lam Tat, who was a Politburo member before he was killed in 1960, were hawkers; Lam himself was a member of the Democratic Servants Union, and is believed to have been employed as a cook or a manservant to a European family before the war, about the time he affiliated with the Party. Another prominent communist, active in the Malayan Races Liberation Army (MRLA) in Negri Sembilan at the time he was killed in 1956, worked as a cook and houseboy for the manager of a large oil palm corporation in Johore before the Japanese invasion.

The local Chinese have been of greater value to the movement than those born elsewhere, because they were more familiar with local conditions and also less exposed and therefore less vulnerable than their counterparts born and educated abroad. But they have been handicapped in the quality of their education. Standards in the Chinese schools in Sarawak and in the Federation have been deplorably low, and they are only somewhat better in Singapore. The Malaysian-born communists have also suffered in the quality of their Party indoctrination and training, because the Party has never been able to maintain free communication with more flourishing parties elsewhere. On the other hand, the China-born communists have never been more than a limited asset to the movement because of their extreme vulnerability. Unlike the Malaysian-born worker who could be arrested, serve a few years in jail, and return as an experienced veteran, the China-born communist was liable to deportation at the first sign of questionable political activity.

In spite of this, there have been a number of China-born Chinese who have occupied critical positions in the communist movement in Singapore, in the Federation, and in Sarawak. Probably because of their superior education, a high proportion of these served in some aspect of the public opinion or communications fields. Few are left in Malaysia today, but a number are known to serve in Peking as advisers on overseas affairs or in a liaison capacity for the Malayan Communist Party. Li On Tung, who was born in China but brought to Singapore at an early age, became a Party member in 1935, a Central Committee member in 1946 and, by 1948, a member of the Politburo. Li, who was responsible for propaganda in the Party, reportedly left for China in 1953 but apparently returned to the border area, at least for a time.

Two men, apparently China-born and -educated, who edited the Party-controlled *Min Siang Pao* in Kuala Lumpur between 1945 and 1948 and were members of the Central Committee, now serve in Peking. Lam Fong Sing, a veteran newspaper editor,[21] appeared in China as early as 1951, where he was assigned as assistant director of the South Seas Research House attached to the Commission on Overseas Chinese Affairs. Liew Yit Fun, a Eurasian who was detained in 1948 and deported in 1955, was assigned to the Chinese Party's United Front Work Department. Another prominent Malayan communist who was born in China and apparently received some education there was Lu Cheng, who commanded the 4th Regiment of the MPAJA and was active in the communist-dominated labor front before his deportation in 1946. In China, he subsequently worked with the propaganda section of the All-China General Labor Union. Later he joined the Communist Party of Malaya's Representative Group in China and for some years has been prominent in overseas Chinese affairs in Peking. The Malayan Group in China incidentally was joined in 1962 by a half-dozen Sarawak Chinese who were either deported or who requested permission to leave after being placed under restricted residence orders. These included Wen Ming Chuan, the editor of *Sin Wen Pau* of Kuching and an assistant secretary-general of the SUPP, and Bong Ki Chok and his wife, both officials of the SUPP, in whose possession was found a quantity of Chinese communist documents.

It is hardly surprising that J. H. Brimmell found the leaders of the Malayan insurrection, whom he described as "much inferior to Mao and his associates," lacking in efficiency, adaptability, and finesse.[22] Chen Ping, like most of his colleagues, was deficient in formal education and limited in his understanding of the realities of the communist revolution in China, which he tried to imitate in Malaya; apparently his outside contacts were confined to a few months' residence in Hong Kong not

long after the Japanese war.[23] Whether the CPM leaders have been able
to remedy their deficiencies during their exile in Thailand is not clear.
They have apparently learned the value of caution, and reports indicate
that they have gained valuable experience in working among the Malay
peasantry. At the same time, however, their isolation from outside contacts has been reinforced and their ranks depleted.

The problems of leadership have certainly been less acute in Singapore. Defections in the non-Chinese sector have been high, with the result
that this phase of activity appears to be at a standstill. Within the Chinese
movement, however, not only have defections been low but also there
has been a substantial pool of potential leaders coming from the middle
schools and from Nanyang University.

It is too early to evaluate the quality of leadership in Sarawak.
Undoubtedly, many of the Sarawak officials suffer from the same handi-
caps that the insurrectionary leaders in Malaya did, and they are far less
schooled in terrorist tactics than their Malayan counterparts were in
1948. Nevertheless, it appears that their indoctrination has been quite
thorough, and they have had the advantage of substantial assistance from
outside. Ironically, the cream of the Malaysian communist leadership
appears to be in none of these places, but in China itself, where the top
echelon of the Malayan communist movement may render valuable services to the overseas movement but certainly cannot provide the essential
day-to-day direction.

Recent Communist Policy in Malaysia

The Campaign for a Patriotic Front

We noted earlier that, from 1951 onward, the Communist Party of
Malaya recognized that armed insurrection was not achieving its objectives and therefore initiated a campaign of mass action intended to regain
popular support. This campaign, carried out by the *Min Yuen,* or civil
arm of the Liberation Army, undertook to infiltrate "grey" organizations,
to build new organs of support, and to foster the idea of a national united
front against imperialism. Secret documents of this period indicate that
the Party was not abandoning its reliance on armed struggle but, rather,
seeking mass support for it.

The peace feelers of 1955 [24] which led to the Baling talks were a tacit
admission that the armed struggle could not much longer serve a useful
purpose. The failure of the talks at Baling constituted a failure to effect
the united front which Chen Ping sought with patriotic elements, and it
denied to the communists the opportunity to move from illegal and secret,
to open and legal, forms of struggle.

By 1960, the Malayan Communist Party and the Liberation Army were still committed to the two-pronged policy of violent struggle to be undertaken side-by-side with legal and open struggle where possible. The Party continued at this time, however, to advocate an end to hostilities and to seek popular support to compel the Malayan government to negotiate. And it insisted that it had made numerous efforts in recent years to reopen peace talks, all of which had been sabotaged by the British. Indeed, at this point the communists were insistent that the British had started the war and that all Malayan political parties wished to see it ended—by negotiations between the "opposing forces locked in armed conflict," and without foreign interference of any kind. Recognition of the "right of self-determination" for all Malayans, including Communist Party and MNLA personnel, was also to be a condition for any negotiations.[25]

In one of the important policy papers of 1960, Musa Ahmad, on the thirtieth anniversary of the founding of the Malayan Communist Party, reiterated the five points of the Party's 1957 program. This appears to be the most recent program formulated by the Party, and apparently is still considered valid today:

1. Strengthen and safeguard the independent status of our country; pursue an independent and self-determined foreign policy of peace and neutrality; establish diplomatic relations with all countries; oppose war and uphold peace; refrain from joining any military bloc; unite and cooperate with Afro-Asian countries; strive for the reunification of Singapore with the Federation of Malaya.

2. Foster unity and mutual support among the Malays, Chinese and Indians, etc. with the Malays as the pivot; protect the legitimate rights and interests of the various nationalities in the country.

3. Safeguard the democratic rights and liberties of the people; release all patriotic prisoners; extend legal status to all political parties and public organizations which pledge loyalty to the Malayan fatherland.

4. Protect and develop national industries, agriculture and commerce; improve and develop culture; enforce universal education and ameliorate the living conditions of the people.

5. Terminate the war; repeal the Emergency Regulations and restore internal peace.[26]

It should be noted, however, that the thesis of Musa Ahmad's statement was that the Alliance government was thwarting this program by adopting policies hostile to China and other socialist and Afro-Asian countries, by discriminatory policies aimed at the Chinese and Indians (and poor Malays), by creating myths about the communist threat, and by protecting feudal interests and encouraging foreign monopoly capitalists.

A manifesto issued on the fourth anniversary of the Baling talks shows clearly the emphasis of the Party's propaganda efforts through 1960. The Baling talks had failed because all nationalities of the country had not developed a broad enough patriotic and anti-imperialist national united front based on a worker-peasant alliance. The manifesto therefore called on:

> people of all nationalities and strata, irrespective of their political affiliations, political views and religious beliefs, to unite under the banner of the patriotic and anti-imperialist united front and strive unflinchingly for bringing an end to the anti-people's colonial war, for attaining complete national independence, for realizing full democratic rights and for re-unifying Singapore with the Federation of Malaya.[27]

The Communists denied that events were going against them at this time. The *Malayan Monitor* insisted that the National Liberation Army had continued to strike hard at the imperialists in 1960 and that the Party's policy and line of action had been vindicated in the important advances made by the national liberation movement. The *Monitor* outlined two objectives for 1961: first, continued struggle for national liberation, unification, peace, and democracy through a united front; and second, "fighting for a clear-cut anti-imperialist foreign policy," again along united front lines.[28]

It should be observed that, in spite of the Party's protestations, its terms for ending the armed conflict were hardly a measure of its negotiating strength at that time. Even if the government had been willing to amnesty the guerrillas who surrendered, there was little reason for expecting that it would accord legal status to the Malayan Communist Party or "rights of self-determination" to Liberation Army personnel. One may conjecture that Party spokesmen were well aware of this and used the campaign to end hostilities more for its propaganda value than in the expectation of achieving peace. However, it is significant that, with the development of the Malaysia controversy in 1961, the Party ceased to call for the cessation of the armed struggle, although it did step up its campaign for an even broader front against imperialism and neocolonialism.

The Threat of Malaysia

The issue of Malaysia has been intimately tied in with the question of the delicate balance of Malays and Chinese in the Federation and the anticipated effect upon this balance of the addition of Singapore's predominantly Chinese population. This threat to racial balance weighed heavily with the Federation's conservative leadership against direct union, as did also the extremist nature of Singapore politics. On the other hand, Singapore's vulnerability, both economically and militarily, argued strongly for *some* type of political union with the Federation as an alternative to independence as a city-state.

The Alliance government in Kuala Lumpur viewed uneasily the prospects of having an independent Singapore, perhaps under strong Peking influence, as an immediate neighbor, and the Malayans were extremely cool to the campaign in Singapore for reunification. In Singapore, however, there was no significant segment of the population which opposed merger. The possibility that independence might well mean the severing of all economic and political ties with Malaya was one that even the militant left-wing Chinese could view only with dismay, however much they might resent the alternative of Malay hegemony.

The break within the ruling People's Action Party in Singapore came, then, not on the issue of Singapore's joining the Federation but on the nature and extent of the concessions which the Lee government was to grant to gain merger. A Malaysian federation in which Sarawak, North Borneo, and Brunei were to serve as counterbalances to Singapore was Tengku Abdul Rahman's answer to appeals that Singapore be allowed entry in the Malay federation. Even this was not to constitute a direct merger of the five territories, however. Instead, Singapore was to be granted autonomy in certain fields, and some concessions were to be made to her in regard to economics and finance. In return, however, her citizens were to be denied the privileges of citizenship in other parts of Malaysia, and Singapore's representation in the federal parliament was to be scaled down considerably compared to that of other parts of the projected federation. It was over these terms of merger that Singapore's militant left parted company with Lee Kuan Yew and the PAP and set up a new party and a new trade union federation: [29] the Singapore Association of Trades Unions (SATU). In the fight over Malaysia which followed, Lim Chin Siong and the *Barisan Sosialis* were able to gain a substantial following, not only among the communists and others of the militant left, but also among non-English-speaking, noncommunist Chinese upon whose fears for the future the communist leadership was able to capitalize. Significantly, the Front also gained allies among the Sarawak Chinese and in the Brunei Party *Ra'ayat*, and—for different reasons—in the Indonesian government.

The Malayan Communist Party did not issue a statement on Malaysia until September 20, 1963. In this statement, the Party vigorously opposed Malaysia as a neocolonialist intrigue and supported the people of "North Kalimantan" in "their sacred right to national self-determination," thereby giving CPM approval to the Borneo separatist movement.[30] However, exhaustive treatment of the communist position on Malaysia had earlier been offered by the *Malayan Monitor*, which had treated the new federation as not merely a British plot but also as one in a complex series of intrigues by the imperialists to "extend their global anti-Communist, anti-national liberation, anti-national sovereignty and anti-peace bloc."

Thus, in 1961, when Abdul Rahman invited Lee Kuan Yew to talks on Singapore's future, the *Monitor* charged that "Rahman had already received orders from the SEATO Headquarters in Bangkok to hasten the formal setting up of the Association of Asian States [ASA] on 31st July. The stage had thus been set for linking the imperialist-sponsored ASA states . . . with Rahman's 'Greater Malaysia' alignment." [31] Nor was this the full extent of the intrigue; for "Japanese 'Panzers' . . . armed and nurtured by American imperialists in Okinawa for 'duties' in Southeast Asia" were ready to move, apparently to infiltrate the Asian Common Market.

The "popular demand for genuine reunification" of Malaya, the *Monitor* contended, contained somewhat different ingredients:

> Unite all forces in both territories of Malaya [i.e., the Malayan Federation and Singapore] to secure the immediate withdrawal of all foreign military forces; the dismantling of all foreign bases; the abolition of the imperialist-dominated "War Council" in the Malayan Federation and of the "Internal Security Council" in Singapore; and dissociation of both territories of Malaya from SEATO and all its adjuncts; the scrapping of the unequal humiliating and extremely dangerous "Treaty of Military Alliance and Mutual Assistance" between Britain and the Malayan Federation; the abolition of the so-called "Internal Security" legislation imposed by the imperialists on both territories of Malaya.[32]

This program of struggle was to lead to a new national constitution guaranteeing "all political Parties and individuals the right to elect a national Parliament" and to the rights of freedom of speech, assembly, organization, and publication.

During the two years which elapsed between the Lee-Rahman talks and the realization of Malaysia in September, 1963, the communist mood fluctuated between outrage at the fresh indignities which the imperialists were attempting to perpetrate and elation at the difficulties which Malaysia encountered. There was consternation over the split within the PAP and particularly over Lee Kuan Yew's exposé of the militant left as communist-led. Faced with a "new 'monster' called the People's Socialist Front," the *Monitor* said, Lee wanted "to 'prove' that the Front is 'Red'; everybody opposing him is 'Red'." [33] Consternation mounted higher in November, 1961, when the initial merger agreement was signed in London, with its extension of the existing United Kingdom-Federation defenses agreement. This agreement, it was said, had extended the foreign military occupation of Malaya, intensified the "joint Rahman-Commonwealth-SEATO operations" against the Malayan and Bornean liberation movements and increased the "cynical use" by the Malayan government of racial antagonisms.[34] Later it was charged that the Malaysia plan would not only stir up racial troubles by setting Malay Malayans against

Chinese Malayans but also encourage chauvinism by arrogantly imposing the "imperialist 'greater nation' dictate on the people of the 3 Borneo territories." [35]

Neither the communists nor the Socialist Front in Singapore could draw much comfort from the results of the plebiscite held in Singapore in September, 1962, on the merger agreement. The *Monitor* was, however, able to cite the editorial opinion of the *London Times* in support of its contention that there was not, properly speaking, a referendum on the agreement at all. As for the *Barisan,* Lim Chin Siong announced that it would not accept the results of the "sham referendum," since it did not reflect the true wishes of the people, whom the government had intimidated.[36]

The involved series of events which commenced with the abortive Brunei rebellion in December, 1962, and climaxed with the Manila summit conference at the end of July in the following year was generally received as evidence that the east wind was indeed prevailing. The elation of the anti-imperialists was somewhat subdued, however, following the large-scale arrests in Singapore in February, 1963, which led to the detention of Lim Chin Siong, Fong Swee Suan, and many other top officials in the *Barisan* and the SATU unions and of a number of Nanyang University students and graduate officers. The communists, from the Thai border [37] to Peking, hailed the Brunei rebellion as a genuine national liberation effort directed against the neocolonial Malaysia intrigue [38] and, as such, requiring the support of all fellow anticolonialists. Indonesia's confrontation of Malaya, and subsequently of Malaysia, was welcomed as the courageous reaction of an "enraged giant" to the imperialist threat of encirclement by Malaysia.[39] Finally, Brunei's decision to remain outside of Malaysia and the difficulties which arose in the last-minute negotiations between Singapore and the Federation in London were taken as a vindication of the communist position that the Malaysia scheme had been doomed to failure from the start. In June, Malaysia was "in shambles" [40] and by August, when its inauguration was postponed, the "rotting corpse" was only awaiting burial.[41]

Not all the barriers erected in the path of Malaysia, however, met the anticolonial test. The Philippine claim to North Borneo was a machination of the "Yankee imperialists" who coveted Kalimantan's resources and "openly incited the Philippines to make a claim to Brunei" [sic].[42] Nor were the two Manila conferences or the agreement on Maphilindo greeted with enthusiasm. Both the Federation and the Philippine governments were too well-known for their anticommunist views to be accepted into the Afro-Asian circle by the communists.[43] For the record, the *Monitor* opposed the alignment on the grounds that Indonesia was the only one of the Maphilindo powers which had attained sufficient national independence and sovereignty to be able "to possess and use the democratic machinery to record the sovereign will of the people." [44] True, two of the three Maphilindo states opposed Malaysia. The Philippine motive for opposition was suspect, however, being based not on anticolonialism but on an unproved claim to Brunei which, "the world knows for a fact," had been "incorporated into the Unitary State of Kalimantan Utara." The idea of Maphilindo confederation was doubtful also because a number of its advocates saw it as a counter not to Malaysia but to the anti-Malaysia movement. "A kind of 'Balkan Federation' of the imperialist-cum-Tito mould aimed not at the imperialists but at giving the imperialists a foothold within the anti-imperialist threshhold!" [45] Ironically, the decision taken at the Manila summit to make use of a United Nations fact-finding mission to ascertain the views of the people of the two Borneo territories was greeted as a "victory for the popular forces who had resolutely and ceaselessly hammered at 'Malaysia'." [46]

Such internal consistency as the communist arguments possessed derived in large part from the *Monitor's* thesis that the Southeast Asia Treaty Organization (SEATO) was the chief agency of imperialist intrigue in the region and that Malaysia constituted only one, albeit a key, aspect of the SEATO plot. According to this thesis, Malaysia's chief *raison d'être* was to give the SEATO powers bases from which to launch their operations against national liberation forces in southeast Asia, and Abdul Rahman and Lee Kuan Yew were merely puppets of the imperialists in this enterprise. Because the Treaty Organization was "hated throughout the length and breadth of Malaya," the Tengku could not commit Malaya to it openly. Nevertheless, it was charged, he had made facilities available to train personnel for antiliberation campaigns in Vietnam, Laos, and the Thai border region, and Lee and Abdul Rahman had allowed Malayan bases to be used as staging grounds for troops and combat aircraft committed to SEATO operations outside Malaya.[47]

The SEATO test was also a convenient one for identifying the friends and foes of the Malayan communists, although here as elsewhere it sometimes required some interesting extensions. Indonesia's identification as an anti-imperialist ally was, of course, well-established, and the Malayan communists went to great lengths to demonstrate their support for her West Irian claim.[48] On the opposite side, Germany became a part of the SEATO plot—like Japan, by a process of association—in this instance by way of ASA and NATO. On the issue of the Sino-Indian border dispute, the convolutions required were even more involved in view of Nehru's long association with the cause of Asian nonalignment. Nevertheless, by late 1963, the Nehru government was thoroughly implicated by the *Monitor* in both the "British imperialist 'Malaysia' plot" and in

SEATO. As to the Indian government's links with the Malaysia scheme, "its policy of 'non-aligned' alignment with U.S. and British imperialism against China and Pakistan," it was said, was clearly "being extended into the 'Malaysia' region (via the Nicobars and the Andamans) on promise of a jackal's share of the spoils should the imperialist plot in Asia succeed." [49] On India's role in the SEATO, the *Monitor* asserted:

> It is now known that the enforcement of "Malaysia" is part of the Western imperialist scheme to extend the operational range of SEATO, one flank of which is being extended in league with the Nehru Government (via the Nicobar and Andaman Islands), while the eastern flank is being widened by the direct participation of the American 7th Fleet in the "encirclement" of S.E.A.

The assignment to SEATO of a major role in the Malaysia plot has, it will be noted, had the interesting corollary of elevating the United States to a leading part in the production. According to the *Monitor*, American imperialists had a threefold interest in Malaysia: first, "to join in 'strangling' Indonesia"; second, "to 'assist' Britain in 'strengthening' 'Malaysia'" in the hope of gaining the proprietary role there when British imperialism collapsed; and third, to acquire a "military-economic base" near Indochina to stave off their imminent defeat in Laos and Vietnam.

How prevalent this idea of American interest at work in Malaysia was could be seen in the Singapore elections of September, 1963, in which the *Barisan* charged that American dollars were being used to split the vote of the extreme left in order to defeat *Barisan* candidates.[50] In addition, the uneasiness caused in Malaya by the United States government's policy of releasing stockpiled rubber and tin and thus holding down world prices has been exploited by the communists. However, this issue has been used chiefly for its value as an irritant, with only awkward attempts being made to fit the American policy in with the plot thesis.

"What is Necessary at this Stage"

It appears that the communists' strategy was to foster opposition to the Malaysia plan, from any direction possible, but to avoid actual commitments until they were reasonably sure of adequate assistance from noncommunist quarters. The available evidence also suggests that until July, 1963, they pinned their hopes on Malaysia being thwarted without overt communist intervention. Beginning at that time, however, they began to advocate a more open program of resistance and they received overt support from Peking in this advocacy.

Singapore's open front had, of course, attempted to block Singapore's participation in Malaysia by utilizing the legal channels. At least, in the referendum of September, 1962—in which there were three alternatives, but no way of voting against the merger—they tried to induce voters to register a protest by submitting unmarked ballots. (Contrary to its previously announced policy, the government did not count blank votes as votes for the Lee-Rahman agreement but tallied them separately.) Subsequently, some of the *Barisan* leaders, including Lim Chin Siong, held conversations with Sheikh Azahari when the latter was laying the groundwork for the Brunei rebellion, but apparently they decided against offering him any form of assistance. The *Barisan* did, however, offer public support for the rebel cause after the rebellion began, a fact which was utilized by the Internal Security Council when it instituted the massive arrests of February, 1963. In the aftermath of Operation Cold Stores, *Barisan* efforts to regain the initiative were seriously hampered, chiefly because the Front was deprived of its most competent leaders. Both in the elections and in their wake, the left-wing parties were consistently outmaneuvered by the government, which had admitted its readiness to use communist tactics to suppress communism. By the end of October, Dr. Lee Siew Choh, the *Barisan* chairman, reminded a rally that Lim had called for constitutional struggle as long as there were "constitutional means left" for their struggle, but Lee concluded that the PAP was doing everything possible to "close all doors of constitutional struggle." But his public conclusion, that future emphasis must be on mass work—that is, on the organization and education of the masses [51]— hardly seemed to be the alternative which Lim had in mind.

In contrast with the situation in Malaya, there were a number of factors in Sarawak which inclined the communists there toward armed struggle. One of these was the acuteness, for Sarawak, of the issue of independence versus merger with Malaya. Many of Sarawak's citizens, both Chinese and Ibans, felt that Malaysia was sprung upon them without warning and that their future was being committed without their being given a voice in the matter; and neither group relished the idea of Malay hegemony, which they associated with the old Brunei sultanate. The timing of Malaysia, which was designed to prevent the opposition from mobilizing, required, from the communist point of view, that action to keep Sarawak out of Malaysia be immediate. In a second sense, also, the communists were impelled toward armed subversion by the course of events, since both the Brunei revolt and Indonesia's confrontation offered fortuitous assistance which any avowed revolutionary movement would have found difficult to resist. But it is also a fact that the general situation in Sarawak and the nature of the movement there particularly inclined the Sarawak communists toward armed struggle. As we have noted earlier, this movement was characterized by the extreme youth

of both its organization and its membership; and the degree of frustration, both intellectual and economic, was extremely high among its
members. Under these circumstances, a high proportion of the Sarawak
communists were emotionally attuned to revolutionary activity.[52]

The communist organization and the labor and political fronts
through which it operated presented a solid front of opposition to Malaysia
at a time when there was little informed opinion in other segments of
the populace on the subject; and they employed some of their most
colorful invective to describe it:

> Seeing their approaching doom, the colonialists are terrified. When the
> Malaysia Plan was proposed these degenerated politicians and the slaves
> and running dogs of the British in the 5 states behaved as if they had
> come across a precious jewel. They immediately cried out and sprawled
> before the Tengku begging for the preservation of their lives as dogs. . . .
> We want to remind this group of slaves and running dogs that we shall
> be able to clean away this whole group of political rubbish.[53]

Whether or not the Sarawak communists were informed beforehand
of the Azahari plot concerning the Borneo states, they did not take part
in the rebellion in December, 1962. Rather, it appears that the decision
to embark on limited armed struggle dated from that event. A document
seized by the police offered this justification for the resort to violence:

> Since the outbreak of Brunei, the colony has suppressed the people of our
> country. We can see very clearly that in the revolutionary struggle of our
> country, it is impossible to strive for the independence of our country by
> peaceful constitutional means. If we want to achieve true independence
> and liberation, then we have no recourse but to tread on the road of
> armed struggle.

At the same time, however, the Borneo organization was not willing
to commit the error, committed by the Party in Malaya in 1948, of cutting
itself loose from the legal phase of activity. In another document on the
organization's purposes in contesting the elections in 1963, we find these
significant assertions:

> One hand actively preparing for armed struggle, another hand continuing
> to carry out constitutional struggle, this is our proposal today. We, in lay-
> ing stress on the road to arms have not and cannot, under the present day
> circumstances, let go our constitutional struggle. Therefore we must and
> should participate in this year's elections and at the same time fight for
> victory in the elections. . . .
>   When the people are still backward (especially the natives) they
> are infatuated with constitutional struggle (especially the bourgeoisie).
> As regards the armed struggle, at a time when they either know nothing
> or little about it, or become very frightened, to let go constitutional strug-

gle will mean giving up the fight to win the people over and lead them, isolating ourselves and damaging the racial united front.[54]

On the question of the future of the united front, this document was equally candid. The left wing of the Sarawak United People's Party had been weakened by security action. Therefore, for the present, the communists must continue to work with the "reactionaries" led by the "Ong XX" group,[55] in the meantime, however, exposing them and preparing, if necessary, to form a new party. It is quite obvious that Azahari's rebels, who specifically sought to restore the Brunei sultanate for all of northern Borneo, were operating at cross-purposes with the Sarawak communists, and the communists were presumably aware of this fact. However, it was less obvious that the cause of Indonesian confrontation was not the cause of Sarawak communism. It appears, for example, that hundreds of young communists who crossed the border expecting to be welcomed fraternally by members of the *Partai Komunis Indonesia* (PKI) faced disillusionment on the other side. Instead of PKI agents, the border recruits found Indonesian Army men training them in guerrilla warfare and hardly according them the treatment they had anticipated. What was particularly remarkable, however, was that the spokesmen for Malayan communism, from London to Peking to the Thai border, blandly asserted the legitimacy of the Azahari "unitary state" without weighing the effect of this claim on the Sarawak movement; Sarawak Chinese could hardly be expected to fight for the domination of Brunei as an alternative to Kuala Lumpur, and yet this is precisely what the endorsement of the Azahari claim implied.

However, in September, when Malaysia came into being, the *Monitor* abandoned its policy of caution and boldly proclaimed a program of action which was to include all elements opposing Malaysia. Significantly, in this they received extensive support both from the press and radio in Peking. The *Monitor,* in an editorial entitled, "The 'Malaysia' Explosion," indicated that what was both necessary and feasible at that stage of the anti-Malaysia, anti-imperialist struggle was a "broad united front of the people within each given country concerned, coupled with a broad, closely coordinated movement among the peoples of the various countries directly concerned." There were to be four aspects to this program:

(a)   the consolidation and extension of the broad anti-'Malaysia', anti-imperialist united front on a national scale in Malaya;

(b)   the consolidation and extension of the broad anti-'Malaysia', anti-imperialist united front on a national scale in the three Borneo territories, coupled with the extension of the guerrilla war carried out by the Kalimantan Utara National Army;

(c)   the consolidation and extension of the broad anti-'Malaysia', anti-imperialist struggle programme of confrontation on a national scale as outlined by the Indonesian Government and people.

(d)   the setting up of a joint operation council or command to co-ordinate the day-to-day implementation of the common strategy of the anti-'Malaysia', anti-imperialist campaign throughout the region.

This editorial was quoted extensively in the Peking *People's Daily* on October 8, with the conclusion, "What is Necessary at this Stage," cited in full, and a much condensed version of the same editorial was broadcast on Radio Peking a day later.[56] By the year's end, however, in spite of continued exhortations to the Malayan people to meet the challenge with struggle—"determinedly, unswervingly, and with the clear orientation of overthrowing every apparatus, personnel and scheme directly or indirectly connected with imperialism,"[57] there was little evidence that the Malaysian communists themselves had succeeded in forming a consolidated front. Indeed, in spite of the basic similarities between the Party statement on Malaysia in September and the position taken by the *Monitor* and endorsed by Peking, the statement did not actually constitute a call for action, although it did assert that the struggle against Malaysia would continue. Either the government was keeping the communists in Singapore and the Federation too tied down to be able to move, or they were still waiting for signs that the time was propitious for action.

The Malayan Communist Party and the Sino-Soviet Dispute

Nowhere has the Communist Party of Malaya shown its complete subservience to the Chinese communists so much as on the question of the split within the international communist movement. In fact, on this question it appears that the Malayan communist line may be literally made in Peking. This requires little elaboration. The Central Committee itself is on record, in a series of letters to fraternal parties, as supporting Peking's position against Moscow's.[58] Mao's thinking is the "common treasure of the international Communist movements and of all oppressed nations throughout the world," illuminating the way for the "peoples of Asia, Africa and Latin America in their struggle against imperialist oppression and enslavement and for freedom and liberation." Comrade Mao's conclusion that "imperialism and all reactionaries are paper-tigers" and his idea that one must slight the enemy strategically while taking full account of him tactically had "heightened the Malayan people's confidence in victory and helped them to better grasp the art of struggle."[59] The 1957 Moscow Declaration and the 1960 Moscow Statement are the common programs for the international movement. The modern revisionism of Tito is the main danger facing the international communist movement. And the Malayan communists hope that a reasonable solution to the Sino-Soviet differences "may be found through equal and comradely consultations" in accordance with criteria establshed in the 1960 Statement.[60]

The *Malayan Monitor* expounded at greater length on specific aspects of the controversy, publishing, for example, a six-page defense of China's position on the three-power nuclear treaty.[61] They also tilted with modern revisionists, both identified and unidentified, on a number of issues, including the border dispute between China and India; and the *Monitor's* views on these issues have been cited at some length by Radio Peking. None of this, however, has contributed any new dimension to the quarrel since the Malayan position *is* the Peking position. If the *Monitor* has added anything new to the dispute, it has been simply its finding that the modern revisionists, otherwise unidentified, have joined with the imperialists and their stooges, "certain heavily aligned 'non-aligned' 'neutralists'" and the "raggle-taggle brigade of faint hearts" in suggesting that confrontation be ended.[62]

Conclusion

The circumstances which surrounded the inauguration of Malaysia were hardly auspicious. They should not obscure the fact, however, that the birth of Malaysia marked the end of the era of British colonialism in Asia, and with it any advantage the communists had in the fight for independence. This does not mean that Malaysian communists will abandon the issue of neocolonialism, even if Malaysian differences with Indonesia and the Philippines are resolved. It does mean that patriotism has a new connotation, which the communists, in opposing the existing government, cannot utilize.

The issue of Chinese chauvinism is another matter. So long as there is evidence that the Chinese are victims of discriminatory policies, whether culturally or politically, they will be potential targets for communist propaganda. As we have noted, communism in Malaysia has thrived most of the time almost exclusively within the overseas Chinese communities, and the temptation for the communist leadership to appeal to Chinese sentiments is therefore overwhelming. The issue of Chinese nationalism is, nonetheless, not a simple one for the communists. Chinese sentiment has itself undergone a radical change during the lifetime of the Malayan communist movement; the desire to preserve things Chinese remains, but the sense of expatriation has virtually disappeared. Malayan Chinese may take pride in China's position today, but they are Malayans as well as Chinese and therefore concerned primarily with conditions in Malaya; Sarawak Chinese are similarly oriented to their state of residence.

The demands of expediency, then, as well as their ideological commitments, prevent the communist leadership in Malaysia from fully exploiting Chinese chauvinism. A program which threatened to disrupt the present relations among ethnic groups in Malaysia would cost the communists support both at home and in the Afro-Asian world. Nevertheless, the issue remains—and it could become crucial, if economic conditions, for example, sharpened existing racial differences.

The communists appear to be tied down on the peninsula and in Singapore. In Sarawak, they constitute a major threat only as long as they receive assistance from Indonesia. Malaysian prosperity is a deterrent to any significant resurgence of communist strength. Nevertheless, the number of communists and communist sympathizers is significant, particularly in Singapore and Sarawak; any change in the economic situation which carried with it an increase in unemployment and a decrease in the rate of government expenditures would certainly bring renewed communist activity. A prolonged crisis with Indonesia might also produce the same result.

Communism in Malaysia: A Multifront Struggle

1. I.e., Burma, Indochina, Indonesia, Malaya, and Thailand.
2. Virtually the entire prewar leadership was wiped out by the Japanese in mid-1942, in separate actions in Singapore and the peninsula; and it remains in doubt whether the Party Secretary, Loi Teck—who survived the war—wanted the Party to succeed. In any event, he was subsequently charged—after he had absconded with the Party's funds—with having betrayed it to the Japanese.
3. J. H. Brimmell, *Communism in Southeast Asia* (London: Oxford University Press, 1959), p. 82, alleges that it was the interests of the Soviet Party, rather than those of the local parties, which led to the call for insurrection in 1948. It is supremely important, of course, to recall the 1948 Calcutta communist conference in which the signal for a switch to militant tactics was given by Cominform agents. This had almost immediate repercussions—in terms of stepped-up guerrilla warfare—in all parts of southeast Asia.
4. Also known as the Malayan Races Liberation Army.
5. Singapore Legislative Assembly, *The Communist Threat in Singapore*, Cmd. 33 of 1957, 15 pp.
6. Sarawak Information Service, *The Danger Within* (Kuching: 1963), p. 3.
7. *Ibid.*, p 5.
8. Cited from a captured document entitled, "How to Educate the Masses," in *Communism and the Farmers* (Kuching: Sarawak Government, 1961), p. 4.
9. I.e., it was given recognition on Radio Peking. *Ibid.*
10. A variety of contacts with China are possible by both direct and indirect means, and Radio Peking can be readily picked up anywhere in Malaysia. Radio Peking undoubtedly furnishes much of the communist study material used in the area; it also may provide an important medium for transmission of CPM policies within Malaya. See note on *Malayan Monitor, infra.*
11. Chen Ping's own presence in the border area has not been definitely established. There have, however, been indications which point to his presence

there: e.g., reports by surrendered terrorists of persons assigned as Chen's bodyguards, and so forth. One recent newspaper report from Alor Star indicates that, according to police sources there, the communist guerrillas are split into two groups, and that Chen Ping is believed to be with the elite group which operates in the deep jungle. *Sunday Mail* (Singapore), September 8, 1963.

12. See speech by Dato (Dr.) Ismail bin Dato Abdul Rahman, Minister of Internal Security, on Television Singapura of November 3, quoted in *Straits Times* (Singapore), November 4, 1963. Ismail said on this occasion that he could "assure" his listeners that the powers of preventive detention would only be used on "communists, their sympathizers and others who threaten the security" of the country.

13. *Ibid.*

14. Although the Rhios are very close to Singapore, they are Indonesian-owned.

15. *Straits Times* (Singapore), November 17, 1963.

16. A reproduction of a speech by Liu Shao-chi on organization and disciplinary self-cultivation was among the communist materials found in the possession of a Chinese couple from Kuching who submitted to deportation in 1962. Copies of this speech published in Malaya were captured in the Federation a decade ago, although it does not appear to have ever been published in China. See H. F. Schurman, "Organizational Principles of the Chinese Communists," *China Quarterly,* Vol. I (1960).

17. *The Danger Within;* also Council Negri, *Subversion in Sarawak* (Kuching, 1960).

18. A history of the communist movement in Malaya, seized in December, 1962, which was apparently prepared in the border region for indoctrination purposes.

19. See, e.g., Brimmell, *Communism in Southeast Asia,* pp. 97ff., 330ff. Brimmell comments that the communist insurrection took on in many ways the "aspect of a concealed war between Malays and Chinese."

20. Wu reportedly has been with the Twelfth Regiment in southern Thailand since 1956.

21. He edited *Nanyang Siang Pao* before the Japanese war and is the author of a book entitled *Problems of Malaya.*

22. *Communism in Southeast Asia,* pp. 320-39⁻ *passim.* Brimmell comments, for example, that their 1955 program was "certainly far too subtle" for them to have evolved—and probably also to have carried out—unaided.

23. Chen Ping's destination on this occasion was China, where he expected to confer with Party leaders. Circumstances in China prevented him going beyond Hong Kong, it is believed; however, it is not known who his contacts there were.

24. Originating in the so-called Ng Heng letter of May 1 to Malayan political leaders.

25. *Malayan Monitor* (London), June 30, 1960. See also "For a Just Settlement of the Malayan War," a CPM statement of September, 1959. *Ibid.,* January 31, 1960.

26. "Forward Along the Path Toward Complete Independence," statement of April 30, 1960. *Ibid.,* September 30, 1960. Contrary to usual practice, this statement was not issued in the names of Chen Ping and Musa Ahmad jointly, but only in Musa Ahmad's.

27. "Manifesto of the Communist Party of Malaya on the Fourth Anniversary of the Baling Talks," December 28, 1955." *Ibid.,* April 30, 1960.

28. This was to be a foreign policy "in keeping with the national aspirations and the interests of the Malayan people: namely, a foreign policy which strictly upholds the 5 principles of peaceful coexistence among nations with different

social systems, respects the UN charter; develops and extends friendship and mutually-beneficial intercourse with all friendly countries, including the Socialist countries, and which entirely dissociates Malaya from SEATO and all other imperialist-sponsored 'hot' or 'cold' war commitments." *Ibid.,* January 31, 1961.

29. The SATU was deregistered in 1963.

30. "Malaysia: Statement of the CP of Malaya," *Malayan Monitor* (London), January 31, 1964, pp. 1-2.

The *Malayan Monitor,* although not an official publication, publishes policy statements of the Central Committee of the CPM, as well as Party greetings to fraternal parties and communist governments. Moreover, it is recognized as an authoritative spokesman for Malayan communism both in London, where it is published, and in Peking. On current questions, it has the advantage of access to sources denied to the Party itself; moreover, it appears to reflect Singapore communist preoccupations far more than does the Central Committee. Lim Hong Bee, its publisher, helped organize the Malayan Democratic Union in Singapore in 1945, and went to London in 1947 as a representative for the PUTERA-AMCJA front. He has since been barred from re-entry.

31. *Ibid.,* August 31, 1961. The *Malayan Monitor* not only blurs the distinction between organizations with some deliberation, but is also guilty on occasion of glaring errors in fact—whether accidentally or not is unclear. Thus, on numerous occasions, it has asserted that the Philippine claim was to Brunei rather than North Borneo; and recently it claimed that the ill-fated Southeast Asia Friendship and Economic Treaty superseded ASA when, in fact, it preceded it.

32. *Ibid.*

33. *Ibid.,* October 31, 1961.

34. *Ibid.,* November 30, 1961.

35. *Ibid.,* April 30, 1962.

36. *Ibid.,* September 30, 1962.

37. A statement on Brunei attributed to the Central Committee of the CPM and dated December 15, 1962, was published by the *Malayan Monitor* in the same month, together with statements on the Sino-Indian dispute and on the Cuba incident, both dated November 30. The fact that these documents, and particularly the Brunei one, were issued by the Central Committee and released abroad so soon after the events to which they relate raises interesting questions about their origin, particularly since one of them was signed. It is significant that translations of these documents, both in Chinese and in *Jawi* (i.e., Malay script), were sent from the Thai border area into the Federation, but only some months after the London release.

38. The *Monitor* explained that after the Azahari forces achieved their "initial purpose," they "withdrew to prearranged areas, leaving the oil installations, all properties and all personnel taken prisoner unharmed." December 31, 1962.

39. *Ibid.,* November 30, 1963.

40. *Ibid.,* June 30, 1963.

41. *Ibid.,* August 31, 1963.

42. *Ibid.,* December 31, 1962.

43. The *Monitor* noted critically a statement by the Tengku that, en route to his meeting with Soekarno in June, 1963, he had agreed in Manila that the Philippines and Malaya should jointly contain communism. Curiously, however, no notice was taken of the press reports from Manila at the close of the foreign ministers' meeting that the three powers had agreed to cooperate in solving their Chinese problems.

44. *Ibid.,* September 30, 1963.

45. *Ibid.*

46. *Ibid.*, August 31, 1963.

47. E.g., in May, 1962, a flight of British fighters and bombers was allegedly sent from Singapore to Thailand "for direct aggression against Laos." *Ibid.*, May 31, 1962.

48. In an unusual burst of zeal, the MNLA proclaimed that it would "send its commanders and fighters to Indonesia whenever circumstances permit to join the volunteers army to liberate West Irian and to fight shoulder to shoulder with the Indonesian people so as to drive away the Dutch imperialists . . ." Malayan National Liberation Army's Statement of June, 1962, *ibid.*, September 30, 1962.

49. *Ibid.*, October 31, 1963.

50. *Barisan* campaign posters and streamers graphically portrayed an American tank from which the Statue of Liberty held aloft a missile, Uncle Sam handing out dollars to the head of another left-wing party, and other propaganda of this nature.

51. *Malayan Monitor*, November 30, 1963. In another message at the beginning of 1963, Lim had written:
    "*There can be no harmony, no development, and no progress for our nation so long as the left-wing is excluded from the arena of constitutional politics by police repression. Only with the free and unhampered participation of the progressive forces can the constructive energies of the people be released. However, the ruling clique in the Federation are heavily committed to the imperialists and will pursue an anti-democratic policy in the hope of maintaining themselves in power indefinitely.*
    "*If the forces in the Federation who are pressing for increased recourse to police terror have their way, then a turning point in this country's political development will have been reached. The country will then be set on a course that must lead to a fascist and military dictatorship. The left-wing forces must then make the necessary judgement on the matter.*" [Emphasis in original text.] *Ibid.*, February 28, 1963.

52. The emotional appeal to armed struggle is apparent in a number of the captured materials, such as this poem found in possession of a female cadre:
    The graceful and beautiful rivers and mountains of the fatherland
    Lie across North Kalimantan,
    Bordering the South China Sea in the North and Indonesia in the South.
    British imperialism sucks dry our blood and sweat
    Oh, the labouring people suffer from hunger and hardship.
    The heroic and brave people
    Have to pick up shotguns to fight them.
    We want to chase away British imperialism
    With determination and perseverance.

53. From an issue of the *Workers' and Farmers' News*, seized in June, 1962. Quoted in a press release, Sarawak Information Service, August 22, 1962.

54. Press release, Sarawak Information Service, July 31, 1962.

55. A reference to the moderates within the SUPP, led by Ong Kee Hui. Ong, who was educated in the English stream, was of considerable importance to the SUPP because he had the contacts, through many years of government service as an agriculturist, to bring large numbers of Ibans to the Party rolls. (Although claiming to be multiracial, the SUPP was in fact effective only among the Chinese at the polls.)

56. Simultaneously, the China bimonthly *World Knowledge* published two articles on Malaysia. The first, entitled "Oppose the 'Federation of Malaysia' Which Has Been Assembled by Imperialism," gave China's three-point stand against Malaysia. The second, " 'Malaysia': A Product of Neo-Colonialism," accused the United States of trying to take over British interests in Malaya.

57. *Malayan Monitor,* October 31, 1963.

58. This was true, for example, even when other parties in the area were denying that the rift was significant (e.g., see "The Communist Party of Malaya Greets the 7th (Extraordinary) National Congress of the Communist Party of Indonesia." *Ibid.,* June 30, 1962.)

59. "Greetings of the Communist Party of Malaya to the Communist Party of China on its 40th Anniversary" (June, 1961). *Ibid.,* October 31, 1961.

60. "Letter of the Delegation of the Malayan Communist Party to all Delegates Attending the Sixth Congress of the German Socialist Unity Party" (January 17, 1963). *Ibid.,* April 30, 1963.

61. *Ibid.,* August 31, 1963.

62. *Ibid.,* November 30, 1963. The *Monitor's* charges against the modern revisionists bear a strong resemblance to charges recently aired in Hanoi by the weekly *Thong Nhat (Reunification).* This "organ of struggle for the liberation of South Vietnam" was reported as identifying the opponents of Hanoi's war effort as "the revisionists and rightist opportunists who have been so frightened by America's nuclear force that they have highly publicized the bourgeois pacifist thoughts about these mass-destruction weapons." Quoted in the *Saigon Post,* March 16, 1964.

Selected Bibliography

Brimmell, J. H., *Communism in Southeast Asia: A Political Analysis.* London: Oxford University Press, 1959.

Communism and the Farmers. Sarawak, Kuching, 1961.

Hanrahan, Gene Z., *The Communist Struggle in Malaya.* New York: International Secretariat, Institute of Pacific Relations, 1954.

Malayan Monitor (London).

Miller, Harry, *Menace in Malaya.* London: George G. Harrap and Company, Ltd., 1954.

Pye, Lucian W., *Guerrilla Communism in Malaya: Its Social and Political Meaning.* Princeton, N.J.: Princeton University Press, 1956.

Subversion in Sarawak. Council Negri. Sessional Paper No. 3. Kuching, 1960.

The Communist Threat in Singapore. Singapore, Legislative Assembly, Cmd. 33, 1957.

The Communist Threat to the Federation of Malaya. Federation of Malaya, Legislative Council. Paper No. 23. Kuala Lumpur, 1959.

The Danger and Where It Lies. Federation of Malaya, Information Services, Kuala Lumpur, 1957.

The Danger Within. Sarawak Information Service, Kuching, 1963.

Indonesia: The PKI's "Road to Power"

Guy J. Pauker

The United States government's annual
estimate of communist party organizations comprised, in 1963,
91 parties, excluding splinter groups. The membership
of all communist parties was estimated to be over 43 million,
of which the 14 parties in communist
states accounted for 39 million, or 90 per cent.
The largest parties outside the communist
orbit are the Indonesian and the Italian, which together
account for about three-quarters of the total membership
outside the communist bloc.
In October, 1961, the Italian Communist Party claimed
a membership of 1,729,000; but in 1963
it admitted a drop to 1,543,754 members.

The State Department does not accept even this figure and estimates the size of the Italian Communist Party at only 1.3 million. Similarly, the State Department reduces the membership figure of the Indonesian party from the 2.5 million it claimed in December, 1963, to an estimated 1.9 million.[1]

Unlike the Italian Communist Party, which has declined in size since April, 1951, when it claimed over 2.5 million members,[2] the Indonesian Party has been expanding. On June 26, 1964, a delegation of the Central Committee of the *Partai Komunis Indonesia* (PKI) presented the Indonesian government with information on the Party in accordance with Presidential Regulation No. 13 of 1960. It publicly claimed 3 million members, although no exact figure was released.[3] Even if the much lower State Department estimate were correct, the PKI would still be the largest communist party outside the communist orbit.

Like the Italian Communist Party, the PKI is a creative Party, confident of its ability to fit Marxism-Leninism to the specific conditions of its country. The Italian Communist Party has been directing its appeal, under the leadership of the late Palmiro Togliatti, to the population of a politically advanced Western country. It favors the "peaceful road to socialism." In matters of doctrine, it sides with the Communist Party of the Soviet Union (CPSU) in the latter's dispute with the Communist Party of China, but at the same time it asserts its organizational independence. The PKI, however, increasingly expresses agreement with the Chinese and hostility toward the Russians, although it is striving in fact to formulate its own methods for the seizure of power, which may be less remote from the Italians' than verbal differences would lead one to believe. In both instances primary reliance is neither on parliamentary struggle nor on armed combat, but on constant efforts to become accepted as parties of government. Endorsement of Soviet or Chinese arguments may have to be accounted for primarily by the nature of the audience. Apparently the Italians prefer to promise gradual changes, while the Indonesians seem to favor revolutionary-sounding phraseology. The Italian communist leader, Giuliano Pajetta, trying to explain why the views expressed by the PKI "differ markedly" from those of the Italian party, had this to say following a visit to Djakarta in April, 1963:

> It is hard to explain the [PKI's] prejudice against the "peaceful paths" unless it has something to do with the danger of rightists in a party that follows so skillful and prudent a policy. Quite frankly, though, if we keep in mind the political line the Indonesian comrades follow and remember that they actually operate like this, these explanations seem inadequate, and views such as theirs [appear as] a symptom and manifestation of formalism.[4]

One of these two largest communist parties outside the communist orbit exemplifies the problems facing communism in a Western environment, the other in a non-Western environment. What the two parties have in common is the intellectual vigor and political shrewdness of their leaders, who have motivated and inspired dedicated cadres able, in turn, to recruit substantial followings and thus to build up impressive mass parties. In countries such as France and India, by contrast, the relative sterility of the leadership seems to be reflected in parties of only moderate vigor and size.

Within about 13 years, the present leaders of the PKI have succeeded in transforming a small and politically bankrupt party into one of the world's significant political movements. Their ultimate purpose, of course, is the establishment of a communist Indonesia. The purpose of this paper is to examine how they go about it and whether they are likely to succeed.

Successful communist parties have followed a variety of roads to power. In many cases, victory came in a way which had not been planned. The Chairman of the PKI, D. N. Aidit, was an early advocate of the thesis that there are various roads to power. He stated on May 23, 1952, when Stalin was still alive:

> The people of Indonesia must be oriented toward the socialist Soviet Union and not toward imperialist America. This does not mean that the state structure of the Soviet Union, that is, the Soviet system, should be followed by all nations, including Indonesia. Certainly not. On the contrary, *each nation will travel its own road toward socialism*, on the basis of the development of its national situation, its political situation, its economy, and its culture. [Emphasis supplied.] [5]

In 1961, I characterized the road to socialism followed by the PKI as one of seeking to obtain power by "acclamation." Power is to be won by:

> building up [the Party's] prestige as the only solid, purposeful, disciplined, well-organized, capable political force in the country, a force to which Indonesia will turn in despair when all other possible solutions have failed. In building up this image, it is important that the PKI demonstrate its power, skill, and influence at all levels of public life.[6]

Developments since 1961 have strengthened the author's impression that the PKI's preferred strategy is to establish itself as Indonesia's last hope. In an increasingly anti-Western and radical-nationalist political climate, the communists are likely to be the major beneficiaries of a situation in which the range of options available to the Indonesian political elite has narrowed considerably. The economic stabilization program, formulated in 1963 by international experts, has been abandoned.

Foreign economic assistance is not likely to be forthcoming in significant amounts as long as Indonesia maintains an aggressive posture in southeast Asia. The concentration of the elite's attention on foreign policy, in the context of a continuous struggle against imperialism, colonialism, and neocolonialism, favors an atmosphere of intolerance toward all moderate views, which are being denounced as counterrevolutionary.

In the atmosphere of permanent excitement created by economic crisis and international conflict, the interests of the masses are neglected by the established political elite, which includes the leaders of the major governmental parties, the higher echelons of the bureaucracy, and the senior members of the officer corps. Meanwhile, the PKI leaders and cadres are establishing themselves as the true friends and protectors of the masses, and as persons of honesty, integrity, and dedication in a country where inflation has turned corruption into a way of life. In this political environment, the masses—as they become mobilized by the direct communist political action which is compounding the general impact of modernization—are likely to provide the PKI with enough popular support to make its claim to power irresistible.

This hypothesis assumes, of course, that the established political elite, including the armed forces, will have lost their will to resist a communist take-over. Careful scrutiny of political developments in Indonesia in recent years makes this assumption increasingly plausible. Since the Sukarno regime has stifled free political debate, the Indonesian political system lacks the protection of healthy criticism. In the distorted mental environment thus created, political forces which are less disciplined than the PKI, and which lack the appeal conferred on the PKI by participation in an international revolutionary movement, are languishing both ideologically and organizationally. There is little or no evidence that the PKI's major rivals, such as the Nationalist Party (PNI) and the Moslem Nahdatul Ulama Party, are generating leaders, cadres, and mass support capable of offering the Indonesian people truly attractive alternatives.

And while the PKI has less and less to fear from political competition, it also is meeting less resistance from the armed forces. The Indonesian officer corps has been and still appears, at least superficially, anticommunist. Senior officers have opposed admission of communists to the cabinet. Yet the will of the military to assume power in their own right has proved weak, both during the quasi-parliamentary regime before 1959 and under President Sukarno's "guided democracy." Confidence in their capacity to govern alone has never been great among the Indonesian officers. In recent years, it has been undermined by the experience of assuming a substantial part of the burden of government during a worsening economic and administrative crisis.

The Sukarno regime has forced the officer corps to cooperate, however grudgingly, with the PKI, in the name of national solidarity. Since the other political parties appear less and less attractive associates, and the country's problems appear too complex for the military to tackle alone, are the officers likely to oppose indefinitely the partnership which the PKI offers them? A forecast of Indonesia's political future hinges on an accurate answer to this question.

In formulating his own answer, this author is led to assume, on the basis of mounting evidence, that the PKI expects to come to power by default and by popular acclamation. It can hope to be acclaimed as the only political group that has not yet been given an opportunity to extricate the country from its difficulties. It can expect that its demands will ultimately be accepted by the other, demoralized political groups. A situation favoring PKI fortunes could develop during the present regime, especially if the country's endemic crisis were exacerbated by some calamity; or, more likely, it could develop in the struggle for succession that will follow the death of President Sukarno.

Conceivably, the other political parties may regain their vitality. A firmly anticommunist group might take control of the armed forces, or President Sukarno might appoint in his lifetime a successor capable of rallying massive support. Then too, Sukarno, yielding to pressures from the political parties, could decree the holding of elections and thus reopen "the parliamentary road to socialism." Yet another possibility is that militant elements in the PKI, intoxicated by Chinese doctrine, will prompt the Party to forego the patient course of action followed by the Aidit group since 1951, and thus plunge the country into civil war. While these possibilities cannot be ignored, none of them seems very likely to materialize.

The road to power pursued by the PKI leaders since 1951 may appear, to those familiar with communist doctrine, as ultragradualist. But considering the circumstances, Aidit and his associates can be said to have shown skill, realism, imagination, and boldness. In their search for an Indonesian road to socialism they may have pioneered the new strategy of "national democracy," based on the "extension of Communist influence on the nationalist government" [7] of an excolonial, underdeveloped country, which was adopted at the 1960 Congress of the 81 Communist Parties in Moscow.

The present strategy of the Aidit group was formulated between January, 1951, and March, 1954. At the end of that period, the Fifth National Congress of the PKI approved a Party program which, after stating that "the PKI has taken part and will continue to take a most active part in the parliamentary struggle," added that "the parliamentary struggle alone is not sufficient to achieve the goal of the formation of a government of people's democracy." At that time Indonesia was getting ready for her first general elections, which were held eventually in September, 1955, and which established the PKI as one of the four major parties in Indonesia. It obtained 6,176,900 votes, 16.4 per cent of all votes cast.

Aidit's skepticism concerning the parliamentary road was vindicated in March, 1956, when despite the PKI's electoral success, the coalition cabinet that was formed included the other three large parties but excluded the PKI. This Aidit explained as follows:

> The Indonesian reactionaries, in cahoots with the foreign imperialists, never stop trying to weaken the force of the Indonesian people, especially by preventing revolutionary cooperation among Islamic, nationalist and Communist parties, as desired by the vast majority of the people and as proposed by President Sukarno. What weakens our national force is the anti-Communist, anti-unity policy of the obstinate members of the Masjumi-PSI [Partai Sosialis Indonesia] party.[8]

In the summer of 1956, the PKI leaders, sadder but wiser, had reasons to be vigilant. Aidit told the PKI:

> In connection with the argument concerning the possibility of a shift to socialism via the parliamentary system as contained in the report of the Central Committee of the CPSU to the 20th Congress of the CPSU, the question has often been put to the Communists: Can the shift to socialism in Indonesia be accomplished peacefully through the parliamentary means? . . .

> The reply of the Communists to this last question is: It is a possibility, and one whose realization we must do all in our power to achieve. Therefore, if it were up to the Communists, the best means, the ideal means of change to the system of a people's democracy, the preparatory stage of the socialist system, would be peaceful, parliamentary means. . . .

> The question now arises: Will the other groups and parties permit the shift to a people's democracy by peaceful, parliamentary means?[9]

Although not expecting political miracles from parliamentarism, the PKI leaders favored the existence of a parliamentary system that had proved beneficial to the growth of their party and added to its protection by consecrating the legitimacy of political parties. At the same time, the leaders had to search realistically for a more promising political strategy. Since the PKI had twice, in 1926 and in 1948, experienced the armed suppression of ineptly organized communist rebellions, Aidit dismissed, for public consumption at least, the possibility of armed struggle: "Only the reactionaries obstinately persist in saying that the Communists see only one way to reach their goal, i.e., internal warfare."[10] He then explained to his audience the PKI's preferred strategy:

The PKI's work is not limited solely to the parliamentary struggle, but consists also, and primarily, in activity among the masses of workers, peasants, intelligentsia, and all other democratic masses. *Basically, the PKI's activity is to change the balance of power* between the imperialists, landlords, and other compradore bourgeoisie on the one hand, and the people on the other, by arousing, mobilizing and organizing the masses.[11]

On the surface, the political strategy of the PKI appears similar to that of the Italian Communist Party, which also emphasizes mass struggle and a progressive altering of the balance of power among classes.[12] But whereas in Italy the emphasis seems to be on "structural changes" induced by the politically conscious struggle of the laboring masses, in Indonesia it is primarily on the subtle political calculus of a small elite, adept at palace intrigues and capable of patience, flexibility, imagination, and correct assessment of changing opportunities and conditions in the country. The PKI leadership can succeed in this task only if it is at liberty to pursue its aims rationally, without yielding to the emotional pressures of the Party's rank and file and of the masses, and without succumbing to provocation by its enemies.

As long as the Indonesian masses were still largely quiescent and therefore unlikely to rise to the defense of the PKI, the communist leaders were largely confined to maneuvers among the political elite and had to take constantly into account that a hostile coalition might emerge to destroy them. The primary purpose of these maneuvers was to make it possible to work with the masses and thus to create the political reserve that would give the PKI the electoral strength to pursue the parliamentary road, the popular enthusiasm to help it succeed by acclamation, or a sanctuary in the event of armed struggle.

As the effort to mobilize and organize the masses succeeds, the PKI's political environment is being gradually transformed from an elitist to a popular one. This, in itself, is bound to change the rules of the game by which the distribution of power is determined. Eventually, the PKI may no longer need the protection of President Sukarno, but at this moment the PKI leaders are probably still adhering to the cautious approach which Aidit explained publicly in May, 1953, as follows:

The PKI uses Marxism-Leninism as a constant guide in determining the character of its policy; *it also bases its decisions on the existing balance in social forces.* The PKI is obliged to continuously calculate the balance in the unstable social forces in Indonesia. [Emphasis supplied.] [13]

The Aidit group seems to have followed this basic intuition since January, 1951, when it took control of the Politburo at a plenary session of the Central Committee of the PKI. In trying to change the balance of political forces in Indonesia, it concentrated at first on the task of seeking allies within the *bourgeoisie* ("the tactics of separating the national *bourgeoisie* from the ultra-reactionary *compradore bourgeoisie*").[14] This resulted in PKI support of the Wilopo Cabinet formed in March, 1952, and of the Ali Sastroamidjojo Cabinet formed in July, 1953. The goodwill of these two Cabinets controlled by the Nationalist Party of Indonesia (PNI) allowed the PKI to turn into a nationwide mass movement and to establish itself at the September, 1955, elections as one of the country's four big parties.

In choosing their strategy and tactics, the PKI leaders have demonstrated political wisdom particularly remarkable in so young a group. In 1951, Aidit was 28 years old; Lukman, 31; and Njoto, 26. While their age may have led them to believe that they could afford to wait to succeed to the leadership of the Indonesian revolution, it is nevertheless remarkable that they were temperamentally capable of embarking on the slow and tenacious process of altering the balance of political forces in Indonesia, and that they had the sagacity to understand the futility of the parliamentary road in a country without the strong constitutional traditions that would guarantee the transfer of power from one group to another by the mechanical operation of parliamentary majorities.

As practiced by the Aidit group, changing the balance of forces is a subtle and complex operation which has involved eliminating (or at least neutralizing) irreconcilable enemies, creating an atmosphere in which potential enemies are at least passively resigned to accepting the transfer of power to communist hands, inducing lukewarm friends to lend active support to the PKI, and having a Party apparatus sufficiently well-organized and disciplined to get an iron grip on state power once control of the government is secured. This, of course, is bound to be a slow and gradual process. The Party leadership cannot know in advance when the situation will be ripe for the take-over. Whether the final phase will involve a popular election or street demonstrations that would give party rule legitimacy by acclamation, will depend on circumstances. In either case, resort to violence should be only sporadic and of marginal importance.

The strategy of changing the balance of forces in order to make the PKI ultimately acceptable as a governmental party requires infinite patience on the part of the leaders. They must not antagonize any group other than the principal target in the current phase of the Party's operations. While the Party has to prevent its hotheads from giving its enemies an excuse to crush it, as happened in 1926 and 1948, it also has to generate sufficient revolutionary *élan* to sustain the militancy of its cadres. The PKI has had to find ways to mingle freely in Indonesian society, but without losing its separate identity. As one might expect, "patience" was the key word used by Aidit in the article he published in *Pravda*

commemorating the fortieth anniversary of the PKI.[15] Over the years, the
PKI leaders have been obliged repeatedly to explain to their cadres why
progress has been so slow. In December, 1958, for instance, they stated:

> Since the demand for a National Coalition Government is just, it will
> definitely become a fact. But even so this does not mean that, at this very
> moment, it can be realized in full. The decisive thing in this question is
> the balance of forces. This is why, while not abandoning the demand for
> a National Coalition Government, the revolutionaries must adopt a real-
> istic attitude and must be able to recognize what sort of government can
> be formed at any particular time. It is from this point of view that we
> must analyze our attitude towards the Djuanda Cabinet.

> Thus it is clear that the feasibility or otherwise of the formation of a
> National Coalition Government depends on the work of our Party in
> building the national front, in developing the progressive forces and aim-
> ing well-directed blows at the die-hard forces. The participation of Com-
> munists in the cabinet depends upon the real balance of forces at any
> particular time.[16]

Five years later, the imperturbable Aidit was still explaining the
facts of political life to his Party:

> Some of our comrades are wrong who only seem to be clever at finding
> fault with President Sukarno in connection with the unfulfilled realiza-
> tion and formation of a mutual cooperation cabinet based on NASAKOM.
> They say President Sukarno is only talking nonsense because up to now he
> has not formed a mutual cooperation cabinet based on NASAKOM. . . .

> However, we are not after something which is philanthropic. Authority
> and power revolve around the real balance of forces. Do not expect one
> class to share power voluntarily with another.[17]

In other words, the PKI strategy involves methodical and sustained
action at all levels in Indonesian society until the PKI's enemies have been
rendered helpless and the others have become willing to accept the communists as saviors, or, at least, to give them a try. The very fact that the
PKI has not made more rapid progress on the road to power, despite
President Sukarno's sympathy and encouragement, attests to the seriousness of the obstacles it has to overcome. But the communists have bene-
fited immensely from the protection and support received from President
Sukarno, who has banned his and their major enemies, the *Masjumi* and
Socialist (PSI) parties, prevented the Army from blocking the growth of
the communist mass movement, harangued the population against
communist-phobia, and given the PKI leaders the prestige of ministerial
positions (without portfolio) and well-publicized involvement in policy
formulation. Although the PKI does not have executive control of any
departments of government at present, its influence throughout the Indo-

nesian governmental machinery is constantly spreading as a result of the special assignments given by President Sukarno to the communist members of his Cabinet and to the increasing role of the National Front, in which the communists play a very active part. The balance of political forces is gradually changing in Indonesia, not only because of the skill of the PKI and the ineptitude of its opponents, but perhaps primarily because of the finger that tips the balance.

If present trends continue, the PKI is likely to obtain eventual control of the Indonesian government. But what if President Sukarno were to disappear before the PKI consolidated its gains? Would its enemies not be in a position then to destroy the party? To answer this question, it is necessary to view the current position of the PKI as a growing mass movement in Indonesian society, and to appraise the influence gained by its leaders and cadres among the political elite.

The PKI as a Mass Movement

At the beginning of 1952, the PKI claimed 7,910 members and candidate members, although Arnold C. Brackman, a veteran reporter of the Asian scene, indicated that "it was doubtful if it had half that many." [18] A national party conference decided, at that time, to increase membership in six months to one hundred thousand. In October, 1953, D. N. Aidit, then Secretary of the Central Committee of the PKI, reported to a plenary session of the Central Committee that the plan had been overfulfilled and that the party had now 126,671 members and candidate members.[19] At the time of the September, 1955, elections for Parliament, the PKI had at least one million members, following the membership drive instituted by the Fifth National Congress held in March, 1954.[20] During the December, 1963, plenary session of the Central Committee of the PKI, Chairman Aidit reported "over two and a half million members." [21] Then, on June 15, 1964, Aidit made a statement "in the name of three million Indonesian Communists." [22] Currently, all party references use the figure of three million.

Similarly, on May 3, 1964, the National Committee of *Pemuda Rakjat*, or People's Youth, endorsed, "in the name of 1.5 million members," a proclamation by President Sukarno. On June 15, Aidit greeted "two million members of People's Youth" and, in late July, People's Youth protested, "in the name of two million members," the communiqué signed by President Johnson and the Malaysian Prime Minister.[23]

Sobsi, the federation of labor unions led by PKI Politburo member Njono, claimed 1,561,757 members in 1952 and 2,732,909 by the end of 1959.[24] At the time of its sixteenth anniversary on November 29, 1962, Sobsi claimed no less than 3.1 million members, and, at its Fourth National

Congress, which opened in Djakarta on September 17, 1964, the figure quoted was "more than 3.5 million."[25]

Women play an important role in Indonesian public life. Aware of this, the PKI has concentrated, since about 1959, both on increasing the percentage of women among party members and on expanding the communist front organization for women known as *Gerwani*. In October, 1962, *Gerwani* claimed 1,125,000 members. By February, 1963, the figure quoted was 1.5 millon, and since February, 1964, there have been several references in the party press to 1.75 million members.[26]

The most impressive figures claimed by the PKI are those marking the growth of *Barisan Tani Indonesia* (BTI), the Indonesian farmers' front. At the time of the Fifth National Congress of the PKI in March, 1954, the decision was made to intensify revolutionary work among the peasants. Aidit stated at that time:

> We cannot possibly speak of a real, broad and strong united front until the peasants have been drawn into it because, in our country, the peasants comprise more than 70 per cent of the population. The non-participation of the peasants means the non-participation of the majority of the Indonesian people and this is a very great weakness in our united national front. As yet, only about 7 per cent of the peasants are organized. This is a very small amount. Because of this, the primary task of the Communists is to draw the peasants into the united national front.[27]

Figures about the growth of BTI were given by its General Chairman, Asmu, in November, 1963. At the time of its Fourth National Congress in September, 1953, BTI allegedly had 800,000 members. At the time of its Fifth National Congress in September, 1957, it had 3,390,286. By the time of its Sixth National Congress in July, 1962, it had 5,654,974 members. By August, 1963, BTI claimed 7,099,103 members; in April, 1964, 7.5 million members; and at the BTI national conference held in Djakarta in September, 1964, BTI emphatically claimed 8.5 million members.[28] The last figure was used by President Sukarno himself in addressing the delegates, who held their deliberations at the *Istana Negara,* Sukarno's state palace. The symbolism of this event is not likely to escape the peasant masses.

The reliability of the figures quoted above is extremely difficult to assess. Of course, these millions are not indoctrinated communists. But the usefulness to the PKI of a massive recruitment effort is obvious. While membership figures appearing in the Party press may have been inflated in order to create a bandwagon effect, even conservative estimates reveal the PKI as a formidable factor in present-day Indonesia. Whatever the true figures may be, the very fact that the PKI and its front organizations can claim constant gains in membership reflects the growing strength of the communist movement in Indonesia. The growth of the

PKI also dramatically underlines the lack of meaningful alternatives available to the Indonesian masses today. The communists are filling a political vacuum.

In 1954, 43 million Indonesians were registered to vote under an electoral law that gave the franchise to all citizens who were either over 18 or married. A crude estimate, assuming a low population growth of only 2 per cent per year, indicates that, for 1964, the corresponding figure could be 52.5 million registered voters. If, in order to reduce double counting, one assumes that all members of the PKI and of *Pemuda Rakjat* are also members of at least one of the front organizations, and if one accepts PKI figures at face value, it would appear that up to 14 million persons, or *more than one-quarter of all potential voters, are linked organizationally to the PKI.* To this figure, one would have to add those over whom PKI and front organization members have direct influence. The conclusion is inescapable that the PKI should be able to mobilize a very substantial fraction of the population for political purposes.

In 1955, only one-sixth of those who voted for the PKI were Party members, a proportion comparable to that which prevailed in France from 1946 to 1951, when the French Communist Party obtained from 28.4 to 26.5 per cent of the total votes cast. There, too, only from one-seventh to one-sixth of all communist voters were Party members.[29] Obviously, the six-to-one ratio is no longer relevant to present-day Indonesian conditions. With 3 million members in the PKI and 2 million in People's Youth, such a ratio would point to a potential communist electoral strength of 30 million out of 52.5 million. Aidit does not claim that much. In a speech on May 4, 1964, he said, "Should there be general elections, it can be proved that the number of Marxist followers will not be less than one-third."[30] This confirms what the author learned in November, 1963, when he last visited Djakarta. Conservative estimates credited the PKI with 9 million followers and granted it the capacity to command 30 per cent of the popular vote, counting only persons affiliated directly or indirectly with the communist movement.

The very size of the PKI has become its best defense. The author believes that, Indonesian political culture being what it is, the Indonesian political elite is not likely to stomach the harsh measures that would be necessary to destroy the PKI, now that it has millions of followers. Even after the Madiun rebellion of September, 1948, the communists were ostracized only temporarily. The summary execution of some of their leaders by the Army in that period was primarily the result of the panic created by the Dutch armed attack on the Republic. In August, 1951, the *Masjumi*-controlled Sukiman Cabinet arrested some 2,000 communists and other radicals, but it released them after a few months without pressing charges. Today the only political figure who could still turn the tide against the PKI, namely President Sukarno himself, is not likely to want to do so.

Were the communists to lose Sukarno as a protector, it seems doubtful that other national leaders, capable of rallying Indonesia's dispersed and demoralized anticommunist forces, would emerge in the near future. Furthermore, these forces would probably lack the ruthlessness that made it possible for the Nazis to suppress the Communist Party of Germany a few weeks after the elections of March 5, 1933, an election in which the Communist Party still won five million votes, almost 13 per cent of the total.[31] The enemies of the PKI, including the remnants of various right-wing rebellions, the suppressed political parties, and certain elements in the armed forces, are weaker than the Nazis—not only in numbers and in mass support but also in unity, discipline, and leadership.

Whether the PKI is stronger today than the Communist Party of Germany was in 1933 is more difficult to assess. Little is known about the militancy of PKI cadres, members, and sympathizers. Opportunities to test their revolutionary fervor have been lacking. Should one assume that, in a country which 20 years ago experienced a war of national liberation, latent militancy is still high and that the PKI would resort to armed struggle if it could not secure power otherwise or had to fight for its existence? I do not know whether in recent years the PKI had been storing weapons or training paramilitary forces, but on January 14, 1965, the Party took a bold step in proposing to the President the arming of peasants and workers "in reply to the large-scale military build-up of the British imperialists in Malaysia." [32] Although Sukarno told foreign correspondents the same day that he had rejected the demand, Aidit repeated it publicly at a meeting of the National Front on January 17:

> I have submitted a proposal to President Sukarno to arm immediately the workers and peasants, the pillars of the revolution. No less than 5 million organized workers and 10 million organized peasants are ready to take up arms. This is the only correct reply to the British and American aggression.[33]

This new departure can only mean that the Party has decided to prepare openly for a possible armed clash with its opponents. But even if this maneuver is countered successfully, one should not lose sight of the fact that few revolutions were won by forces militarily trained and equipped in advance. In any case, the efforts of the PKI leaders in their quest for power are still focused primarily on making armed struggle unnecessary.

Another question is occasionally voiced in discussing the prospects of communism in Indonesia: is the PKI not likely to remain permanently in opposition, like the Italian Communist Party, which won 25.3 per cent of the votes in the April, 1963, elections, or like the French Communist Party, which won 21.8 per cent of the votes in November, 1962? [34] In my opinion the experience of western Europe is not applicable to Indonesia. In Italy and France, communism is the way of life for a very powerful but isolated minority group that is unlikely ever to come to power on its own terms, or even to share power with groups whose world views sharply conflict with its own.

Unlike western Europe with its black-and-white ways of thinking, Indonesia is a country characterized by syncretistic thought patterns. This is well-illustrated at the very top of the social pyramid, by President Sukarno himself. He claims to be, at the same time, a nationalist, a Marxist, and a religious man, and would like to see these ideological streams merge in a torrent of national solidarity. Accordingly, he is waging a persistent campaign to overcome what he calls "Communist-phobia" and to have PKI members accepted in all sectors of national life.

Sukarno's efforts will probably succeed, as they are compatible with Indonesian national character. While ethnic, religious, and regional particularisms are strong in Indonesia, the national culture seems to favor tolerance and the acceptance of logically conflicting views. Consequently, the communists are not, as in the West, an isolated sect living by their own lights and segregated from the rest of the population. On the contrary, they pervade Indonesian society. Some years ago (and perhaps more recently) communist and anticommunist members of Parliament could be seen drinking coffee together; communist and anticommunist newspaper editors were personal friends and even roommates. Ideological divisions are bridged by family ties as well as by social relations. For instance, Politburo member Sakirman and the Chief of Indonesian Army Intelligence, Major General S. Parman, are brothers.

There are, therefore, no sharp cultural or social barriers opposing the penetration of the PKI into the total fabric of Indonesian society, except for the resistance of the Western-thinking Islamic modernists and the socialists, whose political parties, the *Masjumi* and the PSI, were banned in 1960. Unlike the politically and culturally isolated communist parties of Italy and France, the PKI is increasingly accepted and active in Indonesian society at large. A few years ago, the PKI seemed to be primarily a Javanese party. Since 1958, it has made progress in the other islands, although the precise measure of its diffusion is difficult to assess.

Aidit, Lukman, and Njoto, the three most important leaders of the PKI, have ministerial rank and the *Harian Rakjat* never fails to mention these titles which add to the national stature and prestige of the party. In the regional and local administration of the country, the PKI is represented on the various appointed bodies. At the bottom of the political and administrative structure, PKI representatives have access to all significant activities as participants in Sukarno's National Front. Their position is constantly improving. On March 16, 1964, the President issued instructions[35] that the local policy-making bodies, known as *Tjatur Tunggal* (i.e., four-in-one), consisting of the military commander, the police chief, the civil governor and the district attorney, should become the *Pantja Tunggal* (i.e., five-in-one) by including a representative of the National Front. This order gave the PKI access to the local power centers.

It is difficult to assess accurately the extent of the communists' penetration into various sectors of Indonesian social life. A few years ago, their presence in the bureaucracy, the armed forces, and educational institutions was small, but in the very recent past their influence in all these bodies seems to be on the rise. Among students, for whom communism until recently had little appeal, the influence of the PKI is increasing.

The PKI is also trying hard to establish itself as a cultural force and as a patron of arts and letters. Through the Institute for People's Culture (*Lekra*), it tries to influence and support all forms of cultural activities. On July 7, 1963, the Party organ *Harian Rakjat* started publishing a Sunday issue devoted to cultural matters. In the countryside, it appears that the PKI and its front organizations provide the only entertainment and information available to the masses, who have no direct access to newspapers, radio, movies, or travel. It is even argued that the success of communist membership drives is due largely to the attraction of Party-sponsored activities to which a membership card represents an admission ticket.

The PKI's efforts to mobilize the peasantry and rally its support is, again, testimony to the Aidit leadership's ability. Until the communists, perhaps emulating their Chinese comrades, turned their attention to them, the rest of Indonesian society had ignored the villages. The best that can be said for the Indonesian government's agrarian policy since independence is that it stopped the exactions of the colonial administration. But the government treated the peasants as objects, rather than subjects, of politics. The PKI's appeal to the peasants is based not exclusively on obvious agrarian grievances, but also on recognition of their human dignity and cultural importance in the national community.

In the first half of 1964, Aidit personally led research teams which studied the situation of the Javanese peasants. The first teams went into the villages of west Java in February, 1964, and Aidit discussed the results in a lengthy report published in May.[36] In April and May, 1964, the research was extended to east and central Java.[37] No other Indonesian parties have undertaken similar efforts. Indeed, the Indonesian authorities themselves are probably less informed about the problems of the Indonesian peasantry (72 per cent of the nation) than the communists.

These studies may be genuinely intended to help a future communist government formulate an agrarian policy realistically fitting Indonesia. They also have obvious propagandistic value at a time when the Party is more interested in obtaining political support from the peasantry than in alleviating its economic plight.

To foster greater militancy and daring on the part of its supporters, the PKI promoted throughout 1964 a Unilateral Action Movement (*Gerakan Aksi Sefihak*), inciting the Javanese peasants to implement by themselves the 1960 basic agrarian law and the law on crop-sharing agreements. Although decrees had been issued, the Sukarno regime had primarily paid lip-service to the idea of agrarian reform, as local authorities tended to side with the existing vested interests. Unilateral actions took such proportions that Acting President Dr. Johanes Leimena found it necessary on June 15, 1964, to order the Department of Home Affairs to prevent such actions by seeking the best possible settlement of agrarian disputes through mutual consultations.[38]

BTI, in defiance of the government's appeal, announced that it was planning more intensified and consolidated actions against the landlords and demanded the dismissal of officials who took a tough attitude toward the peasants. The first National Conference of the PKI held in Djakarta from July 3–5, 1964, adopted a special resolution supporting the unilateral actions of the peasants in strongest terms, condemning "the despicable slanders of the despotic landlords and their apologists who are against the basic agrarian law and the law on the crop-sharing agreement." It also requested the establishment of land reform courts which should include representatives of communist peasant organizations, and the release of arrested peasants.[39]

On July 10 a special court in Klaten, Central Java, opened the trial of a group of BTI members, arrested after violent clashes with the police. President Sukarno, in his August 17, 1964, Independence Day address, while avoiding to endorse the *Aksi Sefihak* movement explicitly, expressed his concern with the fate of the peasant and ordered the immediate completion of the basic agrarian law on Java, Madura, and Bali. On September 24, 1964, the cabinet presidium created a committee to expedite agrarian affairs, consisting of Police Brigadier General Mudjoko and PKI vice-chairman Njoto, both ministers attached to the presidium, and R. Hermanses, minister for agrarian affairs. The same day the establishment of land reform courts including peasant representatives was announced.

These efforts on the part of the government did not stop unilateral actions in Java. Clashes between BTI members and local authorities continued throughout the last months of 1964. Particularly violent riots involving 2000 BTI-led peasants took place at Indramaju, West Java, on October 15 and 16, concerning the distribution of public forest lands.

Several policemen were injured and sixty-four peasants were held for trial. It seems clear that the PKI is currently more interested in creating an atmosphere of militancy in the countryside than in agrarian reform.

While these very recent developments suggest that the communist leadership is making preparations for a possible future showdown with the Army, it also appears that the PKI is leaving the door open for circumstances under which the Army might give up its opposition to the communists and accept a genuine partnership rather than the shotgun wedding which President Sukarno has failed so far to bring about. On the one hand, the PKI voices firm opposition to the idea of military dictatorship and attacks those members of the officer corps who, since 1958, have played an important role in the economic enterprises taken over from the Dutch. On the other hand, PKI leaders never fail to stress the principle of *Dwitunggal Angkatan Bersendjata dan Rakjat* (i.e., unity of the armed forces and the people).[40]

In the weeks preceding the abolition of the parliamentary regime, the PKI was clearly concerned about the danger of a military dictatorship. On May 23, 1959, Aidit stated:

> If it proves impossible to prevent a military dictatorship, that is if nevertheless one is set up, our task is to resist it, and we are convinced that in the end we shall be victorious because the people do not like military dictatorships. . . . There has never yet been nor will there ever be, anything to prove that a military dictatorship can save the people and further advance world development.[41]

Even stronger have been the PKI's attacks on the role of the officer corps in the economic life of the country. In a statement of the Politburo dated July 8, 1960, which was immediately suppressed by the military authorities, the PKI applied the Chinese communist term "bureaucratic capitalists" to the officers-turned-managers of former Dutch enterprises:

> These enterprises are controlled by certain cliques who, in addition to not being competent to run them, are adopting a worse attitude towards the workers than the foreign employers did. The domination of these cliques has brought into being a bourgeois group that is in control of State apparatus and is using it for their own economic interests, they have brought into being bureaucratic capitalists who in addition to suppressing the workers are also suppressing the national bourgeoisie, and there is already proof that they are becoming a channel through which the imperialists are continuing with their policy of exploitation and extortion.[42]

The PKI has also relentlessly carried on its efforts to reduce the administrative role of the military. Throughout 1962, it continued to press for the abolition of martial law.[43] When President Sukarno finally decreed, on December 19, 1962, the lifting of the state of emergency "in order that revolutionary people's forces be given a part in the consummation of efforts to achieve the objectives of the Indonesian revolution," this was greeted by the Politburo in its 1963 New Year message as a "victory most significant for the people's struggle for the enlargement of democratic rights and the improvement of living conditions." [44] Then, anticipating maneuvers on the part of the military to continue to exert, informally, the authority they had enjoyed under martial law, Aidit warned, in his Political Report of February 10, 1963, to the first plenary session of the seventh Central Committee:

> The bureaucrat capitalists and the other reactionaries are doing everything in their power to prepare a series of plans and measures to rob the people of the democracy they will obtain with the lifting of the state of emergency. They have been working for a long time to create a situation of "SOB without SOB." [45]

Unlike the July 8, 1960, attack on the Army, this one was not suppressed, although the military's emergency powers did not expire until May 1, 1963, nearly three months after Aidit's report.

While attacking bureaucratic capitalism and militarism, the PKI has carefully kept open the possibility of an alliance with the armed forces. As early as July, 1956, in his General Report to a plenary session of the Central Committee, Aidit had said:

> Although the reactionaries have tried hard to change their composition and spirit, the majority of the Armed Forces of the Republic of Indonesia still have the spirit of the 1945 August Revolution. . . . For this reason, it is difficult to imagine that the Armed Forces as a whole could now be made a tool for oppressing the people: on the contrary, it is proper for the people to want the TNI and other Indonesian Armed Forces to be protectors of the people.[46]

On February 11, 1957, Aidit had stated in the course of a debate in Parliament:

> It is an open secret that in the general elections for Parliament as well as for the Constituent Assembly, more than 80 per cent of the Armed Forces voted for the democratic parties and *30 per cent of their votes went to the PKI.* The PSI and MASJUMI received less than 20 per cent, fewer even than the PKI or the PNI individually. The PSI, which is influential among the high-ranking officers, ranks fifth in the Armed Forces. While the MASJUMI, because of its pro-DI policy, ranks sixth. [Emphasis supplied.] [47]

Today, more than seven years later, it is anybody's guess what the true situation is in the armed forces. It seems hard to believe that an Army living among a population of which up to 15 per cent is affiliated with communist organizations has remained completely impervious to the communist appeal, especially in a period when the PKI projects the image of being in the forefront of militant, radical nationalism. During the campaign for West Irian, and even more so in the current confrontation with Malaysia, the military must have been given much food for thought by the almost complete identity of outlook between themselves and the PKI with regard to Indonesia's role in southeast Asia.

Significantly, since 1962, Aidit and other PKI leaders have been invited repeatedly to address the staff and command schools of the Army, Navy, Air Force, and Police Academy.[48] These invitations may have been, initially, the result of orders from the President, but now that the ice has been broken, communist access to the officer corps is bound in time to influence some of the military.

Support from the military should be one of the PKI's major targets. It would be naive to assume that a group of men as shrewd and patient as Aidit and his associates could hope to proceed far on the road to power without securing, if not the cooperation, at least the neutrality of the armed forces. In this respect, trends seem to be in the PKI's favor. The most militantly anticommunist officers were eliminated from the armed services before and during the 1958 to 1960 rebellion. Many of the senior officers, loyal to the Sukarno regime but known for their anti-communist views, have been gradually deprived of command positions since 1960. It can be expected that by the time the PKI is ready to assume power, the armed forces will have lost the will and ability to resist such an assumption.

Part of the PKI's strategy to make communism acceptable to Indonesian society involved an interesting departure, a proposal made at its first national conference, in July, 1964, to study the development of religion in Indonesia "as a basis for better NASAKOM cooperation."[49] The PKI had already prepared the ground for a flexible attitude toward religion by amending, at its Seventh (Extraordinary) National Congress held in April, 1962, the Preamble to the PKI Constitution of 1959. At that time, it added the following paragraph:

> The PKI accepts and defends the 1945 Constitution which contains the *Pantja Sila* in its Preamble as the basic principles of the State, aimed at building a just and prosperous society in accordance with Indonesian national identity.[50]

The *Pantja Sila* makes "belief in one God" one of the five basic principles of the republic. By proclaiming its allegiance to the *Pantja Sila* (requested by Presidential Decisions No. 7/1959 and No. 13/1960), the PKI took the first step toward overcoming the hostility of religious groups. Currently, the PKI is prepared to go much further. On September 27, 1964, addressing the mass rally concluding the Fourth National Congress of *Sobsi* in Djakarta, Aidit warned communists not to be antireligious. He asked his audience to report immediately to Party officials any communist conducting antireligious campaigns, and promised that the offender would be promptly expelled from the Party.[51]

Parenthetically, it is interesting that the two largest communist parties outside the communist bloc attempt to overcome religious opposition. In formulating Theses for its Tenth Congress in September 1962, the Italian Communist Party proclaimed that "aspirations for a socialist society can be fostered in men holding religious beliefs."

The PKI Apparatus and Its Influence

In planning for the conquest of power, the PKI leaders have to concern themselves not only with the pursuit of correct strategy and tactics and with the development of a mass movement, but also with the formation of able and militant cadres capable of formulating and implementing meaningful policies at all levels. To this end, the PKI initiated its first three-year plan on August 17, 1956. At the time of the Sixth National Congress in September, 1959, the PKI claimed that 270,000 cadres and activists had graduated from Party schools or had finished a Party course.[52] A second three-year plan was completed in April, 1963, but there seems to have been some difficulty in imposing true Party discipline on members, especially with regard to payment of dues.

A "four-year plan for culture, ideology, and organization," initiated on August 17, 1963, was aimed at increases in membership and intensified indoctrination.[53] The PKI has understood the intense thirst for education of the Indonesian people. It offers education in people's universities (called *Universitas Rakjat*) which teach Marxism and economics in major cities such as Djakarta, Bandung, Jogjakarta, Semarang, Surabaya, and Medan, in Party-organized schools at the senior and junior high school levels, and in elementary school subjects in the villages. One of the party's goals is that, by the end of the four-year plan, its older members will be literate. In addition, the PKI is organizing regional training centers for all cadres. These offer theoretical discussion of ideology as well as practical research into the economic and social problems of the region. The goals of the plan also include doubling the membership during the four-year period and collecting sufficient dues to be able to equip all Party organizations adequately.

The PKI leaders attribute great importance to ideological training. Aidit explained, on the thirty-ninth anniversary of the PKI during the first three-year plan:

Party cadres cannot possibly thoroughly understand the general line and policy of the Party if they do not understand the philosophy of Marxism-Leninism. They cannot possibly understand thoroughly why, for example, the nature of the Indonesian revolution at the present time is not socialist but bourgeois-democratic, why the PKI supports President Sukarno's Concept, why it supports the idea of "guided democracy" and the idea of "back to the 1945 Constitution" if they do not understand Marxist-Leninist philosophy. They can say that the Party's general and political line is good and correct but they cannot explain why.[54]

How successful the effort to train cadres has been is naturally not easy to ascertain. What is apparent to an outside observer is the presence, in party circles, of an intellectual ferment that is lacking elsewhere. The PKI press contributes substantial material to the discussion of Indonesia's problems at a time when the general level of political discourse in Indonesia is very low, partly, of course, because all voices hostile to the Sukarno regime have been silenced.

In the past, communist strength was based almost exclusively on Java, which in 1955 gave the PKI 88.6 per cent of its parliamentary vote.[55] In 1958, at the time of the states rights rebellions in Sumatra and the Celebes, which had strong anticommunist overtones, it was widely assumed that a communist take-over in Djakarta would lead to the secession of the Outer Islands and thus to the starvation of overpopulated Java. (Since then Java's economic situation has continued to deteriorate, to the point where Aidit felt compelled to advise the National Conference of BTI on September 10, 1964, to "turn rats into food for the peasants, as Bung Karno [Sukarno] and I have already enjoyed rat meat.")[56]

The PKI leaders are unlikely to seek power in Djakarta without being reasonably certain that they can draw on the economic resources of the Outer Islands. Consequently, the PKI will have to secure the cooperation of the armed forces against possible secessions and make major efforts to gain political support in the Outer Islands. Reliable information about the real political situation in various parts of the Indonesian archipelago is scarce, but there are indications that the PKI and its front organizations are making progress while the other political forces, with some exceptions in South Celebes and Atjeh, are not more vigorous than on Java.

The organizational structure developed by the PKI for the purpose of extending its influence throughout the Indonesian archipelago has as its principal bodies the Greater Regional Committees, identified as *Comite Daerah Besar* (CDB), *Comite Pulau Besar* (CPB), and *Comite Djakarta Raya* (CDR), known before 1957 as *Provincial Committees* (Provcom) and currently totalling 27 units. At the second level are the *Section Committees* (CS) responsible for regencies, or *Kabupaten*, and for larger towns, as well as *Subsection Committees* (CSS), responsible for districts, or *Ketjamatan*, and for smaller towns. Each of these bodies has an executive committee and a conference. Below the CSS are the *Resort Committees* (RC), based territorially (i.e., in villages or urban sectors) or institutionally (i.e., in factories, mines, offices, or schools). These have less than 100 party members each and are the basic organizations of the PKI, to which the cells (GRUP) are responsible.

In his Political Report of December, 1963, Aidit announced that "only West Irian is still without a PKI Greater Regional Committee in view of the fact that guided democracy in this area has not yet progressed and parties are still prohibited from forming." He then stated that Section Committees exist in 93 per cent of the regencies and larger towns, Subsection Committees in 83 per cent of the districts and smaller towns, and Resort Committees in 62 per cent of all villages or their equivalents.[57]

In this period of deep and bitter controversies among and within communist parties, the PKI leadership has carefully avoided any public schism, in order to project an image of reliable strength. For more than ten years, following the consolidation of the Aidit leadership at the October, 1953, plenary session of the Central Committee, there has been no public indication of factionalism. Only recently, at the first national conference of the PKI, on July 3, 1964, has Aidit indicated that problems did exist, when he told his comrades:

> The internal contradictions in the Party cannot be avoided but must be faced, taken care of and terminated. In settling in the right way the Party's internal contradictions, the skill and quality of the leadership increases. Bringing to an end the internal contradictions of the Party is an absolute condition for increasing the ability of the Party to terminate external contradictions.[58]

Following this national conference, the Central Committee of the PKI was expanded. Whether this represented a quiet balancing of contending factions or the continuation of an earlier tendency to promote the most able cadres to top positions cannot be determined. In any case, no purges have taken place, and the remarkable stability at the top of the PKI hierarchy has continued. Of 14 men who were Central Committee members in January, 1951, 11 were still on the Central Committee by 1961. One, Bachtarudin, had died; and two, Alimin and Tan Ling Djie, had been dropped from the Central Committee but not expelled from the Party.[59]

The Central Committee and the other executive organs of the PKI usually contain a number of secret members. But so far as is known, the composition of these bodies has hardly varied since September, 1959, when the Sixth National Congress installed a greatly enlarged Central

Sukarno addressed the Party in an hour-long nationally broadcast speech in which he stated that "from the time of his youth till the present he had always cherished feelings of close friendship with the PKI." [66] Aidit, answering him on that occasion, waxed lyrical:

> We, who are obliged by the Party to study the history of the Party and the struggle of the Indonesian people, know just how close are the spiritual ties between the PKI and Bung Karno. It was none other than Bung Karno, still then very young, who warmly welcomed the heroic 1926 rebellion.[67]

Whatever the true relationship between President Sukarno and the communist movement may have been in the 30 years before 1956, the past 8 years have been characterized by the President's increasingly close cooperation with the PKI domestically, and with the communist bloc internationally.

Since 1956, numerous exchanges of visits have taken place between Indonesian officials and those of communist countries. The possible impact of the frequent appearance of Sukarno in the company of foreign communist dignitaries is suggested by the fact that Voroshilov's state visit to Indonesia in the summer of 1957 was interpreted by many observers as contributing to the 34 per cent increase (over 1955) of the electoral strength of the PKI in the regional elections held at that time.

In the absence of elections since 1957, of any public opinion surveys, and of freedom of the press, the current state of Indonesian public opinion cannot be assessed, but it is clear that not only the personal authority of Sukarno but also the instrumentalities of the state are used to increase popular acceptance of communism. Not only is the PKI free to propagate its views but, through its hold on the National Front, other parties and organizations are maneuvered into espousing similar positions on most issues of public concern.

It is far from clear how the present relationship between Sukarno and the Aidit group developed. It is conceivable that initially the PKI leaders solicited only protection against their enemies in exchange for their support, and then took advantage of their increasing intimacy with the President to try to convince him that they were the logical heirs of his regime. But it is also possible that, sometime after the 1955 elections had revealed to the President the PKI's potential as a revolutionary mass party, a secret understanding was reached pledging PKI support to Sukarno during his lifetime in exchange for a special role for the communists as vanguard of the Indonesian revolution. After February, 1957, the PKI mobilized mass support for Sukarno's guided democracy. Following the creation of the new regime, in July, 1959, Aidit, as chairman of a committee of the Republic's Supreme Advisory Council, played an important role in shaping the character of the emerging state ideology.

A comparison between the President's Independence Day addresses of 1959 and 1960 suggests a crucial increase in communist influence during that year.

Whatever the chain of events may have been, it is quite clear that some of the major political guidelines of the regime that took shape after 1957 appear to have been drawn several years earlier by the PKI. For instance, the concept of a *Nasakom* cabinet, which Sukarno made into a national issue at the beginning of his campaign for guided democracy in February, 1957, and for which he has pleaded ever since, has the specific purpose of bringing the PKI into the government. The idea, without the acronym later devised by Sukarno, originated in a decision of the Central Committee of the PKI taken in November, 1954:

> Cooperation between the Party and the Communist masses and the Nationalist and Islamic parties and masses is not something which is to last only until the forthcoming elections have been held, as Nationalist and Islamic leaders often declare. We favour cooperation after the elections as well, regardless of who wins. This is in keeping with the slogan of our Republic, *Bhineka Tunggal Ika* [i.e., unity in diversity].[68]

At that time the PKI made no reference to the fact that, in 1926, Sukarno had published in *Suluh Indonesia Muda* an article entitled, "Nationalism, Islamism, and Marxism," urging cooperation between the major currents in Indonesian politics.[69] Only since October, 1962, has the PKI given publicity to that forgotten text, which it reprinted in pamphlet form in 1963. Now Aidit argues that the *Nasakom* concept "created by Sukarno in 1926," his *Pantja Sila*, formulated in June, 1945, the 1945 Constitution, reestablished by decree on July 5, 1959, and the Political Manifesto (*Manipol*) which outlined on August 17, 1959, the basic principles of the new regime of "guided democracy," are "part of one unit which cannot be separated in the efforts of the Indonesian people to finish the national-democratic revolution and proceed toward Socialism."[70] In other words, participation of the communists in the government of Indonesia is an essential component of the political tradition gradually revealed by the national prophet Sukarno.

President Sukarno has succeeded in creating in Indonesia a political symbolism that pervades the country's public life. It is entirely possible that this verbal superstructure will persist for some time after his death. The magic power of words is particularly great in a country deeply imbued with mysticism. The PKI leaders, by treating the President's formulations with quasi-theological reverence and making him the object of their cult of personality, are showing shrewd political judgment concerning their long-term interests. In the last couple of years, the speeches of Aidit and of other PKI leaders appear more and more generously adorned with quotations from "The Great Leader of the Revolution," as

Sukarno has been called since 1960. This not only satisfies the President's boundless vanity but also helps convince the masses that the communists are his true disciples and, therefore, also his most deserving political heirs.

It can be expected that the PKI, in the period of transition following Sukarno's death, will present him as a father-figure whose ideological legacy they are anxious to honor as good Indonesian patriots. However insincere such a maneuver may be, the prospect of it may well appeal to the President, not only because it now mobilizes the communist propaganda machinery on his behalf, but also because it promises him the political immortality which he so obviously seeks.

By accident or design, the PKI leaders can use their doctrine to convince Sukarno both of the sincerity of their current cooperation with him and of his future place in their history books. As early as October, 1953, the Aidit group formulated a PKI program, afterwards ratified by the Fifth National Congress in March, 1954, which provides a suitable basis for a political alliance with Sukarno. In arguing for "a government of the people's democracy," the 1954 PKI Program said that this government:

> will be a government of a united national front, formed on the basis of the alliance of workers and peasants under the leadership of the working class. Taking into account the country's backwardness, the Communist Party of Indonesia considers that this government must not be a government of the dictatorship of the proletariat but a government of the dictatorship of the people. *This government will effect not socialist but democratic reforms. It will be a government capable of uniting all anti-feudal and anti-imperialist forces.* [Emphasis supplied.] [71]

With only a minor juggling of concepts, the PKI should have found it relatively easy to convince Sukarno that this indispensable stage of the anti-feudal and anti-imperialist revolution must be led by him as head of a *Nasakom* or united national front government. This argument must have carried even greater conviction after Premier Khrushchev's visit to Indonesia in February, 1960, and the Soviet Union's massive aid commitments, and especially after the Declaration of the 1960 Congress of the 81 Communist Parties in Moscow pledged support to "independent national democracies," a category which Sukarno could take to include the political system he wants to create:

> The Communist parties are working actively for a consistent completion of the anti-imperialist, anti-feudal, democratic revolution, for the establishment of national democracies, for a radical improvement in the living standard of the people.[72]

Aidit and his group show considerable intellectual resourcefulness and political sophistication in the way they handle their relations with the President. By developing in all their public statements the thesis that Indonesia's economic ills are the result of "the remnants of imperialism and feudalism," [73] the communist leaders imply the blamelessness of the Sukarno regime, but at the same time build up their own claim to power as the only group truly capable of coping with these hostile forces. PKI public statements strengthen Sukarno's self-confident belief that he is not the cause of the country's suffering, but a necessary stage in the Marxist dialectic of history. The latter feeling was clearly reflected in Sukarno's Independence Day address for 1964, entitled "A Year of Dangerous Living." In a country still deeply imbued with magic-mystical thinking, one should not underestimate the impact on the masses of statements such as this:

> Please do not think that Sukarno is a clairvoyant person. Do not think that Sukarno is in the possession of some magic power! No! Whenever I predict this or that, my prediction is based on my knowledge of the objective laws of the history of society. If there is any magic in my possession, it is because I know the Mandate of the Suffering of the People, because I know conditions, and because *I know a science which is efficacious, namely Marxism.* [Emphasis supplied.] [74]

Many Indonesians constantly search for magical formulas that will secure them happiness, health, wealth, or power. To be told by their President that his success is due to the science of Marxism should be worth a great deal to the PKI. But the like-mindedness between Sukarno and the PKI, evinced by the above address, goes further than general endorsement of the science of Marxism by the President. It follows the PKI in sorting political groups as die-hards, middle-of-the-roaders, and progressives, and describes the Indonesian revolution in classic communist terms: a national-democratic stage to be followed by a socialist stage. His 1964 Independence Day address endorses communist positions on all major domestic and international issues raised in Indonesia during the preceding year. The achievements in which Sukarno takes pride are, without exception, goals also advocated by the PKI. Positions taken by the President in current national debates conform to the stand publicly expressed several months earlier by the PKI. Detailed scrutiny of current policies of the Sukarno regime suggests that the PKI, despite its lack of formal executive prerogatives, has already considerable influence on the policies of the Sukarno government.

A most revealing episode in the Sukarno-PKI interplay took place in the last months of 1964. Around September 1 a group of extreme-left nationalist radicals, with impeccable revolutionary records, led by Minister of Trade Adam Malik, former *Murba* Party chairman and ex-ambassador to Moscow, and by the publisher of *Merdeka*, ambassador B. M. Diah, created a "Body for the Propagation of Sukarnoism" (BPS). The group wanted to expound a non-communist interpretation of Sukarno's political views and thus counter PKI efforts to exploit the ideology of the regime for its purposes. Forty newspapers pledged support to this campaign.[75] The Army made it clear that it welcomed the Sukarnoist movement. So did six of Indonesia's ten legal political parties, namely *Murba*, IPKI, the Protestant Party (*Parkindo*), the Catholic Party, and the Moslem parties, PSII and PERTI. PKI, the Nationalist Party (PNI) and *Partindo* attacked the BPS, while the *Nahdatul Ulama* Moslem Party remained neutral.[76] On December 12 the President summoned the representatives of all ten parties to Bogor to discuss the issue and convinced them to accept a statement saying: "We are unanimously determined to foster and maintain the revolutionary and progressive unity with *Nasakom* as its core." [77] Five days later, on December 17, the BPS was banned by Presidential decree.[78] Whether the anti-PKI forces will rally again after this defeat is questionable.

Indonesia's current external orientation also favors the PKI. Soviet military aid and well-publicized communist bloc diplomatic support to Indonesia's campaigns for West New Guinea and against the Federation of Malaysia, created, especially since 1960, the impression that Indonesia's best and perhaps only friends abroad were the communist countries. This trend was reinforced by the concept of the "new emerging forces," expounded by President Sukarno since the September, 1961, Belgrade conference of non-aligned countries, which introduced a new version of the communist two-camps theory of international relations, by pitting jointly communist and excolonial countries against the "old established forces" of imperialism, colonialism, and neo-colonialism. This concept, widely disseminated by the Indonesian press, eroded the neutralist tradition established in Indonesia since independence until it became possible, after Communist China's nuclear detonation of October 16, 1964, to reveal the Indonesia-Chinese *rapprochement* which had taken place during the preceding year creating the foundations of a new Peking-Pyongyang-Hanoi-Phnom Penh-Djakarta axis.

Of late President Sukarno has become quite candid about the future of communism in Indonesia. He was asked by a CBS team interviewing him for the January 31, 1965, *Face the Nation* program whether present trends do not point toward a communist Indonesia. Sukarno answered: "I do not care as long as they do not make trouble for the Indonesian state." This can only mean either "as long as the take-over is peaceful" or (and more likely) "as long as they do not make trouble for Sukarno."

In view of this situation, the proud and self-reliant posture of the PKI both at home and vis-à-vis the international communist movement becomes understandable. In his Political Report to the second plenum of the Central Committee, held in Djakarta in December, 1963, Aidit dis-

cussed the question whether communist parties "can be successful without assistance from socialist countries." He answered:

> If Lenin and the great October socialist revolution teach us anything,
> they teach that if the people are united and in complete accord to strug-
> gle and to gain ultimate victory, not only will the imperialists be thrown
> out but also the capitalist system can be destroyed. *The Soviet Union was
> established by Lenin and the proletariat without aid from socialist states,*
> because the Soviet Union was the very first socialist state. [Emphasis
> supplied.] [79]

In the same speech Aidit also said:

> Among the Communist groups in other countries, there have also been
> people who have not been so enthusiastic concerning the PKI's inde-
> pendent attitude. In fact some brotherly countries have charged the PKI
> with being "nationalistic." They look upon the slogan "Give an Indo-
> nesian Image to Marxism-Leninism" as a slogan which is in contradistinc-
> tion with Marxism-Leninism. . . . Supposing Marx, Engels, and Lenin
> were still alive: would they be angered [by] or partial to the fact that
> certain Communist Parties have reformulated their teachings in powerful
> and creative ways? [80]

These are not the words of Soviet or Chinese puppets but of a new
breed of radically nationalist communist leaders, much more likely to be
accepted in their own societies than were the Comintern agents of earlier
days. The odds are that under these leaders the PKI will come to power
in Indonesia. But, by the same odds, they are not likely either to turn
their country into a satellite or to create a carbon copy of previous communist regimes.

The PKI's "Road to Power"

1. Department of State, Bureau of Intelligence and Research, *World Strength of
   the Communist Party Organizations* (Wash., D.C.: Government Printing Office,
   1964), p. 1.
2. Aldo Garosci, "The Italian Communist Party," in *Communism in Western
   Europe,* ed. Mario Einaudi (Ithaca, N.Y.: Cornell University Press, 1951),
   p. 200.
3. *Harian Rakjat, People's Daily* (Djakarta), June 27, 1964, p. 1.
4. Giuliano Pajetta, article in *Rinascita,* Rome, June 8, 1963, pp. 14-15. Translation published by U.S. Department of Commerce, Office of Technical Services,
   Joint Publications Research Service [JPRS]. No. 22592/1964, p. 13.
5. "Menempuh Djalan Rakjat" ("Embarking on the People's Road"), speech to
   commemorate the thirty-second anniversary of the PKI, in D. N. Aidit, *Pilihan
   Tulisan (Selected Works),* Vol. I, Djakarta, 1959 (JPRS Translation No.
   6551/1961, p. 43).
6. Guy J. Pauker, "Current Communist Tactics in Indonesia," *Asian Survey,* May,
   1961, p. 30.

7. Richard Lowenthal, "On 'National Democracy': Its Function in Communist Policy," *Survey*, London, April, 1963, p. 127.

8. D. N. Aidit, "Bersatulah Untuk Menjelesaikan Tuntutan Revolusi Agustus 1945" ("Unite to Complete the Demands of the 1945 August Revolution"), General Report to the Fourth Plenary Session of the Central Committee of the PKI, July, 1956, in *Pilihan Tulisan*, Vol. II, Djakarta, 1960 (JPRS Translation No. 8886/1961, p. 25).

9. *Ibid.*, p. 49.

10. *Ibid.*, p. 48.

11. *Ibid.*, p. 50.

12. See "Theses of the Tenth Congress of the Italian Communist Party," published in *L'Unita*, Rome, September 13, 1962 (JPRS Translation No. 15,679/1962, pp. 25, 28).

13. D. N. Aidit, "Menudju Indonesia Baru" ("Toward a New Indonesia"), speech on May 23, 1953, to commemorate the thirty-third anniversary of the PKI, in *Pilihan Tulisan*, Vol. I, Djakarta, 1959 (JPRS Translation No. 6551/1961, p. 88).

14. D. N. Aidit, "Djalan Ke Demokrasi Rakjat Bagi Indonesia" ("The Road to People's Democracy for Indonesia"), Report to the Fifth National Congress of the PKI, March, 1954, in *Pilihan Tulisan*, Vol. I, Djakarta, 1959 (JPRS Translation No. 6551/1961, p. 169).

15. *Pravda*, Moscow, May 23, 1960.

16. PKI, *Material for the Sixth National Congress*, Djakarta, December, 1958, pp. 31, 32 (published in English by the PKI).

17. D. N. Aidit, *Kobarkan Semangat Banteng!* (*Rouse the Wild Buffalo Spirit!*), Political Report to the Second Plenum of the Seventh Central Committee, December 23, 1963, Djakarta, 1964 (JPRS Translation No. 23,639/1964, p. 67). *Nasakom* is an acronym introduced by President Sukarno, in 1960, to symbolize the cooperation of nationalist, religious, and communist forces.

18. Arnold C. Brackman, *Indonesian Communism: A History* (New York: Frederick A. Praeger, Inc., 1963), p. 149.

19. Departemen Agitprop, Central Comite Partai Komunis Indonesia, *Putusan-Putusan Sidang Pleno Central Comite Partai Komunis Indonesia* (*Decisions of the Plenary Session of the Central Committee of the Communist Party of Indonesia*), Djakarta, 1953, p. 45.

20. *Bintang Merah* (Red Star), Djakarta, February-March, 1956, p. 112.

21. D. N. Aidit, *Kobarkan Semangat Banteng!* (JPRS Translation No. 23,639/1964, p. 62).

22. *Harian Rakjat*, June 17, 1964.

23. *Harian Rakjat*, May 4, June 17, July 30, 1964.

24. *Laporan Umum Dewan Nasional SOBSI Kepada Kongres Nasional Ke-III SOBSI* (*General Report of the National Committee of SOBSI to the Third National Congress of SOBSI*), Djakarta, 1960 (JPRS Translation No. 7456/1961, p. 53).

25. *Harian Rakjat*, November 30, 1962; September 18, 1964.

26. *Harian Rakjat*, October 17, 1962; February 7, 1963; February 13, June 1, June 11, 1964.

27. D. N. Aidit, "The Road To People's Democracy for Indonesia," General Report to the Fifth National Congress of the PKI, in *Problems of the Indonesian Revolution* (Demos, 1963), p. 252. This volume, published probably in Peking, contains a selection, in English translation, of Aidit's major pronouncements.

28. *Harian Rakjat*, November 27, 1963; April 13, 1964; September 7 and 8, 1964.

29. Jean-Marie Domenach, "The French Communist Party," in *Communism in Western Europe*, p. 113.

30. *Harian Rakjat,* May 6, 1964.

31. W. L. Shirer, *The Rise and Fall of the Third Reich* (New York: Simon and Schuster, Inc., 1960), pp. 195-201.

32. *Antara* News Agency, January 14, 1965.

33. *Harian Rakjat,* January 19, 1965.

34. U.S. Department of State, *World Strength,* pp. 12, 14.

35. *Harian Rakjat,* March 17, 1964.

36. D. N. Aidit, "Kaum Tani Djawa Barat Mengganjang Setan-Setan Desa" ("The West Javanese Peasantry Crushes the Village Devils"), *Harian Rakjat,* May 11, 13, 14, 15, 16, 1964.

37. Aidit described this research program in a speech on July 28, 1964, published in *Harian Rakjat* on August 1, 1964. 3,300 PKI and BTI cadres studied villages in 124 typical subdistricts in Java, using the "3 Togethers" method: work together, sleep together, and eat together with the peasants.

38. *Antara* News Agency, June 24, 1964.

39. *Harian Rakjat,* July 15, 1964.

40. E.g. Aidit, speech of April 29, 1964, at the Naval Academy in Surabaya, *Harian Rakjat,* May 9, 1964. See also the PKI pamphlets *PKI dan AD, PKI dan AURI, PKI dan ALRI, PKI dan Polisi* published in 1963.

41. *Review of Indonesia* (Djakarta, published in English by the PKI), June-July, 1959, Supplement, pp. 4, 5.

42. PKI, "An Evaluation of the Kerdja Cabinet After One Year in Office," mimeo., Djakarta, 1960, p. 4. For use of the term "bureaucratic capitalists" by the Chinese, see Mao Tse-tung, "The Present Situation and Our Tasks," in *Selected Works,* Vol. IV, Peking, 1961, p. 167.

43. Aidit stated, on November 23, 1962: "The Communists demand abolition of martial law precisely because they love the Army," *Harian Rakjat,* November 27, 1962.

44. *Antara* News Agency, December 19, 1962; *Harian Rakjat,* January 1, 1963.

45. D. N. Aidit, *Dare, Dare and Dare Again!* (Peking: Foreign Languages Press, 1963), p. 8. This is the first PKI document circulated by the Communist Party of China in English translation. SOB are the initials by which one refers to martial law in Indonesia since Dutch colonial days.

46. Aidit, *Pilihan Tulisan,* Vol. II (JPRS Translation No. 8886/1961, p. 35).

47. *Ibid.,* p. 80.

48. *Harian Rakjat* published on July 2, 1963, and on July 7 and 8, 1964, the full texts of Aidit's speeches at the Army's *Seskoad;* on July 17 and 18, 1963, the full text of a speech at the Navy's *Seskoal;* on March 23 and 24, 1964, the full text of a speech at the Air Force's *Seskoau;* on February 28, 1963, the full text of a speech at the Police Academy.

49. *Harian Rakjat,* July 6, 1964, p. 2. Aidit stated recently (*Harian Rakjat,* August 20, 1964) that there are more Moslems in the PKI than in one of the smaller Moslem parties.

50. *Madju Terus! Dokumen-Dokumen Kongres Nasional KE-VII (Luarbiasa) PKI (Carry On! Documents of the Seventh [Extraordinary] PKI National Congress),* Djakarta, 1963, p. 319. The title of the volume is based on President Sukarno's exhortation to the PKI in addressing the closing session of that congress.

51. *Antara* News Agency, Djakarta, September 28, 1964.

52. Donald Hindley, "The Communist Party of Indonesia, 1951-1961: A Decade of Aidit Leadership," Ph.D. dissertation, Australian National University, Canberra, 1961, p. 170.

53. *Harian Rakjat,* August 19, 1963.

54. *Review of Indonesia,* Djakarta, June-July, 1959, Supplement, p. 7.

55. Herbert Feith, *The Indonesian Elections of 1955,* mimeo., Modern Indonesia Project (Ithaca, N.Y.: Cornell University, 1957), p. 62.

56. *Harian Rakjat,* September 11, 1964, p. 1.

57. D. N. Aidit, *Kobarkan Semangat Banteng!* (JPRS Translation No. 23,639/1964, p. 70).

58. D. N. Aidit, "Dengan Semangat Banteng Merah Mengkonsolidasi Organisasi Komunis Jang Besar" ("With the Spirit of the Red Buffalo Consolidate the Big Communist Organization"), in *Harian Rakjat,* July 6, 1964, p. 3.

59. Hindley, "Communist Party of Indonesia," p. 118.

60. *Harian Rakjat,* July 8, 1964, p. 1.

61. *Harian Rakjat,* February 13, 1963.

62. E.g., Aidit's speech on communist ethics to the Christian University *Satya Watjana,* full text in *Harian Rakjat,* November 23, 26, and 27, 1962.

63. *Harian Rakjat,* May 20, 1963.

64. George McT. Kahin, *Nationalism and Revolution in Indonesia* (Ithaca, N.Y.: Cornell University Press, 1952), p. 292.

65. Hindley, "Communist Party of Indonesia," p. 490.

66. *Review of Indonesia,* Djakarta, November-December, 1959, p. 41.

67. *Review of Indonesia,* September-October, 1959, p. 12.

68. D. N. Aidit, "The Birth and Growth of the Communist Party of Indonesia," in *Problems of the Indonesian Revolution,* Demos, 1963, p. 100.

69. Ir. Sukarno, *Dibawah Bendera Revolusi* (*Under the Flag of the Revolution*), Vol. I, 1959, pp. 1-23. When this collection of Sukarno's early works was being published, probably in Peking, the 1926 article was rediscovered.

70. Lectures at the *Gerwani* Training Center, October 23 and 27, 1962, on "Marxism in Practice," *Harian Rakjat,* October 29, 1962.

71. Quoted in *Problems of the Indonesian Revolution,* p. 94.

72. *New York Times,* December 7, 1960.

73. D. N. Aidit, "DEKON Dan Sjarat-Sjarat Pelaksanaanja" ("The Economic Declaration and Conditions for its Implementation") in DEKON, Djakarta, 1963 (JPRS Translation No. 19,833/1963, p. 5).

74. "A Year of Dangerous Living," address by the President of the Republic of Indonesia, August 17, 1964, English translation by *Antara* News Agency, Djakarta, p. 10. The speech was distributed in pamphlet form as a supplement to *Harian Rakjat* of August 19, 1964. Its Indonesian title is *"Tahun Ber-Vivere Pericoloso,"* a slightly ungrammatical reminiscence of Mussolini's slogan, *Vivere Pericolosamente,* inspired, in turn, by Nietzsche. In accordance with current Indonesian practice, this year's address is to be referred to by the acronym *Tavip,* joining *Manipol* (1959), *Djarek* (1960), *Resopim* (1961), *Takem* (1962), and *Gesuri* (1963).

75. *Merdeka,* Djakarta, November 9, 1964.

76. *Far Eastern Economic Review,* Hong Kong, December 24, 1964, p. 598.

77. *Harian Rakjat,* December 14, 1964.

78. *Harian Rakjat,* December 18, 1964.

79. D. N. Aidit, *Kobarkan Semangkat Banteng!* (JPRS Translation No. 23,639/1964, pp. 45, 46).

80. *Ibid.* (JPRS Translation, p. 59). The PKI leaders again showed their wisdom on August 10, 1964, when the Agitprop Department of the Central Committee of the PKI announced in *Harian Rakjat* the initiation of a "movement to eradicate the disease of self-satisfaction" from the Party and warned: "Self-

satisfaction is the mother of retreat and defeat. Humility is the mother of progress and victory."

Selected Bibliography

Brackman, Arnold C., *Indonesian Communism: A History*. New York: Frederick A. Praeger, Inc., 1963. A study by a veteran reporter of the Asian scene.

Feith, Herbert, "Dynamics of Guided Democracy," in *Indonesia*, ed. Ruth T. McVey. New Haven, Conn.: Human Relations Area Files Press, 1963.

———, "President Sukarno, the Army and the Communists: The Triangle Changes Shape," *Asian Survey*, August, 1964.

———, "President Sukarno and the Communists: The Politics of Domestication," *American Political Science Review*, December, 1962.

Hindley, Donald, *The Communist Party of Indonesia*. Berkeley, Calif.: University of California Press. [In press.] A detailed account of the first decade, 1951 to 1961, of the Indonesian Communist Party under the leadership of the Aidit group.

———, "The Indonesian Communist Party and the Conflict in the International Communist Movement," *The China Quarterly*, July-September, 1964.

McVey, Ruth, "Indonesian Communism and the Transition to Guided Democracy," in *Communist Strategies in Asia*, ed. A. Doak Barnett. New York: Frederick A. Praeger, Inc., 1963.

———, *The Rise of Indonesian Communism*. Ithaca, N.Y.: Cornell University Press. [In press.] An important study of the history of the Indonesian Communist Party before 1927.

Pauker, Ewa T., "Has the Sukarno Regime Weakened the PKI?" *Asian Survey*, September, 1964.

U.S. Department of Commerce, Office of Technical Services, Joint Publications Research Service [JPRS], *Translations on South and East Asia*. This serial publication includes selections from *Harian Rakjat* and various Indonesian communist periodicals. JPRS publishes translations of important Indonesian Communist Party documents.

The Communist
Parties of Burma

John H. Badgley

The communist movement in Burma is as
splintered in 1964 as at any period in its chaotic lifetime. Three
communist or protocommunist parties are extant, and
within each organization long-existent personal dissension
has been exacerbated by the Sino-Soviet
split. None of the communist parties have obtained
Cabinet seats since Burma achieved independence.
Perhaps this is chiefly because of communist belligerence
and, also, skillful governmental manipulation of the
competition within communist leadership.
Directly below Ne Win's Revolutionary Council, however, there
are civilian advisers who have been active in the
communist movement and who model their developmental

programs after those of communist states. Some of these advisers encourage authoritarian measures resembling steps taken in eastern Europe during the early communist years, namely, imprisonment of political opposition, suppression of the critical press, nationalization of industry, and reorientation of the educational system to emphasize Marxist doctrine.

Despite these indications of leftist influence, it would be an error to consider the current Burmese government communist, or, at least, communist in any traditional sense. The government belongs to no communist military alliance; pursues an active neutralist foreign policy; supports the test-ban negotiations and treaty; encourages China to accept India's demands in the Sino-Indian border dispute; and imprisons and harasses communist leaders within Burma. In short, the current strength of communism in Burma rests more on the inherent persuasion of communist ideology expressed by independent Marxists than it does on the group of splintered party organizations; and the indigenous development program reflects more the influence of general socialist ideas than the power of a monolithic communist party.

Origins and Development of the Communist Parties in Burma

The current weakness in the organization of the communist parties in Burma is an accentuation of organizational difficulties which appeared in the 1930's, when communist ideas were first introduced into Burma. At that time, diverse extremist ideologies were seized upon by younger Burmese nationalists who regarded dyarchy and the continued British presence as the greatest of political evils. A number of radical organizations were founded, although no communist party of national significance appeared until 1943. Communist activity began with study groups instigated by Thakin Kodaw Hmaing and other publicists in the period from 1930 to 1935. In the mid-Thirties, communist classics first appeared in translation and active agitation began with the student leadership of a university boycott and the Indian riots of 1936.

The most active student political group, the Thakins, was influenced by writings of Marx, Lenin, and Stalin. Many members called themselves communists, but no party discipline was imposed and no widely accepted leadership emerged to unite these self-styled communists. Hence, a broad organizational base was not created. Kodaw Hmaing, then in his early fifties, and Thakins Soe, Ba Hein, and Pe Htay, who were in their late twenties, were among the first committed Burmese communists, but none of these men sought to synthesize communist theory to fit the indigenous circumstances, as did M. N. Roy in India, Tan Malakka in Indonesia, and Ho Chi Minh in Indochina. No Burmese traveled to Moscow or established ties with the Communist International; indeed, in the Thirties, Burma's communists were relatively isolated from foreign communists and the Comintern.[1]

Communism in Burma took root untended and unappreciated by the outside world. This unique quality set the movement on a stormy course from which the Burma communist parties have yet to recover: a course plagued by lack of cohesive leadership and almost devoid of international legitimation.

Notwithstanding difficulties encountered in creating a single communist authority, the movement did prosper at the intellectual level in Rangoon. The imprisonment of boycott and riot leaders in 1936 threw older communists into jail with younger students who, during the subsequent months, were tutored and enlisted in various communist causes. For example, U Nu, Aung San, and Than Tun were persuaded by Thakin Soe to assist in translating *The Communist Party of the Soviet Union* and the *Communist Manifesto* into Burmese.[2] A Marxist study group, formed by 13 Thakins in 1938 near Rangoon University, may be considered the first communist cell in Burma as well as the initial core of the Communist Party of Burma.[3] Thakin Ba Hein published *The Capitalist World* in 1939, and provided through it an indigenous communist interpretation of colonialism as it affected Burma. Although the government confiscated those communist materials they could find, most of the younger active nationalists had read various radical tracts prior to the Japanese invasion of 1942.

Japanese involvement in the Burmese independence movement, which commenced in 1940, precipitated the first basic division among the communists. The embryonic communist movement suddenly found itself basically divided over the nationalist issue.[4] Trouble developed when many Thakins decided to seek foreign support for a proposed insurrection against the British. Japanese agents encouraged the notion and offered promises of support, an option which caused a three-way division among the Thakins: One group favored an appeal to the Chinese Communist Party; another supported the Japanese proposal; a third element—the doctrinaire communists—opposed fighting the British on the grounds that Japan should first be defeated. Thakin Kodaw Hmaing met secretly with the Japanese in March, 1940, to work out a strategy involving Japanese support. Subsequently he and Dr. Ba Maw encouraged the young Thakin, Aung San, to establish contact with Japanese agents in China.[5] Meanwhile, the more radical political parties—including the Thakin Party, the Fabian Party (a moderate Marxist group), the People's Revolutionary Party (subsequently the Socialist Party), and the nationalistic Myochit Party of U Saw—clandestinely espoused a variety of strategies to achieve independence by violent means. Speaking of this period after the war, Aung San wrote:

> It was true that I was one of the original members of the Communist Party. But that party at first existed more or less in name, its members being exceedingly small. Than Tun, who is today one of its leaders, did not belong to it at that time . . . [Later] when I met Thakin Soe secretly in August 1944 to hammer out the anti-Jap movement and organization, he urged me to join the Communist Party formed by him [the previous year]. I agreed to join it finally, but I left it afterwards as I disagreed with some of his views and with his sectarianism. . . .[6]

In Aung San's statement rests the fundamental problem of party discipline, namely, the lack of a consensus among the leadership. Only briefly, from August, 1944 to October, 1946, did the communists work together as a part of the united front Anti-Fascist People's Freedom League (AFPFL) in the drive for freedom. Within the AFPFL, over which Aung San presided, clustered political, communal, and functional organizations. The Chairman of the Communist Party of Burma (CPB), Thakin Soe, hoped eventually to dominate the coalition, for the CPB had earned the goodwill of both the British and most Burmese by actively fighting the Japanese throughout the war. However, Soe's aspirations were frustrated when the Socialist Party, the core of the AFPFL leadership, agreed to negotiate rather than fight for independence.

Thakin Soe withdrew his faction of the CPB, a group henceforward called the Red Flags, early in 1946, and some months later took a small band underground to initiate the insurrection which he continues to fight 18 years later. Thakin Than Tun then formed a new Communist Party of Burma, the White Flags, which continued to cooperate with the government until August, 1947, when U Nu, the Premier-designate following Aung San's assassination, refused to include any communists except Thein Pe Myint, a deviant CPB member, within his shadow cabinet. Militancy gained the ascendancy within the CPB (i.e., White Flag) Politburo thereafter, and in March, 1948, only three months after independence, Than Tun announced that he would follow Thakin Soe underground.[7]

The White Flags quickly amassed a substantial guerrilla force. The party had extensive contacts in the districts and, after 1951, it operated in loose alliance with the Red Flags as well as with the People's Volunteer Organization (PVO), an ex-militia led by rurally oriented politicians who, like the two communist parties, had broken with U Nu over the distribution of cabinet posts. These three insurgent forces, with several thousand Karen insurgents, dominated central Burma between 1948 and

1952, controlling the countryside and most small towns, fighting together in the early years but, after establishing sectors of control for taxation purposes, becoming increasingly suspicious of one another. Gradually, a revitalized Burmese Army, under the command of Ne Win, reasserted Rangoon's control over the towns and transport routes. By 1954, the two communist forces were cut off from their economic bases and had begun to disintegrate. By 1958, 38,000 insurgents had surrendered.

Meanwhile a third group of communists, members of Parliament who had remained loyal to the government, split from the AFPFL over the issue of Burma's support for the United Nations' policy in the Korean War and formed a new political party in January, 1951. This new Burma Workers and Peasants Party (Red Socialists, or BWPP) competed with the AFPFL in the next two elections, retaining its seats in Parliament and generally demonstrating that a communist, or at least a radical socialist, position could obtain wide support. Two popular newspapers, the *Mirror* of Rangoon and *Ludu* of Mandalay, publicized BWPP policies.

Prior to the 1956 elections, the BWPP joined the loosely structured National United Front (NUF), obscuring their own communist orientation within a relatively moderate platform. The NUF was indeed successful, capturing over 40 per cent of the popular vote, but the Red Socialists were unable to improve their position in Parliament. Of 239 contested seats, the NUF captured only 48. The next election, which was delayed by the Ne Win caretaker government, was held in February, 1960, and despite a split within the AFPFL and U Nu's creation of his own National Union Party, the NUF lost electoral support and won only 30 seats. NUF influence in Parliament declined, and the old problem of divisiveness within communist leadership returned to split the BWPP into moderate and radical factions, some loyal to Moscow, others pursuing the Peking line, and a significant minority independent of any foreign line.

During the same decade that the Red Socialists were building their organization, another faction of the White Flag communists, originally led by Than Myaing, had taken residence in China and established Burma's first close relationship with a foreign party. Some 32 members of this faction, led by Bo Zeyya and Yebaw Htay, returned in three groups to Burma in July and August, 1963, to help in the negotiations for termination of the communist insurrections. The meetings broke down in November, and Yebaw Htay took the Peking group into rural Burma to join and attempt to dominate Than Tun's White Flags. The Red Flags, long since isolated from the rest of the communist movement, were branded as Stalinist by other communists and seemed destined to obscurity. But in the spring of 1964, a split developed within the White Flags and a faction led by Goshal allegedly joined the Red Flags in opposition to Than Tun's "moderate" revisionism.

Communist Leadership and Organization

The diverse leadership within the several communist organizations should not obscure the dominant position held by the White Flags since 1950. This position was partially legitimized by contact with the Indian, British, and Soviet communist parties. Than Tun established relations with the Communist Party of India (CPI) through his theoretician, Thakin Ba Tin (i.e., Goshal), a Burmese of Bengali extraction who associated with the Ranadive faction in the CPI during the Japanese occupation. Goshal retained his Indian Party membership and was for several years the chief liaison between the CPB and the CPI. Then, in 1946, a Chinese communist visiting India, Thang Fa, sent official felicitations from Mao Tse-tung. The Soviets established communications through the Yugoslavs attending the 1948 Calcutta conference and maintained this channel through a series of Burmese communists in Moscow, the first of whom was Yebaw Aung Gyi, a current member of the White Flag Politburo.

Than Tun himself remained inside Burma and was neither internationalist in outlook nor particularly concerned about foreign assistance. His strongest qualities, from the outset, were his ideological flexibility and his capacity to attract better-educated Burmans to his cause. All but two or three of his Central Committee members had attended universities. Tun had these men teach in his Central Political School for cadres, which offered dialectical materialism, Marxist economics, and the philosophy of the Cominform as major courses; subsequently they instructed party organizers at district and township levels. The White Flags proselytized students at Rangoon University and in district high schools, and from these students came the cadres to serve as their political militia.

After the insurrection began, the White Flag structure resembled that of the Chinese communist guerrilla organization. Key village areas were established as economic bases. The Central Committee represented regions, and within each region were district, township, and village circle cadres. Each command position was shared by a military and political leader, and local leaders who were sympathetic to the White Flags were usually made chairmen of the People's Courts. Than Tun also maintained liaison officers with the Red Flags and the PVO command in Pyinmana district during 1949, in Prome district in 1950, and in Pakokku and Lower Chindwin districts thereafter. However, the Central Command Post actually exercised little influence over the other insurgent groups, particularly the PVO factions.

The Red Flag communists were much more the product of a charismatic leader than were the other communist parties in Burma. Thakin Soe was the first Burmese to publish translations of the Lenin and Stalin classics, but his faith in his own dogmatic interpretation of this literature became intolerable to his contemporaries and, between 1946 and 1952, his Red Flag forces were relatively isolated from the other communists. Then, following the formal alliance of the communists in 1952, Than Tun met frequently with Thakin Soe, while the communists' influence waned in the face of the government's increasing control over towns and major villages. Soe proposed creation of a single liberation army and, nominally, this proposition went into effect. In practice, however, no single command chain was established. After 1951, both the above- and below-ground communists espoused a popular democratic front idea; again, however, words and deeds differed, for both the White and Red Flags continued to follow the tactics of militancy, rejecting all government overtures.

The division between Burma's two insurgent communist parties made military victory more difficult and was clearly endangering the entire communist movement by 1954. The two Politburos, however, persisted in their rigidity. Personal rivalries were also a significant factor preventing unification. Than Tun was accused of being unrealistic and excessively theoretical by second-line leaders, who began to surrender in increasing numbers. "He organized the party, not the masses, and made slow headway in raising the political consciousness and establishing a people's army." [8]

The underground communists attacked both the domestic and foreign policy of U Nu's government, especially the American aid program, and sought to associate it with alleged U.S. aid to the Kuomintang forces in the Shan States. This latter issue was generally accepted as valid, but other insurgent propaganda conflicted with specific government accomplishments in the economic sector, further alienating the insurgents from the public.[9] The government restricted trade between Army-controlled and insurgent territory, placing the villagers in communist districts on a subsistence existence. Finally, surrendered White Flags complained that the rural cadre generally fell short of even minimum qualifications as "good communists." Few were effective among the villagers; those assigned this most basic task were often "unsuited for any other activity," since village work was the least prestigious job in the party organization. In my own interviews, village leaders complained of excessive terrorism practiced by both communists and AFPFL organizers, but the brutality of the Red Flags was most outstanding in the minds of villagers a full decade after the Red Flags had evacuated north-central Burma. The refusal of the better-educated workers to live and serve within village communities was, therefore, a general problem that plagued communist and noncommunist parties alike.

Burma's third communist party, the Burma Workers' and Peasants'

Party, was popularly known as the Red Socialists. Their major support came from one faction of the trade unions, although they also claimed to be a peasants' party. Rural factions of the PVO, as well as BWPP town organizers, were able to win votes for Red Socialist candidates who campaigned on a platform more akin to Khrushchev's communism than to Mao's or Stalin's. The top leadership resided in Rangoon and normally traveled to their districts only before elections; thus BWPP influence rested on their relationships within the elite rather than on powerful rural associations such as the PVO and the White Flag organizations had. The more prominent Red Socialists were scarcely distinguishable from the socialist faction of the AFPFL, in terms of their education; most were lawyers in Rangoon. Only their ideology was markedly dissimilar, for it displayed considerable Soviet influence, particularly in later years. The BWPP gained its greatest influence shortly before the 1956 elections, when it allied with other opposition groups to form the National United Front and, again, for a few months in 1958, when U Nu retained his Premiership only through their support in Parliament. Ne Win's caretaker regime, U Nu's brief return, and the Revolutionary Council all worked against the BWPP organization. In December, 1962, the old BWPP and NUF combined to form a new leftist party, the National Democratic United Front. In November, 1963, most of the Rangoon and district organizers were arrested, disintegrating the party structure, and in March, 1964, this party, along with others except the Burma Socialist People's Party (BSPP), was declared illegal.

The protocommunist student associations in Rangoon and Mandalay universities are a fourth leftist grouping in Burma. The tradition of radical student associations extends back into the 1920's. However, as communist-dominated organizations, their history begins in 1951, when they first contested the elections for the Rangoon University Students Union. They were defeated the initial year by U Kyaw Nyein's socialist-supported student association. However, the following year, the several factions of communist students united to form the Progressive Students Organization (PSO) and staged a successful strike against the University administration. This group won the student elections at Rangoon University in 1953 and then began the construction of a national organization among district students.

The Progressive Students Organization, like the senior communist parties, was unable to retain its unity. In 1954, it split along the three major communist party lines then existing in Burma, namely, the Red Flags, White Flags, and Red Socialists. Rather than publicly reveal the cleavage, the leaders formed the Rangoon University Students United Front (RUSUF), a more autonomous association of "sympathizers and neutrals" to replace the PSO. The new slate of communist candidates again defeated the government-backed student organization and continued to control official student government until the Army came to power in 1958, at which time the core leadership was imprisoned. These students were released during the 1960 to 1962 administration of U Nu. In July, 1962, the RUSUF-led students rioted on the campus, causing Ne Win to dispatch troops who fired upon the massed students, killing some 30 of the demonstrators. The Army then dynamited the student union building, symbol of organized student opposition, reducing it to rubble. All student political activity was then banned by the Revolutionary Council and the universities were twice closed, in 1963, in an effort to destroy the students' organization—a policy which may have affected the character and status of the University more than the strength of the communists within the student body.

The students of Burma are the most volatile of all politicized groups, for they have been deeply affected by the vast social change now enveloping the land. Within their ranks is the specific discontent of unemployment: They are a group educated for a modern society yet living in a traditional agrarian state. This very practical problem is directly related to the question of who constitutes Burma's communists today.

The Socioeconomic Character of the Communists

Interviews of town and village leaders in central Burma in 1962 provide a typology of the communist leadership. Even though I was unable to meet with any active White or Red Flag communists and the interviews were confined to NUF leaders, these sources and the press interviews of amnestied communists published over the past decade provide relatively clear distinctions. The majority of communist leaders, apart from the Red Flags, have been educated to the high-school level or beyond. All higher leaders come either from higher-income village families, merchant families in towns, or, as in the cases of Ba Nyein and Thein Pe Myint (both of whom are independent communists and are now the civilian "theorists" serving the Revolutionary Council), are sons of clerks in the British civil service. In their youth, therefore, these men enjoyed a much higher status and standard of living than the normal villager or townsman. Nearly all prominent leaders in the White Flag organization were political activists in high school or university and joined the CPB as students or soon after leaving school.

Even at the district level, the older communist leaders are not peasants, although the ranks of both the White and Red Flags have been filled with villagers who served as militia. Younger leaders, usually recruited in town high schools, are sent to villages to organize cadres or militias, a policy differing from that practiced by the PVO and all former legalized parties which built upon the existing village power structure or a minority faction within the village.

The Red Flags, the most extreme of the communist parties, have attempted to dissolve the traditional family and village structure in their drive to achieve a complete revolution. In areas under Red Flag control, Buddhist priests have either relinquished their authority or have been shot, in the same fashion that landowners have either donated their property to the party or have risked death. Such terror has been sanctioned by Thakin Soe, who has preached militant egalitarianism, elimination of Buddhism, and the imminent attainment of communism in Burma. The Red Flag cadres have operated as military units seeking to mobilize entire villages, both men and women, into a communist militia. Thakin Soe promoted a number of women to high rank in his army; indeed, his chief negotiator with the Ne Win regime was a woman, and his advocacy of female equality has become one of his most spectacular policies. Like an evangelist, Thakin Soe recruited devotees, not members, and defections from his organization have been incredibly few, considering the hardship and failure that have characterized its history. For two decades, the Red Flag forces have been driven from village to village in the poorest section of Burma, and finally separated from all popular support. In a certain sense, the Red Flags echo the rebel tragedy of a century ago, when Burman guerrilla fighters fought along the fringes of the Arakan Yomas and Chin Hills against the British for a quarter of a century before they were extinguished.

While the insurgent communists operate more as armies than as political parties, the Red Socialists function as a party striving to win votes on issues and personalities. As the major opposition for 12 years, the BWPP was not able to gain the financial support that the AFPFL or U Nu's Union Party obtained; consequently its organization was always limited by financial stringency. Members of the party, if not the organization itself, turned to the Chinese and Soviet embassies as well as to Chinese merchants for aid, and their press made abundant use of Tass and *Jen-min jih-pao* materials. The Russian defector, Kaznacheev, reports a fascinating method of planting imaginative, but false, stories in the other Asian papers about Burma, then republishing them in the Burmese *Botataung* and the *Mirror* as reliable foreign reports concerning capitalist imperialism within Burma.[10] Of course, there was also evidence that the right-wing faction of the AFPFL and the anticommunist press in Burma was not without its foreign aid. Propaganda from both sides filled the bookstores throughout the country until the Revolutionary Council banned foreign propaganda distribution in 1963.

The problem of financing political parties may well have been the immediate reason for the collapse of Burmese democracy in 1962, and the earlier corruption that resulted from the scramble for the limited funds available for party coffers became most apparent within the BWPP. The Red Socialists seem to have set out to be an independent, nationalist-communist front. They attracted to the lightly disciplined BWPP many of the legitimate intellectual leftists in Burma. The heritage of this group of college graduates, lawyers, and professionals was similar to that of the top AFPFL leaders except for their personal wealth. Eventually, however, the BWPP became so compromised by its dependence upon outside support that Burmese untutored in the Khrushchev-Mao debate had difficulty discerning the difference between Red Socialist and White Flag ideology.

Current Ideologies and Relations With Other Political Forces

In considering the variety of Burmese communists, some observers have wondered whether the apparent complexity of the movement was merely a guise concealing a basic unity. Such a strategy was pursued successfully by Ho Chi Minh and by several eastern European communist parties. Since 1952, moreover, the Chinese communists have strongly urged such an approach for all national liberation movements. Since the CPB (i.e., White Flag) has had intimate relations with the Chinese, is it not probable that Chinese tactics do indeed prevail? One cannot answer these questions with complete certainty. But if one bases the answer upon the behavior patterns of the leaders, there can be little doubt that the cleavages among the Burmese communists are real and politically significant.

The top leaders have been unable to tolerate the discipline of a single party because of the higher value they have placed upon their own absolute command. In this respect, the communists have behaved like other Burmese politicians, all of whom have had extreme difficulty in defining political authority. Who is entitled to power within any party? The question remains unanswered nearly two decades after independence. In Burma, modernity is still so seriously challenged by traditionalists that every political party represents nothing less than a replica of the total culture. Thus, power contestants must operate within the pattern of the village community and the central administration, those two monarchal traditions later reinforced by British colonial policy. As yet, the political party has no legitimate function as a nexus of conflicting interests which can be compromised. No method of compromise, whereby politicians and lobbyists can agree to disagree and thus coexist within a single organization, has been accepted within the Burmese political process. If one can neither command nor follow, then one withdraws.[11]

In the splintering of the communist parties, ideological positions are often connected with personal rivalries and are frequently taken to rationalize a pre-existing antagonism toward another leader. For example, Thakin Soe renounced Kodaw Hmaing's support in 1940 over the single issue of acceptance of Japanese aid, and he never again heeded the old man's authority even though the difference of opinion became irrelevant after the war and Kodaw Hmaing eventually received the greatest international communist recognition awarded a Burmese, the Lenin Peace Prize. Thakin Than Tun split with the more senior Thakin Soe over the British negotiation issue, yet even after both leaders were underground and jointly attacking the government, they could never be successfully reunited. Thakin Lwin, a leading Red Socialist, dissented from Than Tun's insurrection policies. Still, in later years, after the BWPP became a protocommunist party and both leaders were propagating an ideology that was markedly similar in content, neither man was willing to join the other's organization. U Ba Nyein, for a decade Thakin Lwin's colleague in the BWPP, split with him in 1962 over the question of supporting the Revolutionary Council. Today, Ba Nyein is Secretary in the Finance Ministry and Thakin Lwin is in jail. In short, questions of power, of gaining or retaining command, and of personal relations have often been more significant than ideology.[12]

Despite the qualification just placed upon the meaning of ideology, however, there are valid differences in the party lines. Once these are identified, one can see clearly the deep cleavage between the majority White Flags and the other left- and right-wing parties within the movement.

Since 1950, the White Flags have propagated in foreign affairs an ideological position nearly identical to that of Peking. In that year they published, in Burmese, a 36-page document edited by U Ba Win and entitled "The First Year's Journey of the New Republic of China," which argued that "500 million Chinese are now ready to take action in any condition of foreign interference in the Far East." The White Flags consistently opposed economic aid from any Western power and, like the Chinese communists, were particularly incensed over the United States' presence in the Southeast Asia Treaty Organization (SEATO), Korea, Vietnam, and Laos. The U Nu and Ne Win neutralist positions and Burma's role in the test-ban negotiations have recently been condemned in White Flag statements. Except during the four months of amnesty negotiation in 1963, the White Flag radio and pamphlet propaganda considered the Revolutionary Council a "fascist dictatorship."

The Red Flags have advocated the same policy towards the West and have been even more vitriolic in their condemnation of the various Burmese governments. However, Thakin Soe has been most bitter in his denunciation of Khrushchev's coexistence policy and has even admonished

Mao Tse-tung for not actively supporting liberation movements since the 1948 uprisings. He has advocated a united peasant revolution throughout Asia and Africa to cast out the capitalist influence which he believes still controls politics outside of China. This stance has earned Thakin Soe the epithet of "Trotskyite"; nevertheless he views himself as the only legitimate heir to Lenin's revolution.[13]

Most Red Socialists have supported close economic and political ties with the socialist camp but have followed Khrushchev's lead in favoring peaceful coexistence and the test-ban treaty. In domestic policy they have differed even more with the insurgent communists, for they were willing to operate in the open within the bounds of the 1948 constitution until its demise in the 1962 coup. The Red Socialists initially declared their support for the Revolutionary Council, an action refused by the more leftist parties, and they indicated a willingness to join in one monolithic party, the Burma Socialist People's Party, in which ex-PVO leaders would have the dominant civilian position. Red Socialist participation in the BSPP was strongly opposed by the underground parties, and a majority of the BWPP finally pulled out and sought to reestablish their own district organizations. The arrest of the entire BWPP leadership in November, 1963, and the outlawing of all parties within the National Democratic United Front in March, 1964, at least temporarily destroyed their influence and, of course, convinced the White Flags even further that they had no hope of cooperating with the military regime.

The dramatic collapse of the negotiations between the several communist parties, and the temporary elimination of over 500 BWPP politicians, opened a new phase in the extended communist-nationalist conflict in Burma. For the first time since March, 1948, a clear division exists between the socialist, and even Marxist, theorists who are essentially nationalists and those communists who have undetermined and varied loyalties to foreign interpretations of communism. Internment of all significant politicians, including leaders of the National Union Party and the National United Front, has cut off the insurgent communist parties from any potential political support within Rangoon, except from military factions or the BSPP. However, there is scant opportunity for the communist parties to influence or permeate this remaining legitimate party. Men like Colonel Saw Myint, Organizing Secretary to the Central Committee, and adviser Bo Htein Lin are as sensitive to communist subversion in Burma as any individuals Ne Win could have selected for such key posts.

Bo Htein Lin was one of the two leading PVO commanders during the PVO nine-year insurrection, and he attempted to work with the Red and White Flags for four years after the insurrection commenced. PVO guerrillas eventually flushed the communists out of north-central Burma, after rejecting further cooperation because of communist efforts to penetrate the PVO and their excessive dependence upon violence during the insurrection. Many PVO commanders were schoolmates of the new Burmese Army commanders, some had been Thakins, and most had fought together in the Burmese Independence Army against the Japanese in 1945. Thus, although the Burmese Army constructed by Ne Win after 1949 was theoretically fighting the PVO as well as the communists, and although PVO propaganda was flavored with Marxist jargon, there were seldom major engagements between PVO forces and Army companies. From 1953 onward, moreover, the forces lived in mutual respect of one another, encouraging commerce across one another's territory and eventually developing a situation of mutual trust which enabled them to work out a mutually advantageous amnesty.[14]

Ne Win called Htein Lin and other key socialist politicians to Rangoon two weeks before the March, 1962, coup to serve as political advisers. Since that time, the BSPP has been slowly expanding its organization into rural towns across central Burma and into Karen territory in the delta and in Karenni State. District politicians from other parties have had no choice except to cooperate with or fight the BSPP. Given the intimate ties between the military and the BSPP leadership, moreover, there has been little opportunity for any political opposition to form, apart from the demonstrations arranged by Buddhist monks opposing the secular, authoritarian development program.

Both the Red Flags and White Flags now find themselves dependent upon communal political forces. Since the November break, they have apparently sought to exploit the tensions that have matured among the Shans and Kachins as the Burman military has consolidated its grip on the central government. The current relationship between the communist parties and the non-Burman insurgent forces may be summarized as follows. During most of the 1950's, Thakin Soe's Red Flags were allied with the delta faction of the Karen National Defense Organization (KNDO), the Karen nationalists who went underground in 1949. Thakin Soe allegedly converted to communism Mahn Ba Zan, the delta Karen commander, and was able to utilize the superior arms and numbers of the Karens for many of the Red Flag operations against the Burmese Army. Following the 1962 coup, Ne Win opened a new series of negotiations with the KNDO and offered amnesty terms which included significant contributions to the economy of the Karen State. The KNDO commander, Saw Hunter, continued discussions for over a year, finally coming to Rangoon in June, 1963, and he has remained there with Mahn Ba Zan, who headed the tripartite discussions and who renounced his allegiance to Thakin Soe. The success of these discussions means termination of the Karen revolt which has seriously weakened Burma's government since 1949.

To the north, however, the military faces an incredibly nationalistic Kachin Independence Army (KJA) which controls Kachin State and which has become increasingly militant since the collapse of the government's negotiations with the communists. As was once the case with the Karens, one or another of the communist parties seems to be in a position to exploit the separatist sentiment and, until the Revolutionary Council can offer satisfactory conditions for amnesty, the KIA is likely to remain a chronic and serious political opposition force to any unifying efforts in northern Burma.

The White Flags could obtain unlimited armaments from the Chinese if Peking chooses to exploit this weakness on her border, and unconfirmed reports have suggested that Kachin leaders who fled to Yunnan a decade ago have returned to command the KIA. Confirmation of such assistance, however, would seriously undermine the Chinese communist effort to identify with nationalist sentiment in Burma and southeast Asia. More likely is the possibility that U.S. arms captured in Vietnam or sold in Thailand have been purchased by Kachin agents on the Shan border. Certainly, any hint of U.S. support of the KIA would be equally serious for American relations with Burma. The aid the U.S. at one time supplied Kuomintang Chinese forces in the Shan States has remained to haunt American efforts to cultivate Burmese friendship.

There has been no evidence of cooperation between the insurgent forces in the Shan State and any of the communist parties. There is little chance that the Shan separatist movement can be resolved without major changes in the structure of Burma's government, for the depth of the Shans' distrust and antagonism toward the Burmans, most recently reawakened by the internment of leading Shan politicians in 1962, has its roots in the fifteenth century. Meanwhile, a younger Shan leadership is emerging within the underground forces operating out of northern Thailand, and the possibility that these men might align themselves with the KIA and White Flags certainly exists.

The key to the eventual solution of the communal difficulties, from the Kachin and Shan vantage point, obviously does not lie in the creation of a Chinese satellite in Burma. Burmese minority groups are in an excellent position to learn of the outcome of Chinese nationality policy from refugees who have fled across the border in the past 15 years. In the long run, the border minorities must seek a solution through a government in Rangoon, and this cannot be a Maoist-type communist government if they are to achieve their goals. Therefore, it is most likely that the KIA and Shan insurgents, like the KNDO before them, will try to use the communist parties, if at all, for their own ends. Once the government in Rangoon offers terms politically and economically acceptable to the minority leaders in these semiautonomous states, the communist parties will have lost this remaining bastion of popular support in Burma. Until such terms are offered, popular leaders dedicated to the cause of their particular ethnic group will continue to push the campaign against Rangoon, frequently aligning themselves with other dissidents.

Impact of the Sino-Soviet Split

Perhaps the growing division in the communist world did not have the same significance for Burma as for other southeast Asian states, because the Burmese communists were already divided between Khrushchev, Mao, and Thakin Soe. It seems very likely that the White Flags have been strongly influenced, although not totally controlled, by a Peking faction since 1952 and that, but for Than Tun's influence, they would have become as subservient as the North Korean Workers' Party.

Competition for influence over the BWPP commenced in Burma with the visits of Chou En-lai in 1954, of Bulganin and Khrushchev in 1955, and of Chou En-lai again the same year. Kaznacheev reports that the Chinese were exceedingly cool to the Russian efforts to aid the Red Socialists, and it may be that the legalized Burmese communists felt the first impact of Sino-Soviet competition. Both Soviet and Chinese agents attempted to work with the BWPP, and both achieved limited success. Later, and all within one year, there occurred the attempted defection of the Russian military attaché, the southeast Asian Tass representative's bumbling attempt to libel a leading newspaper editor as having accepted a bribe from the United States, and finally the successful defection of Kaznacheev. Soviet influence over the Burmese communists could scarcely have been lower.

The most significant question concerning White Flag relations with Peking, which is the depth of Than Tun's loyalty to Mao, must go unanswered. There is reason to believe that the Chinese encouraged the Peking faction of the Burmese communists to return in August. Yebaw Htay and Bo Zeyya flew into Rangoon from China only a few months after Liu Shao-ch'i's visit to the country in April, 1963, which suggests that Ne Win may have brought some pressure to bear upon the Chinese to help solve the problem of communist insurgence within Burma in exchange for Burmese understanding in the Sino-Indian border conflict. Subsequent action by Ne Win, who flew to Delhi apparently to act as an intermediary between Nehru and Chou En-lai after the latter's return from Africa, supports this hypothesis. The Chinese communists may well have taken a leaf from their experience in Laos, where a coalition government was created in 1962, and sought to encourage in Burma a united front government in which the White Flags would participate as the Pathet Lao did in Laos. But Ne Win sent the Peking faction of the White

Flags packing two months after their return from China, which suggests that the Chinese are now in an awkward position, their strongest pressure group within Burma having been publicly discredited.[15]

Summary

The communist movement in Burma in the mid-Sixties consists of three heads (Thakin Soe, Than Tun, and the imprisoned Red Socialist leadership), four arms (the Red Flags, White Flags, Red Socialists, and the student organizations), and no body or legs upon which to move. Like other political parties in this still traditionalist country, the communists have failed to bridge the gap between peasant and government, tradition and modernity, and leader and follower. They have suffered from disciplinary problems and ideological confusion even more severely than the noncommunist parties. This is not to say that the communists have not drawn intelligent, capable leaders into their movement; indeed, one of the most plaintive comments I have heard in Burma is the observation that "our best leaders have followed the wrong cause." An ill-defined but deeply felt Burmese nationalism is the dominant political mood of Burma today. Any variety of international communism or unusual loyalty to any foreign political system is sufficient cause to create suspicion and popular distrust.

Only those aspects of communism that can be admixed with Burmese nationalism as it develops in the future under military leadership are likely to gain acceptability. It is significant that only those deviant Marxists from the BWPP and the PVO have secured power within the Ne Win military regime. A clear line has been drawn between internationalists and nationalists among the communists, as it has in Yugoslavia and India, and only the national communists have achieved respectability. The essential position of these leaders, that central government must assume responsibility for all production if Burma is to progress economically, is similar to that of the current Revolutionary Council. In agriculture, as in industry and services, these leaders have advocated a guided economy, and for two years their policies have been followed. 1965 will be a crucial year, a test of whether socialist tenets will yield larger harvests and more rapid industrial growth. If improvements are not forthcoming, there is a strong possibility of a reaction against recent revolutionary measures from within the military itself as well as from the alienated business community.

The influence gained by the few national communists has not modified Burma's foreign policy; on the contrary, there seems to be a heightened awareness of the dangers of neoimperialism as practiced by both the Soviet Union and the Chinese People's Republic. Both the Soviet and Chinese consulates have been removed from upper Burma, in Mandalay and Lashio, and foreign communist propaganda is missing from the bookstalls. Burma has intensified its diplomatic activity with its non-communist neighbors, particularly Thailand, and continues active participation in the Colombo Plan, ECAFE, the Geneva disarmament discussions and, of course, the United Nations. The bedrock of Burma's foreign policy, independent neutralism, remains firm as the military leadership continues its search for a nationalist philosophy that will be compatible both with its desire for modernity and its continuing commitments to traditionalism.

The Communist Parties of Burma

1. Young Thakins were most influenced by writings of Indian and British communists in the late Thirties. There was contact with the Indian Party, but we have little documentation of the extent of communication.
2. Thakin Mya Than, *The Return From Two Islands,* Rangoon, 1962.
3. An interview by the author with Than Maung, editor of the *Mandalay Sun,* February, 1958.
4. Aung San, *Burma's Challenge,* Mimeograph, Defence Service Historical Institute (DSHI). Rangoon address of August 29, 1945. Personal copy received from U Thein Naing, Research Director, DSHI.
5. Hachiro Takahashi, "The Great Asia War History: Secret of Establishing A Country." English translation in DSHI. Aung San resided in the International Settlement at Amoy for two months prior to his move to Tokyo. He made a feeble effort to contact the Chinese communists, but failed, and was finally traced by Japanese intelligence and given free transport to Japan.
6. Aung San "President's Statement," March 3, 1946. Archives, Defence Services Historical Institute, Rangoon.
7. From March to May, 1948, U Nu and Than Tun negotiated intensively in an effort to resolve the issue. Nu extended a 15-point proposition which promised the White Flags more than the AFPFL was prepared to give. Thein Pe Myint played a key role in these discussions, earning the permanent enmity of the insurgent communists in so doing. Earlier, in December and January, Thakin Than Tun and other southeast Asian communists met in Calcutta with eastern European and Soviet Party delegates who encouraged the uprisings that occurred the following spring throughout southeast Asia. See my article, "Burma's Radical Left," *Problems of Communism,* March-April, 1961.
8. Chit Than Tun, ex-Central Committee member of the White Flags, quoted in *The Nation,* January 14, 1954.
9. Burma's economy has failed to advance as rapidly as its population growth over the past two decades. However, land reclamation, crop diversification, and small-scale industry have been moderately successful projects. For a detailed study, see Louis Walinsky, *Economic Development in Burma 1951-60* (New York: Twentieth Century Fund, 1963).
10. Aleksandr Kaznacheev, *Inside a Soviet Embassy* (Philadelphia: J. B. Lippincott Company, 1962), pp. 173-78.
11. See Lucian Pye, *Politics, Personality, and Nation Building* (New Haven, Conn.: Yale University Press, 1962), pp. 177-207. Pye, in exploring this tendency, offers the hypothesis that male child-rearing techniques cause such behavior. My own observations of Burman family life cause me to agree about the importance of this factor but, also, to suggest that this political phenomenon derives from a more fundamental cause, an ethical system which demands that

any individual reject secular authority when it seems to challenge his integrity or self-identity. Theravada Buddhist emphasis upon self-realization and concern for future existence provides sanction for the individual who acts to reject or overwhelm any secular authority which seems to theaten his will. The courage to take such a step is a highly prized virtue and is expected in a leader. Thus, the more powerful the leader, the more compulson from his followers that he should assert his will.

12. Perhaps the best example of ideological flexibility in Burma is Thein Pe Myint, who has undertaken government-sponsored tours in the Soviet Union, China, and the United States. He has assumed an incredible variety of ideological postures since publishing his first Marxist essay just before World War II, and at one time or another has been on close terms with most of Burma's major communists, as well as being available for conversations with visiting political observers who want inside information about Burmese politics. All of Thein Pe Myint's major works are in Burmese. The most significant of his recent publications include *Experience in Politics*, 1956; *The Eastern Sun Is Rising*, 1958; *Kyaw Nyein: A Political Biography*, 1961; and *Experiences as a Candidate*, 1962.

13. Following Stalin's death, Thakin Soe claimed his mantle of authority and, during the 1963 amnesty discussions with the government, Soe met the press with a framed picture of Stalin on the desk before him. He criticized Peking for lack of courage in denouncing Khrushchev: "While it dared to make repeated attacks on the treachery of Tito, it failed to attack the real culprit of Soviet revisionism by name." Also, Thakin Soe blamed China for double-talk when it condemned the twentieth CPSU Congress but still subscribed to the 81-Party Declaration which was based on that Congress. Press Conference, August 13, 1963. Reported in *The Nation*, p. 1.

14. Information about the PVO was gained through interviews in Lower Chindwin district and Burmese government documents in the Rangoon Defense Services Historical Institute. I met with Bo Htein Lin on several occasions prior to, and following, the coup.

15. The Revolutionary Council published the entire transcript of the "Internal Peace Parley" which was conducted between June 11, 1963, and November 11, 1963.

Selected Bibliography

Butwell, Richard, *U Nu of Burma*. Stanford, Calif.: Stanford University Press, 1963.

Cady, John, *A History of Modern Burma*. Ithaca, N.Y.: Cornell University Press, 1958.

Johnstone, William, *Burma's Foreign Policy*. Cambridge, Mass.: Harvard University Press, 1963.

Pye, Lucian, *Politics, Personality, and Nation Building*. New Haven, Conn.: Yale University Press, 1962.

Revolutionary Council, Union of Burma, *The Philosophy of the Burma Socialist Programme Party*. Rangoon: Government Printing Office, 1962.

————, The Peace Parley. Rangoon, 1963. (Mimeographed.)

Shway Yoe, *The Burman: His Life and Notions* (4th ed.). New York: The Macmillan Company, 1963.

Tinker, Hugh, *The Union of Burma*. London: Oxford University Press, 1959.

Walinsky, Louis, *Economic Development in Burma: 1951-60*. New York: The Twentieth Century Fund, 1962.

Revisionism and Dogmatism in the Communist Party of India

> "The unity of the party has been com-
> pletely broken. . . . We are in the midst
> of the most serious inner-party crisis
> in history . . . the party is on the verge
> of complete disruption and split." [1]

Ralph Retzlaff

In its drive to attain power in the world's
second largest country, the Communist Party of India (CPI)
has been obliged to respond to imperatives arising from
its ideological commitment to the international communist
movement, while also seeking to retain
a legitimate status within the Indian nationalist
movement and the freedom struggle. The
often delicate balance between these two conflicting forces
has been rendered more complex in recent years. Deep-seated
divisions have developed over the appropriate
strategy and tactics to be adopted in respect to both international
and domestic problems. Domestically, the Party
is sharply divided as to the nature and degree of opposition

comparable to that of the INC, which also opposed the involvement of India in the war though for quite different reasons. When the international communist line shifted radically in the wake of the Nazi invasion of the Soviet Union, however, the CPI began to call for cooperation with the British and support for "the people's war," and a complete rupture of relationships between the CPI and the INC took place. This was further intensified in 1942, when the INC began the Quit India agitation while the CPI was calling for full cooperation in the war effort. As the war began to draw to a close in late 1944, and many INC leaders were being released from jail, the CPI sought a reconciliation with the INC, but to no avail. As a result, its influence in Indian politics on the eve of independence was negligible. In the elections to the provincial legislatures held in 1946, it succeeded in capturing only 3.6 per cent of the valid votes polled, and 8 of 1,477 seats.[8]

During the period immediately prior to the granting of Indian independence, the CPI was forced to face the need to define precisely its position in Indian politics and, in particular, its attitude toward the INC. In the absence of clear guidance from the CPSU or the CPGB, a split began to develop within the Party. In one form or another, that split has persisted down to the present day. A radical wing, which called for a turn away from positions of cooperation or conciliation with the INC and for the adoption of a militant line, emerged. It advocated a reversal of the wartime policy of restraining mass activity of a revolutionary character and called instead for a policy of insurrection and guerrilla activity. The Zhdanov speech of September, 1947, which signaled the advent of cold-war policies by the CPSU, and the advice of the Yugoslav Cominform delegates who attended the Second CPI Congress (in February and March, 1948, in Calcutta) and strongly urged militant action, set the seal of international approval on insurrectionary tactics. As a result, B. T. Ranadive, the prime exponent of this view, replaced P. C. Joshi as General Secretary, and the CPI embarked upon an adventurist line of action which did not end until 1951. Ranadive was strongly influenced by the Russian model of revolution and consequently directed principal attention to the urban working classes. Thus, shortly after India attained independence and while the Nehru government was struggling to consolidate and stabilize its position, the CPI launched a series of violent agitations and once again placed itself in direct opposition to Indian nationalism.

It was during this adventurist phase that one of the earliest indications of a potential basis of Sino-Soviet controversy over the ideological direction and control of the CPI emerged. The Andhra Pradesh unit of the CPI, under the direction of C. Rajeshwar Rao, came out in vigorous criticism of Ranadive's adherence to a Russian-style revolution, calling instead for emulation of the Chinese experience under Mao's concepts of "new democracy." In June, 1949, when the CPSU gave tentative approval to this latter approach as applicable to Asian communist parties, its move was interpreted as supporting the replacement of Ranadive as General Secretary. This was carried out in May, 1950. While the emphasis under Rajeshwar Rao, who became the new General Secretary, shifted from urban to rural areas, the use of violent insurrectionary tactics continued. Party membership declined sharply throughout this adventurist period, and several of the state units of the CPI were declared illegal.[9]

Several factors facilitated the shift away from adventurism. First, the widespread failure of militancy in Asia (the Philippines, Malaya, Indonesia, Burma, Japan, and India), together with the internal changes in the U.S.S.R. after Stalin's death, led to conditions in which such a shift was called for or at least strongly urged by the CPSU. In addition, while Stalin was still alive, the Soviet Union's attitude toward India began to undergo a change in the light of India's position on the Korean War. R. P. Dutt, of the CPGB, directed a letter to the CPI which advised a shift away from adventurism and a reassessment of the Nehru government. Also, within India, the imminence of the first general elections to be held since independence under universal adult suffrage forced the CPI to consider participating in the elections and subsequently in the legislatures. Inside the CPI, an attack was directed at the adventurist line by P. C. Joshi, the former General Secretary, and several other important Party leaders, including S. A. Dange and Ajoy Ghosh. Ultimately Ajoy Ghosh was selected General Secretary, replacing Rajeshwar Rao, and the party began its first tentative steps toward a return to "constitutional communism."

The role of Ajoy Ghosh, who continued as General Secretary of the CPI to the time of his death in January, 1962, should not be underestimated.[10] He derived his strength within the Party from the balancing role which he played at the national level. He was not closely identified with any state unit of the Party, nor with its emerging left and right factions. Under his leadership the CPI gradually, albeit reluctantly, came to support the view that communism could come to power in India through peaceful parliamentary means. This position was formally adopted by the Party in the wake of its electoral triumph in Kerala in the 1957 elections.

The Organization of the CPI

The formal organizational structure of the CPI is set forth in the constitution adopted at the Extraordinary Party Congress held at Amritsar, Punjab, in April, 1958. This document is the high-water mark of the Party's adherence to constitutional communism and parliamentary government. It states in part:

> The Communist Party of India strives to achieve full democracy and Socialism by peaceful means. It considers that by developing a powerful mass movement, by winning a majority in Parliament and by backing it with mass sanctions, the working class and its allies can overcome the resistance of the forces of reaction and insure that Parliament becomes an instrument of people's will for effecting fundamental changes in the economic, social, and State structure.[11]

The constitution provides for a five-tiered structure, with units at the national, state, district, local, and branch levels.[12] The supreme authoritative body is the All-India Party Congress, which normally meets every two years.[13] One of its principal functions is to elect the National Council, the highest authority between Congress sessions. Apart from those individuals designated as representing the Party center, the remainder of the members of the National Council are grouped under various state units of the Party, each state unit having a minimum of two members.[14]

The National Council elects, from among its members, a Central Executive Committee which is the highest authority of the Party between meetings of the National Council. It also elects a General Secretary and a Secretariat.[15] In addition, the National Council nominates the Central Control Commission, which is formally elected by the Party Congress. Along with counterparts at the state level, the Central Control Commission is responsible for investigating breaches of Party discipline. Its decisions are normally final, although in special cases the Central Executive Committee may refer a case to the National Council for special consideration. The organizational structure of the CPI at state and district levels parallels that at the national level. The precise structure of the local and branch units of the Party is dependent to a considerable extent on Party strength and on variations in local institutions and political and administrative structures.

One of the most useful indices of CPI strength throughout India is to be found in the results of the general elections to the State Legislative Assemblies held since 1951-52.

Table 1

PERCENTAGE OF VALID VOTES POLLED BY THE CPI IN STATE LEGISLATIVE
ASSEMBLY ELECTIONS

| | *Election Year* | | |
State	1951-1952 [a]	1957 [a]	1962 [c]
Kerala	17.5%	35.3% [b]	39.1% [b]
West Bengal	10.4	17.8	25.0
Andhra Pradesh	22.8	29.5	19.3
Orissa	5.7	8.4 [b]	8.0 [b]
Madras	9.8	7.4	7.8
Punjab	6.2	13.6	7.1
Bihar	1.1	5.2	6.3
Assam	2.4	8.1	6.3
Maharashtra	2.5	6.3	6.0
Uttar Pradesh	0.9	3.8	5.4
Rajasthan	0.6	3.0	5.4
Mysore	1.4	1.9	2.3
Madhya Pradesh	0.7	1.6	2.0
Gujarat	2.5	0.8	0.2

Note: The states have been ranked by the the percentage of CPI votes polled
in the last Legislative Assembly election. All figures have been rounded to one
decimal place.

[a] *Source:* Phillips Talbott, "The Second General Election: Voting in States,"
American Universities Field Service (mimeograph) (India-PT-6-'57), pp. 31 and 49.
With the exception of Gujarat and Maharashtra, the 1952 figures have been adjusted
to reflect the reorganization of states which took place in 1956. The figure cited for
both Gujarat and Maharashtra is that for the State of Bombay prior to bifurcation.

[b] *Source: Seminar* (New Delhi), "Your Vote," 29 (January, 1962), p. 15. The
1962 votes listed for Kerala and Orissa are for the special midterm general elections
held in February, 1960, and May, 1961, respectively. The vote secured by the CPI
in the parliamentary elections held in 1962 in these two states was: Kerala, 35.5%;
Orissa, 5.1%. See *Indian Affairs Record*, VIII, No. 3 (March, 1962), 87.

[c] *Source: Indian Affairs Record*, VIII, No. 4 (April, 1962), 115-18.

It is evident from the data in Table 1 that support for the CPI is
not uniformly distributed throughout India. The main areas of Party
strength are in Kerala, Andhra Pradesh, and West Bengal. In the next
eight states listed, the party polled between 5 and 8 per cent of the
popular vote. In the remaining three states, it polled less than 2.5 per cent
of the vote. It is also clear that the CPI has maintained a modest but
measurable increase in popular support in the majority of the states over
the period of the three general elections, and that the pattern of differential distribution of support has been fairly constant. There is no
indication, in terms of nationwide electoral support, how much damage
the Party suffered as a result of the Chinese invasion in 1962, but it is
well to bear in mind that, during the mass agitation against the Kerala

CPI Ministry in 1959, the CPI actually increased its popular vote from 35.3 per cent to 39.1 per cent despite the fact that it lost its majority in the Legislative Assembly.

It is difficult to generalize about the mass or elite character of the CPI. If votes given to the Party are used as a rough indicator of its mass support, then the CPI is a mass Party in some states. The figures from the last Legislative Assembly elections for its three main areas of strength are: Kerala, 3,171,732; West Bengal, 2,379,953; and Andhra Pradesh, 2,257,748. In other states the Party is clearly elitist in character, having both a small formal membership and a relatively small base of popular support.

One factor which has considerable influence over the fortunes of the various state units of the CPI has been their tendency to seek alliances—not simply with other Marxist and left-wing socialist parties in electoral contests and mass agitations, but with a wide range of groups which span the socioeconomic and ideological spectrum. This is in part due to the wide variations in both the patterns of political organization as well as in the social and economic fabric of Indian society in the various states. An example of the confusion which results can be seen in the recent General Elections. While the Uttar Pradesh state CPI unit supported left-wing INC candidates when it had no nominees of its own contesting in a constituency, the Kerala Party uniformly opposed all INC candidates.

The socioeconomic groups to which the CPI has been able to turn for support have varied considerably from state to state. Thus, while in Andhra Pradesh it has drawn heavily upon members of the Kamma and Reddy castes who are large landholders in the middle and upper ranges of the social hierarchy, in Kerala it has drawn its main support from the Ezhavas, a landless, low-caste group at the bottom of the social hierarchy. These and many other differences have led state units of the CPI to press for a considerable degree of flexibility in tactical and strategic lines. While pressure for regional political flexibility often occurs within nations having federal political systems, it is clear that, in the CPI, these pressures are extreme and have produced a severe strain upon Party unity, discipline, and control.[16]

The Shift in CPI Policy from 1951 to 1958

The gradual shift in the attitude of the Soviet Union toward the Nehru government in India between 1950 and 1955 had two perceptible effects upon the CPI. First, it brought about a gradual and very reluctant reorientation of the CPI's official line toward the Nehru government. As late as 1950, the CPI officially denounced both the foreign and domestic policy of the Nehru government in the strongest possible terms. Gradually, under pressure from the CPSU, and with the abandonment of its adventurist phase, the CPI came to acknowledge that there were some positive aspects in what was still generally viewed as an undesirable foreign policy. Subsequently, its emphasis shifted to the view that while the Nehru government's foreign policy was good, its domestic policy was bad. Finally it came to the position of acknowledging that there were favorable features in both the domestic and foreign policies of the Nehru government.

The policy shift regarding the Nehru government was not accomplished without considerable internal conflict within the CPI, however. Even in 1957, a hard-core left faction remained unconvinced that either the domestic or foreign policies of that government merited CPI support. As the right faction within the Party gradually adjusted itself to the CPSU line, it was increasingly separated from the left faction, which refused to acknowledge the validity of the CPSU assessment, although at this point it did not directly challenge Soviet authority.[17]

In 1954 and 1955, Nehru exchanged visits with both the Soviet and Chinese leaders. During this period, several important statements appeared in international communist party journals, causing considerable debate within the CPI. The first of these was an article by R. P. Dutt, of the CPGB, which appeared in October, 1954.[18] In it, Dutt implied strong support for both the domestic and international policies of the Nehru government. Since the article had been written by the CPGB's main spokesman on India, it threw the CPI into a quandary. At first, the Central Committee of the CPI almost rejected the Dutt article. It argued that the line which emerged from it was one of increasing support to the Nehru government and of "lining up behind it on a plea of national freedom, . . . [which] . . . would have weakened the movement for full freedom and . . . the economic and political struggles of the masses." [19] Subsequently, in a second resolution, the Central Committee took a wait-and-see attitude, seeking further guidance in the hope of resolving the deep internal dispute that had developed.[20]

The second article which influenced CPI policy was an editorial appearing in *Pravda* on January 26, 1955. It praised not only the foreign-policy accomplishments of the Nehru government, but also commented favorably on Nehru's domestic policy. This article appeared one month before the special elections in Andhra Pradesh in February, 1955. It was used widely by the INC, to the detriment of the CPI, which was badly defeated.

In 1956, another article caused deep consternation within CPI ranks.[21] Written by Modeste Rubenstein and appearing in *New Times*, it went even further than previous Soviet statements and adopted the view that for many years the Nehru government had been following a peaceful path to socialism, strongly implying that it, rather than the CPI, might lead the way to socialism in India. Ajoy Ghosh, then General Secretary, who had played a key role in bringing the CPI around to limited support of the Nehru government, took strong exception to the Rubenstein article.[22] The CPSU withdrew from the extreme position taken in the Rubenstein article, which had failed to acknowledge a possible constructive role for the CPI in the development of Indian socialism. However, the tendency characterized by the Dutt and *Pravda* articles toward the recognition of positive aspects of the Nehru government carried with it the strong implication that the CPI should play a constructive and cooperative role vis-à-vis the INC. As we mentioned earlier, a segment within the CPI comprising, in part, those who were identified with the adventurist period, such as B. T. Ranadive, strongly resisted this pressure for a shift in attitude which emanated from the CPSU. Throughout this entire period, inner Party differences continued to grow in strength and to pervade all aspects of Party operation and activity.

By the Fifth Congress of the Party in 1958, however, the leadership of the CPI exuded confidence that the parliamentary takeover in Kerala could be repeated in other states and, eventually, at the center. It expressed support not only for the foreign policy of the Nehru government, but also for substantial segments of its domestic policy. The militant leftist faction of the Party viewed this dual tendency of support for constitutionalism and parliamentary action, coupled with support given specific INC policies, with increasing disfavor. Rather than rejoicing in the CPI electoral victory in Kerala, it felt that this victory restricted its ability to engage in militant mass activities in other parts of India where this was regarded as essential. Nevertheless, the internal situation made it necessary for the leftists to bide their time.

The Shattered Image of the CPI

The adoption by the CPI of its new constitution at Amritsar in 1958 marked the culmination of a process whereby the Party gained increasing respectability on the Indian political scene. The liabilities which the Party had incurred in the past as a result of its antinational stands and its adventurist phase faded from public consciousness. Under Ajoy Ghosh's leadership, the CPI gave increasing evidence of being able to cope successfully with the conflicting demands of national and international loyalties.

In 1959, however, three events brought about a marked transformation of the political scene and served to shatter the image of respectability which the CPI had built up. By the end of 1959, the CPI once again found a very broadly based and active hostility directed toward it within India. This, in turn, provided the basis for the reemergence of vigorous intra-Party conflict along right (i.e., nationalist) versus left (i.e., internationalist) lines.

The uprisings by Khampa tribesmen in Tibet, which culminated in the flight of the Dalai Lama to India in April, 1959, resulted in the expression of widespread concern within India about the Tibetan situation. In mid-March, Nehru made two statements in Parliament. He sought, on the one hand, to assure Indian public opinion of the government's concern over events in Tibet; on the other hand, he sought, through cautious wording, not to arouse the Chinese. However, in late March, the official Chinese news agency issued a communiqué that set off a wave of anti-Chinese sentiment in India. First, it stated that the Tibetan rebellion was being directed from Kalimpong on Indian soil; and second, it charged that reference to developments in Tibet made in the Indian Parliament amounted to an interference in the internal affairs of China by India. With the exception of the CPI, all political parties joined the Prime Minister in a vigorous denial that Kalimpong was being used as a base for subversive activities by the Indian government and supported Nehru's view that the Indian Parliament had the right to discuss any matter which it found fit for such discussion.[23] The Secretariat of the National Council of the CPI, however, issued a statement on the Tibetan situation essentially supporting both of the Chinese charges.[24] This resulted in criticism of the CPI and the assertion that the Party was playing an antinational role in Indian politics.

Even as the controversy over the CPI's position on Tibet developed, a second attack upon it began to take shape. The actions of the communist ministry which had taken office in the state of Kerala in 1957 were strongly criticized. The focal point of the controversy was the Kerala Education Bill, which proposed basic changes in both public and private school administration in Kerala.[25]

In January, 1959, after the Act received the assent of the President of India, the Nair Service Society, a caste Hindu organization, spearheaded a statewide campaign against it. In May, it convened a conference of all communities and noncommunist political parties and, acting in concert, they initiated a mass agitation. The ostensible purpose was to cause the withdrawal of the Act, but in fact (as later admitted by the leader of the Nair Service Society) the true aim was to bring about the downfall of the Kerala government. Widespread violence occurred throughout the state in connection with the antigovernment agitations in June and July. Finally, over the vigorous objections of the Kerala government and the national CPI, the President of India, acting under the emergency provisions of the Indian Constitution, signed a proclamation dissolving the state legislature and dismissing the government. The Governor took over administration of the state and retained control until February, 1960, when a united front of anticommunist parties succeeded in defeating the CPI in a special election.

These events strained the CPI's continued adherence to the Amritsar thesis and the acceptance of parliamentary democracy as the principal avenue through which the Party would secure power in India. Nehru's affirmation at a press conference that the communists could rule again if they won the elections in Kerala was clearly aimed at encouraging continued CPI adherence to democratic methods. And, in the wake of the CPI's defeat, E. M. S. Namboodiripad, the former Chief Minister, indicated that the Party in Kerala would continue to function as a constructive and responsible opposition in the Assembly.[26] Nevertheless, the successful overthrow of a communist government by anticommunist forces gave added support to the leftists within the Party who argued that the INC would never allow a communist government to institute a program of socialist reforms.

While the flight of the Dalai Lama and the overthrow of the Kerala government were incidents to which the CPI was capable of adjusting, albeit with some difficulty, the third aspect of the changing scene in 1959 posed a much graver challenge. For some time there had been indications that differences about the demarcation of the border existed between India and China. In August, 1959, the Chinese occupied Longju in the Northeastern Frontier Area (NEFA) and the dispute became serious. Shortly afterward, the Secretariat of the National Council of the CPI issued an equivocal statement "regretting" the incident.[27] Subsequently, the Central Executive Committee (CEC), meeting at Calcutta, adopted a resolution on the border issue in which it advised the government of China not to insist upon the acceptance of its maps and advised the government of India not to press for the McMahon line. The CEC expressed its confidence that socialist China could never commit aggression against India, just as India had no intention of committing aggression against China.[28] The resolution was designed to meet the mounting pro-Chinese sentiments of the internationalist wing but also stressed that the CPI stood with the rest of the people of India for the territorial integrity of the nation, thus establishing its *bona fides* as a true national party. However, the resolution did not satisfy the external critics of the Party nor its left (i.e., internationalist) or right (i.e., nationalist) factions. Intra-Party tensions continued to mount.

Ajoy Ghosh, the General Secretary of the CPI, led a five-man delegation to China in early October to participate in the anniversary celebrations of the founding of the Chinese People's Republic. Upon his return to India on October 18, he stressed that the Chinese leaders were extremely anxious that the border dispute be settled as quickly as possible. With a timing that succeeded in seriously embarrassing Ghosh, the Chinese attacked an Indian patrol in the Konga Pass in the Ladakh region of Kashmir on the 21st of October. By the end of that month, intra-Party conflict within the CPI emerged into public view. S. A. Dange, a leading rightist, explained to a public meeting that he was not in full agreement with his Party's views on the Sino-Indian question. He urged that the CPI recognize the McMahon line in order to meet the increasing criticism leveled at it and stop the estrangement of the Party from the rest of India. The CPI National Council, meeting at Meerut in mid-November, formally accepted the McMahon line and stated that the areas south of it were and should remain a part of India.[29] This represented a clear victory for the right, even during the tenure as General Secretary of Ajoy Ghosh, who still sought to maintain a centrist position in the Party. It failed to stop the dissatisfaction voiced by the leftists within the Party, who felt that the CPI was abandoning the requirements of proletarian internationalism. By late 1959, the CPI leadership was on the defensive. A tendency toward polarization between its nationalist and internationalist elements had reemerged within the Party.

The Sino-Soviet Dispute

The rise of the Sino-Soviet dispute and the consequent breakdown of ideological unity in the international communist movement has had a marked effect upon the CPI, as it has upon all other communist parties. The evolving official position of the CPI regarding this dispute can best be seen against the background of the Twentieth Congress of the CPSU in 1956, the 1960 Congress of 81 Communist Parties in Moscow, and the Twenty-second Congress of the CPSU in 1961.

Two major lines set forth at the Twentieth Party Congress of the CPSU were the concept of peaceful transition to socialism and the de-Stalinization campaign. Both were sources of major discussion and controversy within the CPI. After hearing Ajoy Ghosh's report on the actions taken at the Twentieth Party Congress of the CPSU, the Fourth Party Congress of the CPI adopted a resolution which, recognizing the gravity of the issues raised by the CPSU, called upon all Party committees to discuss Ghosh's report, and in conjunction with this, required that the Central Committee of the CPI make available to all Party members an editorial which appeared in the Chinese Communist Party (CCP) organ, the People's Daily, on April 5, 1956, entitled "On the Historical Experience of the Dictatorship of the Proletariat," which supported and justified many actions taken by Stalin in the Soviet Union.[30]

In an exchange of correspondence with Jaya Prakash Narayan, a former Socialist Party leader, Ghosh elaborated his views on the de-Stalinization campaign:

> We agree that we were wrong in idealizing everything in the USSR. We should have paid more attention to the criticism of the USSR made by Socialists and non-Communist democrats. We agree that among us and in other Communist Parties, the tendency developed of defending everything done by the USSR, of condemning everyone who criticized any aspect of Soviet policy. We are deeply conscious of the damage this has done to the cause of Communist-Socialist unity and even to the cause of Socialism. We are determined to abandon this attitude.[31]

In the context of the Sino-Soviet dispute, the implication of Ghosh's remarks suggested a desire on his part to support a much more flexible and nationalist line.[32] Despite the Party's electoral triumph in Kerala, the left internationalist faction within the CPI continued to oppose the support extended by Ghosh to the possibility of a peaceful transition to socialism and to the de-Stalinization campaign. The events of 1959 and, in particular, the surfacing of the Sino-Indian dispute greatly exacerbated inner Party conflict. As was only natural, the two contending factions sought to buttress and legitimize their internal quarrels by seeking support from the great external debate between the CPSU and the CCP. Thus, in 1960, as the Sino-Soviet dispute emerged into full view and competition began for the loyalties of the world communist parties, the CPI factional quarrels, which had been heightened by the events of 1959, took on an added intensity and were interwoven into the international communist quarrel.

The World Federation of Trade Unions (WFTU) meeting in Peking in June, 1960, and the Bucharest conference held in conjunction with the Third Congress of the Rumanian Workers Party in the same month, provided indications of the conflicting positions held by groups within the CPI on the Sino-Soviet dispute. Interestingly, whereas the CPI delegation to the WFTU meeting in Peking was headed by S. A. Dange, a leading rightist, the CPI delegation at the Bucharest Conference consisted of two leftists who were members of the CPI Central Secretariat, namely, Basavapunniah and Bhupesh Gupta.[33] While Dange is reported to have strongly supported the CPSU at the Peking Conference, the leftists at the Bucharest Conference reportedly avoided taking an open position on the Sino-Soviet quarrel.[34]

At the 1960 Congress of 81 Communist Parties in Moscow, Ajoy Ghosh delivered a lengthy speech in which he sought to explain the position of the CPI with respect to both the Russians and the Chinese.[35] In his speech he sought, to a limited extent, to conciliate the CCP and to assure it of the cooperation of the CPI; nevertheless, he made it unmistakably clear that he strongly supported the CPSU in the internal conflict in the communist world and that he opposed the CCP in the Sino-Indian border dispute. By mid-1960, factional quarrels within the CPI had reached a point where several of the state units of the Party began to consider resolutions concerning the attitude of the CPI toward the CPSU, the CCP, and the border dispute.[36]

Among all of the CPI units, the most staunchly leftist has been the largest, that in West Bengal. This fact has not been lost upon the Chinese. Reportedly, a two-man CPI delegation attended the Vietnamese Communist Party Congress in September, 1960. It consisted of H. K. Konar, a leading West Bengal leftist, and K. Damodaran, a rightist from Kerala. While snubbing Damodaran, the CCP sought out Konar, and reportedly explained to him the nature and character of the Chinese position in the Sino-Soviet dispute. Konar has continued to be one of the staunchest members of the pro-Peking group within the CPI.

In late 1961, when the Twenty-second Congress of the CPSU took place, Ajoy Ghosh led a seven-man delegation consisting of both rightists and leftists. Upon his return from Moscow, he admitted at a press conference that serious differences continued to exist within the ranks of the CPI over the intensified de-Stalinization campaign in the Soviet Union. These differences soon broke out into the open. E. M. S. Namboodiripad, in a press conference in Calicut, Kerala, remarked, "We Indian Communists have experienced only the result of what is positive in Marshal Stalin." [37] Shortly afterward, the Secretariat of the West Bengal unit of the CPI accused the leadership of the CPSU of a "direct violation" of the principles of the 1957 Moscow Declaration in its attack on the Albanians.[38] Party divisions on matters of basic ideological importance found the center group led by Namboodiripad, and the left group led by the West Bengal CPI unit ranged in open opposition to Ghosh, who had the support of the right group led by Dange. These divisions, moreover, were a reflection of the open split which had manifested itself within the CPI at its Vijayawada Congress earlier that year.

In the spring of 1961, the CPI had held its Sixth Party Congress. The events of the Congress, as well as those leading up to it in the Central Executive Committee and in the National Council, gave ample indication that neither the left nor right factions within the Party were in a mood for compromise. While the rightist faction of the Party had a majority in both the Central Executive Committee and the National Council, it did not feel that its position was sufficiently strong either to purge the left faction or to force its ideological position upon the entire Party.[39] Thus, when the National Council completed its meeting on February 22, 1961, prior to the Vijayawada Congress, it adopted with only minor modifications the political thesis sponsored by Ajoy Ghosh, the General Secretary of the Party. This was a thesis supported by the Dange group. But the Council also agreed that the rejected thesis of the leftists headed by B. T. Ranadive should be circulated to the Party Congress as a minority document. In fact, a third document, prepared by E. M. S. Namboodiripad and critical of both the extreme right and left was also circulated at the Congress.[40]

The principal distinctions among the three draft resolutions placed before the CPI at Vijayawada centered on the Party's attitude toward the INC and the Nehru government. The official draft, put forward by Ghosh and supported by the rightists, argued that the INC could not be regarded as a force of reaction. It advanced Ghosh's view that the CPI should oppose INC measures considered to be reactionary and support those considered to be progressive. The leftist draft, sponsored by B. T. Ranadive and others, gave credit to the INC for some of the work which it had done, but nevertheless regarded it as a force of reaction and consequently urged vigorous opposition. The Namboodiripad draft sought to create a distinction between two sections of the *bourgeoisie* within the INC. It argued that, although one section had obvious connections with both foreign and indigenous monopoly capitalism, another section was clearly anti-imperialist and antifeudal in its outlook and that it was with this section of the national *bourgeoisie* that closer contacts should be forged in order to win them to the side of the CPI.[41]

The conflict at Vijayawada over the ideological line to be adopted by the Party was paralleled by a comparable struggle for organization control. This ultimately resulted in an expansion of the National Council from 101 to 110 members, the additional members being evenly divided between the right and left factions.[42]

In June, 1961, the National Council chosen at the Vijayawada Conference elected a 25-member Central Executive Committee.[43] An examination of the new, outgoing, and continuing members reveals that the right faction continued to maintain a slight position of dominance within the Party but faced a fairly substantial leftist opposition.

The split within the CPI over internal issues was reflected in the stands taken by the right and left factions in the growing dispute within the world communist camp. The CPI was thus obliged to turn its attention to the Third General Elections, scheduled for the spring of 1962, in a state of deep division. Ajoy Ghosh, in his election statement, remarked:

> . . . our attitude toward the Government of India's foreign policy is . . . one of general support, together with the demand that it should become firmer and more consistent.

[In regard to domestic policy] the Communist Party considers that in the forthcoming elections it is of utmost importance that the "anti-people" policies of the Congress are exposed, the damage done by them is explained and the people rallied to weaken—and where possible to break—the Congress monopoly of power. . . . That would be for the good of the Congress itself since it would help honest Congressmen to fight the evils that have crept in with greater chances of success. . . . We do not, however, advocate the breaking of the Congress monopoly of power for its own sake and by any methods. We do not want merely the defeat of the Congress—no matter at whose hands. Our attitude toward the Congress has nothing in common with the attitude of parties, groups and elements of the extreme Right. . . . In contrast to [them] . . . we combat the policies of the government with a view to bring [sic] about a move to the Left—toward democracy, social advance and consistent anti-imperialism.[44]

Ghosh's views were honored in the breach as CPI state units each sought to secure that balance of electoral alliances and mass action most in keeping with the demands of the local situation. While the CPI's support of V. K. Krishna Menon was consonant with this position, the actions of state units in Andhra Pradesh, Madras, Punjab, and West Bengal, for example, were much less unambiguous. To some extent, the CPI was aided in its electoral campaign by the fact that mass attention had been diverted from the Sino-Indian border dispute by the Indian government's occupation of Goa. The CPI strongly supported the Goan action, a move that had also brought forth warm praise from the Soviet Union. The outcome of the Third General Elections (see Table 1 for detailed statistics) showed that the CPI did not suffer a setback in mass support; rather, with few exceptions, it continued its modest but steady gains in percentage of votes polled throughout the country. In three states, Andhra Pradesh, Kerala, and West Bengal, the CPI remained a major factor in the political scene.

Far more serious, however, was the death of Ajoy Ghosh in mid-January of 1962, on the eve of the elections. The intensity of intra-Party conflict between the left and right factions, as well as the unsettling conditions which existed during the elections, seriously complicated the CPI's search for Ghosh's successor. It was not until a meeting of the National Council on April 29, 1962, that a compromise was reached between the left and right factions. A new position, Chairman of the Party, was created. It was given to S. A. Dange, the leading rightist; and E. M. S. Namboodiripad, the centrist, was made the General Secretary.[45] This proved to be an uneasy and ultimately unsuccessful maneuver. Throughout early and mid-1962, as the right and left factions of the Party continued to jockey for control, signs of an approaching conflict between India and China in the border regions increased. Finally, on

October 20, 1962, Chinese troops invaded Indian territory in both NEFA and Ladakh and pressed onward into previously uncontested territory in NEFA. The ties of Indian nationalism and of proletarian internationalism were directly and intensely confounded. The main offices of the Party in New Delhi were stoned and sacked by mobs, and demands were raised by opposition parties that the CPI be abolished as an antinational group.

Three days before the Chinese invasion, the National Council had adopted a resolution on developments in NEFA in which it strongly supported the notion that the McMahon line was the border of India and that Chinese forces which had reportedly crossed it had thus violated Indian territory. The CPI had nevertheless refused to condemn China as an aggressor.[46] Even Dange, on October 19, 1962, the day before the Chinese invasion, refused to label Chinese action on the border "aggression," preferring rather to speak in terms of Chinese violation of Indian territory.

The intensity of the split within the CPI over the invasion is indicated by the fact that it was not until November 1, 1962, almost two weeks later, that the National Council was able to adopt a resolution on the Chinese invasion.[47] In it, the Party specifically termed the Chinese action "aggression" and called upon all sections of the Indian people to "unite in defense of the motherland." [48] The adoption of the November 1 resolution had an immediate impact on the inner Party conflict. Jyoti Basu (of West Bengal), P. Sundarayya (of Andhra Pradesh), and H. K. S. Surjeet (of Punjab)—three leading leftists—resigned from the Central Secretariat immediately after the adoption of the resolution.

On November 20, 1962, the Central Secretariat addressed to all fraternal parties throughout the world a letter in which it sought to explain and justify the stand taken in its November 1 resolution. In particular, it attempted to meet criticism directed at it by the leftists of the Party that it had violated the rules of proletarian internationalism through its attack upon the CCP. The letter asserted that the CCP had acted in "total disregard" of CPI advice on the Indian situation. It further charged:

> . . . it is evident that at the root of their understanding and policy lie certain narrow nationalistic considerations and some distorted and incorrect approach and line following thereon.[49]

Two features of the letter are particularly noteworthy. First, the extent to which the CPI Central Secretariat justified and supported *all* aspects of the foreign policy stand taken by the Nehru government in the Sino-Indian border dispute. Second, the fact that the letter was signed not only by Dange, Bhupesh Gupta, Z. A. Ahmed, M. N. Govindan Nair, and Yogindra Sharma, all rightists, but also by the important centrist, E. M. S. Namboodiripad.

In mid-November, the government of India began a selective crackdown on the CPI left wing, arresting over 957 top and middle cadres of the Party in almost all the states by January 10, 1963. Significantly, Namboodiripad, who was taken into custody on November 22, was released one week later.[50] All opposition parties continued to mount an attack on the CPI, which was virtually in a state of collapse. By mid-December, there were indications that the CPI front organizations had for the most part either declined or disappeared.[51] From December 9, 1962, to January 6, 1963, Dange went abroad on an "explaining mission" in which he visited both Moscow and London. Reportedly, in Moscow, Khrushchev strongly criticized Dange for falling "easy victim to the chauvinism of the reactionary forces." He condemned the CPI resolution of November 1, which had accused the Chinese of committing aggression. He is said to have argued that it would rather have been advisable for the CPI to charge Peking with "misconceiving a situation on its border and invading India." [52] Immediately thereafter, Dange went to London. At a public meeting there, he said that both India and China had accused each other of aggression. In general content, his speech marked a return to the pre-November 1 National Council position on China. This caused considerable consternation among the rightists in the CPI.

It is at this juncture, early 1963, that a radical transformation took place within the Party. In the wake of the Chinese invasion, the West Bengal unit had been seriously affected by the large-scale arrests of its members. The Central Secretariat, therefore, took steps to create a Provincial Organizing Committee (POC) which superseded the formal state Party unit. A similar reorganization took place in Punjab, and there is indication that reorganizations had taken place in Andhra Pradesh and Madras prior to the arrests of CPI members.[53] The West Bengal POC was clearly controlled by rightists who supported Dange. The left faction was not slow in reacting. First in West Bengal and subsequently in other states, they set up what has become in essence a parallel organization, called the PCZ in West Bengal.[54] In early February, 1963, as the organizational splits within the CPI continued to deepen and the situation regarding the factional loyalties of many of the Party members remained fluid, the National Council met in an eight-day session and adopted two resolutions which served to worsen relationships between the CPI and the Chinese Communist Party. The National Council, over the strenuous objections of the party leftists, most of whom were in jail, adopted two resolutions.

The first resolution, "On Certain Ideological Questions Affecting the Unity of the International Communist Movement," [55] clearly aligned the formal leadership of the CPI with the position taken by the CPSU in the Sino-Soviet debate. Specifically, the National Council resolution charged the CCP and the Albanian Party of Labor (APL) with violating the 1957 Moscow Declaration and the 1960 Moscow Statement, and also with violating the norms of proletarian internationalism with respect to relations between fraternal parties.[56]

The second resolution, "On the Political Situation," dealt with a wide range of national and international issues. It supported Khrushchev's actions in the Cuban missile crisis and reiterated the specific charge that the Chinese had committed aggression against India, although significantly the charge was made in a much less strident tone. The National Council once again strongly supported Nehru's position on international issues, while attempting to isolate certain domestic policies of the Nehru government for criticism and specific opposition.[57]

Less than a month later, on March 9, 1963, the Chinese Communist Party unleashed its strongest attack up to that point on the CPI. It published an editorial in *People's Daily* titled "A Mirror for Revisionists." [58] In it, the Chinese referred to "the Dange clique" which had:

> seized the leadership of the Communist Party of India . . . [and] betrayed Marxism-Leninism and the proletarian revolution, betrayed the revolutionary cause of the Indian proletariat and the Indian people and embarked on the road of national chauvinism and class capitulationism, thus creating complete chaos in the Indian Communist Party [59]

It specifically charged Dange with: (1) replacing the theory of the class struggle by the slogan of class collaborationism; (2) replacing proletarian socialism by bourgeois socialism; (3) defending the dictatorship of the *bourgeoisie* and the landlords; (4) giving unconditional support to the Nehru government in its policies of hiring itself to United States imperialism; and (5) of trampling underfoot the friendship of the Chinese and Indian peoples and acting as buglers for Nehru's anti-China campaign.[60] In closing, the editorial made a thinly disguised bid for support from the leftists in the CPI:

> The Chinese Communist Party and the Chinese people have a deep concern and a profound sympathy for the Indian Communists who are persisting in their struggle for the Communist cause and for the Indian proletariat and the Indian people who have a glorious revolutionary tradition. No reactionaries, no revisionists can block the advance of the Indian people. . . . History will prove that those who are firmly upholding truth and justice and firmly adhering to Marxism-Leninism and proletarian internationalism are the genuine representatives of the interests of the Indian people and the Indian nation. India's future is in their hands. . . . In the last analysis nobody can undermine the friendship between the peoples of China and India or the friendship between the Chinese Communists and the Indian Communists. [61]

On April 21, 1963, a month and one-half later, *New Age* published a reply by Dange, titled "Neither Revisionism nor Dogmatism Is Our Guide." [62] Dange's reply to the CCP attack bears close reading by all students of the Sino-Soviet split. In a most frank and open fashion, Dange reviewed in great detail not only the Sino-Indian border dispute which served as the catalyst for the breakdown in relations between the CCP and the CPI, but also placed it in the context of the fundamental differences which had evolved in the world communist movement. Addressing himself directly to the Chinese bid for support of the CPI leftists he argued:

> Contrary to the interests of the world Communist movement, the Chinese leadership has, through [its] . . . allegations virtually given a call for a split within the ranks of the Communist Party of India. . . . We, of the Communist Party of India, will leave no stone unturned to defeat every splitting move and uphold the banner of Communist unity. [63]

But Dange was unable to match his statement with actions. The situation within the CPI was progressively deteriorating as the leftists continued to develop their parallel organization outside the disciplinary channels of the main CPI structure.

The spring and early summer of 1963 was a period of intense maneuvering within the Party. Immediately following the National Council session on February 12, E. M. S. Namboodiripad submitted his resignation as General Secretary of the Party. Presumably no final action was taken on the matter until the National Council meeting of June 26 to July 6, when it was announced that he had formally resigned and that the duties of the General Secretary would be taken over by Chairman Dange. At that meeting, which preceded the ill-fated Sino-Soviet ideological discussions of July in Moscow, the National Council of the CPI proceeded to take up several matters. One was the organizational problem posed by the actions of the left group within the party; the other was the adoption of a political resolution. [64]

The main attention of the National Council session centered on the organizational issue. The resolution on organizational problems, put forward by M. N. Govindan Nair and Yogindra Sharma, strongly urged that the leftist faction was no longer an innocent minority. It had started functioning as a rival all-India party with its own discipline, organization, and leadership. It had been issuing circulars in West Bengal asking members of the CPI to defy the National Council and the POC appointed by it. The resolution further charged that the PCZ was distributing anti-Khrushchev literature among CPI members and was bringing out several weeklies in various parts of India to preach the "dogmatist, sectarian line." Despite this and other evidence presented at that time, Dange and the rightists were unwilling to move directly against the entire leftist faction and risk an open split. Instead, the matter of a parallel party was referred to the Central Control Commission for investigation, and a show-down was thus postponed.

Dange did move in a limited fashion against the left by having the National Council take notice of the complaints against A. K. Gopalan. The charges against Gopalan were that he had been visiting several states and holding meetings with CPI members without consulting the official leadership of the party, and acting in general in support of the leftist faction within the Party. It did not, however, take any formal action against Gopalan at that time.[65]

Emboldened by the inability and unwillingness of the National Council, controlled by the right wing, to precipitate an open split, the left forces supporting the PCZ in West Bengal intensified their activity. The first step was a secret meeting, called on September 1st at the Muslim Institute in Calcutta, organized in violation of a POC directive. Over 1,000 persons are reported to have attended from all over West Bengal, admission being through special cards issued by the PCZ.[66] Subsequent to this, a mass public rally was held by the PCZ in Calcutta. Ostensibly convened by a front group called the Democratic Convention, the demonstration was again organized in defiance of a directive from the POC and was addressed by A. K. Gopalan. One of the main themes was the demand for release of the communist *détenus*, who were largely leftists.[67] Even before Gopalan addressed the Democratic Convention, a move had been underway to dislodge Gopalan from his position of leadership of the 31-member CPI delegation in the central Parliament.[68] In addressing the Democratic Convention, he forced the Dange group to confront a painful choice—either strict enforcement of Party directives and policies at the risk of a split or continuance of the Party as a faction-ridden organization. As the right-wing group contemplated making formal charges of Party indiscipline against Gopalan, reports continued to appear in the press of the growing strength of the PCZ groups in Kerala, Andhra Pradesh, Punjab, Madras, and West Bengal. In each case, it was apparent that the PCZ had been successful in gaining the support of a substantial segment of the state Party unit.

When the National Council met in New Delhi in mid-October, it had available to it five punishments which it could levy against Gopalan—warning, censure, temporary suspension, removal from post, and expulsion from the Party. Originally, the demand had been made that Gopalan be removed from his position of leadership of the CPI in Lok Sabha and suspended from membership on the National Council. At the National Council session, a resolution was moved which demanded public censure and temporary suspension of Gopalan. The final action taken clearly showed that Dange, while still in nominal control of the CPI, dared not go beyond a certain point. The resolution adopted by the National Council, by a vote of 49 to 22, was a simple public censure.[69]

> That it could not suspend [Gopalan] . . . from the party or take some other drastic action has been interpreted as proof of the inherent strength of the pro-Peking group in the party. A too reckless wielding of the disciplinary rod will break the party to pieces and Mr. Dange knows it only too well.[70]

Shortly after the National Council session, Gopalan, in company with E. M. S. Namboodiripad, toured Kerala and vigorously attacked the Nehru government's policies.[71]

By December, 1963, it was clear that the Party contained two parallel organizations. One, the rightist faction, controlled the formal units of the Party; the other, the leftist faction, was operating a parallel party center and commanding the loyalty of significant segments of virtually all of the state Party units. During the fall of 1963, the government of India had begun releasing communist *détenus* in several states and, by December, it had released a substantial number of *détenus* in West Bengal. Most of these men were allied with the left. Within West Bengal, the two principal factions existed together with a much smaller, centrist group. Jyoti Basu, who had been a member of the left and associated with its leaders in jail, upon his release sought to contact Namboodiripad, reportedly with the proposal that together they should "gather a third force which might help in building up party unity."[72] Namboodiripad flew to Delhi from Kerala and began conversations with a range of Party leaders.

The leaders of the leftist faction met in Delhi prior to the meeting of the Central Executive Committee, reportedly drew up a ten-point indictment of Dange, and planned to issue it at the session of the CEC, thereby forcing a split in the Party. This they did not do. Two important factors undoubtedly conditioned the tactics of the CPI left wing at this juncture. First, the sudden, serious illness of Prime Minister Nehru; second, a secret directive attributed to Peking, which called for a split in the world communist movement.[73] The state of confusion existing within the CPI is clearly indicated in an analysis of the four principal measures discussed and acted upon at the CEC meeting of mid-January, 1964. On two resolutions—one, the question of support to INC candidates in the coming Madras municipal elections and two, an attack on Aidit for his statement describing the Dange clique as spies for Nehru—the CEC was sharply divided. On a third resolution, welcoming the recent INC decision to give stronger support to socialist policies, the CPI surprised itself by coming to an almost-unanimous agreement, although the left itself split.

On the fourth and final issue, concerning the control of the organizational structure of the Party, a right-left split again ensued. The left pressed for a vote on the resolutions regarding the Madras municipal elections and the Aidit statement. After heated debate, the meeting reportedly voted, 16 for and 11 against, these resolutions, indicating an almost even division in the CEC.

The CPI's attitude toward the INC was clearly complicated by the increasingly strong stand taken by Congress elements on behalf of socialism and the support of bank nationalization by the INC left wing headed by V. K. Krishna Menon. The CPI left, in particular, was shaken by these events. Thus, the official CEC resolution called for joint action by like-minded people inside and outside the Congress to redress popular grievances and promote socialist ideals. It emphasized that the voice of the leftist elements within the INC—their strong stand against monopolies and for socialist ideals—was more significant than the specific content of the INC's "democratic socialism" resolution.[74]

On the matter of internal Party organization, however, the near consensus previously achieved was shattered. The CEC considered two questions: the specific status of the West Bengal unit; and the matter of convening the next Party Congress. It finally voted to restore the West Bengal State Council of the CPI which had been replaced by the Provincial Organizing Committee (controlled by the Dange group). But in doing so, it fixed three conditions: The revived State Council should: (1) propagate sincerely and wholeheartedly the earlier decisions of the National Council; (2) publicly denounce the PCZ; and (3) support all disciplinary actions taken earlier by the POC with the concurrence of the National Council.[75]

The debate on the convening of a Party Congress was critical. Many saw it as intimately related to the increasing demand by Peking for a split within the CPI. The leftists in the Party were unanimous in demanding that the Congress be held in April, 1964.[76] They also demanded that the 1960 membership rolls be the basis for the election of delegates of the Congress, rather than the 1962 membership rolls which would have worked to their detriment. On both these issues, they were defeated. The CEC voted to convene the Party Congress in October, 1964, and to hold it on the basis of the 1962 membership rolls.[77]

Throughout the CEC meeting, reports persisted that Namboodiripad made an unsuccessful attempt to achieve a *rapprochement* between the two principal factions of the Party in view of the desperate need for Party unity.[78] The CEC appointed a commission to draft documents on ideological, political, and organizational issues to be placed before the National Council and the Party Congress to be convened in October. The commission was comprised of the Central Secretariat and six other members from the Central Executive Committee. Among the latter, reportedly, were three leftists, Jyoti Basu, P. Ramamurthi, and M. Basavapunniah. All three are understood to have refused to serve.[79]

The National Council meeting in New Delhi in April, 1964, was the scene of a full-scale effort by the leftists and several centrists to oust S. A. Dange as Party Chairman. The immediate issue was a letter that Dange had purportedly written to the British authorities prior to independence offering to work for the government in exchange for his release from prison. The National Council's refusal to consider this allegation led to a walk-out by 32 members, including all the hard-core leftists as well as Namboodiripad and Jyoti Basu, who issued an appeal to Party members to repudiate "Dange and his group" and their "reformist political line" and "factional" organizational methods. On April 15, the National Council suspended from Party membership all the signatories of this appeal.

This marked the final split in the Party, even though several unsuccessful efforts were made in the next three months to bring the two factions together. In July, 1964, the Leftists and Namboodiripad met at Tenali to formally establish a separate party structure, though one which claimed to be the legitimate Communist Party of India. On September 14, the CEC of the Right CPI struck off the Party rolls the names of all those who had participated in the Tenali meeting or had joined the new Party subsequently.[80] In the last quarter of 1964, India witnessed the curious spectacle of two Communist parties holding what were claimed to be the 7th All-India Party Congress—the Left CPI in Calcutta in the first week of November and the Right CPI in Bombay in late December and early January. The central issue at the Calcutta session, at least in public, was the party program drafted by Basavapunniah and Ramamurthi. Namboodiripad introduced a number of amendments to the draft, reportedly with the support of Jyoti Basu, which concerned the composition of the "People's Democratic Front" (PDF) proposed as the basis of an anti-imperialist, anti-monopolist united front. These amendments differed from the official draft in noting "contradictions" within the ruling class which might lead dissident sections to align themselves with the PDF. The significance of this controversy, which was eventually won by Namboodiripad, was kept ambivalent in the public discussions, but presumably the Party's attitude to the INC was the real issue. In any case, the program as finally adopted did not constitute a declaration of all-out war on the INC and the "ruling class" as it would have under the original draft.

The Left CPI also demonstrated some concern with its image as an extremist party wedded to revolutionary rather than evolutionary tactics. In his opening address, Ramamurthi admitted that the 1948 policy (which he blamed on the Dange "clique"!) had been a serious miscalculation. He did not want to commit the Party to "armed insurrection," he declared, but preferred "parliamentary and extra-parliamentary activities." [81] Nevertheless, it is significant that the Party's Constitution, as revised at the Calcutta meetings, did not include the preamble adopted at the 1958 Amritsar session which emphasized the possibility of peaceful transition to socialism.

The Leftists also repeatedly denied that the establishment of their Party had been instigated by the Chinese, but was the result, they claimed, of differences that had existed in the CPI since 1947 on the role of the *bourgeoisie*. The proceedings at Calcutta, however, were unlikely to mitigate the Left CPI's reputation as a pro-Peking party. The 1962 Chinese invasion of India was described merely as "the October clashes on the border." In defeating the leftist position on this question, the political report declared:

> While the minority gave support to the Government's measures of defence of the border, it refused to toe the line of the Government in looking upon the Chinese as an invader intent on grabbing our territory or subjugating our people.

The Dange clique's "unambiguous call for all-out (ideological, political, and military) attack on the Chinese" was denounced as "the logical outcome of their revisionist and class collaborationist outlook." [82]

Indeed, despite the few minor concessions to the more moderate elements affiliated with the Left CPI, the general tone of the resolutions and reports adopted was such as to enhance the Party's isolation within India's political party system. Certainly it was not conceived to assist the Kerala State Unit in its search for allies in the Special Legislative Assembly elections scheduled for early 1965.

Nor were the Party's differences with the Right CPI narrowed significantly, as was evident from the proceedings at the National Council meetings at Trivandum in November and the Rightists' own version of the 7th All-Party Congress at Bombay in December, 1964. A resolution adopted at the latter meeting was vehement in its denunciations of the "narrowness and sectarianism" of the Left CPI's political program. In contrast, the Right CPI made several overtures to the "progressive" elements within the INC. One prominent leader, P. C. Joshi, referred to the "healthy differentiation" taking place inside the INC "between the Right on the one side and all the rest on the other." The CPI, he declared, would cooperate with both the centrists and the leftists within the INC "against every compromise with the Right and surrender to its pressure." [83] Obviously, there is little in common here with the Left CPI's view of the INC as an instrument of the big *bourgeoisie*, landlords, and monopolists, at least from the viewpoint of party tactics.

The Right CPI carefully reiterated its position on the international communist movement at the Bombay meetings. China was condemned, and by name, for having repudiated the common policy outlined in the 1960 Moscow Declaration and for initiating disputes which had led to the splitting of the Communist movement. Peking was also denounced for its "narrow nationalistic and chauvinist attitude" on the Sino-Indian border question, and for its efforts to create a wedge in the CPI—obviously a reference to the China connections of the Left CPI.

By the beginning of 1965, therefore, there were two mutually antagonistic Communist parties competing for the support of cadres and local and state units. It was at this stage that the Government of India decided to intervene in an effort to influence developments within the Indian Communist movement. Wholesale arrests of Left CPI leaders commenced in late December, 1964. More than 750 had been imprisoned by the first week of January, 1965, including all the front-line leaders except Namboodiripad and Jyoti Basu, who represented a more moderate element in the Left Party and one less tainted with the suspicion of pro-China sentiment. In a broadcast to the nation, Home Minister Nanda charged that the Left CPI "was to serve as Peking's instrument in creating conditions of instability in the country and to facilitate the promotion of Chinese designs against India" by promoting "an internal revolution to synchronise with a fresh Chinese attack." [84] But the Government's well-timed intervention may also have a crucial effect on the fortunes of the two Communist parties by depriving the Left CPI of most of its leadership at this crucial organizational stage, particularly in regard to the forthcoming Kerala elections.

Summary

The Sino-Soviet dispute has not created the deep-seated divisions within the Indian Communist Party. Indeed it is extremely doubtful, even were that conflict ended, that CPI factionalism would be significantly altered. The split in the CPI stems from the internal history of the Party and from issues that are largely indigenous to the Indian scene. The principal dilemma relates to the tactics and strategy that should be adopted toward the Indian National Congress—the degree of accommodation or antagonism to be directed toward it. The fact that both the foreign and domestic policies of the Indian Government have won increasing approval from the Soviet Union has added further complications for the CPI. But overlaying these problems are certain basic indigenous considerations—the diverse origins of Party units and the varying social origin of Party members—factors which contribute extensively to the differences between state Party units. The CPI has not escaped the pervasive influence of Indian regionalism, which affects every party in

India. It also shares the problem of factionalism so common in Indian politics.

In an immediate sense, the single most important fact contributing to the breakdown of CPI unity has unquestionably been the death of Ajoy Ghosh. For over a decade, Ghosh succeeded in keeping in check the various contending forces within the Party. The only CPI leader who had the potential to play a similar role within the Party was E. M. S. Namboodiripad, perhaps the Party's most talented ideologist. In March, 1963, Namboodiripad published a review, in *World Marxist Review,* of a collection of speeches and writings of Ajoy Ghosh, using this as an opportunity to discuss his own ideological position. He clearly eschewed the extreme tendencies of both right and left and placed himself firmly in support of the pragmatic and flexible policies which had enabled Ghosh to rebuild the Party after its post-independence adventurist period. Namboodiripad put his finger squarely on the central issue confronting the CPI today when he said:

> The main question before the party after the Chinese aggression was how to integrate patriotism of Indian Communists as Indians to their sense of proletarian internationalism as Communists.[85]

In spite of Namboodiripad's best efforts, the CPI was split into two parties in 1964, forcing Namboodiripad to ally himself, at least temporarily, with the leftists. There is one variable, however, which could measurably alter the entire character of the factional conflict within the CPI. Prime Minister Nehru's death in May, 1964, has brought new leadership to the fore in both the INC and the Government. Dange, and before him Ajoy Ghosh, justified their position of extending partial support to the INC on the basis of its socialist policies and tendencies. Should the transition from Nehru's leadership eventually yield a more conservative INC, the basis of Dange's ideological position and a major source of conflict within the CPI would be removed. The Left CPI position vis-à-vis a violent, revolutionary strategy versus a constitutional, democratic strategy would be greatly strengthened and a reunified party, under left-centrist leadership, might emerge. This would undoubtedly be strongly supported by the Chinese Communist Party.

Revisionism and Dogmatism in the Communist Party of India

1. This quotation is attributed to E. M. S. Namboodiripad's 72-page essay, "On Revisionism and Dogmatism," and is quoted in another inner-Party document, "The Threatening Disruption and Split of the Party," prepared by M. Basava-punniah and 16 other leftists in the CPI. See *Thought* (weekly) (New Delhi), February 22, 1964, pp. 3-4.

2. Most students of Indian communism agree that the CPI was organized in December, 1928. See G. D. Overstreet and M. Windmiller, *Communism in India* (Los Angeles, Calif.: University of California Press, 1959), pp. 133-34. Some sources date the founding from May, 1933, and credit P. C. Joshi, who became its first General Secretary, with an important role in its formation. S. A. Dange, the present Chairman of the CPI, was one of those involved in the events in 1928. The CPI has two principal national publications, *New Age* (weekly) and *New Age* (monthly). A recent statement in *New Age* (weekly), June 9, 1963, cited December 26, 1925, as the date, a move some observers took as critical of P. C. Joshi. See *Thought* (weekly) (New Delhi), June 15, 1963, p. 4.

3. In Bengal the Anushilan Samiti and the Jugantar Party; in Punjab the Ghadr Party and the Hindustan Socialist Republican Army. Overstreet & Windmiller, *Communism in India*, pp. 44, 235.

4. For an analysis of the role played by these elements in the present leadership struggle within the West Bengal Communist Party unit, see Asok Mitra, "Plebian Revolution," *Seminar* (New Delhi), No. 51 (November, 1963), pp. 33-36. See also N. C. Bhattacharyya, "Leadership Problems in the Communist Party of India: With Special Reference to West Bengal," Paper presented at International Political Science Association, Round Table, Bombay, January 4-10, 1964, passim. (Mimeographed.)

5. The CSP had been formed in 1934 as a separate party within the Indian National Congress. Its leadership at that time was predominantly Marxist.

6. The All-India Kisan Sabha, the All-India Trade Union Congress, and the All-India Students Federation, respectively.

7. Overstreet & Windmiller, *Communism in India*, p. 357.

8. Asoka Mehta, *The Political Mind of India* (Bombay: Socialist Party, 1952), pp. 84, 86-87.

9. CPI membership declined from an estimated 89,263, in 1948, to 20,000 in 1950. By 1954, after the party had rejected the adventurist line, its membership once again climbed to 75,000, and by 1957 it had reached 125,000. Overstreet & Windmiller, *Communism in India*, p. 357.

10. See *Link* (weekly) (New Delhi), January 21, 1962, pp. 12-14 for a perceptive and sympathetic analysis of Ghosh's role in the CPI. See also the interesting comments by E. M. S. Namboodiripad in *World Marxist Review*, VI (March, 1963), 74-77. [This periodical is now titled *Peace, Freedom, and Socialism*.]

11. *Constitution of the Communist Party of India Adopted at the Extraordinary Congress, Amritsar, 1958* (New Delhi: Communist Party of India, 1958), p. 4. Less than a year after the adoption of this constitution, a united front of noncommunist political parties launched an agitation against the communist ministry in Kerala which resulted in its dismissal in July, 1959. This placed a serious strain upon the CPI's continued adherence to constitutional and parliamentary action. Nevertheless, the party's official organizational structure still is governed by the 1958 constitution.

12. Administrative districts in India generally range in population from 500,000 to 3,000,000, although some are as large as 6,000,000 and as small as 20,000. The local units may be formed at either the town level, or at various other subdistrict administrative levels. Branch units (formerly cells) are organized on either a geographic or functional basis. There is little available data on the degree of articulation of the infrastructure of the CPI.

13. There were 454 voting delegates, of whom 439 actually attended, at the Sixth Party Congress held at Vijayawada, Andhra Pradesh. (*New Age* [weekly], April 23, 1961, p. 1.) The CPI indicated that these delegates were elected on the basis of the Party's 1959 membership, given as 177,501.

14. The distribution, by states, of members elected to the National Council in 1961,

apart from the 14 members elected to represent the Party center, was as follows: 15 (Andhra Pradesh, Kerala); 12 (West Bengal); 9 (Madras); 6 (Bihar, Maharashtra, Punjab); 5 (Uttar Pradesh); 3 (Orissa); 2 (Assam, Gujarat, Mysore, Madhya Pradesh, Rajasthan). In addition, the centrally administered territories of Delhi, Himachal Pradesh, Manipur and Tripura, are each represented by 2 members. This totals 109, the actual figure given in *New Age* (weekly), April 23, 1961, p. 4. The name and state represented by the 110th member was not given, nor was it subsequently available.

15. For a listing of the 25-member Central Executive Committee and the 5-man Secretariat elected following the Vijayawada Congress, see *New Age* (weekly), July 2, 1961, p. 6.

16. For an interesting account of the regional variations in the units of the CPI see S. S. Harrison, *India: The Most Dangerous Decades* (Princeton, N.J.: Princeton University Press, 1960), pp. 178-245.

17. This growing gap between the right and left in the CPI can be seen in the Third Party Congress at Madurai, 1953. See *Communist Conspiracy in India* (Bombay: Democratic Research Service, 1954). The Fourth Party Congress at Palghat, 1956, provides additional substantiation. See *Communist Double-talk at Palghat* (Bombay: Democratic Research Service, 1956).

18. "New Features in National Liberation Struggle of Colonial and Dependent Peoples," *For a Lasting Peace: For a People's Democracy*, October 8, 1954.

19. "Draft Resolution for the Emergency Session of the Central Committee, New Delhi, October 29, 1954," in *Communist Double-talk at Palghat*, pp. 139-44.

20. "Central Committee Resolution on Comrade R. P. Dutt's Article, New Delhi, November 6, 1954." *Communist Double-talk at Palghat*, p. 145.

21. Modeste Rubenstein, "A Non-Capitalist Path for Underdeveloped Countries," *New Times*, Nos. 28 and 32 (July 5 and August 2, 1956). Reprinted in *New Age* (monthly), October, 1956, pp. 19-28.

22. Ajoy Ghosh, "On India's Path of Development," *New Age* (monthly), October, 1956, pp. 6-18.

23. See *The Hindu* (Madras), March 31, 1959.

24. *New Age* (weekly), April 5, 1959, pp. 1, 20.

25. The Kerala Education Bill, one of the first measures adopted by the communist-controlled Kerala legislature, was passed on September 2, 1957. After considerable legal delay the President of India gave his final consent to the Bill in January, 1959, and it was then published as the Kerala Education Act in the *Government Gazette*. The situation came to a head in March, 1959, when the government published rules framed under the Act which, among other things, sought to prohibit school teachers and students from taking part in antigovernment agitations. For an analysis of some problems which arose within the Kerala CPI and the Party in general on this issue, see N. C. Bhattacharyya, "Leadership Problems in the Communist Party of India," p. 15.

26. *Hindustan Times* (New Delhi), February 19, 1960, p. 9.

27. *New Age* (weekly), September 20, 1959, p. 1.

28. See "Resolution Adopted by the Central Executive Committee of the CPI, Calcutta, 25 December 1959," in *The India-China Border Dispute and the Communist Party of India* (New Delhi: Communist Party of India, July, 1963), pp. 8-11. (Marked "For Party Members Only.")

29. *The India-China Border Dispute*, p. 15.

30. The text of Ghosh's report to the Fourth Party Congress of the CPI is in *Communist Double-talk at Palghat*, pp. 104-127. The report was printed in a pamphlet by the CPI, along with the *People's Daily* editorial and the resolution of the CPI Fourth Party Congress specifying their joint distribution. See *On the Twentieth Congress of the CPSU* (Delhi: Communist Party of India, 1956).

31. See *New Age* (weekly), November 18, 1956, p. 7, and November 25, 1956, pp. 1, 8-9, for the texts of the Narayan-Ghosh letters.

32. For an interpretation which supports this point of view see *Link* (New Delhi), January 21, 1962, pp. 12-14.

33. During this period, Bhupesh Gupta took an essentially opportunist position within the party, shifting his allegiance in accordance with his estimate of group strength at the state and national levels, and his judgment of how his own prospects were affected. (See page 326, where he is listed as a member of the rightist faction.) The rapidly changing character of developments within the West Bengal unit of the CPI added to this tendency to change allegiances.

34. *Link*, July 31, 1960.

35. The text of Ghosh's speech at this conference is now available in *The India-China Border Dispute*, pp. 28-52.

36. An instance of this took place on October 22, 1960, when the West Bengal unit of the CPI adopted, by a vote of 67 to 10, a resolution, which rejected the Moscow line of peaceful coexistence. See *Indian Affairs Record*, Vol. 6, No. 10, 229. For other examples, see *Indian Express*, June 22, 1960; and *Hindustan Times*, November 14, 1960.

37. *Indian Affairs Record*, VII, No. 11, 253.

38. *Ibid.*, VIII, No. 1, 8-9.

39. One report gave the strength of the three factions as follows: right, 56; left, 36; and followers of E. M. S. Namboodiripad (who at the time held a centrist position), 18. See *The Hindustan Times* (New Delhi), April 17, 1961, pp. 1, 6. When the actual split in the Party took place, however, only 33 members of the National Council sided with the leftists. This discrepancy is most probably due to several factors. First, an overestimate of leftist and centrist strength within the Council; second, a shift in position by those whose loyalties to the left group were less intense; and third, an unwillingness on the part of some, despite their pro-leftist convictions, to face the prospects of actually going "into the wilderness."

40. A year earlier, at a meeting in Calcutta of the Central Executive Committee, Ghosh had remarked to a press correspondent: ". . . we differ from a *bourgeoisie* party. We never fall apart because of differences among us; the minority always yields to the opinion of the majority." *The Statesman* (New Delhi), May 6, 1960. By the time of the 1961 Congress, this interpretation of democratic centralism was being severely strained.

41. For a discussion of the Vijayawada Congress, see Savak Katrak, "India's Communist Party Split"; also *Indian Affairs Record*, Vol. 7, Nos. 4-5, p. 771; and the issues of the *Hindustan Times* (New Delhi) and *The Hindu* (Madras), from April 7 to 17, 1961. The full text of the final version of the political resolution adopted is contained in *New Age* (weekly), May 7, 1961, pp. 5-8, 13-16. It explicitly sets forth Ghosh's view that the relationship between the CPI and the INC ". . . will inevitably be one of unity and struggle . . ." It acknowledges that, while the INC is the organ of the national *bourgeoisie* as a whole, it is necessary for the CPI to forge links both ". . . independent mass activity . . . combined with fraternal and genuine united front approach so that on each issue the maximum possible support is mobilized—such has to be the tactics." *New Age*, p. 14.

42. While no fraternal delegation attended from China, a formal delegation from the CPSU, headed by Mikhail Suslov, attended for the first time in CPI history. Suslov's role at the Party Congress is believed to have been one of counseling moderation to the dominant right faction, urging it to avoid an open party split.

43. See *New Age* (weekly), July 2, 1961, p. 6, for the composition of the new Central Executive Committee and the new Central Secretariat.

44. S. L. Poplai, ed., *1962 General Elections in India* (New Delhi: Allied Publishers, January, 1962), pp. 46-47, 50. This volume contains several useful documents, including the statement on the Third General Elections, prepared by Ajoy Ghosh less than three weeks before his death, from which this quote was taken. It also contains the CPI election manifesto and the resolutions adopted at the Amritsar and Vijayawada Conferences.

45. See *New Age* (weekly), May 6, 1962, pp. 8-9; and May 27, 1962, pp. 1 and 4, regarding CPI resolutions on these changes. The change in leadership of the Party was followed a few months later by a change in editorship of the weekly and monthly editions of *New Age*. P. C. Joshi, who had been editor of the weekly was replaced by Namboodiripad. B. T. Ranadive, who had been editor of the monthly edition, was replaced by S. A. Dange.

46. For a text of the National Council resolution of October 17, 1962, "On Developments in NEFA," see the *India-China Border Dispute*, pp. 61-62.

47. Many commentators refer to this as the resolution of November 2 but, in fact, it was adopted on November 1. See *New Age* (weekly), November 4, 1962, pp. 1 and 12, for the text. The Chinese, in their attacks upon Dange and the CPI, refer to it as the resolution of November 1.

48. One of the most serious charges made against the Chinese by the CPI was omitted in the published version of the November 1 resolution (quoted from *The India-China Border Dispute*, p. 67:
"The behavior of socialist China toward peace-loving India has most grossly violated the common understanding in the communist world arrived at in the 81 Parties' Conference in 1960 in relation to peaceful coexistence and attitude to newly liberated countries and the question of war and peace. Socialist China has fallen victim to narrow nationalistic considerations at the cost of the interests of world peace and anti-imperialism, in its attitude towards India."

49. *Ibid.,* p. 87.

50. In subsequent factional disputes, the left-wing leaders of the Party have charged that the Home Ministry and the police were acting on lists supplied by the right wing of the Party, which sought to use this opportunity to destroy the left wing. For a breakdown, by state, of persons arrested under the Defense of India Rules, see *New Age* (weekly), February 24, 1963, p. 4.

51. *Thought,* December 22, 1962, p. 4.

52. *Ibid.*

53. Dange, after a meeting of the National Council on February 12, 1963, indicated that steps were being taken to organize the work of the Party in West Bengal since the majority of the members of the State Council were in jail. See *New Age* (weekly), February 17, 1963, p. 3. A report in *Thought* (New Delhi), January 26, 1963, indicates that Party reorganizations had taken place in four states: West Bengal; Punjab; Andhra Pradesh; and Madras. In Andhra Pradesh and Madras, the reorganizations were of an *ad hoc* character and presumably had taken place before the widespread government arrests.

54. Among those reported to have been involved in the creation of the parallel party are: Promode Das Gupta, Jyoti Basu, Muzaffar Ahmad, and H. K. Konar (of West Bengal); H. K. S. Surjeet (of Punjab); B. T. Ranadive (of Maharashtra); P. Ramamurthi (of Madras); and P. Sundarayya (of Andhra Pradesh). Information available to the Dangeite leadership of the CPI in late December indicated that at that time there were parallel parties in at least five states: Andhra Pradesh, Kerala, Punjab, Madras, and West Bengal. Each had its own officers, couriers, and agit-prop machinery. In addition, the leftists have brought out the following regional weekly newspapers in vernacular languages: *Desh Hitaishi* (West Bengal); *Janashakti* (Andhra Pradesh); *Spark* (Madras); and *Chinta* (Kerala). See *Thought* (New Delhi), January 25, 1964, p. 4.

55. For the text, see *New Age* (weekly), February 17, 1963, pp. 1, 12. The CPI also reprinted, in the same issue of *New Age,* an editorial appearing in *Pravda*

56. of February 10, "For Marxist-Leninist Unity of the Communist Movement: For Cohesion of Countries of Socialism," which was a sharp attack on the CCP. *Ibid.*

57. For the text, see *New Age* (weekly), February 24, 1963, pp. 5, 10.

58. The text is available in *Peking Review*, March 18, 1963. It was also reprinted by the CPI in *New Age* (weekly), March 31, 1963, pp. 5, 14.

59. *Idem.*

60. *Idem.*

61. *Idem.*

62. Supplement to *New Age* (weekly), April 21, 1963, p. xiv.

63. *Idem.*

64. For a coverage of the events surrounding these National Council meetings, see *Link* (New Delhi), June 30, 1963, p. 9, and July 7, 1963, pp. 9-10. See also the columns by Sathi in *Thought* (New Delhi), immediately before and after the National Council session, for a very detailed discussion of internal developments. The political resolution finally adopted, while emphasizing the danger of right reaction, called for the unity of all progressive elements, including Congressmen. An alternative political resolution, put forward by a left-wing delegate, Ram Piara Saraf of Jammu, charged that the Nehru government had shifted rightward, had made heavy concessions to reactionary vested interests and had adopted anti-people policies. It was overwhelmingly rejected.

65. Note that at the June and July session of the National Council of the 110 members, approximately 54, less than a majority, are reported to have attended. Of these, 6 are said to have voted for the alternative political resolution put forward by Ram Piara Saraf. Thus Dange was no longer able to muster an absolute majority in support of his position in the National Council. See *Indian Affairs Record*, IX, No. 8, 259.

66. *Thought* (New Delhi), September 7, 1963, p. 4.

67. Press reports indicated that many of the speeches were directed as much against the attitude of the Party leadership, under Dange, toward the *détenus'* fate, as against the West Bengal government which had imprisoned them. See *Times of India* (New Delhi), September 30, 1963, p. 1.

68. *The Tribune* (Ambala), September 26, 1963, p. 1.

69. *The Tribune* (Ambala), October 23, 1963, p. 4. A slightly different breakdown is given in *Thought* (New Delhi), November 16, 1963, p. 4. 30 of the 110 members of the National Council were in jail. Of the remaining 80, 52 voted in favor of the resolution, 21 voted against, and 3 abstained. 4 absented themselves at the time of voting.

70. *The Tribune* (Ambala), October 23, 1963, p. 4.

71. *Times of India* (New Delhi), October 22, 1963, p. 3.

72. *The Statesman* (New Dehli), December 28, 1963, p. 13.

73. *Thought*, January 25, 1964, p. 4. An earlier indication of Peking's position on the matter of a split in the international communist movement appeared in the *New York Times* (West Coast edition), January 6, 1964, p. 1, which reported that a line calling for "the establishment of separate splinter groups or parties" was laid down in an ideological speech made by Chou Yang, Deputy Director of the Propaganda Department of the Central Committee of the CCP, before an October meeting of Chinese communist ideologists and intellectuals. See also the *New York Times* (New York edition), February 4, 1964, p. 1, where reference is made to an editorial published in *Hung Chi*, the ideological journal of the Central Committee of the CCP, which laid down a theoretical justification for the formal break with Moscow and the formation of an independent communist movement.

74. *The Statesman* (New Delhi), January 19, 1964, p. 1.

control of the governmental machinery—with the possible exception of Indonesia—has enjoyed such favorable conditions for growth and development. And yet the results to date have been unimpressive, even on a comparative scale. To explain why this is the case, we shall briefly survey the history of the communist movement in Nepal and analyze the factors that have made it habitual for the Party to waste opportunities and concentrate on nonessentials.

Most contemporary Nepali political movements had their origin in India in the years immediately following World War II, as the situation under the autocratic Rana regime inside Nepal was scarcely conducive to political activity. A large number of Nepalis resident in India prior to 1947 participated in the Indian struggle to oust British rule on the assumption that independence for India was the necessary prerequisite to the ouster of the Ranas in Nepal, in view of the vital support the regime had long received from the British rulers of India. It is also probable, however, that many Nepalis, both in Nepal and India, were emotionally involved in India's struggle for independence because of the close historical and cultural ties between the two peoples. And, indeed, vociferous as Nepali communist criticisms of India may often be, it is nevertheless Indians (and not just their Indian comrades) with whom Nepali communists have the most in common and with whom communication is most simple and comprehensible. It is for this reason, presumably, that communist verbiage in Nepal tends to be a close reflection of that currently preoccupying the communist movement in India, for the arguments and symbolisms used are frequently borrowed directly from the Indian Communist Party even though they may not be particularly relevant to objective conditions within Nepal.

The close relationship between the two parties extends back into the preindependence period when a few Nepalis were admitted to membership in the Communist Party of India (CPI). This occurred most widely in a few urban centers such as Calcutta, Banaras, Gorakhpur, and Patna, where there were a number of Nepali students, and in the tea-plantation areas of Darjeeling district, where there were large communities of migrant Nepali workers among whom communist-dominated labor unions had made some inroads.

Subsequently, a subtle divergence in attitude between these India-trained Nepali communists and the other leaders of the Party who had confined their political activities to Nepal during the Rana period can be perceived. Divisions within the Party since 1951 would sometimes appear to have been influenced by this factor. It is probably not entirely coincidental that most of the Nepali communist leaders currently in exile in India had been active in India in the period from 1947 to 1951, while most of the leaders who have remained in Nepal since the banning of all political parties in December, 1960, are those who did not affiliate with the Party until after the overthrow of the Ranas in 1951.

This is not to imply, of course, that the Nepali communist leaders currently in India are pro-India and that those in Nepal are anti-Indian. Indeed, the communist faction in exile is the Party group to which is usually attributed pro-China sentiments. What may be significant in this instance are the close ties that were developed between Nepali and Indian communists during this earlier period. These appear to have continued despite wide subsequent differences in their tactics and ideology. According to reports, for instance, a leader of the extremist, reputedly pro-China faction of the Nepali Party now in exile in India has his closest personal relationship with a leader of the moderate, pro-Soviet and anti-China wing of the CPI.

Moreover, the CPI appear to maintain the closest ties with all Nepali communist factions, whether in Nepal or India. The establishment of Russian and Chinese embassies in Kathmandu may have provided the Nepali communists with alternative channels of contact with the world communist movement, but it is questionable how much these have actually been used. There are occasional reports of contacts between Nepali communists and the Chinese in Tibet. While these should not be discounted, the sheer physical obstacles to such contacts would seem to make it unlikely that they play anything but a minor role in the CPN's communications with the external communist movement. All parties are illegal in Nepal today, and it would certainly be embarrassing to the embassies to be approached too openly or too frequently by communist leaders. It is also somewhat ironical that most of the reputedly pro-China communist leaders are currently in exile in India and are, thus, denied easy access to the Chinese either in India or Nepal, except possibly through the pro-China faction of the CPI, which may not be too reliable or eager a channel.

The Early Years

By 1947, Nepali members of the CPI were active in Nepal, participating in a "no-tax" campaign among the tenants in the eastern Terai (a plains area at the foot of the hills) and in a strike among mill workers at Biratnagar in southeastern Nepal.[1] The Nepali communists were also actively attempting to infiltrate other Nepali political organizations in India, in particular the Nepali National Congress (NNC) which had been founded in Calcutta in 1946. Most of the leaders of the NNC, however, were closely associated with the socialist wing of the Indian National Congress—a group that had turned bitterly anticommunist because of their betrayal by the communists during the united front period prior to World War II and by the Communist prowar policy after the German invasion of the Soviet Union in 1941. Rejected by the NNC, the Nepali communists finally decided to establish their own party. On September 15, 1949, five Nepalis [2] met in Calcutta and formed the Communist Party of Nepal.

The new party continued to reiterate the necessity for a united front of all anti-Rana political organizations, but met with an unenthusiastic response from the Nepali Congress, which had been formed in March, 1950, by a merger of B. P. Koirala's NNC and the Nepali Democratic Congress headed by Subarna Shamsher. Their overtures having once again been ignored, the communists denounced the Nepali Congress as representative of the "national-capitalist *bourgeoisie,*" and as a tool of the "reactionary" Nehru government in India.[3] The anti-Rana revolution launched by the Nepali Congress in November, 1950, placed the CPN in a quandary. The party met the situation squarely by straddling the fence—the CPN never formally announced its support of the movement, but a number of communists participated, apparently on a personal basis, in the struggle. The Party's position on the compromise agreement that terminated the conflict in February, 1951, was somewhat more forthright. The Nepali Congress was accused of having betrayed its own revolution by agreeing to join a coalition cabinet headed by the Rana Prime Minister. It was alleged that this solution had been imposed upon Nepal by the government of India and "Anglo-American imperialists." [4] The communists did their best to encourage dissident forces within the Nepali Congress, such as the K. I. Singh group in western Nepal, which refused to accept the cease-fire agreement and continued the struggle. The suppression of these factions by Indian constabulary and military forces at the request of the new Home Minister, B. P. Koirala, added volumes to communist criticisms of the Nepali Congress and the Indian government.

Despite their discontent with the political compromise that ended the revolution, the communists immediately hastened to Kathmandu once the new government had removed the ban on Party activity and had released political prisoners. Aware of its own intrinsic weakness, the Party moved to strengthen its position in two ways: by agitating for a united front of all "progressive forces" opposed to the Nepali Congress-Rana coalition government,[5] and by forming a number of front organizations through which the communists could work more effectively in certain segments of Nepali society.[6] During Nehru's visit to Kathmandu in June, 1951, the communists cooperated with Tanka Prasad Acharya's *Praja Parishad* Party and some elements of the pro-Rana *Gorkha Dal* in organizing a "black flag" demonstration. Student demonstrations were also organized in the fall of 1951, culminating in the arrest of several communists. The united front policy achieved its most notable success in October, 1951, with the formation of the *Jatiya Janatantrik Samyukta Morcha,* or National Democratic United Front, by the CPN, the *Praja Parishad,* and a number of communist front organizations, as the basis for a "national front of all progressive forces." [7] In its Manifesto, the *Morcha* denounced the newly established Nepali Congress government, headed by M. P. Koirala, as a tool of the Nehru government and condemned the "expansionist war-mongering camp of America and Britain." [8] Except for some of the usual anti-Rana cliches, the manifesto was diffident on the subject of a domestic program, probably a reflection of the basically different composition of the *Praja Parishad* and the CPN.

The first serious setback to the communists resulted, ironically enough, from a situation that was primarily not of their own making. In February, 1952, some supporters of K. I. Singh in the Nepali Congress military unit, the *Raksha Dal,* organized a coup against the M. P. Koirala government. From available sources, it would appear that the CPN played no part in the planning and launching of the coup but that it did attempt to take advantage of the situation. Announcing its support of the K. I. Singh demand for an all-party government, the CPN hastily organized a few demonstrations that did little except to confuse the situation further. K. I. Singh and several of his followers fled to Tibet on February 24, and the coup collapsed. On the following day, the CPN was banned because of its complicity in these events, and the Party leaders had to go underground to avoid arrest.

Though illegal, the Party still had several avenues for legal activity through the various front organizations that had not been banned, and through the united front. Tanka Prasad found the alliance with the CPN an obstacle to his efforts to form alliances with other political factions, however, and in October, 1952, the *Praja Parishad* withdrew from the *Morcha.* Deprived of its two main components, the united front was eventually discarded. Isolated in the Nepali political spectrum, the CPN temporarily reduced the emphasis on the united front policy in favor of unilateral action. A new political front organization, the *Jana Adhikur Surakshi Samiti* (JASS, or People's Rights Protection Committee), was founded. The JASS devoted comparatively little attention to civil-liberty issues, however, and concentrated its attention on questions of foreign relations, helping to organize anti-American demonstrations in August, 1954, and anti-Indian demonstrations the following month.

The illegal status of the CPN did not seriously hamper the activities of the Party leaders and workers, most of whom were only nominally underground since the government seldom attempted to enforce the warrants for arrest that had been issued.[9] The Party openly supported a number of candidates in the Kathmandu municipal elections in September, 1963. Six of their candidates won. This was the largest number from any party and an unexpected show of strength in the nation's capital. A few months later, in January, 1954, the First All-Party Congress of the CPN was held in Kathmandu, with representatives from many parts of Nepal present. A constitution was adopted, outlining the Party's organizational structure (see Table 1) and specifying the conditions under which members were to be recruited. The Congress also approved a Party program which included three controversial provisions: (1) "continuous struggle" against the "feudalist" royal regime; (2) replacement of the monarchy by a republican system framed by an elected constituent assembly; and (3) confiscation of large and middle-sized land holdings without compensation.[10]

The Party's critical atttiude toward the monarchy was expressed in a resolution passed by the Politburo shortly after the conclusion of the Party Congress, which declared:

> The King, who represents the feudal landlord interests as well as the former ruling Ranas, has opposed any advancement of the cause of democracy in the country.[11]

In the current Nepali political context, these were bitter words indeed.

The left-sectarian character of the 1954 platform contributed substantially to the further political isolation of the CPN. The demand for the abolition of the monarchy, particularly, alarmed other political leaders, who were then busily currying favor with the palace on the assumption that this was the most plausible route to high office. In adopting this platform, the CPN was implicitly admitting that two announced objectives—a united front with progressive forces and an all-party coalition cabinet—were unfeasible. It is also probable that the platform served to dissuade the government from even considering lifting the ban on the Party.

It was soon apparent to several CPN leaders that the 1954 platform had been a serious mistake. At their insistence, an all-party conference[12] was held in November, 1955, to reconsider policy questions. A new political resolution was adopted. As interpreted in a widely circulated article by the Central Committee entitled "Why the Changes in the Party Program?"[13] this resolution marked a substantial transition toward a more moderate policy stance. The Party admitted that its attitude during the 1950 revolution, its policies of continuous struggle against the subsequent governments, and the demand for an all-party coalition government had been serious errors which had only served to strengthen the power of the monarchy and other feudalist elements. While still maintaining that "the republican idea [is] more suited to Nepal than monarchy or constitutional monarchy," the Party admitted that it was futile to raise antimonarchical slogans "as long as the peasants and the majority of the people . . . are not united for a struggle against the monarchy." [14] The Party's position on monarchy and upon land confiscation were admitted to be major obstacles to the formation of a "broadbased joint front." It was stated that such a front was the prime objective of the Party, and that "controversial measures that are unnecessary and impractical at present" should not be given undue emphasis.[15]

Legal Once Again: 1956 to 1960

The trend toward moderation in the CPN's policy received added stimulation in January, 1956, when King Mahendra appointed Tanka Prasad Acharya, the Party's old ally in the united front of 1951 and 1952, as Prime Minister. The chances for the legalization of the Party were greatly enhanced and, indeed, Tanka Prasad entered into negotiations with CPN leaders on this question shortly after assuming office. As the price for lifting the ban, the new Prime Minister insisted upon the acceptance of constitutional monarchy by the Party.

The CPN Central Committee was still badly divided on this question. The majority, moderate wing headed by Keshar Jang Rayamajhi was ready to accept constitutional monarchy, but a minority faction headed by Pushpa Lal Shrestha insisted that the goal of a republic should not be totally abandoned. The Central Committee finally agreed on a compromise by which the Party tentatively accepted constitutional monarchy, leaving the ultimate decision to the Constituent Assembly which was scheduled for election in 1957. While this statement did not precisely meet Tanka Prasad's conditions, the Prime Minister advised the King to legalize the CPN, and the ban was lifted in April, 1956.

Operating openly once more, the CPN adopted a dual tactical approach primarily intended to improve the Party's position in the long-awaited general elections. Tacit support was extended to the *Praja Parishad* government throughout its period in office, particularly in foreign relations issues, since Tanka Prasad's abandonment of the special relationship with India for equal friendship with India and China was enthusiastically endorsed by the communists. At the same time, the CPN sought to end its isolation within the Nepal political movement. An alliance with the *Praja Parishad* might have seemed logical, but in fact this was precluded by the *Praja Parishad's* own efforts to establish working relations with other, more conservative political factions. In these circumstances, the *Praja Parishad* would have found an alliance with the CPN an embarrassing encumbrance, as well as likely to raise questions about the governing party in the royal palace. The communists, therefore, had to look elsewhere for potential allies and, as usual, it was the Nepali Congress that received the first overtures. In August, 1956, the

Table 1

ORGANIZATIONAL STRUCTURE OF THE NEPAL COMMUNIST PARTY UNDER
THE 1954 PARTY CONSTITUTION

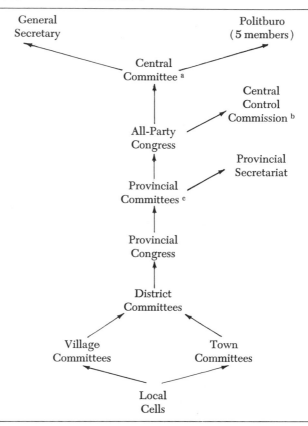

[a] The size of the Central Committee is left to the discretion of the All-Party Congress. So far the Central Committee has had 17 to 19 members.

[b] The Central Control Commission is given the task of maintaining Party discipline, guaranteeing that all Party units implement the decisions of the higher level committees.

[c] There are seven Provincial Committees: (1) East Kosi; (2) West Kosi; (3) North Gandak; (4) South Gandak; (5) Middle Gandak; (6) West Gandak; and (7) Karnali.

CPN Central Committee instructed lower units of the Party to cooperate with the Nepali Congress political action program. The Congress was no more inclined towards cooperation with the communists now than it had been in the past. Indeed, the CPN was almost completely ignored, both by the palace and the political parties, in the dramatic political developments surrounding the dismissal of the Tanka Prasad Cabinet in August, 1957, and the appointment of K. I. Singh in his place.

The vacillation evident in the Party's tactics at this time was probably a reflection of the serious rifts that had long divided the Central Committee. These centered around the question of policy toward the monarchy and, as the necessary corollary, the Nepali Congress, still the major political party in the country. The moderate Rayamajhi faction argued that the Party should accept constitutional monarchy, at least temporarily, since conditions under a royalist regime were more conducive to the growth of communist strength than a government headed by the Party's main rival, the socialist Nepali Congress. Alliances with the Congress for limited purposes might be feasible under certain conditions, but only if this served the ultimate purposes of the Party. The extremist faction headed by Pushpa Lal maintained that the destruction of all "feudalistic" remnants, including the monarchy, should be the immediate as well as the ultimate goal of the Party and that the CPN should align itself with all "progressive" forces that might contribute to the fulfillment of this task. Not all factions of the Party aligned themselves on exactly this basis, of course, but this was the general pattern. The Rayamajhi faction, with broad support throughout Nepal, usually controlled a majority on the Central Committee. The leftist opposition was centered in the powerful North Gandak Regional Committee, which includes Kathmandu, but it also received substantial support from other regional and local Party units, particularly in the eastern Terai.

The struggle within the Party reached a critical stage at the Second All-Party Congress, held in Kathmandu in May and June, 1957. The Central Committee presented to the Congress a draft resolution which reflected essentially the views of the Rayamajhi faction. The most controversial items in the draft were the clauses that condemned the "permanent revolution" concept as "adventurist" and "suicidal" and which termed the demand for nationalizing land without due consideration of the interests of the middle-class peasant as "infantile leftism." This was a direct challenge to the left sectarians, who were bitterly critical of the draft and who were apparently able to prevent its adoption by the Congress, at least in the form presented.[16]

In his opening remarks to the Congress, the Acting Secretary-General, Keshar Jang Rayamajhi, stated the moderate position very clearly:

> In prevailing backward conditions, it is not only impractical but foolish to talk of socialism. As long as the basis for the exercise of democracy by the people is not created, that is, as long as capital is not accumulated in the country through industrial development, it would be difficult to find the way to republican democracy, not to talk of socialism or communism. Therefore, at present it will be the aim of the Communist Party to bring about the development of democracy.[17]

That the leftists had not accepted Rayamajhi's thesis was clearly demonstrated when, shortly after the close of the Second Congress, Pushpa Lal told a public meeting at Kathmandu that the CPN would place a resolution before the Constituent Assembly, when elected, calling for the abolition of the monarchy.[18]

King Mahendra's postponement of the first general election caused another uproar in Nepali politics in the last quarter of 1957. The Democratic Front—originally organized by the Nepali Congress, *Praja Parishad,* and the Nepali National Congress to oppose the K. I. Singh government—decided to launch a civil disobedience movement in December to protest the King's decision. The CPN applied for admission to this select group, but once again was coldly rejected. The communists characterized this as "political narrow-mindedness," but nevertheless the Central Committee, under leftist pressure, decided to pledge its support to the movement.

Over communist objections, the Democratic Front terminated its campaign on December 15, once King Mahendra had agreed to new dates for the election. Having failed to influence the Democratic Front parties, the Central Committee of the CPN suddenly switched tactics and virtually came out in support of King Mahendra. In explaining the new party policy, Rayamajhi declared:

> We believe in constitutional monarchy. We are against any action which will affect the prestige of the Supreme Leader of the nation. The date that he has fixed for the election is quite reasonable. Attempts by the Democratic Front to resume the civil disobedience movement should be considered as mischievous.[19]

To show that his support of constitutional monarchy had not been a slip of the tongue, Rayamajhi repeated the substance of his argument in the Party journal, *Navayug,* asserting that the sovereignty of the King was inevitable under prevailing conditions, since the King was the Supreme Leader of the country.[20]

Naturally, the leftist faction was not prepared to accept Rayamajhi's statements. The controversy became even more intense when King Mahendra suddenly issued a proclamation on February 1, 1958, stating that the elections, then scheduled for February, 1959, would not be for a constituent assembly, as he and his predecessor had promised, but for a parliament that would function under a constitution bestowed on the country by the King. Some leftists argued that the Party should refuse to contest the elections under these conditions and should instead launch a movement to force the King to hold the elections for a constituent assembly. The North Gandak [i.e., Kathmandu] Regional Committee met on Febrauary 4 and approved a resolution to this effect. On March 2, however, the Central Committee rejected this proposal, and voted to accept the Royal Proclamation with some reservations. In its resolution, the Central Committee declared that:

> The combined efforts of the democratic forces in the country can turn a Parliament into a powerful body. In order to achieve this objective, the Communist Party's slogan from now on will be that the constitution to be granted by the King must be democratic.[21]

A second plenary session of the Central Committee, held in Rautahat in June, once again endorsed the decision to contest the election,[22] though only over the strong opposition of the North Gandak Regional Committee representatives. The moderate policy attained an unexpected political reward when in June, 1958, the King appointed two communists to the Advisory Assembly set up to advise the government until the election had been completed. It was the first time any communists had received direct recognition of this sort from the palace.

The Central Committee met once again in September, 1958, to discuss election tactics and to complete the Party's election manifesto. It was decided to support "democratic" candidates in constituencies in which the CPN did not have a candidate. As this policy actually worked out, however, only a few friendly political leaders, such as Tanka Prasad, and several independents received communist support. At one stage, the CPN had approached the Nepali Congress for an election alliance, but had met with the usual negative response. No Nepali Congress candidate received communist support, even in constituencies in which the Congress' main opponent was the reactionary *Gorkha Parishad.* Indeed, most of the CPN's election propaganda was directed against the socialist Nepali Congress rather than against more conservative parties. The CPN's election manifesto was innocuous in the extreme for a communist party, not even mentioning the monarchy or some of the more radical land-reform programs previously supported.[23]

The election results were a tremendous victory for the Nepali Congress, which won over two-thirds of the seats, and a bitter disappointment to the communists who ran 46 candidates but won only 4 seats. Party leaders have usually attributed their lack of success to a shortage of funds, but this is probably more an excuse than a reason. It would appear that the rift in the Party leadership, which by now extended down to the local units in some areas, was a more important factor in the defeat of communists in several constituencies where the prospects had seemed encouraging.

The poor showing of the Party in the elections led to increased criticism of its moderate leadership. Nevertheless, the Rayamajhi faction was able to retain a tenuous control at the plenary session at Janakpur in June, 1959. It was decided that the Party's attitude toward the Nepali

Congress government should be one of selective support or opposition, depending upon the issue at stake. In point of fact, most of the Communist Party's criticism of the M. P. Koirala government was directed at its foreign policy, which was alleged to be pro-Indian. Usually the communist M.P.'s supported the economic, social and administrative reform measures of the Nepali Congress, though describing them as inadequate. This was also a relatively peaceful period, internally. Even the September, 1960, meetings of the Central Committee which formulated draft resolutions for the Third All-Party Congress scheduled for February, 1961,[24] did not result in the usual wrangle. The Party made no progress, however, in its constant search for political allies, as was demonstrated in November, 1960, when all the opposition parties in the Parliament except the communists held a series of meetings in an effort to form a united opposition to the Nepali Congress government.

The CPN Divides

A new crisis occurred on December 15, 1960, when King Mahendra suddenly dismissed the Nepali Congress government, and arrested all of the Congress Ministers and many other party leaders in Nepal. Ten days later, the King placed a total ban on all parties and political activities—a move that probably affected the other parties more adversely than the communists, since the CPN had years of experience in operating underground. Moreover, King Mahendra directed most of his attention to destroying the Nepali Congress organization, and paid comparatively little attention to the communists and other parties. Several communist leaders were arrested at the time of the coup, but were released shortly thereafter.[25] Warrants were issued for several others, but no real efforts were made to apprehend them. Many communist leaders and workers were allowed to continue their political activity virtually undisturbed, thus giving the CPN a tremendous advantage over the Nepali Congress, most of whose workers, even on a district and local level, were imprisoned or forced into exile.

Despite these initial advantages, however, the communists have not been able to reap full benefit from the situation, primarily because of their chronic inner struggle for power.[26] The first signs of a fundamental disagreement within the Party over the 1960 coup became evident early in 1961. The communists had been as surprised by the King's action as had the other parties, but appear to have recovered their poise more quickly. Before long, the Party was operating underground in much the same fashion as it had prior to 1956.

Because of Rayamajhi's absence in Moscow at the time of the coup, the first public reaction of the Party to the King's move reflected the views of the Pushpa Lal faction. On December 24, 1960, a cyclostyled circular was distributed, ostensibly in the name of the Politburo, demanding the cessation of "military terror" and a conference of all parliamentary parties. By mid-January, 1961, however, Rayamajhi and other moderate communists had returned to Nepal, and the struggle for control of the Party machinery began in earnest. The moderate faction was able to gain approval for a more cautious policy toward the new royal regime. In the latter part of January, the Party issued another press note, this time reflecting the views of the moderate faction. While cautiously critical of the December coup and demanding the release of political prisoners, the lifting of the ban on political activity, and the restoration of fundamental rights, the note did not insist on the reconvening of the Parliament, thus by implication accepting the new regime.

The dispute reached a critical stage at a secret plenary session of the Central Committee (held at Darbhanga, India, in March, 1961) which was also attended by 54 delegates representing 24 district units of the Party.[27] In these stormy meetings, the Rayamajhi faction argued that the Party's immediate objectives should be limited to: (1) the restoration of fundamental rights; (2) the release of political prisoners; (3) the withdrawal of the ban on political parties; and (4) the election of a new Parliament in the near future. The Pushpal Lal faction, supported by the North Gandak (i.e., Kathmandu), Gorkha, and Bandipur Party organizations, demanded the reconvening of the dissolved Parliament (i.e., the restoration of the Nepali Congress government) and, if necessary, the launching of a communist-led movement to achieve this objective. A third, minor, faction led by the Piuthan Party unit demanded the election of a constituent assembly to draw up a new constitution, and the eventual establishment of a republican form of government. For all practical purposes, the second and third factions were aligned against the moderates.

The plenary session ended in a virtual stalemate, although the Rayamajhi faction was able to retain control of the Central Committee. Eleven of the seventeen members of the Central Committee were reported to be Rayamajhi supporters, while six followed Pushpal Lal's leadership. However, three members of the Rayamajhi faction were in prison in Nepal and a fourth resigned from the Central Committee during the session, thus reducing the pro-Rayamajhi majority at the Darbhanga session to one.

To negotiate the differences between the two factions, the plenum appointed a joint committee which was assigned the thankless task of chalking out a compromise Party program. This proved to be impossible, however, and the two factions continued their bitter debate over the royal regime.[28] There are some reasons for suspecting that the struggle in the Party was not strictly verbal. There were persistent reports in

Kathmandu in July, 1961, alleging that a colleague had attempted to assassinate the leader of the moderate faction.[29] A few days later, Rayamajhi was apprehended by the Kathmandu police under very curious circumstances. What actually occurred has never been clarified, but one Nepali journal with close ties to the communists implied strongly that opposition elements in the Party had betrayed Rayamajhi to the police.[30] Equally intriguing is the government's sudden arrest of the leader of the promonarchy faction of the Nepal Communist Party while the leader of the extremist faction was allowed to wander around Kathmandu, only indifferently disguised. Whatever the reasons may have been, the government apparently reversed itself quickly for, scarcely one month later, Rayamajhi was released from prison, without having had to sign the declaration of loyalty to the King that had been required of other political prisoners.

Rumors of collaboration between Rayamajhi and certain members of the government circulated even more widely in the Kathmandu bazaar in September, 1961, when the communist leader was given a passport and allowed to visit Moscow for medical treatment. His departure did nothing to reduce the tension in the Party and, indeed, may have been partially responsible for bringing matters to a head. The moderates, bolstered by the return of the three members of the Party's Central Committee who had been released from prison at approximately the same time as Rayamajhi, decided to issue a strong warning to the extremists. Pushpa Lal and his associates were threatened with expulsion if they did not mend their ways, accept the decision to support the royal regime, and work within the existing institutional framework.

A serious clash occurred between the two factions at a Central Committee meeting in Kathmandu, held in late November or early December, 1961. Pushpa Lal insisted that the King's rule was "feudalistic" and had to be overthrown by any means required, even revolution. The "bourgeois and reactionary" Indian government was only a slight improvement over the royal regime, Pushpa Lal agreed, but in the circumstances New Delhi could be expected to favor and support "democratic forces" in their struggle to free Nepal from the "King's dictatorship." He also favored an alliance with the Nepali Congress as the necessary prerequisite for a successful revolution. These views were totally unacceptable to the moderates, and the extremists were threatened with expulsion from the Party if they did not cease their anti-Party activities. Shortly thereafter, Pushpa Lal and several colleagues fled to India.

On arriving in India, Pushpa Lal made two tentative offers of cooperation to the Nepali Congress.[31] These were received cautiously by Subarna Shamsher and his colleagues, though it would appear that no outright rejection of the proposal was made at that time. For nearly three months Pushpa Lal toured areas of India in which there were substantial settlements of Nepali migrants—followed very closely, it should be noted, by D. P. Adhikari, then a member of the moderate faction of the Party. Pushpa Lal announced in early April, 1962, that a "Congress of the Communist Party of Nepal" would be held the following month, ostensibly to formulate policy for the Party but actually to set up what amounted to a parallel communist party. The announcement brought forth an immediate denunciation from the Rayamajhi wing of the Party. Speaking on behalf of the Central Secretariat, Kamar Shah issued a statement in Kathmandu (it should be remembered that the Party was illegal in Nepal and all political activity was theoretically proscribed) accusing the Pushpa Lal group of:

> actively conspiring against central leadership, violating the Leninist standard of party life and indulging in factional activities to undermine the very unity of the party.

Despite their "anti-Party" activities, the announcement continued, the Central Committee was "confident that the rank and file of the party, educated in Leninist principles, will defeat the nefarious designs of the Pushpa Lal group to split party unity, and the party will advance further in its goal to serve the people and the country in its glorious past tradition." [32]

The Pushpa Lal group ignored the warnings that accompanied Kamar Shah's statement. Meetings, termed an *Adhibeshan* (General Congress) of the Party, were held in Banaras in mid-May, 1962, and drew representatives from 8 of the 35 districts of Nepal.[33] Seven resolutions were passed, the most important of which called for a revolution against the King's regime. A second resolution expelled ten moderate members of the Central Committee, including Rayamajhi, Shambhu Ram Shrestha, Kamar Shah, D. P. Adhikari, and P. B. Malla, on charges of betraying the Party by supporting the King's "anti-democratic" steps. In their place, a new 19-member Central Committee, including only 4 members of the old Committee, was elected. In addition, a 51-member National Council was formed, and most of these were also newcomers.

The Banaras meetings were an open declaration of the split within the CPN. In late May, the Central Committee (i.e., the Rayamajhi faction) issued a statement condemning the violent activities of the "antinational elements" in India:

> No democratic movement succeeds through violence and terroristic activities. It can succeed only through a mass movement launched inside the country. Violent actions weaken the mass movement. The Communist Party therefore condemns such activities.[34]

This statement, astonishing in view of its source, would seem to be directed more at Pushpa Lal and his supporters in the Party than at its ostensible object—the Nepali Congress. By the summer of 1962, all efforts to prevent the formalization of the split within the Party leadership had come to naught. Finally, in September, the Central Committee (i.e., the Rayamajhi faction) expelled Pushpa Lal, Tulsi Lal Amatya, and Hikmat Singh from the party. Other members of the party who supported these three "deviationists," it was stated, would be dealt with by the appropriate committees of the level on which they worked.

With the revolutionary path to communism discarded, presumably temporarily, the Rayamajhi faction reemphasized the old policy of a "united front of all democratic forces" in Nepal. One of the first indications of the new direction of communist policy was the article in a pro-communist weekly [35] complaining that "no united and organized front had yet been established to meet the challenge" of the "Indian-American puppet forces led by Subarna and Bharat." [36] As the government's ban on political activity was a serious, possibly insurmountable obstacle to the formation of a united front, much of the communists' persuasive talents have been employed in a campaign to convince the King that the dynamics of such a movement were basically in conformity with his own political objectives. In terms slightly exotic even for Nepali communists, one Party spokesman wrote:

> In view of its historical necessity and its probable nature, the leadership of the national front must necessarily be undertaken by His Majesty who is not only the propounder but also the symbol of national unity. The entire country and Nepal's real friends abroad have full confidence and faith in His Majesty. As it would prove highly beneficial to the interest of national unity to utilize His Majesty's great personality, it is in the fitness of things that he should announce the formation of a national front and guide it. Only through such a front will it be possible to achieve the national goal on the basis of a minimum program by establishing political unity in the country. As the national front will not be a political party, His Majesty's leadership thereof will never mean that there will be political partisanship. Rather, this will foster equality of treatment and thus promote the cause of national unity.[37]

To emphasize even further the "royalist" character of the proposed united front, the Central Committee of the Communist Party suggested that the King should call a political conference at the royal palace to discuss the nature of the united front. "All nationalistic and democratic forces standing for different ideologies and policies, with a program for the solution of national problems" should be invited.[38] The use of the adjective "nationalistic" is particularly significant, since in current Nepali political parlance, the Nepali Congress and affiliated "anti-national" elements were automatically excluded. The term "democratic," on the other other hand, is interpreted so broadly in Nepal that it is doubtful if any organization could reasonably be excluded on this basis, thus permitting any of the forces representing traditional and vested interests to join at their discretion.

The relationship between the front and the government was also a delicate question upon which the communists attempted to reassure the King. The front would not be a political party, the Party said, nor would it be entrusted with the task of running the government:

> Of course, it would be indispensable to maintain close contact and hold consultations between such a front and the government. Each will have to respect the other as otherwise there will be no national unity. In case such a front is formed, it will not be able to assume the form of a "party" though its members following different ideologies and principles may work for nationalism, for the country's development and for democracy. Instead, such a front may put an end to mutual rivalry and opposition for the sake of opposition, and pave the way for a healthy competition for constructive work and service to the country.[39]

As described so enthusiastically by the communists, the front would be another instrument through which the government could implement its political and economic programs. Needless to say, there was some skepticism in official circles in Kathmandu about the communists' intention of allowing the front to function in this fashion. There were several aspects of such a front that were obviously advantageous to the communists. It would provide the Party with an organization within which the communist cadres could legally operate even while the Party itself was still banned. Furthermore, the communists would be assured easier access to such administrative institutions as the *Panchayats* and class organizations which they have been assiduously attempting to infiltrate. Finally, the Party could use its participation in the front to seize a central and possibly dominant position among the remnants of the political party movement in Nepal, in preparation for the time when it once again would have to compete with the Nepali Congress.

Recent Developments

China's aggression against India in October, 1962, had a drastic impact on the Nepali communists, on internal policy disputes as well as on attitudes toward the international situation. In the wake of the Sino-Indian conflict, the Nepali Congress leader-in-exile, Subarna Shamsher, terminated the terrorist campaign that had been launched against the royal regime nearly a year earlier. Pushpa Lal's group, which had been active in this campaign, though on an autonomous basis, found itself in a difficult situation. Pushpa Lal's policy had been based on the proposition that the overthrow of King Mahendra should be the primary objective of the CPN, even if the immediate result was a regime dominated by the Nepali Congress. With the collapse of the campaign, it was obvious that this policy was unrealistic and that these tactics had been unavailing.

Reportedly, a number of Party workers who had fled to India became disillusioned, returned to Nepal in 1963, and presumably made their peace with the Rayamajhi faction.[40] A serious rift also developed within the extremist group, which was split into two factions—one loyal to Pushpa Lal, and another which followed the leadership of Tulsi Lal Amatya, until then one of Pushpa Lal's most important supporters. Information on the split is sparse and unreliable but, according to a pro-Rayamajhi journal, there were a number of factors involved.[41] Pushpa Lal supported contacts with Bharat Shamsher (the ex-*Gorkha Parishad* leader who had fled to India and joined the Nepali Congress), which Tulsi Lal opposed. Pushpa Lal was now taking a pro-India position and, indeed, was accused of being a tool of the Dange, pro-Soviet, faction of the Indian Communist Party; Tulsi Lal followed a pro-China line. Pushpa Lal was demanding the restoration of the Parliament and the 1959 constitution; Tulsi Lal wanted only the reconvening of the Parliament. Another communist leader, D. P. Adhikari, was reported to have attempted to mediate the dispute between Pushpa Lal and Tulsi Lal at the instigation of the Indian communists, but to have failed.[42]

How reliable these reports may be is open to question, but it is apparent nevertheless that the challenge to the Rayamajhi leadership has receded in recent months. The proroyalist policy followed by the moderate faction has brought tangible rewards, including Rayamajhi's appointment to the prestigious if powerless *Raj Sabha* by King Mahendra, the appointment of an ex-member of the Party's Central Committee as an Assistant Minister, and the election of a communist as Deputy Speaker of the National Panchayat (i.e., Central Legislature). The CPN has also made some headway in its efforts to infiltrate the new political institutions the King has introduced. An estimated 15 per cent of the members of the National Panchayat are reportedly communists or their supporters,[43] and similar advances have also been achieved in the lower level Panchayats and national class organizations. There are some indications, however, that Rayamajhi's gradualist approach has not been popular with Party workers who are emotionally antimonarchical and action-oriented. The Party would also appear to have lost some of the appeal it formerly had with students and young intellectuals, who are no longer as prone to view the communists, or at least the domestic variety, as the wave of the future.

International Complications

From the preceding analysis it is apparent that internal factors have been primarily responsible for the serious divisions within the CPN, but that international developments, such as the Sino-Indian border conflict and the competition between Russia and China for influence within Asian communist movements, have also had a perceptible impact. It would probably be inaccurate to divide the CPN into intransigent pro-Soviet or pro-China factions, and expect to find any high degree of consistency in their statements and behavior. Like most other Asian parties, the CPN finds it extremely embarrassing to have to make a choice between the two communist giants. The position of the Nepali Party is made doubly difficult by the reality of a major Sino-Indian struggle for influence throughout the Himalayan area, which has now become inextricably enmeshed in the Sino-Soviet dispute and in the divisions of the Indian Communist Party into ostensibly pro-Soviet and pro-China factions.

With commendable caution, none of the major Nepali communist leaders have openly declared themselves in the quarrels dividing the communist world. Pushpa Lal and Tulsi Lal [44] have often been accused of pro-China leanings, but their position as exiles in India makes it imprudent for them to publicly align themselves with the Chinese camp and, indeed, it is doubtful whether Peking would openly welcome them into the fold. Despite its vocal advocacy of radical revolutionary tactics, Peking appears to have encouraged the CPN to follow a moderate, pro-royalist policy, which is more in conformity with its own intensive courting of the royal regime. It would probably be embarrassing to Peking to have a pro-China faction in the CPN that is also advocating armed revolution against King Mahendra.

The compulsion on Rayamajhi is not nearly so great, but an overtly pro-Soviet alignment might well alienate many Party members who are emotionally anti-Indian and, thus, staunchly pro-Chinese in sentiment. In the present context in Nepal, no clear line is drawn between pro-Soviet and pro-Indian positions. Rayamajhi has, therefore, assumed a neutral position in the Sino-Soviet fracas and has carefully refrained from commenting publicly on any of the issues in dispute. Rayamajhi's contacts have been mainly with Moscow, however, and presumably his wing of the CPN would line up with the Soviet Union if ever it became absolutely necessary to choose sides. The Rayamajhi group would appear to follow the Soviet Party's lead on such questions as the test-ban treaty, the proper method for settling disputes between communist parties, and the attitude to be adopted towards the national *bourgeoisie* in still unliberated areas.

Even more surprising, the CPN has cautiously and reluctantly adopted an attitude toward the Sino-Indian conflict that conforms essentially with Soviet objectives and policies. It would be presumptuous to maintain that the Soviet Union adheres to a pro-India position in this dispute, but there are indications that Moscow often prefers to bolster India's position in such areas as Nepal when the alternative is an enhancement of Chinese influence. It is probably not coincidental that the frenetic criticisms of India that were a normal feature of the pro-communist (Rayamajhi faction) press in Kathmandu have largely dis-appeared, and that scarcely concealed criticisms of China now appear with some regularity.[45] Blame for the Sino-Indian conflict, for instance, was placed on China, at least by implication, in one editorial:

> The Nepalis . . . know that if the Chinese had adopted a correct stand on the [Sino-Indian border dispute] and allowed the old slogan of "*Hindi-Chini-Bhai-Bhai*" to be echoed, the grave of the Indian reactionaries would long have been dug.[46]

In another rather startling editorial, it was argued that Indian policy toward Nepal was wrong in some respects and must be resisted, but that "we are resisting India's policy toward us by unnecessarily displaying our dependence on the Western powers *and China*." [Emphasis supplied.] [47] Such a statement would once have been impossible in a pro-communist paper. Speculation on the reason for its appearance now could range over a wide spectrum, but the attitude of the Soviet Union on these questions might well be the most plausible explanation.

The CPN in Retrospect

As noted before, the Nepali communists have not fared as well as might perhaps have been expected, even accepting the thesis that Nepal is still in a primitive stage of political consciousness and is not prepared for anything as modern and sophisticated as dialectic materialism. In this essay, it has been suggested that the inadequacies of the leadership and its division on what are essentially tactical rather than ideological questions (the dividing line is not always too precise) have torn the Party asunder, absorbing the workers' energies and attention.

But perhaps such factionalism inevitably stems from the nature of the leadership. For a Party that prides itself upon an egalitarian and cosmopolitan character, casteism, regionalism, and ethnocentricism seem to play a very important role. Virtually all of the top Party leaders are from the three most prosperous high-caste communities in Nepal—the Brahmans of the Terai and Kathmandu, Vaisya (i.e., commercial) castes of the Newar community of Kathmandu Valley, or the Chettri (i.e., Kshyatriya or warrior, now mostly landowning) castes of the Terai and lower hill areas.[48] The current divisions within the Party leadership are not drawn solely on caste lines, but it is impossible to avoid the impression that caste antagonisms, and particularly those between Brahman and Newar, are a contributing factor.

Such predominance of high-caste leaders is the general pattern within all political parties in Nepal. A list of the 20 most important political leaders in Nepal in 1959, for instance, gives this breakdown, by caste: 10 Brahmans; 3 Newar Vaisyas; 6 Chettris (including 3 Ranas); and 1 Christian (from Darjeeling). As in most of Asia, there is a high positive correlation between political leadership in Nepal and social and economic position and, perhaps more important, education. It was the high-caste communities who were in a position to obtain education and then, subsequently, participate in the anti-Rana movement which, after 1951, provided most of the top political leadership in Nepal.

Presumably, this pattern is in the process of transformation because of the broad expansion of educational opportunities and the gradual nationalization of politics, which has been further stimulated by political developments since December, 1960. One would expect such changes to become manifest in the CPN at an early stage, in view of its emphasis upon peasants and workers. And, indeed, communist leaders have claimed that the bulk of the Party's rank and file outside Kathmandu Valley is drawn from the "peasant class," though the term appears to include middle-landowning groups. The list of members of the CPN District Committees (*circa* 1959) indicates that in some areas, particularly in the western hills, recruits from local tribal communities are in a majority.[49] But these were usually areas in which the Party was weak and where, perforce, local leadership was left in local hands. In the real centers of Party strength—that is, Kathmandu and the Terai—local leadership would appear to have been the prerogative of the powerful high-caste communities which have long dominated these areas.

A survey of the CPN candidates in the 1959 general elections supports this conclusion. The Party ran candidates in 46 of the 109 constituencies. Most of these were concentrated in Kathmandu Valley, the Terai, and a few foothill constituencies,[50] presumably the areas in which Party structure was substantial enough to support candidacies. Of these 46 candidates, at least 15 were Brahmans, 10 were Newar Vaisyas, and 12 were Chettris. In addition, there was 1 Muslim, 3 members of local ethnic groups, and 5 candidates whose caste or ethnic affiliation cannot be determined from available data.[51] The small number of candidates from local ethnic groups, which often constitute a majority in their areas, is very striking. Even in the several eastern hill constituencies contested, where Limbus and Kirantis are in the majority, most of the Party's candidates were Brahmans, who in this area are often large landowners. In the Terai constituencies, most of the Party's twenty-seven candidates were Brahmans or Chettris; there was nary a peasant in the lot despite the long period in which the communist-dominated *Kisan Sangh* had been active in parts of this area. The Newar Vaisyas provided the candidates for Kathmandu Valley, as well as for a number of western hill constituencies in which Newars have long been the most prominent merchant community.

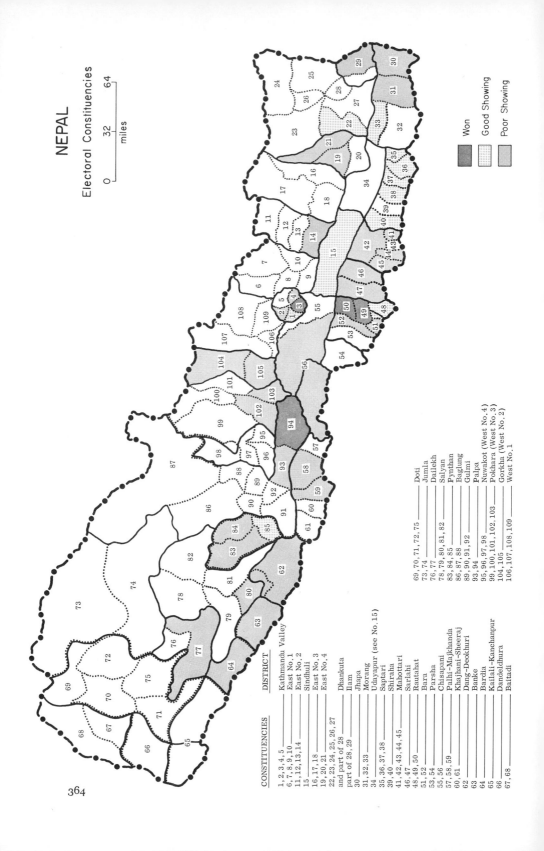

NEPAL

Electoral Constituencies

0 32 64
miles

████	Won
░░░░	Good Showing
▒▒▒▒	Poor Showing

CONSTITUENCIES   DISTRICT

1,2,3,4,5 ————————— Kathmandu Valley
6,7,8,9,10 ———————— East No. 1
11,12,13,14 ——————— East No. 2
15 ———————————————— Sindhuli
16,17,18 —————————— East No. 3
19,20,21 —————————— East No. 4
22,23,24,25,26,27
and part of 28 ————— Dhankuta
part of 28,29 ———————— Ilam
30 ————————————————— Jhapa
31,32,33 ————————————— Morang
34 ————————————————— Udayapur (see No. 15)
35,36,37,38 ——————— Saptari
39,40 ————————————— Shiraha
41,42,43,44,45 ——— Mahottari
46,47 ————————————— Sarlahi
48,49,50 —————————— Rautahat
51,52 ————————————— Bara
53,54 ————————————— Parsha
55,56 ————————————— Chisapani
57,58,59 —————————— Palhi–Majkhanda
60,61 ————————————— Khajhani–Sheeraj
62 ————————————————— Dang–Deokhuri
63 ————————————————— Banke
64 ————————————————— Bardia
65 ————————————————— Kailali–Kanchanpur
66 ————————————————— Dandeldhura
67,68 ————————————— Baitadi

69,70,71,72,75 ——— Doti
73,74 ————————————— Jumla
76,77 ————————————— Dailekh
78,79,80,81,82 ——— Salyan
83,84,85 —————————— Pynthan
86,87,88 —————————— Baglung
89,90,91,92 ————— Gulmi
93,94 ————————————— Palpa
95,96,97,98 ————— Nuwakot (West No. 4)
99,100,101,102,103 — Pokhara (West No. 3)
104,105 —————————— Gorkha (West No. 2)
106,107,108,109 ——— West No. 1

All this discussion points up another major weakness of the CPN—its failure to emerge as a truly national party with operational units in all areas of the country. Party activity is concentrated in Kathmandu and the Terai. There are units in some hill areas, but only in a few places such as Palpa and Dharan has the Party shown much strength. This is apparent not only from the 1959 election statistics, but also from a survey of communist agitational activities prior to 1960 which shows that they were effective only in Kathmandu and the Terai.

Reportedly, the communists have been able to augment their strength in the hill areas since the ouster of the Nepali Congress regime in December, 1960. The inauguration of local, district, and zonal *Panchayats* (or councils) has provided the CPN with a valuable channel for organizational activity which it has not been slow to exploit. In the elections to the National *Panchayat* in 1963, for instance, 18 communists were reported to have won seats; in contrast, 4 succeeded in the 1959 elections. Since all candidates ran as independents and not as Party members, it has not been possible as yet to obtain full information on the successful communist candidates. But the limited data available shows that, in 1963, the communists won in areas where they had been strong in 1959 as well as in several areas where they had run a rather poor second to the Nepali Congress in the first general elections. The communist victories in these areas are probably attributable to the thoroughness with which the royal regime has destroyed the Nepali Congress organization while leaving the CPN virtually untouched. From the long-range communist viewpoint, this may be one of the most hopeful signs for the future.

Another weakness in the Party, and one on which the communists lay considerable emphasis, is the alleged lack of adequate financing. In view of the nonavailability of even remotely reliable data, this question will not be discussed in detail. Bazaar rumors are, of course, numerous, but they are always unverifiable and often inconsistent. It is sufficient to note that all possible sources of support for a communist movement, including some rather improbable ones, have been cited as the financial backers of the Party. Within a three-month period in 1963, for instance, there were confidential reports that the Pushpa Lal group was being financed by: (1) the Dange faction of the CPI; (2) the West Bengal faction of the CPI; and (3) the Chinese embassy in India. Possibly all three rumors were false; or again, perhaps they were all accurate. In any case, they are all unverifiable.

One final comment on the composition and character of the leadership of the CPN may help explain its tactics and attitude. It has sometimes been asserted that membership in a communist party leads to social and intellectual isolation, including the severance of relations with family, caste, and non-Party friends. This may be the case in other parts of Asia, but it would not seem to be so in Nepal. Naturally, Party work absorbs the interests and time of the Party workers, but far from totally. One communist leader estimated that only one-fifth of the members are full-time workers, while the rest go on with their regular activities. Nor is the social and intellectual climate in Nepal such as to lead to expulsion from a family for anything so unessential as political beliefs. Indeed, one would suspect that it is a rare high-caste Kathmandu family that does not have at least one member in most major political camps, all coexisting with relative congeniality and insuring the family against total exclusion from the rewards of any conceivable political changes. Nor is it unusual to see communists participating in family, caste, and religious ceremonies. It might well be difficult for many communists to put into practice some of their "progressive" ideas about society and social relations, even were they in a position to do so.

The Present and Potential Strength of the CPN

If the protestations of the Rayamajhi wing of the CPN were taken seriously, there would be no reason to discuss the present situation of the Party. According to their official line, there have been communists in Nepal since December 26, 1960, *but there has not been a communist party*, since all political activity has been banned since that date and no good communist would consider violating one of His Majesty's ordinances. Objective conditions in Nepal, it is argued, are such that there is as yet no scope for an organized party. The most communists can do is to work to create conditions which would eventually permit the emergence of an organized communist movement. No one takes these protestations too seriously, of course, and even some of the CPN leaders prefer to ignore rather than deny the obvious contradictions between such statements and some of the readily apparent examples of Party activity.[52] To operate under and within the partyless *Panchayat* system, it is necessary to make this disclaimer; otherwise, communists who have attained positions in government and *Panchayat* institutions could be disbarred and imprisoned. All available evidence indicates, however, that the Party structure has been maintained intact since 1960 and that the principles of democratic centralism are still rigorously applied.

Any estimate of the size of the Party in Nepal must be purely speculative. Rayamajhi was reported to have claimed that there were 6,000 full members and 2,000 cadets in 1959.[53] In addition, large numbers of Nepalis were affiliated with the various front organizations at one time or another. The *Kisan Sangh*, for instance, once claimed over 125,000 members (probably a gross exaggeration), and the communist students' organization also had attracted wide support within the student community. These fronts served as valuable vehicles for the recruitment and training of potential members. The abolition of all class organizations in 1961, and the establishment of government-supervised organizations of peasants, labor, women, students, youth, children, and ex-servicemen may have disrupted the Party's recruiting tactic temporarily. But if the infiltration tactics employed by the CPN achieve any significant results, the new class organizations may eventually prove recruiting agencies as valuable to the Party as the fronts once were.

From the viewpoint of future development, possibly the most important objective of the CPN is the further isolation of the Nepali Congress and of the democratic-socialist political movement it represents. The CPN and the Nepali Congress are the only two parties in Nepal that have demonstrated any political potential, for they alone seem to have any conception of the role of parties in modern political systems. It was these two parties that contended for influence in social and class organizations prior to December, 1960, and it is often their party workers, now functioning as independents, who are involved in the new class organizations. A similar contest, though incipient and seldom verbalized, is also evident in the *Panchayats*, even though party politics are still officially in abeyance. When party politics once again emerge in Nepal, it is likely that the real struggle for power will lie between the Nepali Congress (or some similar organization) and the communists.

Obviously, the policies followed by King Mahendra since December, 1960, have given the CPN a decided advantage in its rivalry with the Nepali Congress. But it is probably still too early for dire predictions. Indeed, the communists may eventually find their proroyalist label an embarrassment, even if the existing political system demonstrates more survival capacity than the other experiments that have been tried since 1951. It is still questionable whether the communists constitute a serious menace to the present regime, or to any successor government that might be established in the next few years. It would appear to be too isolated and too fractionalized to offer a real alternative unless, of course, its rule were imposed on Nepal by an external power. In the current political context, it would be possible for a comparatively small but determined group to overthrow the regime and fasten its control on the country, *but only* if it had substantial support from the officer corps of the Army. Despite recurring reports that the CPN is earnestly endeavoring to establish a base of influence among the younger officers, there are no indications that they have met with any success as yet, and this is one group upon whom the King keeps a careful surveillance.

The greatest scope for communist advancement would still seem to lie in the infiltration of political and social institutions, and it is success

or failure in this sphere that will largely determine the Party's prospects
in the foreseeable future. If they are permitted an unchallenged opportunity to shape these institutions to their own purposes, which government policy has virtually assured them until recently, it is not unlikely
that the communists could emerge a few years hence as the most important and, perhaps, the only feasible alternative to the royal regime. But
there are some indications that the privileged position enjoyed by the
communists in this sphere of political activity may be coming to an end.
In a speech before the Narayani Zonal Assembly on April 13, 1964, the
Chairman of the Council of Ministers, Dr. Tulsi Giri, warned that disunity
among democratic elements had encouraged communist propaganda,
and declared that "since our country is a Monarchy, we face a great
danger from Communism." [54] One week later he repeated his warning
and called for unity among democratic elements to meet this danger.[55]

It was considered particularly significant that the Chairman made
such a statement before one of the *Panchayat* bodies. This was interpreted as an indication of the government's intention to combat communist activities and influence within these institutions. If this analysis should
prove correct, it would constitute a major change in government policy
that would undoubtedly have serious consequences for the Rayamajhi
faction of the Party. Dr. Giri's statement would gain added importance
if his appeal for unity among democratic elements included the Nepali
Congress, some of whose local workers were quietly released around
the beginning of 1964, after several years' imprisonment. Political align-
ments in Nepal once again seem to be in a transitional stage, and the
prospects that the CPN might dominate a significant segment of the
political spectrum would seem to have receded since 1963.

Communism Under High Atmospheric Conditions: The Party in Nepal

1. *Jatiya Andolanma Nepal Kamyunist Party* (*Contribution of the Nepal Communist Party in the National Movement*), Text of the Report of the General
Secretary at the First Conference of the Nepal Communist Party, September,
1951. Nepal Communist Party, Kathmandu, 1951, pp. 3-4.
2. Niranjan Govind Vaidya, Narayan Vilash, Nara Bahadur, Durga Devi and
Pushpa Lal (*Jatiya Andolanma Nepal Kamyunist Party, op. cit.,* p. 16). Of
these, only Pushpa Lal subsequently achieved a prominent position in the
Party's leadership. However, a number of other Nepalis, such as Man Mohan
Adhikari, were already active in communist circles in 1949, and apparently
were associated with the new party from the beginning.
3. *Ibid.,* p. 5. During this period the Indian Communist Party was still taking an
uncompromisingly hostile attitude toward the Nehru government.
4. See the May Day, 1951, call for a "People's Front" by the Party's Central Committee. *May Divash ko Avasarma Kamyunist Party ko Ghosanapatra* (*Manifesto of the Communist Party on the Occasion of May Day*), CPN, Kathmandu,
May, 1951, pp. 4-6.

5. *May Divash ko Avasarma Kamyunist Party ko Ghosanapatra, op. cit.*, pp. 4-6.

6. In addition to the all-Nepal Peace Council which had been founded in India, the communists set up the *Kisan Sangh* (Peasants' Organization), the *Mahila Sangh* (Womans' Organization), a Students' Federation, and several other similar organizations in 1951.

7. Letter from Pushpa Lal to Tanka Prasad, 4 July 1951, *Jagaran* (Nepali Weekly), July 12, 1951, p. 19.

8. *Jatiya Janatantrik Samyukta Morcha ko Ghosanapatra* (*Manifesto of the National Democratic United Front*), Kathmandu, November, 1951, pp. 3-5.

9. In 1954, for instance, a communist wedding "was the social event of Kathmandu." Both the groom and the bride were wanted by the police, but nothing was done to interfere with the widely publicized ceremonies. "Nepal in Ferment," *The Statesman* (Calcutta), November 27, 1954, p. 12, col. 4.

10. *Nepal Kamyunist Party ko Karyakram* [*Masauda*], (*Draft Program of the Nepal Communist Party*), CPN, Kathmandu, 1954.

11. *Text of the Resolution of the CPN Politburo Passed at its February 20, 1954, Meeting in Kathmandu* (unpublished typescript copy, circulated only to Party members).

12. It is difficult to ascertain the exact differences between the two All-Party Congresses (1954, 1957) and the two all-party conferences (1951, 1955). The 1954 Party constitution makes no provision for such conferences, and the legal basis for this procedure is unclear. Perhaps the regular biennial Party meetings are termed Congresses and special Party meetings called at the instigation of the Central Committee are called conferences.

13. Political Resolution of the Nepal Communist Party (adopted at the second all-party conference, November 22, 1955), CPN, Sharada Press, Bhagalpur, India, 1955; and *Party Karyakram ma Parivartam Kina?* (*Why Changes in the Party Program?*) CNP Central Committee, Azad Press, Banaras, India, 17 pp. (for Party members only).

14. *Party Karyakram ma Parivartam Kina? op. cit.*, pp. 16-17.

15. *Ibid.*, pp. 12-13.

16. The course of events at the Second Party Congress has never been made public. Apparently the Congress did not accept the draft presented to it by the Central Committee, and this political resolution was never published in its entirety, as were all previous resolutions. Indeed, the only excerpts from the draft appeared in several strongly critical articles published in the leftist-controlled weekly, *Masal*. See: A. N. Rimal and P. N. Rana, "P. B. Dastavejena Hamro Motaved" (Politburo Memorandum: Our Opinion), *Masal*, May 16, 1957, and Pushpa Lal Shrestha, "Prathan Mahadhevisar le pas Gariyeko Karyakram Prati Mero Vichard" (My Views on the Program Approved by the First Congress), *Masal*, May 30, 1957.

17. *Samaj* (Nepali Daily), May 29, 1957.

18. *Diyalo* (Nepali Daily), June 11, 1957.

19. *Naya Samaj* (Nepali Daily), December 26, 1957.

20. *Navayug* (Nepali Weekly), January 5, 1958.

21. Text of the Central Committee Resolution on the Royal Proclamation Adopted at the Central Committee Meeting at Janakpur on March 2, 1958. *Naya Samaj* (Nepali Daily), March 8, 1958.

22. Text of the Resolution Adopted at the Plenum Session of the Central Committee held at Gaur, Rautahat, from June 3-6, 1958. *Halkhabar* (Nepali Daily), June 13, 1958.

23. "Nepal Kamyunist Party ko Chunao Ghosanapatra" (Election Manifesto of the Nepal Communist Party), *Navayug*, November 26, 1958.

24. The history of the Third All-Nepal Party Congress suggests the difficulties im-

posed on the Party by the rift in the leadership. Initially scheduled for Biratnagar in November, 1958, the session was postponed until after the 1959 elections. Rescheduled for February, 1960, at Chitaun, the session was once again postponed, and a new date and locale—February, 1961, at Narayangarh—was announced. The royal coup of December, 1960, intervened before the Narayangarh Congress could be held, however, and a plenary session of the Central Committee was held at Darbhanga, India, in March, 1961, instead.

25. None of the 5 members of the Politburo and only 3 members of the 17-man Central Committee were arrested in the three months following the December coup.

26. It has been charged that the well-publicized division of the CPN's leadership into pro- and antimonarchy factions is nothing but a gigantic hoax, deliberately contrived by the leaders of both factions to guarantee the communists maximum maneuverability no matter what the trend of political developments. While this possibility cannot be discounted, there is no substantive evidence to support it. The issues dividing the CPN, and the policy and tactical arguments advanced, are similar to those disrupting most Asian communist parties today. It is also questionable whether the communist leadership in Nepal is sufficiently subtle and unimpassioned to employ such sophisticated tactics for an extended period, particularly since their own Party workers could not be made privy to the game and would be as badly misled as their political opponents and the royal regime.

27. Source materials on the Darbhanga session of the Nepal Communist Party are both meager and unreliable. The most detailed account of the proceedings was published in the pro-Communist Nepali weekly, *Samiksha* (March 23, 1961). The reliability of this source is somewhat lessened by the fact that it reflects the views of the Rayamajhi faction of the party. Shorter interesting comments on the Darbhanga session can also be found in: *Halkhabar,* March 29 and 22; *Dainik Nepal,* March 27, 1961; and *Nepal Samachar,* March 22, 1961.

28. *Nepal Sandesh,* June 28, 1961.

29. *Motherland,* July 9, 1961.

30. *Pravartak,* July 12, 1961. It is interesting to note that the day after Rayamajhi's arrest, a leader of the extremist faction, Tulsi Lal Amatya, told reporters in Darjeeling that the communists had divided Nepal into five zones and that he had been given the task of organizing the revolution in the eastern districts. (*Nepali,* July 9, 1961.)

31. P. N. Chowdhury, the General Secretary of the Nepali Congress, reported that the Pushpa Lal group had "assured us that it would soon join the movement." (*Nepal Today,* I, No. 9 [April 1, 1962], 93.)

32. Statement by Kamar Shah on behalf of the Central Secretariat, *The Himalayan Sentinel,* April 16, 1962, p. 4.

33. For one of the most complete reports on this meeting, see: C. Kesari Prasai, "Nepali Communists in Wilderness," *Janata* (Journal of the Praja Socialist Party of India), XVII, No. 23 (July 1, 1962), 4:1-3.

34. *Nepal Samachar,* June 1, 1962.

35. As all parties are banned in Nepal, there are no longer any official party organs. However, the *Samiksha,* a weekly published by a former member of the CPN, adheres closely to the policy positions taken by the Rayamajhi faction of the Party. There is, of course, no way of determining whether this journal is actually serving as a Party mouthpiece on any one question. In this essay, we assume that it is unless there is evidence to the contrary.

36. Madan Mani Dikshit, "Rashtriya Prajatantric Yekta" ("National Democratic Unity"), *Samiksha,* August 23, 1962. It should be noted, however, that at least a year and a half earlier, communist leaders had discussed the necessity of a united front that would exclude the Nepali Congress. The *Statesman,* March 13, 1961, p. 6, col. 5.

37. *Samiksha,* October 14, 1962.

38. *Ibid.*

39. *Ibid.*

40. According to the official journal of the Nepali Congress, the CPN-in-exile National Executive had brought out a booklet entitled *Tatkalik Karyaniti* (Short-term Program) in mid-1963 which in essence accepted the Rayamajhi thesis on tactics and instructed Party workers to return to Nepal. No copy of this publication has been available, nor has this report been vertified from other sources. Moreover, it was at this time that Pushpa Lal published a pamphlet which was widely distributed in Nepal and which was still bitterly critical of the royal regime. Perhaps the Short-term Program represented the views of Tulsi Lal Amatya, who had recently succeeded Pushpa Lal as General Secretary of the CPN-in-exile. ("Communist *Volte* Face," *Nepal Today,* II, No. 19, September 1, 1963, 178.)

41. *Samiksha* (Nepali Weekly), July 31, 1963.

42. *Samiksha* (Nepali Weekly), August 28, 1963. D. P. Adhikari, who had previously maintained a position between the Rayamajhi and Pushpa Lal factions, fled to India in the first half of 1963.

43. *The Statesman* (Calcutta), April 3, 1963.

44. In this respect, it is interesting to note that Tulsi Lal Amatya has consistently been a supporter of what in Nepal are considered Maoist views on tactics and ideology. Tulsi Lal's principal activity in the post-1951 period was in the sphere of peasant organization—the *Kisan Sangh*—rather than within the regular Party structure. He has reportedly always taken the position that, given Nepal's peculiar conditions, the peasantry alone could provide a revolutionary potential. On this point he has usually found himself in disagreement with most other communist leaders in Nepal, who have an urban origin, are intellectually oriented, and who accept the more orthodox Marxian position that the working class, supported by the peasantry, must be the instrument of revolutionary change.

45. The *Naya Samay,* a procommunist weekly (not to be confused with the Nepali daily of the same name) that is not affiliated with the Rayamajhi faction, has maintained its anti-Indian, pro-Chinese position—often publishing handouts from the Chinese embassy as news items. The source of financial support for this journal is an open secret in Kathmandu.

46. *Samiksha* (Kathmandu), February 10, 1963.

47. *Samiksha,* October 17, 1963.

48. Only one person from outside these three groups—a member of a well-to-do Kathmandu Muslim family—has as yet achieved a prominent position in the CPN hierarchy.

49. This would not necessarily mean that these members were drawn from the lower economic stratum, however, since there are many landowning families within these tribal communities.

50. See Electoral Constituency Map. The communist candidate in No. 5 constituency, in Kathmandu Valley, withdrew in favor of Tanka Prasad Acharya, the Party's old ally and benefactor. This turned out to be a mistake, since Tanka Prasad lost badly, while the CPN candidate might well have won.

51. With some exceptions, the caste identification of the candidates has been based upon their names, a procedure which, among the highly structured high-caste groups in Nepal, is a relatively simple proposition. Unfortunately, in the name of egalitarianism, some Nepali communists have dropped the use of caste names (a process that must be sternly resisted by social scientists). The five unknowns on this list belong to this category, though from their given names it is probable that they were all Brahmans or Chettris.

52. In one interview, a prominent communist leader in Kathmandu commenced

our discussion with the usual statement that the Party had been disbanded in December, 1960. With a barely perceptible pause, he then went on to discuss some of the Central Committee's plenary sessions that had been held since that date.

53. *Samiksha,* June 11, 1963.
54. *Dainik Nepal,* April 15, 1964.
55. *Swatantra Samachar,* April 23, 1964.

Selected Bibliography

'A Nepali,' "Political Parties in Nepal," *Economic Weekly,* July 19, 1952, pp. 736-39.

Chakravarty, Nikhil, "Nepal's Unfinished Revolution," *New Age,* VI, No. 10 (October, 1957), 54-64.

Mihaly, Eugene, "The Situation in Nepal," *The World Today,* XIX, No. 10 (October, 1963), 431-39.

"Nepal in Ferment," *The Statesman* (Calcutta), November 26-December 3, 1954. A seven-part article.

Red'ko, I. B., *Nepal Posle Vtoroi Mirovdi Voiny. Antifeodol'noe I Antiimperialisticheskol Dvizhenie, 1945-1956. (Nepal After the Second World War. The Anti-Feudal and Anti-Imperialist Movement, 1945-1956).* Moscow: Izdatel'stov Vostochnoi Literatury, 1960. 267 pp.

Rose, Leo E.: *Nepal: Government and Politics.* Human Relations Area Files, New Haven, 1956. 360 pp.

"The Soviet Union and Nepal," *Central Asian Review,* X, No. 3 (1962), 294-96.

The Ceylon
Communist Party

Competition for Marxist Supremacy

Robert N. Kearney

The Ceylon Communist Party is not a powerful force
in the politics of Ceylon. Its membership is small,
its electoral successes have been few, and there
has been little change in its strength since independence in 1948.
The Ceylon Communist Party is one of three Marxist
parties advocating the revolutionary reconstruction
of Ceylonese society and competing for scarce urban-labor
and left-wing votes in Ceylon. The Ceylonese communists suffer
from the unique humiliation of facing a much stronger
Trotskyist party, which regularly wins between two
and three times the popular vote of the Communist Party.
Nonetheless, the Communist Party has been a vigorous
and conspicuous participant in Ceylonese politics. The efforts

election. Their share of votes remained constant in 1952 and declined in 1956. In March, 1960, with the three Marxist parties presenting a record number of candidates, the left vote edged up to about one-fourth of the total. At the election four months later, with the number of left candidates sharply reduced, the Marxists received only 13 per cent of the total vote, the smallest proportion they have ever received (see Table 1).

Table 1

PER CENT OF POPULAR VOTE WON BY MARXIST PARTIES

	1947	1952	1956	March, 1960	July, 1960
Communist Party	4	6 [a]	4	5	3
Lanka Sama Samaja Party	17 [b]	13	10	10	7
Mahajana Eksath Peramuna [c]	—	—	—	11	3

[a] Vote cast for the Communist Party–VLSSP united front.

[b] Includes two factions separately contesting the election.

[c] Called the Viplavakari Lanka Sama Samaja Party until 1959. The VLSSP fought the 1952 election in a united front with the Communist Party and the 1956 election as a part of the *Mahajana Eksath Peramuna* coalition.

Although there has never been a serious prospect of a Marxist parliamentary majority (see Table 2), the cooperation of the left with the SLFP in the elections of 1956 and July, 1960, seemed to be critical to the defeat of the UNP.

Communist Leadership and Organization

The Marxist leadership in Ceylon, as in most of the former colonial areas of Asia, is drawn from the urban, Westernized bourgeois intelligentsia. The left leaders of Ceylon are mostly low-country Sinhalese [5] of wealthy families, who have been educated at British universities or Inns

Table 2

NUMBER OF PARLIAMENTARY SEATS WON BY MARXIST PARTIES

	1947	1952	1956	March, 1960	July, 1960
Communist Party	3	4 [a]	3	3	4
Lanka Sama Samaja Party	15 [b]	9	14	10	12
Mahajana Eksath Peramuna	—	—	—	10	3

Note: Ninety-five seats in the Ceylon House of Representatives were at stake in the 1947, 1952, and 1956 elections. Prior to the two elections of 1960, the number of elective seats was increased to 151.

[a] Seats won by the Communist Party–VLSSP united front. One seat was captured by a VLSSP member and three by communists.

[b] Includes two factions contesting the election separately.

of Court. Several are respected far beyond the ranks of their own parties for their intellectual brilliance and their devoted efforts and personal sacrifices on behalf of the common man.

From its founding, the Communist Party has been dominated by two men, Pieter Keuneman and Dr. S. A. Wickremasinghe. Keuneman has been General Secretary of the Party since its inception, except for approximately one year in 1948 and 1949. Dr. Wickremasinghe was a principal founder of the Lanka Sama Samaja Party and led the fight against LSSP condemnation of the Third International. After his expulsion from the LSSP, he was instrumental in organizing the United Socialist Party and the Communist Party, and has been President of the Communist Party since its establishment.

Pieter Keuneman is usually considered to be the most powerful leader in the Communist Party. While Dr. Wickremasinghe occupies an important position as the party's founder and a veteran Marxist, Keuneman apparently has provided the vigorous leadership. Born in 1917, Keuneman is about a decade younger than the other Marxist leaders. He is a member of a prominent family of the small Burgher community of Dutch and Ceylonese extraction and his father was a respected judge during the colonial period. Like many of the leaders of the left, Keuneman had a brilliant record as a student in Britain. He won Bachelor's and Master's degrees from Cambridge University and was elected president of the Cambridge Union. He worked briefly as a journalist in London and Colombo before turning his full attention to politics. The only communist to serve continuously in Parliament since 1947, Keuneman is a skillful debater and has probably made more frequent and effective use of the question period than any other Member of Parliament. He has been elected to Parliament from the three-member Colombo Central constituency in five consecutive elections, and served for a dozen years on the Colombo Municipal Council. His loss of that seat is the only election defeat of his political career. His consistently strong electoral appeal is often attributed to his tireless service to constituents. Always accessible, he performs innumerable personal services, ranging from mediation with the police or bureaucracy over minor matters to bringing individual grievances to the attention of Parliament. It is freely conceded that few M.P.s cultivate a constituency with more care.

Dr. Wickremasinghe, a member of a very wealthy and prominent family from the Southern Province, is a medical doctor who studied and engaged in student politics at the University of London. He served briefly in the public service, but lost his post in a reduction of force and entered private medical practice. In 1931, he was elected to the colonial legislature. When he failed to win reelection in 1936 he returned to Britain, where he apparently developed ties with British communists. Many years later, he attributed his radicalism to witnessing the stern suppression of communal disturbances by British and Indian troops in 1915, when he was 13 years old.[6] Although defeated in several earlier attempts to enter Parliament, he has served as an M.P. since 1956. In 1952, his British-born wife was elected to Parliament from his home constituency, which he now represents.

Other communist leaders have attracted little public attention. M. G. Mendis, a veteran communist worker and one of the Party's founders, has been a principal organizer of the communist trade union movement. Communist activity among the Tamil-speaking people of the north was organized by P. Kandiah, a former University of Ceylon librarian, who in 1956 became the only Marxist ever to be elected from a constituency containing a majority of the usually conservative Ceylon Tamils. Kandiah died in 1961, at less than 50 years of age. Two other communists were elected to Parliament in July, 1960. One, a member of the Wickremasinghe family from the Southern Province, has been active in local government, rural development societies, and the Communist Youth League in the south. The other, elected from a constituency at the edge of Colombo, is a young lawyer and a lecturer in political science at a Colombo Buddhist university. In 1964, he resigned from the Communist Party in order to join a coalition government formed by the SLFP and LSSP. Party workers and trade union organizers apparently are sometimes drawn from the lower middle-class clerical employees of the public service and private business firms and skilled workers in trades such as printing. However, the top leadership of the Communist Party is predominantly of substantial middle-class professional and intellectual background.

The Ceylon Communist Party is organized along typical Leninist lines. Democratic centralism, rigorous party discipline, and severe condemnation of factionalism [7] help to insure tight control of the Party apparatus by the leadership. Effective control appears to be concentrated in the hands of the General Secretary, the only officer whose powers and duties are defined in the Party constitution.[8] It is to the General Secretary that Party members apparently have looked for guidance on major questions of policy.[9] The National Congress formally is the most powerful party organ. The Congress which met in 1964 was the seventh to be held in 21 years. Between Congresses, control is vested in the Central Committee, which appoints the Party officers, a Political Bureau, and a Secretariat; between meetings of the Central Committee, plenary power is lodged in the Politbureau.[10] Branches, which have replaced cells as the basic organizational unit, are formed on the basis of place of work or residence, the latter reportedly more numerous. According to Party rules, as few as three members may form a branch, but branches are said usually to contain a minimum of ten members.[11]

Although the constitution describes an elite cadre of activists schooled in Party history and Marxist-Leninist doctrine,[12] the 1960 Party Congress called for a "transformation to a mass Communist Party" [13] and, in 1961, the Party claimed the recruitment of 3,000 new members and the creation of more than 60 new branches.[14] In 1962, the Party claimed a membership of about 19,000,[15] but estimates by informed outside sources put the membership at 3,000 to 5,000. More than one-third of the total membership at the time of the 1960 Congress had reportedly joined since the preceding Congress in 1955.[16]

The communist-controlled All-Ceylon Federation of Communist and Progressive Youth Leagues, with a relatively large (claimed to be more than 25,000) but weakly disciplined and impermanent membership, extends the scope of communist activity and influence beyond the Party membership. In 1961, a communist women's organization was created. Another vehicle for enhancing Party influence is the carefully cultivated communist trade-union movement. The Ceylon Trade Union Federation, containing 20 unions having a total membership of more than 40,000,[17] is under communist control as are several unaffiliated government employees' unions. Other organizations which are subject to varying degrees of Party control have been used extensively in disseminating communist and anti-Western propaganda. The Ceylon Peace Council is probably the principal organization through which communists have attacked Western stands on nuclear weapons and nuclear tests.[18] The Afro-Asian Solidarity Association and the Lanka-Soviet Friendship League have also frequently served as forums at which communist leaders speak on peace and anti-imperialism.

Sources of Marxist Support

Marxist political strength is heavily concentrated in the relatively urbanized and modernized southwest corner of the island. Almost all the parliamentary seats won by Marxists since 1947 have been along the southwest coast, from Colombo to the southern tip of the island, and inland from Colombo toward the Kandyan highlands.[19] Communist Party support, as reflected in parliamentary elections, has been even more narrowly concentrated. All but one parliamentary seat won by the Party in the five elections since 1947 have been in Colombo or in a small area of the Southern Province near the south tip of Ceylon. The Party won three seats in each of the first four elections and four in July, 1960. Pieter Keuneman has been elected consistently from the Colombo Central constituency and, in July, 1960, a seat in the Colombo suburbs went to the communists. In each election except that of 1956, two seats in the south were captured by communist candidates. The only constituency outside the Colombo area or the pocket in the south ever carried by a communist was the constituency at the extreme north of the island, carried by Kandiah in 1956. It is believed that caste tensions and the tireless activity of the communist candidate combined to produce this victory.

The geographical concentration of Marxist strength is attributable to a number of factors. The southwest is the area of the longest and most extensive contact with the West. Literacy is appreciably higher there than in any other area of the island except the Northern Province. The Colombo District contains 40 per cent of all persons on the island literate in English. Urbanization has proceeded the furthest. The Western Province, which includes the Colombo District, contains 62 per cent of the island's urban population.[20]

Ceylon's small nonagricultural labor force is largely in the southwest. Since before the founding of the LSSP, the Marxists have expended tremendous energy on trade-union organization, and trade-union activity was the principal means by which the bourgeois intellectuals of the left gained political experience and won a popular following. Their greatest success has been among the urban workers. Marxist efforts to organize and win support among laborers on tea and rubber estates have met with only limited success, although an estate workers' union is the largest of the trade unions affiliated with the communists' Ceylon Trade Union Federation and some leaders of Indian Tamil estate workers' organizations are ideologically close to the Marxists, often cooperating with them. Ironically, the nationalization of commercial enterprises since 1956 has inhibited the political activity of some of the Marxists' most militant supporters. Nationalization has transformed a significant portion of the urban labor force into employees of the government who are prohibited (although not always effectively) from participating in politics. It is not surprising that the Marxists passionately demand political rights for government employees, particularly in the nationalized industries and the schools taken over by the government in 1960.

Except in a few scattered localities, the Marxists have generally displayed slight inclination or ability to forge effective links with the rural population. The communists have recently claimed to be taking steps to contact the peasantry, but their efforts seem to have been perfunctory and productive of few results.[21]

The relatively large public bureaucracy, situated principally in Colombo, has provided the Marxists with an important source of support. Marxist influence is particularly strong among the clerical employees, who occupy an unenviable position in the rigid class structure of the bureaucracy.[22] Their English-language secondary education, urbanization, and contacts with modernization seemingly have produced major frustrations with existing social conditions and aspirations for a living standard which their modest salaries will not accommodate. This may help to explain why the government clerks are among the most volatile groups in politics and labor relations.

Marxist hostility toward the social *status quo* and advocacy of the destruction of caste distinctions have enabled the left to profit politically from protests against the caste system. Minority castes are particularly strong and articulate along the coastal belt extending south from Colombo. Caste protest in Ceylon usually takes the form of opposition to the social and political domination of the Goyigama caste, which is both the highest in status and the most numerous of the Sinhalese castes. The United National Party is commonly believed to be Goyigama-dominated. As the Marxists were virtually the only organized opposition to the UNP immediately after independence and have continued to be the major UNP opposition in the urban and semiurban areas of the Southwest, caste-protest votes ordinarily have gone to the left parties.[23] The caste element in Marxist strength is reflected in a disproportionate representation of minority castes in the leadership of the Marxist parties. Communist strength in the Southern Province probably has a strong caste element. Communist leadership in the south is largely of the Durāva caste which, along with certain other minority castes, is relatively numerous there.

A major element in Marxist strength is the personal esteem and respect accorded individual Marxist leaders. The support the Marxists receive in the villages of the southwest is often attributed to the personal appeal of their leaders and candidates. Nearly all of the prominent Marxists are themselves low-country Sinhalese from this area, many of whom belong to locally prominent families. Regular communist successes in the Southern Province are commonly credited to the local respect accorded to the Wickremasinghe family and to Dr. Wickremasinghe personally.

It is also in the southwest that the Marxists have devoted their principal organizational and ideological efforts since the origin of the left movement nearly three decades ago. Many leading Marxists have been active in local government in the area, especially in Colombo. Dr. N. M. Perera, the LSSP leader, was Mayor of Colombo briefly. Keuneman and his wife have both served on the Colombo Municipal Council. Of the four communists in Parliament since 1960, three have been members of local government bodies.

While the Marxists have been unable to win a strong island-wide following, the concentration of their strength in the strategic Colombo area gives them an element of extraparliamentary political power. May

Day rallies, which are now held by nearly all Ceylonese parties and have become major demonstrations of strength, repeatedly reveal the strong position of the Marxists in the Colombo area. The parades and mass meetings of the Marxists, particularly the LSSP, completely overshadow the efforts of the Sri Lanka Freedom Party and the United National Party, the strength of which is dispersed through the countryside. Marxist influence in the southwest was demonstrated dramatically in 1953, when a left-organized hartal protesting an increase in the price of subsidized rice resulted in an almost total disruption of transportation, communications, and many other activities in the area. Disorder and the destruction of property spread rapidly, and at least 10 lives were lost.

Marxist trade-union strength in the Colombo vicinity has been evident in a number of bitter labor disputes. Strikes in the Colombo harbor by Marxist-led trade unions, particularly those commencing in December, 1961, and December, 1963, demonstrated the vulnerability of the Ceylonese economy to determined trade-union action at critical points. In both cases, military personnel had to be used to maintain essential harbor operations. However, the trade-union following of the Marxists has not always proved to be a pliant and effective political weapon. Most of the strikes which have plagued Ceylon in recent years have been produced by wage demands and workers' grievances, and Marxist and other trade unions have been competing to demonstrate the greater militancy of their leadership. A frankly political strike in March, 1959, by LSSP trade unions, protesting against a public security bill before Parliament, was opposed by the trade unions of the communists and the VLSSP and was not a success.[24] In 1961, when the Sama Samajists and the communists were avoiding opposition to the SLFP government, disputes involving Marxist trade unions erupted in the nationalized bus service and cargo-handling facilities of Colombo harbor. The Marxist leaders sought to support the workers' demands while attempting to prevent a political rupture with the government,[25] but the bitterness engendered by the 51-day harbor strike contributed to altering the attitude of the Marxists toward the government. Thus, rather than using trade-union support to win political objectives, the Marxist leaders found themselves drawn into an altered political position by circumstances their trade unions created.

The Communists and Party Policy

In the view of Ceylonese communists, Ceylon is passing through the first of two revolutionary stages, the stage of national-bourgeois revolution which must precede the second stage of socialist revolution. Therefore, the Party has sought limited demands which have, to a large extent, coincided with the goals of other parties and scant attention has ever been devoted to ultimate objectives of the Party or the precise path to be taken for their attainment.

The communist program of immediate aims has not varied greatly. Common elements are: (1) a foreign policy of independence from the West and support for peace and anticolonialism; (2) economic development and industrialization, particularly with communist-bloc aid; (3) limited nationalization, with emphasis on the nationalization of foreign holdings; (4) modest workers' benefits and labor and welfare legislation; (5) assistance to the rural poor and tenant cultivators; (6) reform of the public service, armed forces, and police; and (7) recognition of nationalist aspirations.[26]

A major problem confronting the communists, and other Marxists as well, has been the rapid growth of Sinhalese nationalism and mass political consciousness since independence. This has been manifested, particularly, in the official-language controversy. Initially, the official language issue arose as a protest against the privileged position of the English-educated classes; but, as sentiment developed to declare Sinhalese the sole official language, it became a contest between the Sinhalese-speaking majority and the Tamil-speaking minority.

The Marxists had first introduced the language issue into politics during the late 1930's in the form of demands that certain administrative matters be handled in the vernacular languages. When the language issue later arose as an explosive and emotional force involving ethnic group status and solidarity, however, the Marxists were caught completely unprepared. The small VLSSP quickly adopted a Sinhalese-only position, but the communists and Sama Samajists continued to insist on both Sinhalese and Tamil as official languages. Both parties lost members through desertions and expulsions produced by the language issue, and Marxist meetings were broken up by Sinhalese-only enthusiasts during the 1956 election campaign. The communists entered the 1956 election committed to a policy of official recognition for both languages. However, they formed an electoral alliance with the Sri Lanka Freedom Party, which was pledged immediately to make Sinhalese the only official language.

By 1960, the Communist Party had succumbed to Sinhalese-only pressure and shifted to a language policy more in tune with the aspirations of the Sinhalese majority. The 1960 communist election manifesto urged that Sinhalese "be the state language," but that the use of Tamil in administration and education in the Tamil-speaking areas be allowed.[27] Later that year, the Party was warned to "guard against the danger of running ahead of the level of understanding of the masses at any given stage."[28]

Communist confusion on the language issue was evident at the 1960 Party Congress. The communists confessed that on this issue a "sectarian attitude" had infected the Party "and especially its leadership." Consequently, "when the struggle over the official language matured in 1956, the Party endorsed wrong slogans and adopted incorrect tactics which temporarily isolated it from the developing movement." [29] The judgment of the Sama Samajists that the influence of their party declined after 1956, principally because of the language issue,[30] might apply as well to the Communist Party.

Unity of Progressives and Ceylonese Foreign Policy

It is the question of tactics rather than policy that has absorbed the Ceylonese communists. Communist literature and speeches abound with tactical discussions and exhortations to tactical moves and contain little discussion of policy, immediate or ultimate. It thus appears that the operative goals of the Communist Party can be determined with more accuracy by examining their tactical positions than by emphasizing their policy pronouncements.

The most consistently voiced tactical objective of the Ceylon Communist Party, since soon after independence, has been the unity of all progressive forces. All other communist objectives, immediate or long-range, have seemingly been subordinated to this end. At independence, early in 1948, the communists were still collaborating with the "bourgeois" politicians who had organized the United National Party and formed the first government of independent Ceylon. Later that year, however, the communist line abruptly changed to one of total opposition to the *compradore bourgeoisie* of the UNP, to whom the communists claimed the British imperialists had handed political power. With the change of line, Pieter Keuneman temporarily relinquished the post of party General Secretary. The shift in tactics was confirmed by the 1950 Party Congress, which issued a call for "unity of the working class and the national-bourgeois forces to defeat the reactionary alliance between imperialism and the UNP," [31] a theme that has been repeated subsequently with monotonous regularity.

In 1951, the Sri Lanka Freedom Party was founded by S. W. R. D. Bandaranaike. Although the SLFP stressed language and religious appeals, it claimed to be a socialist party seeking equality of opportunity and a classless society.[32] It was also anti-UNP. To the communists, the SLFP clearly represented the national *bourgeoisie*,[33] and for a dozen years, the communists insistently demanded united action by the Marxists and the SLFP. Relations between the communists and the other Marxists were usually stormy and acrimonious, and when conflicts arose between cooperation with the SLFP and with other Marxist parties, the communists generally opted for cooperation with the SLFP. In the 1952 election, for example, the Communist Party-VLSSP united front supported SLFP candidates, even against the candidates of the LSSP.[34] Nevertheless, over the years, the communists seem to have attempted to keep open the possibility of cooperation with both the national-bourgeois and Marxist groups. The Communist Party has never totally abandoned its proletarian claims, but has sought simultaneously to capture all "progressive" and "national" support. This unreconciled duality was evident in the Party's 1960 election manifesto, which claimed: "The Communist Party is based on the working class and defends the interests of all progressive sections of the people. . . . It combines the principles of scientific socialism with all that is progressive in national traditions." [35]

Prior to the 1956 election, the communists, Sama Samajists, and Bandaranaike's SLFP agreed to a no-contest pact, to avoid fighting for the same seats and thus splitting the anti-UNP vote. A short time later, the SLFP joined with several much smaller groups, including the apostate Trotskyists of the VLSSP, in the *Mahajana Eksath Peramuna* coalition, which scored a surprise victory over the UNP. The Sama Samajists and communists both extended support to the MEP government formed by Bandaranaike. Although the Sama Samajists soon broke away, the communists continued to support the government until the MEP coalition broke up in 1959, a few months before Bandaranaike was assassinated.

Before the March, 1960, election, the communists sought unsuccessfully to reach agreement on cooperation with the LSSP and the SLFP. Still, they assisted in the defeat of a minority UNP government formed after the March election and promised their support if an SLFP government was formed.[36] When a second election was called for July, 1960, the communists again joined the Sama Samajists and the SLFP in a no-contest pact. The July election produced an SLFP parliamentary majority and Sirimavo Bandaranaike, widow of S. W. R. D. Bandaranaike, became Prime Minister. The Communist Party pledged unqualified support to this government,[37] while the LSSP, internally divided on its attitude toward the government, cautiously offered "critical support" which proved to be of short duration. For some time, the communists urged the LSSP to support the government to prevent the return to power of the UNP. By 1962, however, the communists apparently had become disenchanted with the SLFP government, and their tactics shifted to emphasis on unity with the other left parties.

It seems clear that communist support of the SLFP was closely related to their marked preference for its foreign policy. The UNP governments, in power from independence to 1956, generally maintained close and friendly relations with the West and did not disguise their hostility toward communism. A defense agreement provided for British military assistance, if needed, and allowed the British to maintain naval and air bases in Ceylon. D. S. Senanayake, Ceylon's first Prime Minister, professed to see "mounting evidence that Communism is determined to dominate the world by force and that the only hope of maintaining peace with freedom lies in the rapid increase of the combined strength of the free nations." [38] A later UNP Prime Minister delivered a scathing attack on Soviet imperialism at the 1955 Bandung Conference of Afro-Asian states. [39]

With the creation of the SLFP, an alternative foreign policy was presented. Neutralism, the maintenance of diplomatic and economic relations with the communist bloc, and avoidance of security ties with the West have been basic elements of SLFP policy. The S. W. R. D. Bandaranaike government came to power in 1956 pledged to nonalignment, friendly relations with all countries, and the removal of British bases and military personnel. [40] The new Prime Minister quickly arranged for the liquidation of the bases and established diplomatic relations with the Soviet Union and Communist China. Later, diplomatic relations were established with several communist regimes in eastern Europe, and trade and economic assistance agreements were negotiated with the Soviet Union, Communist China, and other communist states. The SLFP government formed in 1960 was committed to continuing the neutralist foreign policy of Bandaranaike. [41]

The Communist Party has been lavish in its praise of SLFP foreign policy, hailing the shift in Ceylon's foreign relations as the most significant achievement of the change of governments in 1956. The Communist Party organ declared:

> The defeat of the UNP in 1956 marked an important change in the role that Ceylon played in world affairs. As a result of the election victory of the late Mr. Bandaranaike, Ceylon ceased to be a reserve of imperialism and its war plans, as she was under UNP rule, and became an active force fighting for world peace and against imperialism and colonialism. [42]

The importance attached to foreign policy by the Ceylonese communists was indicated by a statement on the main tasks of the Party adopted at the 1960 Congress. [43] The first task cited was: "To strengthen still further Ceylon's contribution to the fight for peace and against colonialism and to develop and consolidate its relations with the socialist and anti-imperialist countries." The remaining three tasks were concerned with organizational and tactical matters, and could be interpreted as instrumental to the completion of the first task.

Shifts in Tactics

The communist tactics based on close support of the SLFP were subjected to considerable pressure in 1962, forcing the Party into its first major shift in alignment in a dozen years. In their support for the SLFP the communists faced a growing problem. Although the Sirimavo Bandaranaike government maintained its neutralist foreign policy,[44] in domestic affairs it progressively alienated the urban population and trade unions and incurred the wrath of the other Marxist parties. Apparently the communists decided that at least a temporary alteration of tactics was necessary to prevent the Party's isolation from all potential allies and the loss of urban and trade-union support. The communists did not abandon their desire for a broad national front of progressives, but their attention shifted from the SLFP leadership to its rank and file, and priority was transferred from cooperation with the SLFP to unity with the other Marxist parties.

The series of strikes by Marxist trade unions in nationalized enterprises in December, 1961, and January, 1962, created a confrontation between the left and the government. Troops were utilized to operate the strike-bound harbor of Colombo, and Mrs. Bandaranaike denounced the Marxists, charging that the strikes were politically motivated.[45] A one-day general strike was called to protest the use of military personnel in the harbor. The mounting tensions abruptly receded on the discovery of a plot by military and police officers to overthrow the government. Communist leader Pieter Keuneman responded: "The main job before the Government and the Left, whatever may be their differences, is to get together and jointly smash this reactionary conspiracy of foreign and local vested interests."[46] However, lingering communist concern with the issues posed during the strikes was reflected in a Party statement for the following May Day. While renewing the usual plea for unity between the SLFP and the Marxists, the statement urged that the government reject "both the hostile attitude to the trade unions and the dependence on the armed forces which dominated its policies immediately prior to the attempted *coup d'état*."[47]

Another crisis in relations between the SLFP government and the Left developed over the budget in mid-1962. Prior to the budget message, the Communist Party had conducted a vigorous campaign for a "people's budget," urging that economic problems be met by nationalizing foreign-owned property rather than by increasing workers' tax burdens.[48] The campaign was intended to influence the government by mobilizing popular opinion, but it failed to move the government or create much public interest. The budget introduced in July, 1962, proposed a sales tax and a cut in the consumer's ration of subsidized rice. The proposals produced an instant outcry both in Parliament and in the streets. A backbench revolt within the SLFP eventually forced the government to withdraw both proposals. Communist disenchantment, however, had already grown. Keuneman charged: "This budget marks a turn in the policies of the SLFP Government. It is a shift to the right." In announcing communist intentions of voting against the government on a major issue for the first time, Keuneman appealed to the SLFP backbenchers "to join the progressive forces outside your ranks in fighting against the fundamental capitulatory policies of your Government." [49]

An apparent decline in SLFP popularity in the urban areas was viewed with apprehension by the communists. A devastating Marxist defeat and a major UNP triumph in a Colombo Municipal Council election in December, 1962, seemed to reflect urban dissatisfaction with the government, directed against the Marxists because of their past identification with the SLFP. A tendency of the SLFP leadership after 1960 to rely exclusively on support from the rural areas, where SLFP strength had always been greatest, was denounced by the communists as an attempt to divide the workers and the rural masses.[50]

Late in 1963, when the tactical shift had been completed and a degree of left unity had been obtained, Keuneman wrote in the international communist theoretical journal *World Marxist Review:*

> Supported by the Left, Mrs. Bandaranaike's government at first pursued the line of weakening the economic and political positions of imperialism and compradore capital. But later, towards the end of 1961, it began to reverse this trend, began to compromise with the foreign and domestic vested interests, to vacillate and retreat; it clashed with the working class and the Left parties, and began to rely more and more on emergency powers and on the support of the armed forces.

Keuneman laid heavy stress on the importance of Marxist and working-class unity and suggested a very limited role for the SLFP in completing the "anti-imperialist and anti-feudal stage" of revolution.[51] This analysis was in sharp contrast to one by Keuneman in the same journal three years earlier, in which the need for close communist collaboration with the national *bourgeoisie* of the SLFP had been emphasized.[52]

Despite a history of distrust and recrimination between the communists and Trotskyists, the idea of left unity has persisted in Ceylon and, periodically, proposals for unity have been advanced. After the election of July, 1960, the Communist Party had claimed that cooperation with the Trotskyist LSSP in the election "helped to some extent to break down old prejudices and suspicions and laid the basis for further unity in the future." Also, rectification of "certain errors arising from the cult of the individual" by the international communist movement following the Twentieth Congress of the Communist Party of the Soviet Union facilitated closer relations between the communists and Sama Samajists. The communists issued a call for united action aimed at "the creation of a single socialist party, based on Marxism-Leninism." [53]

The desire for left unity also existed outside the Communist Party, and was compounded by repeated disappointments with the SLFP and frustration stemming from the Marxists' inability to increase their strength in the 15 years since independence. The first manifestation of the new trend toward left unity was a joint rally of the three Marxist parties in February, 1963, protesting the termination of American aid as a result of the nationalization of the property of American petroleum companies. The following May Day, a common Marxist rally was held for the first time in more than two decades. A joint Marxist May Day resolution condemned the SLFP, and Sama Samajist leader N. M. Perera called for the downfall of the government to make possible a genuine socialist regime.[54] After protracted negotiations, the Communist Party, LSSP, and MEP established a United Left Front in August, 1963. A common program worked out by the Marxists included proposals for the acceptance of Sinhalese as the sole official language, with regional concessions to Tamil; the nationalization of foreign-owned and large Ceylonese-owned enterprises; and worker participation in management.[55]

Left unity, however, proved to be of short duration. With the government under pressure from dwindling parliamentary strength and mounting labor turbulence, the SLFP leaders in 1964 approached the Marxists on the possibility of a coalition government, although the Marxists had been bitterly denouncing the SLFP government throughout the preceding year. The Marxists insisted that a coalition include all three Marxist parties,[56] and negotiations stalled when the SLFP leadership decided to admit neither the MEP nor the Communist Party into the government. Mrs. Bandaranaike was reported to have objected to communist participation because of the communists' international connections and hostility toward religion.[57] The Sama Samajists, however, broke the deadlock by deciding to join the government alone. In June, 1964, three LSSP leaders became cabinet ministers and the LSSP M.P.s joined the government parliamentary group. One of the four communist M.P.'s resigned from the Party to enter the coalition. The communist leaders, their Party by then split by a revolt of pro-Peking communists, were confronted with simultaneous exclusion from the coalition and collapse of the United Left Front as left unity evaporated. After a delay, perhaps indicating communist exasperation, the Party Central Committee resolved to cooperate with the SLFP-LSSP coalition government. The Central Committee, however, denounced the LSSP for abandoning the other Marxist parties and demanded the inclusion of the MEP and Communist Party in the government.[58]

After six months in office, the coalition government unexpectedly lost a vote of confidence in Parliament in December, 1964, when 14 SLFP M.P.s crossed to the opposition. Parliament was dissolved and an election called for March 24, 1965. The fall of the government left Ceylonese politics in a state of considerable uncertainty. The tactics the communists would evolve, after their retreat from their longstanding support of the SLFP, followed by the collapse of left unity, remained unclear but as long as the coalition holds together the alternatives appear to be isolation or as close a relationship to the coalition as they are allowed.

The Peaceful Path to Socialism

As their tactical maneuvers suggest, the Ceylonese communists have sought their goals primarily through parliamentary activity and political alliances. The narrow parliamentary majorities commanded by governments in recent years and the close balance of votes in some constituencies make even the limited strength of the Communist Party of possible parliamentary or electoral significance. The men who have headed the Party are experienced and effective in the parliamentary arena and on the public platform. A typical example of Party behavior under their leadership is provided in a description by Keuneman of a claimed communist triumph. Following the assassination of Bandaranaike, he asserted, a reactionary *coup d'état* was about to occur. The plot was foiled not by an armed uprising or direct action but because "the Communist Party and other progressive forces fearlessly exposed in Parliament the foul conspiracy." [59]

The Party has claimed that it "seeks to establish full democracy and socialism in Ceylon by peaceful means," but the possibility of violence and "extra-Parliamentary struggles" has not been ruled out.[60] Despite the past emphasis on parliamentary and electoral action, a shift in Party leadership or circumstances such as the establishment of a strongly anticommunist government could lead to an attempt to employ violent or disruptive means. However, the Party is probably too small and weak to be capable of effective widespread violence or direct action without the assistance of other groups. Guerrilla warfare seems singularly unsuited either to the geography of Ceylon or to the experience and temperament of the urbane intellectuals who currently lead the Party.

Ceylonese Communism and the Sino-Soviet Dispute

Repercussions of the rivalry between the Soviet Union and the Chinese Peoples Republic for world communist leadership have seriously disrupted the Ceylon Communist Party, leading to a major Party schism early in 1964. A firmly pro-Soviet position was assumed by the leaders of the Ceylonese Party at the first indication of divisions within international communism. At its 1960 Congress, the Party announced that as a result of the victories of socialism, largely attributed to the Soviet Union, "war is not a fatal inevitability." [61] At the Twenty-second Congress of the CPSU in 1961, Pieter Keuneman echoed Khrushchev's attack on the Albanian Party of Labor and praised the Soviet Party's Twentieth Congress as a turning point in the history of the entire communist movement.[62] A later statement by the Central Committee of the Ceylonese Party, issued in April, 1962, proclaimed unequivocal support for the Soviet Union in its developing contest with Albania and, indirectly, China. Peaceful coexistence and competition were endorsed. Efforts by the CPSU to eradicate the Stalinist cult of personality were lauded, although the statement stressed that the evils of Stalinism in no way vindicated Trotskyist claims. The statement concluded with a denunciation of the leadership of the Albanian Party for pursuing a course which "endangers the unity of the socialist camp and the international communist movement." [63]

In September, 1963, the Ceylon Communist Party reaffirmed its staunch support of the Soviet position on issues separating the Soviet and Chinese communists. In a lengthy statement issued by the Central Committee, the Ceylonese communist leaders delivered a sweeping denunciation of Chinese views, professing to be "deeply pained, surprised and alarmed at many of the political positions and deeds of our Chinese comrades in recent times." The statement sharply criticized Chinese attitudes on the inevitability of war, peaceful coexistence, and disarmament, as "both erroneous and dangerous." The Ceylonese attacked the Chinese stress on the role of national liberation struggles and Chinese deemphasis of the likelihood of a peaceful transition to socialism. Dogmatism and nationalism were identified as the immediate dangers to the international communist movement. Chinese suggestions that the Soviet communists were revisionists were labeled "unfounded and unworthy slander." The statement constituted a detailed defense of the CPSU and a severe condemnation of Chinese communist views and acts, which were said to "depart from the agreed general line of the international communist movement, spread confusions within fraternal parties, endanger the international positions and prestige of Communism, and expose the international communist, working class and democratic movements to the danger of splits and disruption." [64]

The unequivocal pro-Moscow stand of the Ceylonese Party leaders had few parallels in Asian communist parties. A partial explanation of this strong support for Moscow may lie in the personal ties and preferences of the Party's top leaders. Keuneman and Dr. Wickremasinghe have been frequent travelers to Moscow, presumably know the Soviet Party officials, and for many years seemingly have identified their fortunes with the Soviet Party. They do not appear to have had similar contacts with the Chinese. In addition, China is not in a good geographical position to aid or influence the Ceylonese communists. To the Ceylonese, China is as distant as the Soviet Union. Because of the Party's relative weakness and lack of spectacular successes, the Ceylonese communist leaders may not have been inclined toward adventures or exaggerating the revolutionary potential of the period, and thus may have found the Soviet line more appealing. Keuneman has disclaimed any special lessons for Asian communists from the Chinese experience, which he attributed to unique historical circumstances in China.[65]

As the Central Committee was restating its support of Moscow, dissension on this issue, which had been rumored for some time, erupted into public view and touched off factional struggles within the Party and communist-controlled organizations. Nagalingam Sanmugathasan, a leading communist trade unionist and Politbureau member, was expelled from the Party in October, 1963, for promoting the Chinese line in defiance of Party policy. Sanmugathasan is General Secretary of the Ceylon Trade Union Federation and of the Ceylon Plantation Workers Union, the largest of the Federation's trade unions. In enumerating the charges against him the Central Committee claimed that, since early 1963, he had repeatedly defied the Party leadership by supporting the Chinese line. He was charged with taking a public position in opposition to that of the Party, attempting to separate the Trade Union Federation from the Party and use it against the Party, and forming a "secret organization within the party" which appeared to be "the nucleus of a new party." He was also charged with attempting to obstruct the formation of the United Left Front. In a public reply to the Central Committee, Sanmugathasan condemned the CPSU and defended the Chinese Communist Party, arguing that the "key to the successful fight against imperialism" lay in "revolutionary struggles" in the underdeveloped areas.[66] A short time later, a second Politbureau member, Premalal Kumarasiri, editor of the Party's Sinhalese-language newspaper, also was expelled for advocating the Chinese line.

The dissidents publicly challenged the pro-Moscow stand of the Ceylon Communist Party leaders with the release of a statement dated October 27, 1963, in reply to the Central Committee pronouncement in support of Moscow the preceding month. The statement, signed by ten Central Committee members, including Sanmugathasan and Kumarasiri, accused the Central Committee majority of "dutifully obeying the baton" in siding with the Soviet Party. Responsibility for the Sino-Soviet ideological controversy was attributed to Soviet attempts "to revise the basic tenets of Marxism-Leninism at the 20th Congress of the CPSU and since." A point-by-point rebuttal of the Central Committee declaration and vigorous praise of Chinese attitudes followed. The statement condemned the veteran Ceylon communist leaders for lack of revolutionary zeal, charging they had "turned their back on the revolutionary struggle and pinned their hope exclusively on the parliamentary method of achieving victory for the working class." [67]

The contest quickly involved the communist-led trade unions and other organizations. A major victory was scored by the pro-Peking faction when it seized control of the Ceylon Trade Union Federation. M. G. Mendis, President of the Federation, walked out of the Federation's annual meeting late in 1963. He accused the Sanmugathasan group of packing the meeting with delegates opposed to the current Communist Party leaders and attempting to split the Federation from the Party.[68] Subsequently, a rival Ceylon Federation of Trade Unions was created under the leadership of Keuneman and Mendis. The Ceylon Trade Union Federation, and apparently a major portion of its constituent trade unions and members, appeared to be firmly in the hands of Sanmugathasan and the pro-Peking group.[69]

The pro-Soviet veteran Communist leaders suffered similar reverses in other communist-led organizations. In November, 1963, the Central Committee of the All-Ceylon Federation of Communist and Progressive Youth Leagues reportedly condemned the expulsion of the pro-Chinese dissidents from the Communist Party and called on the Federation membership to fight party "revisionists." [70] Later, the Federation President and six Central Committee members were dismissed from office, presumably for supporting the Communist Party leaders against pro-Chinese sentiment in the Federation.[71] The established communist leaders lost a simultaneous struggle for control of the Afro-Asian Solidarity Association. Keuneman failed in an attempt to prevent the reelection of Association President Mrs. Theja Gunawardhana, whom he accused of using the Association to propagate the Chinese line.[72] In March, 1964, the contending groups sent rival delegates to an Afro-Asian conference abroad. Later, a meeting of pro-Moscow members "invalidated" the previous election and named as President a pro-Moscow Party leader.[73]

As conflict mounted within the Ceylon Communist Party, indications of Chinese and Soviet support and encouragement for the rival groups appeared. Early in the dispute, the Central Committee attempted to prevent the dissemination by Party members of pro-Chinese literature reportedly obtained from the Chinese embassy and People's Publishing House outlet in Colombo.[74] Five Ceylonese employees of the Tass and Soviet Trade Mission offices in Colombo claimed they had been discharged because of their pro-Chinese attitudes.[75] Both Peking and Moscow made reference to the situation in Ceylon. In reply to Soviet charges of encouraging splits in foreign parties, Chinese Party spokesmen declared their support for "revolutionary comrades who adhere to Marxism-Leninism," among whom they classified Kumarasiri and Sanmugathasan.[76] In a speech to the Central Committee of the CPSU attacking the Chinese Party for dividing the world communist movement, M. A. Suslov cited Ceylon as an example of a country in which Peking had encouraged a split and helped to set up a rival Party.[77]

The contest between communist factions became a complete rupture in 1964, when the two groups held separate Party Congresses, each claiming to be the legitimate Seventh Congress of the Ceylon Communist Party. The Congress of the pro-Peking group was held in January and reportedly was attended by 399 delegates and 149 observers from 109 Party branches.[78] A resolution was approved repudiating the pro-Moscow statement of the Central Committee the preceding September and endorsing the reply by ten Party members in defense of the Chinese positions on the questions in dispute.[79] A Central Committee selected by the January Congress named Kumarasiri to the position of General Secretary and Sanmugathasan to that of National Organizer. The newly created Central Committee solemnly expelled Keuneman, Dr. Wickremasinghe, and 21 other veteran communist leaders from the Party.[80]

The following April, 422 delegates gathered for the Seventh Congress convened by the pro-Soviet Party leaders. Keuneman told the gathering that the Party had withstood an onslaught of "splitters and renegades" who were supported by the Chinese Communist Party. He attacked open Chinese encouragement of schisms in "fraternal parties" as creating "an intolerable and dangerous situation which threatens the ideological, tactical and organizational unity of the international communist movement." [81] Keuneman and the other pro-Soviet leaders were renamed to the major Party posts.

With the meeting of separate Congresses and the establishment of separate Party organs and offices early in 1964, within a few months of the first public indications of Party dissension, the schism seemed to be total. Ceylon possessed two separate and antagonistic Communist Parties, each claiming to be the legitimate party of Marxism-Leninism. The pro-Moscow Party contained the popularly known veteran communist leaders, including the handful of communist M.P.s, and appeared to cling to control of the existing Party organization. It apparently also was recognized outside the Party as the true continuation of the Ceylon Communist Party. This group remained a component of the United Left Front and figured in coalition speculation prior to June, 1964. A bid by the pro-Peking Party to participate in the United Left Front May Day rally in 1964 was rebuffed.[82] The pro-Peking group, however, had achieved considerable success in winning control of ancillary organizations and apparently had been able to create a parallel Party organization. The insurgents' strength in the trade unions and youth groups indicates the greater appeal of the more militant and aggressive Peking line and the weaker bonds of discipline among these Party supporters than among the Party's disciplined regulars.

The Ceylon Communist Party has faced strong competition from other Marxist parties since its founding. A united Party had failed to win impressive popular support or establish itself as the major party of the left. Disruption of the Party and its trade unions and rivalry between competing communist groups seems certain to restrict further the limited role of the Ceylonese communist movement.

The Ceylon Communist Party:
Competition for Marxist Supremacy

1. The Sinhalese term *sama samaja,* literally "equal society," was adopted by the founders of the Party as the nearest equivalent to the English term "socialist." On the history of the LSSP, see Leslie Goonewardene, *A Short History of the Lanka Sama Samaja Party* (Colombo: Lanka Sama Samaja Party, 1960).

2. W. Howard Wriggins, *Ceylon: Dilemmas of A New Nation* (Princeton, N.J.: Princeton University Press, 1960), p. 126.

3. *Forward* (Colombo), June 30, 1961. *Forward* is the English-language weekly newspaper of the Ceylon Communist Party.

4. Conversations with Ceylonese communist during 1961 and 1962.

5. The Sinhalese ethnic community is composed of low-country Sinhalese in the coastal areas of the south and west and Kandyan Sinhalese in the interior hill country. Some cultural differentiation between the two groups resulted from the much earlier and more intense impact of Western influences in the low country, and some sense of separate identification has remained.

6. S. A. Wickremasinghe, "At 13 I was a Communist," *Ceylon Observer* (Colombo daily), November 14, 1961.

7. *Lankā Komiyunist Pakshayē Vyavasthā Mālāva* [Ceylon Communist Party's Constitution] (Colombo: Ceylon Communist Party, n.d.), pp. 12-17. (My translation.)

8. *Ibid.,* pp. 26-27.

9. Thus, at the time the Soviet-Albanian dispute first became public, Party members were reported to be waiting for an expected pronouncement by Keuneman on the Party's position.

10. *Lankā Komiyunist Pakshayē Vyavasthā Mālāva,* pp. 23, 26-27.

11. As reported by communist officials in January and February, 1962.

12. *Lankā Komiyunist Pakshayē Vyavasthā Mālāva,* pp. 5-6.

13. *Draft Thesis for the 6th National Congress of the Ceylon Communist Party* (Colombo: Ceylon Communist Party, 1960), p. 49. This work is hereafter cited as *Sixth Congress Thesis.*

14. K. P. Silva, "Ceylon: Communist Party Safeguards National Interests," *World Marxist Review,* 5, No. 5 (May, 1962), p. 62. Noncommunists give little credence to the claims.

15. Interviews with party officials in January, 1962.

16. *Sixth Congress Thesis,* p. 58.

17. *Administration Report of the Commissioner of Labour for 1960* (Colombo: Government Press, 1961), p. 147.

18. E.g., see *Ceylon Daily News* (Colombo), June 11, 1962.

19. See Wriggins, *Ceylon: Dilemmas of a New Nation,* pp. 134-35.

20. These figures are computed, respectively, from *Census of Ceylon: 1953* (Colombo: Dept. of Census and Statistics, 1957), Vol. 1, pp. 194-196; and *Statistical Abstract of Ceylon: 1961,* p. 26. The Colombo District contains 21 per cent and the Western Province contains 28 per cent of the island's total population.

21. E.g., see Silva, *World Marxist Review,* p. 62. The 1955 Party Congress had called for increased efforts in the rural areas and conceded past failure to work among the peasantry. *Lanka's Way Forward: Political Resolution of the 5th Congress of the Ceylon Communist Party* (Colombo: Ceylon Communist Party, 1955), pp. 25-26.

22. See Richard L. Harris and Robert N. Kearney, "A Comparative Analysis of the Administrative Systems of Canada and Ceylon," *Administrative Science Quarterly,* Vol. 8, No. 3 (December, 1963), 347-49.

23. See Bryce Ryan, *Caste in Modern Ceylon* (New Brunswick, N.J.: Rutgers University Press, 1953), pp. 276-79.

24. See Goonewardene, *A Short History,* pp. 60-61. Politically motivated strikes are discussed by Wriggins, *Ceylon: Dilemmas of a New Nation,* pp. 154-55.

25. Thus, a spokesman of the communist-led Ceylon Harbor Workers Union insisted that the harbor strike was intended only to alleviate workers' grievances, not to undermine the government—*Ceylon Observer,* December 29, 1961. Similarly, LSSP Secretary Leslie Goonewardene denied that a general strike called in January, 1962, to protest the use of troops in the strike-bound harbor was directed against the government—*Ibid.,* January 4, 1962. While the strikes were in progress, the Communist Party newspaper insisted on the necessity for continued Marxist support of the SLFP government—e.g., *Forward,* December 29, 1961.

26. The principal sources used are *Manifesto of the Communist Party* (Colombo: Ceylon Communist Party, 1960); *Lanka's Way Forward; Sixth Congress Thesis;* and *Forward,* April 27, 1962.

27. *Manifesto of the Communist Party,* p. 7.

28. *Sixth Congress Thesis,* p. 43.

29. *Ibid.,* pp. 25-26.

30. Goonewardene, *A Short History,* p. 61.

31. Pieter Keuneman, "Success for the Policy of Unity," *World Marxist Review,* Vol. 3, No. 10 (October, 1960), 73.

32. *Srī Lankā Nidahas Pakshayē Vyavasthā* [*Sri Lanka* Freedom Party's Constitution] (Colombo: *Sri Lanka* Freedom Party, 1958), p. 1. (My translation.)

33. E.g., *Sixth Congress Thesis,* pp. 13, 37.

34. Goonewardene, *A Short History,* p. 41; Colvin R. de Silva, *The Why and the Wherefore* (Colombo: Lanka Sama Samaja Party, 1952), p. 7.

35. *Manifesto of the Communist Party,* p. 2.

36. Ceylon, House of Representatives, *Parliamentary Debates,* Vol. 38, col. 183. Hereafter, the debates of the House of Representatives will be cited as *Debates.*

37. *Ibid.,* Vol. 39, col. 367.

38. D. S. Senanayake, "Foreign Policy; Defence Forces; Internal Security," in U. A. Jayasundera (ed.), *United National Party Independence Souvenir: 1952* (Colombo: United National Party, 1952), p. 21.

39. See Sir John Kotelawala, *An Asian Prime Minister's Story* (London: George G. Harrap & Co., Ltd., 1956), pp. 186-94.

40. *Joint Programme of the Mahajana Eksath Peramuna* (Colombo: *Mahajana Eksath Peramuna,* 1956), pp. 1-2.

41. *Sri Lanka Nidahas Pakshayē Māthivarana Prakāsanaya: 1960* [Sri Lanka Freedom Party's Election Manifesto: 1960] (Colombo: Sri Lanka Freedom Party, 1960), pp. 10-11. (My translation.)

42. *Forward,* January 12, 1962. For similar statements, see *Sixth Congress Thesis,* p. 15; and Keuneman, "Success for the Policy of Unity," p. 74.

43. *Sixth Congress Thesis,* p. 49.

44. After the communists broke with the SLFP government, a visit by Mrs. Bandaranaike to the Soviet Union in late 1963 produced Ceylonese-Soviet declarations of mutual admiration for the contributions both states were making to world peace and anticolonialism, and the Soviet government singled out the Ceylonese policy of neutralism and nonalignment for warm praise. Text of the joint communiqué appears in *Ceylon News* (Colombo, weekly), November 7, 1963.

45. E.g., *Ceylon Observer,* December 12, 1961; January 8, 1962.

46. Pieter Keuneman, *The Politics of the Coup* (Colombo: Ceylon Communist Party, 1962), p. 4.

47. *Forward,* April 27, 1962.

48. *Ibid.,* May 4, 1962.

49. *Debates,* Vol. 47, cols. 2884, 2906.

50. E.g., *ibid.,* Vol. 46, cols. 925-26.

51. Pieter Keuneman, "Towards Unity of the Working Class," *World Marxist Review,* Vol. 6, No. 12 (December, 1963), 10-14.

52. Keuneman, "Success for the Policy of Unity," pp. 73-75.

53. *Sixth Congress Thesis,* pp. 56-58.

54. *Times of Ceylon* (Colombo, daily), May 2, 1963.

55. *Ceylon News,* August 15, 1963.

56. *Times of Ceylon,* May 11, 1964.

57. *Ceylon News,* May 28, 1964.

58. *Ibid.,* July 2, 1964.

59. Keuneman, "Success for the Policy of Unity," p. 74. This emphasis on parliamentary action is typical of the leadership which headed the Party from its founding and which since the split with a pro-Chinese faction has led the pro-Soviet Party. It may not typify the attitude of the pro-Chinese communists.

60. *Sixth Congress Thesis,* p. 52.

61. *Ibid.,* p. 2.

62. *Ceylon Observer,* October 27, and October 28, 1961.

63. *Statement of the Central Committee, Ceylon Communist Party, on the 22nd Congress of the Communist Party of the Soviet Union* (Colombo: Ceylon Communist Party, April 8, 1962).

64. *On Questions of the International Communist Movement: Statement of the Central Committee of the Ceylon Communist Party* (Colombo: Ceylon Communist Party, September 26, 1963).

65. Interview with Pieter Keuneman, January 11, 1962.

66. The Central Committee charges and Sanmugathasan's reply are contained in *Ceylon News,* November 7, 1963.

67. The full text of the statement appears in *Peking Review,* No. 48 (November 29, 1963), 9-16.

68. *Ceylon News,* December 26, 1963.

69. See *Times of Ceylon,* January 20, 1964.

70. "Protesting the Revisionist Leadership of the Ceylon Communist Party," *Peking Review*, No. 48 (November 29, 1963), 17.
71. *Times of Ceylon*, November 21, 1963.
72. *Ibid.*, November 26, 1963; *Ceylon News*, December 5, 1963.
73. *Ceylon News*, April 30, 1964.
74. *Ibid.*, October 17, 1963.
75. *Sunday Times* (London), January 5, 1964.
76. "The Leaders of the C.P.S.U. Are the Greatest Splitters of Our Times," *Peking Review*, No. 6 (February 7, 1964), 18.
77. *Pravda*, April 3, 1964, translated in *Current Digest of the Soviet Press*, Vol. 16, No. 14 (April 29, 1964), 10.
78. *Times of Ceylon*, January 20, 1964.
79. "Revolutionary Leadership of the Ceylon Communist Party Established," *Peking Review*, No. 5 (January 31, 1964), 18-19.
80. *Ceylon News*, April 9, 1964.
81. *Ibid.*, April 23, 1964.
82. See *ibid.*, April 16, 1964.

Selected Bibliography

Abhayavardhana, Hector, "Categories of Left Thinking in Ceylon," in *A Miscellany*, Community Pamphlet No. 4. Colombo: Community Institute, 1963, pp. 31-57.
Draft Thesis for the 6th National Congress of the Ceylon Communist Party. Colombo: Ceylon Communist Party, 1960.
Goonewardene, Leslie, *A Short History of the Lanka Sama Samaja Party.* Colombo: Lanka Sama Samaja Party, 1960.
Keuneman, Pieter, "Success for the Policy of Unity," *World Marxist Review*, III, No. 10 (October, 1960), 73-75.
————, "Towards Unity of the Working Class," *World Marxist Review*, VI, No. 12 (December, 1963), 10-14.
Lanka's Way Forward: Political Resolution of the 5th Congress of the Ceylon Communist Party. Colombo: Ceylon Communist Party, 1955.
Oliver, Henry M., Jr., *Economic Opinion and Policy in Ceylon.* Durham, N.C.: Duke University Press, 1957.
On Questions of the International Communist Movement: Statement of the Central Committee of the Ceylon Communist Party. Colombo: Ceylon Communist Party, September 26, 1963.
Phadnis, Urmila, "United Left Front in Ceylon," *Eastern World*, XVII, No. 11 (November, 1963), 11-12.
Statement of the Central Committee, Ceylon Communist Party, on the 22nd Congress of the Communist Party of the Soviet Union. Colombo: Ceylon Communist Party, April 8, 1962.
Weerawardana, I. D. S., *Ceylon General Election: 1956.* Colombo: M. D. Gunasena & Co., 1960.
Wriggins, W. Howard, *Ceylon: Dilemmas of a New Nation.* Princeton, N.J.: Princeton University Press, 1960.

Index